AUTHORITARIAN NIGHTMARE

AUTHORITARIAN NIGHTMARE

TRUMP AND HIS FOLLOWERS

JOHN W. DEAN
and BOB ALTEMEYER

MELVILLE HOUSE
BROOKLYN • LONDON

AUTHORITARIAN NIGHTMARE: TRUMP AND HIS FOLLOWERS

First published in 2020 by Melville House Publishing
Copyright © John W. Dean and Robert A. Altemeyer

First Melville House Printing: October 2020

Melville House Publishing
46 John Street
Brooklyn, NY 11201
and
Melville House UK
Suite 2000
16/18 Woodford Road
London E7 0HA

mhpbooks.com
@melvillehouse

ISBN: 978-1-61219-934-4
ISBN: 978-1-61219-906-1 (eBook)

Library of Congress Control Number 2020939950

Designed by Beste M. Doğan

Printed in the United States of America

1 3 5 7 9 10 8 6 4 2

A catalog record for this book is available from the Library of Congress

To Mo, Dodi, Franny,
Sally, and Molly—all my favorite ladies.

JOHN W. DEAN

To Jean, who has given me the breathless
pleasure of being her partner for
nearly sixty years. And to Alf Shephard,
who brought me to the University of
Manitoba and kept me, so I could teach
and explore to my heart's content.

BOB ALTEMEYER

TABLE OF CONTENTS

FOREWORD

JOHN W. DEAN

The nightmare is not over. In fact, it could get worse, so the material set forth in this book, and additional analysis added since its original publication, remains strikingly relevant. Out of the Oval Office, Donald Trump is a diminished personality but given his hold on the Republican Party, he remains an important political figure who must be understood. Everything we had to say about Trump in the prior edition remains applicable.

Even more significant, however, is our study of Trump's devoted followers—the millions upon millions of people who voted for him, and want him back in the White House.

Donald Trump's presidency was overwhelmingly political theater, with most of the substance, like selection and appointment federal judges and Supreme Court justices, along with tax cuts, the work of the Republican Congress. Trump himself did not develop nor offer a single legislative proposal during the entirety of his presidency. In fact, the United States has survived the most inept, corrupt, dishonest, and laziest president of my lifetime, which spans fifteen presidents (FDR, Truman, Ike, JFK, LBJ,

Nixon, Ford, Carter, Reagan, Bush I, Clinton, Bush II, Obama, Trump, and Biden—all of whom I have studied.) Because of Trump's striking incompetence, mixed with his narcissism and blundering, he will go down in history as the absolute worst of the modern presidents.

Nonetheless, the material in this book explains why Trump remains the chosen leader of the Republican Party and of right-leaning independents, giving him a wide influence over most of those millions who voted for him in 2020. Trump is an authoritarian leader by disposition, not by leadership skills for he has none, and he arrived on the political scene at a time when the Republican Party had become a resting place for people who want to be told what to think, and how to deal with what they perceive as a threat from the growing global nature of American society. America has become a land of too many people who are not white enough for Trump's supporters. As explained in Chapter Eleven, Trump's followers, and the Republican Party, are the most prejudiced people in America.[*]

I am not sure if Trump himself knows if he will run again for president. Given the number of civil and criminal investigations he must now deal with without the protections of the Office of the President of the United States, and his less than robust health, he cannot know for certain himself. Nonetheless, I have little doubt he will act as if he is running, for two reasons. One, it is a proven ploy to raise money, which he has done to an excess as president. In fact, he appears to have personally pocketed more money than any president in American history. And secondly, running for president is a potential defense to any of the several potential criminal prosecutions which he faces. If and when indicted he will claim it is politically motivated and they are going after him because he seeks the presidency—and if he were just Don the Con they would not bother.

---

[*]   See also "Authoritarianism Among Trump Voters: A Monmouth Study." This follow-up study is also addressed in the new afterword.

But it is difficult to believe he really wants the job. Clearly, he is not a person who finds any pleasure whatsoever in public service and helping others. Trump is only interested in helping Trump. He loves the 24/7 attention of being president. But when he had the job it was obvious he did not particularly enjoy it, and so spent a historic amount of time playing golf—just under a staggering 300 rounds (which cost American taxpayers $142 million)!

Whatever, of this I am certain: As long as Trump remains relatively healthy and does not become the first American president to be confined to a penitentiary for his remaining years (where he should be), he will have a large and slowly declining influence over Republican politics and thereby our political life. Had Trump and the Republican Party lost overwhelmingly in the 2020 election, they would have fallen off the cliff into political irrelevance. Authoritarianism would have been conspicuously rejected, and the wannabe GOP demagogues in the wings would have gone looking for their Mr. Rogers sweaters. But that did not happen, and if American voters fall asleep, or Democrats become too kind, the nightmare of authoritarianism will loom large again.

If there has ever been any doubt of how authoritarians behave, it is only necessary to look at what occurred after Trump was defeated on November 3, 2020, when he refused to transfer power to his successor, inciting an insurrection on January 6, 2021. Trump's exit from office is a deeply troubling capstone to his presidency. His refusal to accept defeat, his conspicuously corrupt effort to overturn state election results to favor himself, his perpetuation of what has become known as The Big Lie, which is now being employed to justify future voter suppression of black and brown Democrats, is all very un-American. Or at least what we thought to be un-American. As this edition is being launched the post-Trump story is still being written. We do not know if it is the end of his undemocratic presidency or the beginning of post-democratic America. Lest we not forget what was involved,

I have gathered its essence in a new afterword for a summary of this ugly underbelly of authoritarianism. This is a portrait of our ongoing American authoritarians, and they are no more attractive here than anywhere else in the world where they have sought power. They are everything our nation's founders warned us to avoid.

The profile of Donald Trump found in Chapters One through Four digest a substantial body of psychological information about the man. I have read most everything written about him, and with the exception of *Too Much and Never Enough: How My Family Created the World's Most Dangerous Man* by Mary L. Trump, his niece and a trained clinical psychologist, I have not found any better fact-based analysis of him than the material assembled in our chapters. This analysis, like all the science spread through these pages, is largely the work of my collaborator, Bob Altemeyer, who filtered the information about Trump's background and influences through his own perspective as a seasoned psychology professional and long-time student of authoritarians. (Mary Trump was not necessarily looking to uncover or understand Donald's proclivities in terms of authoritarianism, but rather to reveal his deeply troubled egomaniacal personality in general, although along the way her work confirmed our finding regarding the outsized role that Donald's father, Fred, had in his life.) Because Trump's future political behavior and politics are certain to be aberrant—i.e., ineffectual, anti-democratic, norm-shattering, and un-American—the explanations set forth in these four chapters provide insights and understanding about his disposition and the origins of his behavior in succinct detail, illustrating the boundaries of his personality.

However, the core of this book remains Chapters Five through Eleven, where Trump's followers and enablers are described and analyzed based on decades of scientific study, information which was confirmed by administering a series of personality tests to a nationally selected panel of just under one thousand participants by the Monmouth Polling Institute. Additional confirmation arrived when Monmouth returned to these participants in December 2020 to determine how their proclivities had played out in the election. Short answer: just as the science had predicted. Accordingly, when Trump provoked his core followers to rampage at the Capitol on January 6, 2021, the Monmouth Polling Institute released these additional findings about these authoritarian followers, which I have addressed in the afterword.

In short, Trump's followers and enablers are a political presence and force to be reckoned with, and they will remain a true influence on American politics and government for the indefinite future. Clearly, their most striking feature is their prejudice, their intolerance of others, along with their tolerance, and even encouragement, of undemocratic ways and means in our government. At this point we do not know the exact number of Trump voters in 2020 who were (and remain) dyed-in-the-wool authoritarians, but the number was substantial enough to give them meaningful significance. Our analysis put the number at 50 million or more, but it now appears that our estimate was on the low side. The point I hope to make is that authoritarianism is a real problem for American democracy, so I hope people who love democracy become familiar with the personalities described in this book. There is a way to deal with them. Call them out, and out-vote them.

Authoritarianism is insidious. I began studying the subject to understand my own experiences at the Nixon White House. When Trump emerged as a candidate 2015, I did not believe the American people would be so foolish as to elect an authoritarian clown their president. Bob Altemeyer, however, thought it very possible, and he, of course, was correct. Unlike many political scientists, sociologists, and psychologists, as well as journalists familiar with authoritarians, he saw a Trump-like character coming. (He continues to update his findings on his website, www.theauthoritarians.org.) What continues to surprise me is why so few social scientists familiar with authoritarianism have remained silent, with only a few exceptions.* This book seeks to address the lack of discussion about the authoritarian nature of Trump's rise and continuing influence, but more importantly, we hope to foster a better understanding of all those Americans who want a Trump-type president, notwithstanding the fact it will destroy our democracy. As the Monmouth surveys establish with clear and convincing evidence, these people—or I should say their mindset—is a significant presence in contemporary American politics. To ignore it, and them, is to not understand what is occurring and why. I find these mindsets are a clear and present danger to freedom-loving Americans. As the psychological profile of this thinking, set forth in the pages that follow, reveals—just as Erich Fromm perceived when he first studied these attitudes in 1941—these are people who seek to escape freedom. They do so, however, at the expense of others, which makes them intolerable to me, and is why I continue to address this subject.

---

* I have addressed one of those exceptions in the afterword. See endnote 23.

INTRODUCTION

Just as we were finishing the first draft of this book, the COVID-19 virus began tearing the whole world apart, and nobody's life—and no new book about Trump—could be unaffected. Donald Trump had faced few challenges but had created much chaos during his first three years in the White House, while the country had been reveling in peace and prosperity. Pensions were padded, payoffs were pursued, parks were packed. Then it all disappeared almost before we knew it was going. A lot of people had worried from November 8, 2016, onward that the end was nigh, and its name would be World War III. Few had figured on a plague. But Trump's dealing with COVID-19 will define his presidency, and we had to deal with his dealing, front and center, in this book because it exemplifies his behavior and that of his followers. The trouble was, we could not wait to see how the emergency turned out, since it would probably still be turning out, or be freshly returning, on Election Day 2020. The closer we get to November 3, 2020, the more it looks like that day will be a pivotal moment in American history, and the more we thought this analysis had to be informed by the president's handling of the COVID-19 crisis.

Then on May 25 a white police officer in Minneapolis slowly and brutally murdered a helpless Black man in broad daylight as onlookers filmed the crime and begged the officer to stop. The country erupted with wider and angrier protests than most Americans alive today had ever seen as the racism that has betrayed America's ideals from its first days was nakedly exposed in all its ugliness. The demonstrations lasted for weeks and were almost always peaceful. Local officials in Minneapolis and the state's governor immediately aligned themselves with the nonviolent protestors and took steps to reduce the anger and try to solve the problems. So did other governors, mayors, police chiefs, and rank-and-file police officers. What did the president do?

Sometimes emergencies bring out the best in leaders, revealing unanticipated strengths and sound judgment. Certainly, Americans needed strong, wise leadership as they woke up every day to the greatest public health crisis in a hundred years and the greatest civil unrest in fifty years. The chief executive of the land has the job of uniting the country in times of perils and using his vast array of experts to advise him. The epidemic gave President Trump the opportunity to demonstrate the massive skills at organization and government that his followers ardently believed he had. And a strong showing would almost guarantee re-election in November. Americans would thankfully give a second term to a president who had just saved the nation from such peril. As for the civil unrest, no one was better positioned than Donald Trump, because of his past, to bring peace to the land by joining the cry that Black lives matter as much as white lives and showing he would work to make African Americans equal partners in a great America.

Instead of turning this political godsend and this opportunity for historic healing into buzz-saw momentum in the election, it seemed to us that

Trump proceeded to make the same mistakes he had been making for the past three years, while his followers, whom this book is mainly about, kept cheering him on. So the White House's handling of the pandemic and the Black Lives Matter protest did not lead us to reframe our analysis of America's situation; rather, it stamped an exclamation point on almost every one of our conclusions.

But can the world possibly need yet another book about Donald Trump? If you Google "books about Trump," the answer seems obvious: "You've got to be kidding!" But while there are many books about the man and his presidency, favorable and not so favorable, we could find no book that explains *why* he acts the way he does. Nor are there any books that explain his base, the source of his power. In fact, many observers have thrown up their hands in despair at Trump's very steadfast supporters. They seem beyond the pale, beyond understanding. Well, give us a chance, for we believe we have solid science-based answers.

First things first. Many people have opined there is something seriously wrong, psychologically, with Donald Trump. If you proudly wear a Make America Great Again hat, you may be offended by the suggestion. For you, as for him, Trump should be immortalized on his own Mount Rushmore, maybe renamed Mount Trump, as America's greatest president. But if you have passed on a twenty-five-dollar official MAGA hat while observing Donald Trump for any time at all, you may believe the man is deeply troubled mentally. Psychiatrists and clinical psychologists have been riveted by his behavior from the outset of his presidential bid. They wondered during the campaign, "Is this an act just to get elected?" But by the time he moved into the White House, many concluded Trump was not "crazy like a fox" but "crazy like a crazy."[1] This point was made by one of the mental health professionals who wrote the bestselling book *The Dangerous Case of Donald Trump*, edited by Dr. Bandy Lee of the Yale School of Medicine.[2] The conclusions of these analysts and therapists varied quite a bit, understandably, since clinical diagnosis remains something of an art. But more than anything, these psychiatrists and psychologists believed that Trump displayed extreme narcissism with more than a touch of psychopathy. He is, as one therapist put it, in a phrase reflecting years of professional training, "a dog with both ticks and fleas."[3]

These professionals have company. Many sophisticated Washington pundits and presidential observers have deep concerns about Trump.[4] Republican leaders and other influential conservatives who hoped he would grow into the job have often been disappointed. Trump's interactions with his cabinet and senior advisors led some of them to expose the man, warts, more warts, and even more warts, to journalists such as Bob Woodward, who compiled them in his bestseller, *Fear: Trump in the White House.*[5] One senior official, "Anonymous," reported strikingly similar information in an op-ed in the *New York Times* on September 5, 2018, and later, a book, revealing that a group of alarmed officials had quietly banded together to keep some of Trump's decisions from being enacted.[6] Other aides, competing with one another for the president's favor, leaked damaging information about their opponents in Trump's inner circle, which implicitly diss Trump for hiring their opponents. The Trump White House "leaks" more than Nixon's did when he formed the infamous "Plumbers" unit to shut off the flow. It appears everybody is trying to get even. John Bolton's book *The Room Where It Happened* revealed just how dysfunctional the White House had become by 2018 and what a terrible manager and decision maker Trump was.

The combination of brutal personal portrayals and the daily drips of West Wing scuttlebutt reported regularly from the White House lawn on the six o'clock news give one pause about the person who lives at 1600 Pennsylvania Avenue. Donald Trump, the most powerful person on the planet, apparently does not have as much influence as he wants, often exploding in anger in the West Wing, not to mention ranting publicly on social media when he does not get his way. He demands all-the-time-on-all-the-issues loyalty from those around him. As a result, most of the cabinet appointees and high administration officials who objected, however privately, to Trump's plans during his first two years in office have resigned or been fired. As Trump entered the last year of his four-year term, he surrounded himself, as much as he could, with advisors who told him he was always right. That action has given us the equivalent of an explosives-loaded freight train with no brakes.

We have no formal training in psychiatric diagnosis, so our two cents' worth of opinion about Trump's mental health might not even be worth the two cents. But we do agree with those who have called Donald Trump an authoritarian leader, and we do know something about authoritarianism from history, from witnessing it in action in the White House, and from the scientific research on it. We will explain what we mean by that term in Chapter 1 and then spend the next three chapters examining how Donald Trump became, over the course of his life, a very flawed authoritarian leader. The next part of the narrative will address Trump's supporters. This is probably the most important contribution we can make, for even if Donald Trump disappeared tomorrow, the millions of people who made him president would be ready to make someone else similar president instead. Their steadfast backing of Trump is understandable on the surface because he has delivered much of what he promised. But he has failed to give them much else that he guaranteed them, even when he had the wind at his back and open seas with Republicans controlling both houses of Congress. Yet his base forgives all. They thrill to the man, and many of them would probably march with conviction into cannon fire for him. A *Guardian/YouGov* poll released on December 2, 2019, reported that 53 percent of Republicans believe Trump is a greater president than Abraham Lincoln, who usually comes in first in surveys of historians and political scientists on presidential greatness. Early in Trump's presidency—when he fired the director of the

FBI, when he took children from their parents along the Mexican border, when he said he was in love with North Korea's dictator, when he sided with Vladimir Putin against U.S. Intelligence assessments that Russia had interfered in the 2016 election—the political analysts and editorial writers thought, *This time he's gone too far. Nobody's going to support that kind of, uh, stuff.* But the polls showed that practically every one of his supporters backed him. Today the pundits simply shake their heads with dumbfounded resignation when Trump's base stands by him no matter what he says or does. *"What are Trump's supporters drinking?"* *"What are they smoking?* *"What are they thinking?"*

Since leaders lead one at a time but followers come in bunches that make leaders, it has been possible to do a great deal of scientific research on authoritarian followers. We know how they are created, where they are concentrated, how they think, why they are so easily led, why they are so aggressive, and even a lot that they do not know about themselves. Social scientists have been fascinated for decades by the authoritarian followers who, as Erich Fromm put it and as Dostoyevsky portrayed in "The Legend of the Grand Inquisitor" in *The Brothers Karamazov*, want to escape from freedom. After all, the followers make someone into a dictator. Donald Trump only has the power to flout American institutions, treaties, and laws because he has a large, dedicated base who will believe whatever he says and do whatever he wants. Accordingly, we spend a lot of time in this book grasping Trump's threat to America by explaining his followers.

We believe the base's endless loyalty springs from the same psychological trait that some observers think runs deeply in Donald Trump himself, authoritarianism. Our understanding of these people is based on decades of research on people who might well support an autocratic takeover of a democracy. Journalists and commentators may find this body of study, presented as the core of this book in Chapters 5 through 11, richly informative about contemporary American politics and the American electorate. Most people have never heard of this body of research, but it appears that its moment has arrived. It provides answers to two questions many concerned people are asking: What is wrong with Donald Trump? How can so many people support him? There is a related third question, the subject of the last chapter of this book: Can this authoritarian movement be contained before it is too late?

We are not alarmists. If you look at our previous work on authoritarianism you will see that we always said: "We still have lots of time; things have not gotten really bad yet." But the past three years have been, well, the past three years, and suddenly there is a real crisis upon us, one unrelated to COVID-19. We do not wish to frighten anyone because that is one of the ways authoritarian leaders operate. Rather, we seek to alert and inform, relying on verifiable facts and the answers nature has repeatedly given in studies about why Trump and his supporters act the way they do. America faces a number of very serious problems right now, made worse by its president. Insight is available and solutions do exist; in fact they have been around for a long time but they will take a long-term commitment.

AUTHORITARIAN
NIGHTMARE

CHAPTER ONE

DONALD TRUMP, COVID-19, "BLACK LIVES MATTER," AND AUTHORITARIANISM

When President Donald Trump learned about the novel coronavirus outbreak in China in January 2020, he dealt with it the way he proudly claims he deals with almost all his decisions: he played it by gut instinct. In this situation, his intuition said it was no big deal, so he took no action. As a result, America, the richest and among the most medically advanced countries in the world, took totally inadequate protective measures and became widely infected with the COVID-19 virus as it spread across the world in January and February 2020. By May, America, which had 4 percent of the world's population, had 29 percent of the world's COVID-19 deaths.[1]

Even his staunchest supporters will admit that Donald Trump is unschooled in matters relating to genetic mutation and viral transmission. He likely does not know the difference between a codon and a condom, which is in no way a condemnation, for we do not choose leaders because they have encyclopedic knowledge.* Instead, American presidents have access to experts in almost every field to advise them on matters outside their

---

* If you have not taken high school biology lately, a codon consists of three adjacent "letters" on a strand of DNA or RNA that tell a cell what to use next as it builds a protein. If you do not know what a condom is, ask one of your many children.

knowledge. Trump supporters also know that the president says he knows more than anybody else about almost everything. Accordingly, he was not inclined to listen to the experts who told him the virus posed a very grave danger to the United States.

By mid-January 2020, when the administration knew the COVID-19 pandemic had arrived in America, Trump was in firm control of the executive branch of government. Although he had been all but indicted for obstruction of justice by Special Counsel Robert Mueller's inquiry into the Russian influence on the 2016 election and had been impeached by the U.S. House of Representatives for the "Ukraine Scandal," Trump had been assured by the Republican-controlled Senate that they would never remove him from office. Thus, his impeachment trial through January 2020 and the first few days of February became more a victory lap than a ride out of town on a rail. By the start of the final year of his first term, he had accumulated more power than any president in living memory. As a result, when his instincts told him that the COVID-19 virus was merely a new version of the flu and of little importance, all the expertise in the many branches of the federal government, as well as that available in the private sector, that could have prepared the country for the upcoming invasion found, maddeningly, that their initiatives were blocked at the top, and little was done. More Americans would die because of this action over the next year than died in the wars in Vietnam and Iraq.

HISTORY OF THE COVID-19 VIRUS

This new coronavirus was quickly recognized by scientists not as another kind of flu, but rather the latest offspring of a family of viruses that had earlier produced the SARS (2003) and MERS (2012) outbreaks. Its origin is unclear. SARS and MERS had originated in animals and spread to humans. The coronavirus disease (2019), or COVID-19, closely resembles a virus found in a species of bats. The virus allegedly first appeared in humans in the city of Wuhan in central China, home to the Wuhan Institute of Virology. The institute conducts research on the animal origins of coronaviruses. So, COVID-19 may have developed in a bat somewhere in China, been collected by the institute, and then a staff member became infected and began the spread among humans. It has been determined that people can carry the disease and not know they have it. It is also possible that the virus passed from an animal host to a "Typhoid Mary" in Wuhan without any involvement of the institute. (A conspiracy theory, favored by Donald Trump, spread that the Chinese government had produced COVID-19 at the institute as a biological weapon. But the laboratory, which has connections with similar laboratories in Texas and Canada and exchanges researchers, is not equipped to perform bioweapon research. An alternate theory holds that Americans developed COVID-19 and took it to China. Help yourself, there is no rule limiting how many conspiracy theories a person can believe.)[2]

Suspicion stuck to the Chinese government like mud to a boot because it had tried to cover up the outbreak. The first known victim entered a hospital in Wuhan in early December 2019 and did not attract much attention. But by Christmas, eight unusual respiratory cases had appeared. The institute was sent samples and identified a new coronavirus, which it found was extremely similar to SARS. It notified the hospital and a local government agency. Wuhan officials, and later national authorities, however, tried to suppress this information, but two doctors described the illness on WeChat. They were told by government authorities on December 30, 2019, to stop talking about it. On December 31, China finally notified the World Health Organization (WHO) that mysterious pneumonia cases had appeared in Wuhan. But the cover-up continued for another week as the Chinese government reported that the disease was not spreading. By January 8, 2020, the Center for Disease Control (CDC) in the United States had been alerted by WHO, which notified American doctors to watch out for patients from Wuhan with a coronavirus.[3]

The first known infected person to enter the United States was a Chicago woman who had traveled to Wuhan and became ill after returning on January 13. A second passenger from Wuhan arrived in Seattle on January 15 with the disease. But it turned out that two persons in Northern California may have contracted the disease even earlier through "community spread." Similarly, a forty-three-year-old Frenchman contracted the coronavirus on December 27, 2019, even though he had not traveled.[4]

THE UNITED STATES SHOULD HAVE BEEN PREPARED

Trump would later insist that no one foresaw, or could have foreseen, a crisis like this coming. That was untrue. For years, many people had warned of such a pandemic. Scientists knew another coronavirus would come along some day and developed models predicting how it would spread and what would be needed to minimize the damage. They knew the best way to protect the country was to keep the new virus from becoming widely established, and that was done through mitigation, by quarantining those who had it and keeping the rest of the population as socially isolated as possible. The Obama administration had learned much from the Ebola virus epidemic in Africa in 2014 and ran a simulated outbreak for incoming Trump cabinet appointees in January 2017 to illustrate the problems sure to arise in such a situation.[5] However, some of the officials reportedly had no interest in the presentation. And those who did, such as Rex Tillerson and John Kelly, had been fired or had quit their jobs by 2020. When asked if the president had been informed about these training sessions, a former official doubted it, stating that it was not the sort of thing Trump was interested in.[6]

Nevertheless, various scientific and medical groups continued to study how to deal with a new plague. A simulation by Johns Hopkins University in October 2019 cosponsored by Bill Gates produced an eerily accurate prediction of what would begin happening just two months later. Scientists and medical officials had been begging the Trump administration to prepare for a new viral infection. But the country's supply of testing kits, face masks, protective clothing, emergency hospital beds, respirators, and ventilators was grossly inadequate when the pandemic appeared.[7] Sometime in January 2020, according to the *Washington Post* (which President Trump denied with a wave of his hand but has not further refuted), US intelligence officials discovered the cover-up in China and warned both the White House and congressional leaders that the outbreak in China was more serious than Chinese authorities were indicating.[8] Trump telephoned China's President Xi Jinping who assured him the situation was well under control (it was not). Trump, as he had with Russia's Vladimir Putin and North Korea's Kim Jong Un, believed Xi because he had a personal relationship with him, and he felt the Chinese leader would not lie to him. Thus, he accepted Xi's word at face value rather than the evidence presented by the American intelligence agencies and took no action. (Later, Trump severely criticized the WHO for believing Chinese misinformation on the virus.)

On January 18, 2020, Secretary of Health and Human Services Alex M. Azar II felt it was his duty to warn the president that a pandemic might arise across the world from the outbreak in China.[9] But the president did nothing, and the message to his staff was clear: he was not interested in the virus. According to many reports his staff knew that they should not bother him with uninteresting things unless they were prepared to be yelled at, cussed out, and "lose access," especially if the news indicated he had made a mistake earlier. Nevertheless, many experts were deeply worried. "Donald Trump may not have been expecting [an outbreak in America], but a lot of other people in the government were—they just couldn't get him to do anything about it," one official acknowledged to the *Washington Post*, noting, "The system was blinking red."[10]

On January 22, 2020, President Trump was asked if there were concerns about a pandemic, and he made his first public statement on the matter when he replied, "No. Not at all. And we have it totally under control. It's one person coming in from China, and we have it under control. It's going to be just fine."[11] But new cases continued appearing elsewhere, and American health officials began saying aloud how unprepared the country was for an epidemic. But Trump, again, portrayed no concern. "It will all work out well," he tweeted on January 24. On January 28, 2020, he stated that Johnson & Johnson was going to develop a coronavirus vaccine.

On January 29, 2020, Chief Trade Advisor Peter Navarro circulated a memo inside the West Wing warning that the coronavirus crisis could cost the United States trillions of dollars and put millions of Americans at risk of illness or death.[12] Trump later denied ever seeing the memo, but the *New York Times* established from multiple sources that he had.[13] That same day, Secretary Azar again phoned Trump and repeated his warning from two weeks earlier. Trump reportedly told Azar he was being an "alarmist." The next day, he said of the spreading virus, "We have it very well under control. We have very little problem in this country at this moment—five [cases]. And those people are all recuperating successfully."[14] Despite being warned by three sources in his own administration during January about the possibility of a devastating epidemic reaching the United States, including twice by the secretary of health and human services, it appears Trump did not even request to be kept further informed on the subject. Instead, he dismissed the warnings out of hand, even belittling an advisor who tried to help him. The same day Trump issued his "We have it well under control" statement, the WHO declared the coronavirus to be a "public-health emergency of international concern," which was its strongest warning yet of a spreading epidemic. The next day, January 31, 2020, the White House announced a remarkably weak protective action: (1) foreigners who had been anywhere in China would not be admitted into the United States, and (2) Americans who had been in the Wuhan area would be quarantined for two weeks when they came back.

This was Trump's "travel ban on China." It was only a travel ban on non-Americans. It did nothing to keep thousands of Americans, who had traveled elsewhere in China where the disease had spread, from re-entering the United States without being quarantined or even checked. Nor did it red-flag travelers, Americans or otherwise, who were bringing the virus into the United States from, say, Italy or Spain. Trump acted like a child home alone dealing with a thunderstorm by closing the front door but leaving all the windows open. Two days later he was asked if he was worried about the coronavirus. Trump replied, "Well, we pretty much shut it down coming in from China." In fact, it was pouring into the country from China and everywhere else it had reached. One might argue that Trump was simply presenting a calm face to prevent panic on Main Street and Wall Street, while he was industriously setting the American government to work behind the scenes to deal with a forthcoming public health crisis. In fact, that is what should have been done. This was the time to act, and no one was more responsible for the safety of the nation than the president. Tens of millions of tests for the new virus needed to be acquired and distributed. Vast quantities of personal protective equipment needed to be stockpiled. Hospital facilities needed to be expanded. Medical ranks of doctors, nurses, and other vital health workers needed to be reinforced. Equipment such as respirators and ventilators needed to be purchased in large quantities. Public information campaigns needed to be planned. Congressional leaders and state governors needed to be brought into the loop. Decisions needed to be made in the broadest terms on the highest level about school closures, large public events, using the National Guard, and so on.

But Trump did almost none of these for the next forty days, during which time various branches of the government kept warning the White House of what was about to take place and pleading that preparations be made. Instead, the country had internal disputes among Trump's staff accompanying his deep reluctance (his fear) to do anything that might trigger a collapse of the stock market and the broader economy. During those many weeks people got on and off cruise ships, full airplanes flew from infected areas into the United States, the Super Bowl and all its parties were held, scads of professional sports and college games were played, people went to movies and concerts and ate out and rode crowded transit systems and coughed nonchalantly at work and did not wash their hands a dozen times each day because they did not know they were risking catching and spreading a life-threatening disease that was sweeping the world the way the Spanish Influenza had done in 1918. As a result, tens of thousands of Americans would die, and almost everybody else's lives would be confined to a box, and the economy would tank, and the country would go, for openers, nearly four trillion dollars more into debt trying to cushion the collapse. To be sure, death and depression and debt were inevitable once the virus appeared, but it affected the United States much more than it needed to. For the most part, it was indisputably down to one man: Donald Trump. Historians, we suspect, will probably decide it was one of the worst blunders in American history.

Note we said, "For the most part." Prominent conservative media voices pitched in and reassured listeners that the issue was unimportant. Rush Limbaugh announced that the coronavirus was just the common cold: "Why do you think this is 'COVID-19'?" Rush asked, answering (erroneously), "This is the nineteenth coronavirus. They're not uncommon."[15] Similarly, various Fox News hosts assured their audiences the disease was unimportant, being blown out of proportion, the flu, a political hoax by the Democrats, and certainly nothing that should affect anyone's lifestyle. Polls indicate their listeners believed both them and Trump as he and Fox played Ping-Pong with this message. As a result, some of these listeners no doubt ignored the advice medical authorities were giving, based on what they could see happening in countries such as Italy; rather these folks carried on as usual and died. We all make mistakes, but news outlets that echo whatever President Trump says are responsible for the demise of thousands of their own listeners whom they ushered into the Valley of Death. We doubt, like Donald Trump, this concerns them whatsoever.

FEBRUARY AND EARLY MARCH 2020: A TIME OF MAGICAL THINKING

Instead of preparation in February "while the coronavirus waltzed right in," as one epidemiologist put it, Trump remained publicly unconcerned. On February 10, 2020, he claimed springtime weather would kill the virus: "Looks like by April, you know, in theory, when it gets a little warmer, it miraculously goes away."[16] He gave the same assurance on February 14: "When it gets warm, historically, that's when it gets able to kill the virus." February 19 brought: "I think the numbers are going to get progressively better as we go along." On February 23, he reassured Americans that things were "very much under control. We had twelve [confirmed cases] at one point. And now they've gotten very much better. Many of them are fully recovered." But the rest of the world was not seeing the rapid recoveries described by Trump. Rather almost every other country hit by the virus was experiencing rapidly climbing infection rates. Italy had shut down eleven municipalities in the north. Iran was reportedly swamped but not talking about it. Japan closed its public schools. By now it was clear that infected people could spread the virus even though they had no idea they were carriers. They could spread it when they had no symptoms, so airport checks had only caught a fraction of the infections, with the asymptomatic hosts spreading the virus far and wide.

Stock markets started falling from record highs on February 13, 2020, and that did worry Trump. However, he did not address the threat of the virus; rather he blamed news networks for worrying investors, who kept selling anyway. Referring to coronavirus cases, Trump protested: "It's going down, not up. We're going very substantially down, not up." But his words better described the stock market. The next day he predicted: "It's going to disappear. One day, it's like a miracle, it will disappear." On February 26, he protested, "This is a flu. This is like a flu," adding, "Now, you treat this like a flu." He insisted, "It's a little like the regular flu that we have flu shots for. And we'll essentially have a flu shot for this in a fairly quick manner." On February 28, he told a campaign rally that the news circulating about the coronavirus was a hoax perpetrated by the Democrats in yet another effort to drive him from office. The following day he promised that a vaccine would be available "very quickly," then he repeated, "very rapidly" and praised his administration's actions as "the most aggressive taken by any country." Various spokespersons said the threat was being "well-contained." "It may get a little bigger," Trump said on television, adding, "It may not get bigger at all."

Meanwhile, American public health experts, doctors, nurses, and other health professionals, who knew otherwise, were battling the fast-growing epidemic day after day that threatened to strike them down too as it had their patients. They became the new first responders, who, like the fire-fighters who rushed into the Twin Towers to save people on 9/11, put their lives on the line for others in this emergency. Some of these health professionals perished while fighting through fatigue and frustration to save others, working without essential testing materials or personal protective equipment—equipment the president said individual states should compete for with other states rather than have the federal government provide. (Trump had declared himself a "wartime President" but bizarrely insisted those on the frontlines find their own ammunition and armour.) As the critical month of February ended, the chances Americans diagnosed with COVID-19 would survive were far better if they headed to countries like South Korea, Singapore, Australia, New Zealand, or Canada, almost any country other than the United States. Through early months of the pandemic Trump (and his inner circle) embraced what some called "magical thinking," which was undeniably divorced from scientific fact, not to mention reality.[17] He insisted COVID-19 was much less dangerous than the ordinary flu. It had a "much smaller range of death," he said on March 2, when it has been proven to be many times more lethal. He continued promising a vaccine "soon." Amplifying this, on March 3, he said the United states would have "not only the vaccines but the therapies. Therapies are sort of another word for 'cure.'" On March 4, he reassured Americans, "We're talking about very small numbers in the United States."

"It's very mild," he stated on March 6, the day he toured the headquarters for the Center for Disease Control and Prevention. "Our numbers are lower than just about anybody." Word was getting out that the United States did not have enough testing kits. Trump bluntly asserted, "Anybody who wants a test can get a test." But many people knew that was not true, as testing kits and the chemical reactant needed to evaluate the test remained in short supply. He also disclosed that he was naturally gifted in microbiology and epidemiology: "I like this stuff. I really get it. People are surprised that I understand it. Every one of these doctors said, 'How do you know so much about this?' Maybe I have a natural ability. Maybe I should have done that instead of running for president."[18] Then he revealed he did not know the ordinary flu killed people (even though his grandfather had died of it).

By now people were leaving supermarkets with carts full of toilet paper, and the Dow Jones Index was falling like a bungee jumper, only without the certainty that it would be pulled back before it hit rock bottom. But on March 7, Trump continued to dismiss the threat, saying, "I'm not concerned at all." And he acted unconcerned, constantly ignoring the advice from public health officials about "social distancing," regularly shaking hands and sharing close space with others in public and setting an example of exactly what *not* to do if the disease was to be contained. On March 10, Trump said, "It will go away. Just stay calm. It will go away."

TRUMP RECOGNIZES THE DANGER, OCCASIONALLY

By mid-March, Trump could no longer fake it, for he surely realized Americans were living in mortal danger. On the night of March 11, he addressed the nation from the Oval Office, reading a speech written by Stephen Miller and Jared Kushner. (His measured and flat reading of someone else's words on the teleprompter reminded many of a hostage video.) He said the situation was very serious; he endorsed frequent hand-washing; and he announced that no one from Europe, save from Great Britain, would be allowed into the United States. This seriously misrepresented the new policy, and aides spent the next twenty-four hours saying things were not as bad as the speech made them seem. But dire times were clearly ahead. The National Basketball Association canceled its future games, and Major League Baseball ended spring training. On March 14, Trump declared a national emergency. Shortly after that, he announced that Great Britain was also included in the travel ban, and flights turned around over the Atlantic. Reporters asked him about the abrupt shift in his message. What changed? He both denied he had changed at all, and then reverted to his previous nonchalance. "Some of the doctors say this will wash through." The "flip" was followed by a "flop."

When asked on March 13 if he was responsible for the problem that had arisen with the shortage of testing equipment for COVID-19, Trump said,

"I don't take responsibility at all." Instead, he blamed President Obama, claiming somewhat strangely that the previous administration had failed to provide the nation with tests to detect a virus that did not exist during Obama's time in office. On March 15, Trump claimed that the United States "has tremendous control" of the virus. But the very next day, he said, "[T]he situation was out of control," and was "very bad." Strict new measures would be introduced and likely last through the summer, and the United States might be headed for a recession. When asked again how he rated his performance in handling the crisis, he gave himself a ten out of ten. On March 16, the White House issued social distancing guidelines designed to mitigate the spread of the disease. The next day Trump declared, "I felt it was a pandemic long before it was called a pandemic." On March 18, he insisted he had "always treated the Chinese virus very seriously." On March 19, he announced that an anti-malaria drug would be made available very quickly because he felt it would work against COVID-19. Medical experts did not agree, so the next day Trump admitted he "just had a feeling" it would work. But he added, "I've been right a lot of times." An NBC correspondent observed that thousands now had the disease and hundreds had died. What would the president say to the American people to help them deal with their fears? Trump answered, "I'd say you are a terrible reporter. That's what I'd say." He broadened his attack to the "fake news" media, saying his job of uniting Americans was difficult because of "dishonest journalists." Later that day he added, "We were very prepared. The only thing we weren't prepared for was the media."

As Americans watched these almost daily news conferences in which the administration's medical experts repeatedly said social distancing was essential for stopping the spread of the virus, they could not help but notice that the experts were standing elbow to elbow behind the microphone in the confined White House briefing room. It was suggested they were "display props," used by the administration to help portray the president as a commander leading his united troops into battle. Unfortunately, the visual lowered the experts' credibility and stepped all over what they were saying to anyone who could see.

TRUMP BACKSLIDES

Trump mostly struck the pose in mid-March of a calm, competent defender of America against "China's virus," and his approval rating rose in the polls. But this "Rally 'Round the Flag" effect amounted to only 3 percent, much lower than the boost leaders in other countries received, and a fraction of what happened to ratings of George W. Bush after 9/11.[19] Trump then announced on March 23, just eight days after issuing the social distance guidelines, that it would soon be time to ease up on the containment restrictions so the economy could recover. He indicated we could accept some future deaths to have a strong economy again. Otherwise masses of Americans would kill themselves soon because they did not have jobs. Medical officials and scientists disagreed, saying that projections about suicide were highly speculative while the virus was still spreading. Mitigation was the best weapon against it. As soon as social distancing and isolation is stopped, the disease will start spreading faster and overwhelming hospitals. And just proposing to lift the restrictions would lead some people to ignore them or expect them to be lifted much sooner than was wise. But Trump wanted to instill hope and confidence in the public, and he admitted it might be necessary to have some people die to improve the economy.

Elderly people, poor people, and people with prior medical conditions were most likely to pay the price, especially if they lived in big cities where the chances of community spread were greatest. Republican Lieutenant Governor of Texas Dan Patrick said the next day that the elderly would willingly sacrifice themselves to boost the economy for their descendants.[20]

Democrats may have recalled that Republicans falsely said Obamacare would create "death panels" that would "kill off Grandma" if they thought it cost too much to keep her alive. Now the GOP seemed to consider Grandma's death an acceptable price for restoring jobs. By the end of March, however, Trump was persuaded by his medical advisors to extend the social isolation guidelines through April. He also framed the situation in terms of how many people would have died if governments had done nothing. He announced he had saved millions of lives, but only compared to what would have happened if there had been no doctors, nurses, hospitals, and so on. An objective observer would have to say that, far from saving lives that would have been lost, the president had increased the death rate over what it could have and should have been.

On April 3, President Trump denied that he had earlier said COVID-19 would be gone by April. On April 4, the New York Governor Andrew Cuomo, after battling with Trump for a week over needed supplies and equipment, announced that China was giving his state a thousand respirators. What was wrong with that picture? On this same day, Trump announced the end of the crisis was in sight. In mid-April, Trump was encouraging demonstrations that demanded the social isolation regulations be removed, even though the states involved had not met his own criteria for ending the lockdown. Accordingly, he urged that Michigan, Minnesota, and Virginia (all states with Democrat governors) be "liberated." He complained that some governors were not sufficiently grateful for the help he extended and told his staff not to include them in future plans. This startled some, as Trump is the president of all the people, and the motto of the country had to be "We are all in this together" if the social isolation measures were to be effective. But Trump kept dividing the nation. He praised Georgia's Republican governor Brian Kemp for ending parts of the state's isolation measures in late April, even though epidemiologists warned it was much too soon. Trump replied that he wanted to start the economy's recovery and continued to build pressure to make states "open up for business as usual" in early May. At the time, the administration knew there were thirty thousand new cases of the disease every day, and that figure would surely go up if social distancing was significantly reduced.[21]

From mid-March on, Trump blamed many others for the fact that the United States had become the epicenter of the COVID-19 outbreak in the world, namely the news media, public health officials, governors (in both parties) who kept saying that his daily portrayal of the situation was filled with lies, the Obama administration, the Center for Disease Control, the World Health Organization, Democrats, and especially China. He never acknowledged that his trusting of his own intuition over the advice of so many experts had been the major reason so many Americans were sick and so many had died. Now he was ignoring their advice once again, rolling the dice that improving the unemployment rate would be worth however many tens of thousands who would die in the process because their government considered them expendable, and it would reignite the epidemic whose spread had been slowed by the very policy he was now abandoning.

Of all things, face masks produced a battleground between medical authorities and Trump supporters. After some inconclusive early findings, it became clear that wearing a face mask in public slightly protected a person from catching the virus, and it helped keep the wearer from spreading the disease to others. This was important because most people who were infected did not know it. Many White House aides were seen wearing a mask, but not the president. People attending "reopen the economy" rallies were conspicuously unmasked, and some carried signs saying they were showing support for Trump by not wearing one. Some told reporters that making people wear masks was "tyranny," and wearing one was a sign you were against the president. Trump did nothing to discourage this belief and thus helped create a division in the country over what ought to have been a straightforward way to control the infection. Undoubtedly, like the pressure he was constantly applying to open businesses and send children back to school, people would die because of this too.

COVID-19 AND AUTHORITARIANISM IN AMERICA: A TALE OF TWO DISEASES

From time to time, American presidents have thoroughly pinned themselves to disastrous positions. Lyndon Johnson's decision to get heavily involved in Vietnam comes to mind, and Richard Nixon's insisting on a cover-up. Donald Trump told the American people over and over that the COVID-19 virus was not worth worrying about. It was just like the flu. He had it completely under control. It was not going to affect anything. And he meant it. He did practically nothing to protect America, and he kept the government from doing much as well, even though its medical officers and scientists were pleading to do something. The United States is projected to lose more than 200,000 lives in 2020 because of Trump, more than we lost in Korea, Vietnam, 9/11, Iraq, and the war on terror *combined*.[22]

No previous president, however, has tried to change history when his actions became an undeniable catastrophe. Lyndon Johnson, for example, chose not to seek re-election in 1968 when he saw how deeply divided the nation was over the war. He did *not* say, "I never said we should send troops to Vietnam." Richard Nixon resigned when he saw he would lose the impeachment vote in the Senate in 1974. He did not say, "I was never involved in a cover-up of Watergate," when his secretly self-recorded conversations said otherwise.

But friend and foe must agree that Donald Trump has tried to deny the undeniable about his reaction to COVID-19. He says he always took it seriously. He says he knew it was a pandemic before anybody else. He says he never said it would miraculously disappear once spring came. He says he reacted perfectly to the danger, "ten out of ten." He has a long list of others whom he blames, but he himself was not at all responsible for what happened to America. Whether you may like or loathe Donald Trump, the record is indisputable that this is simply not true. But as remarkable and unprecedented as his level of mendacity may be, even more remarkable is the fact that about half the country appears to believe this monumentally false rewrite. You can see the average of his daily level of support in public opinion polls at FiveThirtyEight's "How Popular/Unpopular Is Donald Trump?" (a composite based on a wide collection of reliable polls.)* Except for the small bump at the end of March, when his approval rating nearly reached 46 percent, he found favor with about some 43 percent of the Americans surveyed day after day, week after week. Even after he wondered aloud if injecting bleach into people would cure the virus. Even after he said the crisis was over and we should go back to our normal lives, although tens of thousands of new COVID-19 cases were being recorded every day. No matter what he says, roughly 43 percent of Americans remain with him. You must wonder, is there anything he could say or do that would change the minds of his supporters?

TRUMP AND BLACK LIVES MATTER

As the United States was reaching its 100,000th COVID-19 death, a white policeman in Minneapolis was recorded on video (by a passerby) murdering a Black man who was handcuffed and being held down on the paving by a knee on his neck for nearly nine minutes. The man, George Floyd, begged for his life. The policeman, hand casually in his pocket as he pressed his knee on Floyd's neck, showed supreme indifference before cameras as

---

*   See https://projects.fivethirtyeight.com/trump-approval-ratings/.

the onlookers begged him to stop. Floyd's dead body was removed by an ambulance and the video was posted online where it went viral. Small protests broke out that night, May 25, in the city and more occurred the next day. When the horrific video became a national news story, demonstrations against police brutality grew and spread to other cities. On May 27 President Trump tweeted he had ordered the FBI to investigate the killing. The next day he told reporters in the Oval Office that the video of George Floyd's death had been "very shocking" and it was a "very bad thing." But when asked, he refused to say whether the police officers involved should be charged with murder. Reports from the White House suggested Trump was torn between two groups of advisors on what he should do. One group wanted him to be sympathetic with the African American community. The other camp reportedly warned he would lose measurable support from his base if he did not take the side of the white policemen and condemn the demonstrators as radical leftists and terrorists. Trump stood at a potentially historic moment in his presidency when he could have helped rectify 400 years of unconscionable racial injustice and head off the biggest outbreak of racial protests the country had seen in fifty years. He had a chance to do what a president should do, unite the country in time of peril and try to solve its problems. It was most definitely not the time to fan the anger of the Black community, city mayors, and various governors by attacking them. But if you knew anything about Donald Trump and the people in his base whom he wanted to please above all others, you could have predicted which way he was going to turn.

Trump became president with a reprehensible record for dealing with racial matters. For example, in April 1989 a white woman jogging alone in Manhattan's Central Park was assaulted, raped, beaten, and left for dead. But her body was discovered, and she was taken to a hospital in a coma. The police arrested five teenage boys, ages fourteen to sixteen, who had been among a group of youths carousing in the park that night. Four were African Americans and the other was Hispanic. The youths were interrogated all night without attorneys, beaten, and by the morning four of them had signed confessions. When Donald Trump heard of the arrests he took out a full-page advertisement in four New York City newspapers calling for the death penalty for each of the accused. He said in the ad, "I want to hate these muggers and murderers . . . they should be forced to suffer." Later Trump appeared on the Larry King Show, where he was reproached for the hatefulness in his ads. He replied, "Maybe hate is something we need if we're gonna get something done." Trump's newspaper ads ignited public opinion against the Central Park Five and they were found guilty and sent to prison based on their coerced confessions, which they had retracted. In 2002 a notorious serial rapist and murderer serving time for other crimes admitted he had attacked and raped the jogger in Central Park. His DNA matched the semen found in the victim, who had made a stunning recovery but could not remember anything about the attack. The five youths, now young men scarred by years of serving in penitentiaries, were released from custody with apologies and money. But Donald Trump refused to believe he had ruined their lives and he refused to believe they were innocent. He felt the confession by the real assailant proved nothing. He had made up his mind they were guilty, and nothing was going to change him. Donald Trump is so deeply prejudiced the truth does not have a chance.[23]

Given this, no one should be surprised at Trump's behavior in responding to the public reactions to the murder of George Floyd. His feelings became evident after the large and peaceful demonstration in Minneapolis ended with a group who broke off and burned down the local police station, looted stores, and set cars on fire. Trump ignored the peaceful protest, and he especially ignored the underlying issues, and began a non-stop week of demagoguery and threats. Accordingly, in a call to the governors to address COVID-19, Trump ranted about the demonstrators ("looting leads to shooting,") and urging strong-arm tactics ("You've got to dominate the streets!") and recriminations against those who tried to make peace ("You have to dominate or you'll look like a bunch of jerks, you have to arrest and try people . . . you don't have to be too careful . . . get retribution.")[24] These "Black Lives Matter" demonstrations continued, day after day, and night after night, with the president's own front yard soon becoming the focus of the demonstrations in Washington, DC. The largely peaceful but noisy demonstrators assembled around a fenced-off Lafayette Square, the park adjacent the North Lawn of the White House. On the evening of June 1, President Trump gathered the news media in the Rose Garden and delivered a brief televised speech in which he tried to portray the increasingly peaceful demonstrations as riots but said he was an "ally of all peaceful protest." While the president was delivering his remarks, mounted Park Police, National Guard units, and federalized police used pepper spray, billy clubs, and armored vehicles to remove demonstrators from the streets surrounding Lafayette Park, with live television covering it all.

Following his provocative Rose Garden remarks, which conspicuously overemphasized the violence in the demonstrations, the president took no questions from the reporters he had assembled, and disappeared back into the White House. He emerged shortly at the North Portico with a phalanx of senior government officials who all made their way across the street from the White House to Lafayette Park, led by the president. In the front row of the two dozen officials were Secretary of Defense Mark Esper, Chairman of the Joint Chiefs of Staff Mark Milley, Attorney General William Barr, and White House Chief of Staff Mark Meadows, followed by White House Press Secretary Kayleigh McEnany, son-in-law and senior aide Jared Kushner, and his wife, the president's daughter and senior aide, Ivanka Trump, carrying a large white pocketbook. It was not clear, at first, where this parade was headed, but no one had ever before seen the Chairman of the Joint Chiefs of Staff in full battle dress on the streets of the United States. Soon it became clear. Trump was heading for St. John's Episcopal Church, which was boarded up to protect from demonstrators. Ivanka reached inside her white handbag and retrieved a bible, which she gave to her father, who hoisted the bible (upside down) above his shoulder as he posed for his picture to be taken in front of the church. This entire drill, removing the peaceful demonstration by force, assembling the top of the American military and the assorted government officials, parading through the park to the church, was pure political theater, a "photo op," as is known in the news media.

Donald Trump had used the Black Lives Matter protests to flaunt his authoritarian inclinations and put on a show of a would-be autocrat for his base. But he was making unprecedented use of the American military. He had threatened to deploy the United States Armed Forces to the streets of America to end peaceful protests (by making them appear out of control). He had required the Chairman of the Joint Chiefs of Staff to dress in full battle fatigues as part of his political theatre. (Thankfully, both Secretary of Defense Esper and Joint Chiefs Chairman Milley told the president he could not use the active duty military for law enforcement duty anywhere in America. And after heavy criticism from retired military and others, both men publicly apologized for their folly of participating in Trump's political charade.[25]) It was a telling moment in the Trump presidency. He was five months away from standing for re-election and down in the polls. He was playing to his base as a "law and order president," telegraphing that if he is reelected he will use the American military and force governors to stop uncomfortable protests that address difficult but important questions of race relations in America. He was also showing his base that he has moved beyond COVID-19, because none of these government officials were wearing masks; rather they were acting like there was no pandemic. Donald Trump's performance in Lafayette Park should remind all that he is a wannabe dictator conspicuously displaying his inchoate authoritarian rule.[26] If he gets another term as president, he has made clear how he will govern.

THE NATURE OF AUTHORITARIANISM

When you find yourself asking questions about Trump's unwavering support and the loyalty of his base, you have wittingly or unwittingly entered the world of authoritarianism. Stripped to its essentials, authoritarianism happens when followers submit too much to the authorities in their lives. What is "too much," then? When followers choose to believe a leader who demonstrably and repeatedly lies to them, ignore undeniable contradictions in his rationales, and back him to the max when he makes very bad decisions—that's "too much." When they turn a blind eye to obviously immoral and outright unlawful acts he performs, support him when he places himself above the law and repeatedly tries to undermine the nation's founding principles, and they generally think, feel, and do what he tells them to, because he is their leader, that is *way too much*.

Seen this way, authoritarianism involves two kinds of authoritarians, an authoritarian leader and authoritarian followers. Most people mean the first when they say someone is an "authoritarian," but we shall demonstrate that the followers deserve the title too and, in their own way, are the more important element in the compound, the carbon in a carbon-based system. This is the reason this book about Trump's authoritarianism is mainly about his followers. An authoritarian leader will not last long without followers— lots of them. Since entering the political arena in 2015, Donald Trump has been called an authoritarian so many times that the description is in danger of becoming a cliché when it should be an indictment.[27] You will find that at the core of most dictionary definitions of an "authoritarian person" is someone who demands complete obedience and denies individual freedom. The most common synonyms (autocrat, despot, dictator, and tyrant) show that when used as a noun, it refers to a leader who demands that everyone obey him. Autocracy is the simplest and most natural form of government. You find despotism in many animal species. Wolves have their alpha males, for example. Hierarchies form because animals seek advantages that help the fortunate ones and their offspring survive. Early human societies, from tribal units to fledgling nations were likely built around "one-man rule." The very name "kingdom" reveals this. But about twenty-six hundred years ago, a new form of government, democracy, began to develop in Greece. It vests ultimate power in the citizens of a state, and over the centuries since, along a very bumpy road, at a very uneven pace, it has become the preferred form of governance by most thinking citizens of a state. Democracy, however, is much more complicated than autocracy and can be enormously frustrating. Winston Churchill is credited (possibly incorrectly) with saying, "The best argument against democracy is a five-minute conversation with the average voter." But as he more famously put it, "Democracy is the worst form of government except for all those other forms that have been tried from time to time."[28]

Certainly, the average person is much better off in a democracy than being a serf or a slave or a loyalty-swearing citizen in a dictatorship. But people do not always realize that. Democracies get into trouble if their institutions lose support and massive dissent arises. If the traditional political parties continue to fail them, demagogues will spring to the fore.

As political scientists Steven Levitsky and Daniel Ziblatt point out, most of the democracies overthrown since World War II died at the ballot box when authoritarian leaders were voted into power.[29] Usually these totalitarians did not even bother to throw out the country's constitution. They just subverted it bit by bit until they controlled everything, and it became irrelevant. We do not relish playing Paul Revere now, but it seems to us that American democracy is nearly at the point of no return in this process. Americans elected a very traditional type of authoritarian leader with Donald Trump—a demagogue. During the first five months of the 2016 GOP primaries, the *New York Times* was so struck by Trump's demagogic rhetoric they gathered and analyzed "every public utterance" by him, some 95,000 words. They retained historians, psychologists, and political scientists to review the material, and the experts concluded it echoed "some of the [worst] demagogues of the past century." Trump was campaigning in the traditions of segregationist George Wallace and anticommunist red-baiter Joseph Mc-Carthy, "vilifying groups" and "stoking insecurities of his audiences," except the *Times* noted, by contrast, Trump was a more "energetic and charismatic speaker who can be entertaining and ingratiating," thus more engaging than his predecessors, which the *Times* found made his demagoguery "more palatable when it is leavened with a smile and joke."[30] Nonetheless, in words and action, Trump was and is a demagogue, pure and simple, albeit ranked stylistically slightly better by one leading American news organization than his predecessors, like Joe McCarthy and George Wallace.

The *Oxford American Dictionary* (3rd ed.) defines a demagogue as "a political leader who seeks support by appealing to popular desires and prejudices rather than by using rational argument." They almost always crave the role of authoritarian leader. Winston Churchill (again) dismissed demagogues as "soapbox messiahs,"[31] which they are, until they attract a following. Then they can destroy a nation. A demagogue on a soapbox trying to glue together a group of followers usually looks comical, but he is almost always an authoritarian with big plans. He wants to be lifted on high by masses of adoring supporters to supreme authority, so he can take control of everything. He may believe all his spiel, but whether he does or not, demagoguery is just a means to his ultimate end: autocratic dictatorship.

SOCIAL SCIENCE RESEARCH ON AUTHORITARIANISM, BRIEFLY

Academic psychology made a determined effort to understand authoritarianism during World War II and kept at it for more than thirty years. The undertaking, fed then as ever by what the journals would publish and what the funders would support, was set off by Nevitt Sanford and two colleagues at the University of California at Berkeley. In 1950, they published *The Authoritarian Personality*, nearly one thousand pages filled with psychoanalytic theory and preliminary explorations in the fields of personality and social psychology. A fourth contributor, Theodor Adorno, was added to the project by its sponsor after the work was nearly finished.[32] Other American researchers at the time believed that what happened in Germany in the 1930s "could happen here" as well. The experience of McCarthyism soon after *The Authoritarian Personality* was published convinced many social scientists that a large segment of the American public could be stampeded into surrendering the democratic rights the country had just fought to preserve in the war against fascism. Reactions to both the civil rights movement and the protests against the war in Vietnam renewed concern that a sizable number of Americans were just one step short of voting for a dictator-in-waiting who promised law and order by "stomping out the rot."

However, the research on authoritarianism that had been furiously undertaken to safeguard democracy stumbled all over itself from the start. The principal investigators had trouble explaining authoritarianism. They seemed to link it only to right-wing extremism, ignoring dictators and followers on the left plentifully visible on the world scene. The Freudian model of how authoritarianism developed in childhood and operated in adults crashed because unconscious psychoanalytic constructs are difficult to measure scientifically, and the theory had too many "escape hatches" when the data said it was wrong. Most of all, the principal tool Berkeley researchers developed to measure the "pre-Fascist personality," the F Scale, seemed to be terribly flawed. Hundreds of American F Scale studies produced almost nothing beyond an amazing ability to contradict one another. The situation became terminally hopeless when various researchers began using selected parts of the F Scale, which differed from one researcher to another, to measure supposedly the same thing. Standardized measurement, one of the cornerstones of the scientific method, was stunningly ignored. By the mid-1970s psychology was stuck in deep muck in this field, out of gas, and broken from bumper to bumper, and nobody in his right mind wanted anything to do with authoritarianism. It was like an abandoned house in town where someone once tragically died. Devote yourself to it as a scientist, and your career would die too. Nonetheless, a small number of researchers and curious minds stubbornly soldiered on. Bob Altemeyer (coauthor of this book) was among them, as was Sam McFarland of the University of Western Kentucky, John Duckitt of the University of Auckland, John Jost at New York University (later Stanford), and Jos Meloen of the University of Leiden in the Netherlands—among others who have had the deserted house all to themselves over the past decades and who have gone romping from room to room trying to make sense of it all. Progress in understanding authoritarianism was made, but mainstream psychology was not interested. You will not find the subject treated, or even mentioned, in most American textbooks today even at the broadest introductory level. Meanwhile, the thing itself, authoritarianism, has now caught fire and is threatening to burn down the whole town. "It" is happening here. Some people see this and have named it for what it is. But authoritarianism confuses almost everyone, and many wonder if it can be controlled before our country is gone.

Authoritarianism is studied by psychologists, political scientists, and sociologists, with each discipline developing its own focus and definitions while using its preferred methods. We have focused on the psychological research in this field.[33] No one in the media apparently knows about this body of evidence but we do not think it is a secret. Our narrative is largely based on the findings of one academic investigator, who happens to be the person Dean asked to cowrite this book. If that was a mistake, blame him. He, however, believes he has chosen wisely because the data, set forth in the pages that follow, speaks for itself and should not be ignored as America faces the crisis we believe lies immediately ahead.

CHAPTER TWO

DONALD TRUMP'S YOUTH: THE CHILD WHO IS THE FATHER OF THE CHILD

Why do we consider Donald Trump an authoritarian leader? Look at the statements below. Do you think he would agree or disagree with them?

- "Winning is not the first thing; it's the only thing."
- "If you have power in a situation, you should use it however you have to in order to get your way."
- "I would be cold-blooded and vengeful if that's what it took to reach my goals."
- "Money, wealth, and luxuries mean a lot to me."
- "I like other people to be afraid of me."
- "I will do my best to destroy anyone who deliberately blocks my plans and goals."

Donald Trump would probably strongly agree with every one of these sentiments. Not only have his actions betrayed such attitudes almost daily, he has even said them "aloud" in his books, on his Twitter feed, and at his rallies. You could put these statements on a poster captioned, "The Donald Trump Creed." But while these sentiments may capture the core of Trump's outlook on life, he did not compile this list nor was it put together with him in mind. The statements come from a psychological test developed in 1996 called the Power-Mad Scale, which is presented in its entirety in Appendix II.[1] It measures how much a person craves social power, and it was created to study "social dominators"—individuals who oppose equality among people and instead believe in domination. We believe Donald Trump would blow the roof off the Power-Mad Scale because he is an extreme social dominator. The drive to dominate everyone around him is a hallmark of an authoritarian leader. It takes no insight to understand why. Persons who would be king, tyrants-in-waiting, demagogues screaming from their platforms present no mystery. Shakespeare did not spend lots of lines delving into Richard III's motivation. Wannabe autocrats crave power—lots of thick, unchecked power, because power gets them what they want. Be it incredible wealth, borderless fame, the most desirable sexual partners, revenge served hot or cold, even immortality: power commands.

Whether you despise Donald Trump or hold him in the highest esteem, you must admit he has an extraordinarily strong drive for power which shows up in his need to dominate others. Tony Schwartz, who spent eighteen months observing Trump in action in 1985–6 as preparation for writing *The Art of the Deal*, found Trump has "an absolute lack of interest in anything beyond power and money." Schwartz explained: "In countless conversations, he made clear to me that he treated every encounter as a contest he had to win . . . He has spent his life seeking to dominate others, whatever that requires and whatever the collateral damage." These experiences led Schwartz to conclude, "Trump felt compelled to go to war with the world. It was a binary, zero-sum choice for him: You either dominate or you submitted. You either created and exploited fear, or you succumbed to it."[2]

HOW TRUMP BECAME AN AUTHORITARIAN

We believe a great deal of Donald Trump's successes and failures, including those as president, directly resulted from the way he was raised and the experiences he had early in life. In fact, as remarkable as it might seem, if you want to understand why Trump approached the COVID-19 crisis the way he did, you can find the reasons in things that happened to him as a child. We will show you the proof in this pudding in this and the next two chapters. First we look at the seminal events in his childhood and adolescence. In chapter 3 we look at how the themes of those formative years were reinforced and strengthened in adulthood and carried him (so improbably) to the White House. In chapter 4 we consider how what we have learned explains the most disturbing presidency in our modern nation's history.

Donald Trump has never talked to anyone at length about his experience of growing up. Tony Schwartz picked up bits and pieces of the story as he ghost-wrote *The Art of the Deal*. When Schwartz asked him to describe his childhood, "Trump became impatient and irritable. He looked fidgety like a kindergartner who can't sit still in a classroom."[3] Even when Schwartz pressed him, Trump seemed to remember almost nothing of his youth, and made it clear that he was bored doing so. Nearly three tumultuous decades later Trump agreed to be interviewed in 2014 by Michael D'Antonio for a biography. But he only sat for four sessions during which he showed no inclination whatsoever to describe his childhood. "Trump famously avoids discussing the past, resists self-analysis," D'Antonio later explained.[4]

"I don't like to analyze myself," Trump said in one of these interviews, "because I might not like what I see."[5] Yet he did tell D'Antonio a few things about his childhood, who presented them in *The Truth about Trump*, which we have woven into the narrative that follows. But most of our information about Trump's early life was obtained by Michael Miller and Paul Schwartzman, investigative reporters for *The Washington Post*. They interviewed "The Donald's" neighbors, schoolmates, and teachers for *Trump Revealed*, edited by Michael Kranish and Marc Fisher.[6] A very clear portrait emerges from these sources.

TRUMP IS THE CREATION OF HIS FATHER, FRED TRUMP

Donald Trump was born on June 14, 1946, in Queens, New York, the fourth of five children born to Mary and Fred Trump. Trump's mother, Mary Ann MacLeod, had come to New York from Scotland as a young woman and worked as a maid until she married Fred in 1936. She reportedly was very status-conscious and sought to be the center of attention at social gatherings. She would go to considerable lengths to be noticed. Donald told a biographer, "Looking back, I realize now that I got some of my sense of showmanship from my mother. She always had a flair for the dramatic and the grand."[7] Due to complications from her pregnancies Mary Trump became sickly with her fourth child, Donald, resulting in his having a limited relationship with his mother. Donald's childhood friends have virtually no memory of her interacting with him. An early pal, Mark Golding, recalled, "When I would play with Donald, his father would be around and watch him play. His mother didn't interact that way . . . Donald was in awe of his father, and very detached from his mother."[8] Many people, including lots of psychologists, would take note of this. Attachment theory holds that the quality and reliability of the mother-child relationship can profoundly impact a person's life. An "empty" relationship, or one that is suddenly ended during the early years can make it very hard for someone to develop trusting relationships and to love as an adult. They find it much easier to feel sorry for themselves than for those afflicted by tragedy. Someone could easily look at Donald Trump's life through this lens and say, "It figures."

Everyone who knew Donald as a youth, and Donald Trump himself, trace his drive for dominance directly and emphatically to his father. If you look at photographs of Trump seated at the Resolute Desk in the Oval Office, you will notice that for several months he only had one picture on the table behind him: his father's. Later his mother's photo appeared. But it was months later. Fred Trump was the son of a German émigré, and is uniformly described as tough, hard-driving, astute, frugal, and accomplished at "working the system"—in his case getting government support for building modest homes and apartments in Queens and Brooklyn. A 2018 *New York Times* investigation found he amassed a fortune after World War II, which he kept by cheating on taxes he owed the very governments that were financing his real estate ventures.[9] One of Fred's favorite ploys, as he played "catch me if you can" with the Internal Revenue Service, was to transfer his wealth to his children while paying only a pittance of the gift and inheritance taxes. Altogether, with his adult children's help, Fred slipped more than $1 billion dollars (in today's money) to his offspring. His accommodating accountants found nearly three hundred different channels to pass hundreds of millions of dollars to Donald alone. (When the *Times* story broke, Donald's wealthy sister Maryanne Trump Barry, who was a senior status federal appellate judge, resigned rather than face investigation and possible impeachment for a lifetime of tax dodging.[10]) Fred Trump clearly believed that if you could get away with doing something profitable that was illegal, just do it, and he orchestrated a massive family-wide tax fraud that allowed him to accumulate and pass along great wealth. Many suspect the apple of his eye, "Mr. Law and Order" Donald Trump, did not grow up far from the tree.

With his mother largely making "guest appearances" in family life, Donald was parented by his father, or not at all. Tony Schwartz explained to PBS *Frontline* in 2016 that he had the impression Fred Trump did not engage in emotions beyond a disciplinarian's anger.[11] Louise Sunshine, who was Donald Trump's personal assistant and eventual executive vice-president from 1973 to 1985 had a front-row seat at numerous interactions between father and (adult) son. "Fred Trump was a machine," she said in 2017. "I mean, he was a human machine. He was driven beyond whatever the description of 'driven' could ever mean. And when you look at the picture of Fred and you look at Donald, you see the great resemblance between the two. And when you think about Fred's energy, you see how it is channeled through Donald."[12] A boyhood friend of Donald, Sandy McIntosh, remembers Donald's father as being "cold. He was not a warm person. I'd see his father at the beach, even, with a suit and a tie and a hat, a clipped, very kind of military mustache, and simply being correct."[13] He was the kind of parent featured in the old joke about the boy who told his parents he had gotten a 95 on the spelling test: "Who got the other five?"

According to Donald, Fred Trump taught him and his older brother Freddy to be hyper-competitive to the point of being "killers" to become "kings." The father predictably toughened his sons by being hard on them. Freddy was supposed to take over the family business, but he fell far short in dominance. He ended up supervising a maintenance crew in an apartment complex and died of a heart attack at age forty-three, a recovering alcoholic. "Our family environment, the competitiveness, was a negative factor for Fred," Donald told Michael D'Antonio. "Freddy just wasn't a killer, and he didn't defend himself, which was a fatal mistake." D'Antonio concluded that Freddy was a severe disappointment to his father, but another prince was at hand: "Donnie," who wanted to be a king. Donald showed much more interest in their father's business than Freddy, who gladly surrendered the role of heir apparent.

We need to pause here and have some sympathy for the young Donald Trump. While lots of dads (and moms) want their children to be competitive and, furthermore, to win, Fred Trump appears to have demanded it as a prerequisite for the little bits of love he had to give. The intensity of these demands "broke" Freddy, while Donald may have welcomed the chance to become Number One Son. He may also have felt great pressure to be a "killer" if he was going to survive psychologically. What he had to be for his father's love was a life sentence. One cannot say how much of a "winner," a "killer," and a "king" Fred Trump wanted his son to be, but there is no indication that he told his son to ease up, that he had arrived. Instead, Donald said of his father in 1990, when he was middle-aged: "This is a man who never lets you forget he's your father."[14] The message seems to have been, both by tutorage and Fred's own example as he pursued establishing a family dynasty: More, more, get more. It's still not enough. That is a very tough assignment to give your child, one doomed to ultimate failure because nobody gets it all. So, Fred insisted Donald always be a winner and never be a loser, giving him an impossible assignment, for no one can always win. But this dark cloud had a shiny patina. Winning was fun. Dominance was fun. And as Donald acquired more, more, more, he inevitably discovered the joys of status, admiration, wealth, and power. Yes, power was the way to everything else. Ultimately, it becomes the goal in itself.

Donald Trump thinks the drive for power is genetically inherited. He has said often that his successes come from his DNA, that he is a "born winner." He may have inherited a genetic predisposition for dominance from his father, a combination of genetic settings his brother Freddy missed. But Donald was raised, twenty-five hours a day, eight days a week, to intimidate and control others. "That's why I'm so screwed up, because I had a father who pushed me so hard," Trump let slip in 2007, during an instance Tony Schwartz called "a brief and rare moment of self-awareness."[15]

BECOMING A BULLY

Trump told Michael D'Antonio, "When I look at myself in the first grade and I look at myself now, I'm basically the same. The temperament is not different."[16] Which, put another way, means that Donald Trump never grew up. This is a very common observation among people who know him.[17] As our misquoting of Wordsworth in the title of this chapter indicates, the child grew up to be a child. By all accounts, including his own, young Trump was something of a terror as a kid. Wherever it came from, nature or nurture, Donnie Trump reportedly had a mean streak. At age five or six he went into a neighbor's yard where a toddler named Dennis Burnham was sitting unattended in a playpen. When the child's mother came outside, Donald was throwing rocks at her son.[18] Donald Trump's brother, Robert, who was born two years after him, told a PBS *Frontline* interviewer, "Donald was always the kid in the family who would start throwing birthday cake at all the parties, that you would build up a tower of blocks, and he would come knock your blocks down."[19] One day Donald was building a tall structure out of his blocks, but he needed Robert's blocks to finish it. Robert loaned him all his. Trump then judged his building was so wonderful that "I glued the whole thing together. And that was the end of Robert's blocks."[20] The story itself tells us something, but Trump's telling of it when he was in his forties—"and that was the end of Robert's blocks"—tells us even more. He was still chuckling over how he had "screwed" his little brother.

People become bullies for different reasons, but clinical psychologists and social workers would probably not be surprised that the young Donald Trump was one. Often bullies have remarkably high opinions of themselves on the surface, but they are trying to mask an underlying anxiety that they are not up to snuff. And often they are doing poorly in school.[21] When Donald entered elementary school at a nearby private institution, he was following three older siblings, including firstborn Maryanne, who was always an A student. His teachers' evaluations were significantly less glowing, which Trump deeply resented. He became "extremely rebellious," Maryanne remembered, and threw blackboard erasers at his teachers. "Who could forget him?" said his former teacher Ann Trees, eighty-two. She added, "He was headstrong and determined. He would sit with his arms folded with this look on his face—I use the word surly—almost daring you to say one thing or another that wouldn't settle with him."[22] Trump told Tony Schwartz, "Even in elementary school I was a very assertive, aggressive kid." He added he had once punched a music teacher at the school in the face, giving him a black eye.[23]

We must weigh Trump's tales about himself against his rather spotty record for truthfulness. No one can remember hearing about this punch at the time, and Trump had only reached the age of seven when it supposedly happened. He would have had trouble giving Little Lord Fauntleroy a black eye. He told this story in 1986 when he was trying to impress an interviewer with how tough he had been all his life. But there is something else in these school stories that becomes a motif in the adult Donald Trump. He said he punched the music teacher because the teacher did not know anything about music. Well, maybe W. A. Mozart knew a lot about music at age seven, but it is for certain Donnie Trump did not. But Trump may have resented, even as a child, anyone who was smarter than he was. This may have arisen from teachers' unfavorable comparisons with the bright Maryanne. *He* was supposed to be the best. His father told him he had to be, so he was. Children with an inflated, unrealistic sense of how smart they are often react to disappointing grades by saying the teacher is stupid. Ms. Trees's description of a defiant Trump as "surly" fits the bill.

Throughout his life, Trump holds "accomplished" people at arm's length. This is the Donald Trump screaming at the joint chiefs of staff in the Pentagon in 2017 that they are so incompetent, "a bunch of dopes and babies," he would never go to war with them.[24] This is the Donald Trump who refuses to accept the scientific consensus about global warming when he has little understanding of what the scientists are talking about. This is the president who ignored all the recommendations and pleas for action about COVID-19 from medical experts until many Americans began dying of the disease.

Trump used his fists as a child. Always big for his age, he appears to have specialized in hitting people smaller than himself. The character named Scott Farkus in *A Christmas Story*, who harasses Ralphie daily, probably resembles the young Donald Trump quite a bit. The kid living next door to the Trumps, Dennis Burnham, told the *Washington Post* in 2016 that his parents instructed him to stay away from Trump. "Donald was known to be a bully, I was a little kid, and my parents didn't want me beaten up."[25] Trump also told Tony Schwartz that he acquired a gang of followers in grade school, not unusual for a bully. "I was always something of a leader in my neighborhood . . . In my own crowd I was very well liked, and I tended to be the kid the others followed."[26] Another boy who grew up with Trump in Queens, Steven Nachtigall, recalled that Donald and his friends would ride their bikes around and "shout and curse very loudly." He once saw them dismount to beat up another boy. Nachtigall still remembered the attack vividly sixty years later because it was so unusual and terrifying at that age. "He was a loud-mouthed bully."[27]

"I loved to fight. I always loved to fight . . . all types of fights, any kind of fight, I loved it," Donald Trump told D'Antonio.[28] But there is no record or memory, so far as we know, of his ever fighting anyone his own size, or bigger (aside from, supposedly, the music teacher).

There is another likely connection here between the elementary school Trump and the man who became president in 2017. If you go on any schoolyard while a bully and his gang are throwing their weight around, you will likely discover that the bully has given other children nasty nicknames to humiliate them, like "Hey, Dirty Clothes" or "Look, there's Pimple Face." His followers will usually laugh and repeat the taunt. President Donald Trump, despite occupying an office of dignity and decorum, does this to almost everyone who opposes him. He seemingly cannot resist adding insult and injury to disagreement, to make it personal, not just business. It is, for him, a favorite route to obtaining dominance over someone. One also notices how often he chooses epithets that apply more to him than to his target, such as "Lying Ted Cruz" or "Racist Pat Buchannan" or "Nasty (substitute many female reporters who have asked a question Trump does not want to deal with)." Similarly, he often attacks people who criticize him or accuse him of sexual assault as being "publicity seekers." Donald likes people to think he grew up rough and tough on the mean streets of New York City, but his family lived in a twenty-three-room "Southern mansion" with nine bathrooms in the posh Jamaica Estates area of Queens. The Trumps likely prevailed, quietly, for that was Fred's style, as the richest patrons of Donald's school. That may explain why Donald was not kicked out despite his bad behavior and poor grades. Well-coordinated as well as big, he found that being a good athlete also got him out of hot water when he underperformed academically and overperformed at being "a little shit," as the music teacher put it later.[29]

Michael D'Antonio was asked in 2017, "Who is Trump trying to be?" and he replied, "He's trying to be someone like he imagines General Patton was. When he talks about these World War II generals portrayed in the movies, he's explaining something about himself and what he admires. He really does identify with that kind of aggression, that kind of authority. His role models . . . were aggressive bullies who used strength as a tool and as a measure of their own self-worth."[30] Or he wants to be Russia's Vladimir Putin, China's Xi Jinping, Philippine President Rodrigo Duterte, Turkish President Recep Tayyip Erdogan, or Egypt's Abdel Fattah el-Sisi.[31]

TRUMP'S MORAL UPBRINGING

Trump's parents strove to be respected members of their community, and that meant being highly respectable. Not a hint of scandal sullied his parents' sixty-three-year marriage. But the tax-dodging, "fixing" Fred Trump had little regard for morality and left the religious instruction of his children to his wife. It did not work. "The values [my mother] gave to me were strong values," Donald once said to a reporter for the *Sunday Times*. "I wish

I could have picked up all of them, but I didn't, obviously."[32] Mary Trump might have had a strict Presbyterian upbringing, but Donald had only a passing acquaintance with her beliefs. Fred Trump squared his felonious habits with respectable Christian beliefs by selecting a package of Christian beliefs to his liking. On occasions he took the family to Norman Vincent Peale's Marble Collegiate Church on Fifth Avenue in Manhattan. Peale preached a pro-entrepreneur, go-get-'em Christianity that had nothing whatsoever to do with Jesus's teaching that the meek will inherit the earth. Trump admired Peale's sermons and considered him a mentor.[33] Peale wrote in 1957, "It is an affront to God when you have a low opinion of yourself."[34] If that is so, God will seemingly suffer no such affronts from Donald. As for ethics, young Donald probably thought about God and morality as often as his father likely did: once a week, some weeks, but not for long, even then. The commandment he probably learned best as he grew up was the one his father successfully followed all his life: "Don't get caught."

DONALD IS SENT TO MILITARY SCHOOL

However, Donald did get caught by his parents. They saw he was underperforming in school and insolent toward teachers who gave him low marks. He also was a bully, but that probably did not bother his father at all. Then in 1959 they discovered a cache of switchblade knives stashed away in Donald's room. Their thirteen-year-old son was buying them during secret Saturday-morning excursions into Manhattan with a friend.[35] Fred and Mary considered Manhattan far too dangerous for Donald, and indeed it would have many attractions for a thirteen-year-old boy. But we should notice that his parents did not find "girlie magazines" under his mattress, but switchblade knives. What possible need did Donald have of them, especially so many? One of them had a blade nearly eleven inches long! ("Now that's a knife.") There was no reason, really. *West Side Story* was running on

Broadway and may have provided the initial appeal. But once Donald got the knives home to Queens, they would have spelled power with a flick of the thumb. He likely bought them to impress other kids with how tough and dangerous he was.

Fred erupted with anger, probably mostly because Donald had disobeyed and deceived him in making the jaunts. He decided to enroll his son the coming fall in the New York Military Academy, located an hour's drive to the north in Cornwall. Donald surely got the message that he had displeased his father. Most cadets stayed at the school throughout the academic terms, which meant Donald was essentially sent away from home for most of the year at age thirteen. He might have felt banished at first, but by 1959, Fred Trump must have realized his firstborn son, Freddy, then age twenty-one, had no interest in real estate. Donald presented the only path to establishing the Trump dynasty. Fred might even have sent Donald to military school partly to toughen him up even more, to make him as determined, self-disciplined, and ferocious for the tasks down the road as he himself was.

When Donald arrived at NYMA he was assigned to F Company, which was overseen by a thirty-four-year-old World War II veteran named Theodore Dobias. Major Doby had served with the Tenth Mountain Division in Italy and had seen plenty of horrors during the division's long grind up the peninsula. Dobias probably bore a good psychological resemblance to his former commander, General Patton. He greeted freshmen boys with a rough and ready shock treatment of verbal and physical abuse. When the headstrong Donald rebelled at having to make his bed and keep his brass shined, Dobias reportedly slapped and punched him until Donald realized there was no way out and conformed.[36] Once he had accepted his fate, Trump embraced the school ethos with both arms. Author Gwenda Blair told PBS: "He loved military school. He liked the out-front competitiveness of it. There were so many different ways you could excel and get medals and ribbons."[37] And just as he had in grammar school, Trump used his athletic ability to advance himself among his peers and court favor with the faculty. Dobias, who coached football and baseball, later told an interviewer, "He always had to be number one, in everything. He was a conniver even then. A real pain in the ass. He would do anything to win . . .[He] just wanted to be first, in everything, and he wanted people to know he was first."[38] Donald sought to co-opt authority just as his father did, and he directed his efforts on the most powerful person in his life at the school. "I figured out what it would take to get Dobias on my side," Trump later told the *Washington Post*, "I finessed him. It helped that I was a good athlete, since he was the baseball coach and I was the captain of the team. But I also learned how to play him."[39] Trump's academic performance may have improved at the highly regulated academy, but it is difficult to believe he was a very good student given the efforts he has taken to make sure the school never reveals his grades.[40] Fred Trump visited Donald regularly at NYMA, showing a keen interest in his progress. One imagines the boy showed him his latest medal or improved academic grade, hoping to please his hard-to-please father. Dobias probably gave Fred Trump reports on Donald and recalls "The father was really tough on the kid. He was very German. He came up on a lot of Sundays and would take the boy out to dinner. Not many did that. But he was very tough."[41]

THE ORIGIN OF "TRUMP"

Donald Trump was best known among his classmates for his athletic skills. One of his accomplishments in his junior year probably led to TRUMP Tower, the TRUMP jet, the TRUMP helicopter, TRUMP Plaza, TRUMP steaks, TRUMP vodka, TRUMP University, and so on. Donald had gotten a base hit that won a baseball game, and the local paper carried the headline, "Trump Wins Game for NYMA." Donald was transported with delight. "It felt good seeing my name in print," he said. "How many people are in print? Nobody's in print. It was the first time I was ever in the newspaper. I thought it was amazing."[42] One should note two things about his reaction. First, he immediately framed the event in a competitive light. "How many people are in print? Nobody's in print." We have to realize that this is the primary way Trump processes life: "Did I beat everybody else, or did somebody beat me?" Second, he who had grown up in the media center of the world was really thrilled by this headline in a small-town newspaper. That is a little surprising. But suppose you are a sixteen-year-old whose mother has, for all your life, shown little interest in you and whose father relentlessly demands that you be a winner. Would you not find fame and glory the elixir of the gods? You could impress hundreds, thousands of people at a time through a newspaper and become somebody great to people who did not even know you. Do you think there is a chance he showed the newspaper article to his father the next time Fred visited?

Thus, by his own words, Donald fell in love with publicity while still a teenager. And this love has only grown. He told Michael D'Antonio in 2014 that he had a team on his staff who monitored how often he was mentioned in the media. "There are thousands of them a day," he proudly said.[43] A sizable chunk of those stories are extremely critical, even condemning of him. But as Tony Schwartz explained in *The Art of the Deal*, for Trump, "good publicity is preferable to bad, but from a bottom-line perspective, bad publicity is sometimes better than no publicity at all. Controversy, in short, sells."[44] And name recognition is everything. So even though his behavior has led many Americans to have a negative opinion of him, any publicity satisfies his longing for recognition. Donald Trump wants to believe that he matters.

IT ALL COMES TOGETHER ON FIFTH AVENUE

Trump was promoted regularly as the class of 1964 moved through the school's military program, but he was consistently outshone by some of his peers who attained more stripes before he did. Then in the summer of 1963 he was promoted from supply sergeant to Captain of A Company, leaping over others who had previously outranked him. It was not the highest position in the cadet corps, but such a big jump puzzled many. "He was really an afterthought," a classmate said later. "He didn't show much as a freshman, sophomore, or even a junior, because he would have already been more than a supply sergeant."[45] Then one of Donald's sergeants in A Company got in trouble for abusing an underclassman and Donald was deemed partly responsible because he did not supervise his sergeants enough. He lost his command and was transferred to the battalion headquarters staff.[46] Thus Donald's good fortune quickly soured, but then a glorious event occurred that we think tied the threads of his youth into the hard knot of his adult personality. The school had a crack drill team and it was asked to lead the Columbus Day Parade in New York City on October 12, 1963. Donald was not a member of the team, but he was six foot two and could flourish a proud military bearing. Accordingly, he was placed in charge of the drill team for the occasion and marched in front of it down Fifth Avenue, thus leading everyone. It must have been a glorious moment for a boy whose behavior shouted, *Look at me, look at me!* when he threw cake at birthday parties. Now he was heading up the frigging parade straight down the center of Manhattan! He shook hands with Cardinal Spellman at St. Patrick's Cathedral at the end of the route, after which he turned to a fellow officer and said, "You know what, Ace? I'd really like to own some of this real estate someday."[47] It was the first sign we know of that Trump was setting his sights higher than the projects his father built in Brooklyn and Queens.

DONALD DISCOVERS "ARM CANDY" AND LEGENDS

Two very notable features of Donald Trump's adult life began to appear after this trip to Manhattan that, as far as we know, had not appeared before. He began using display to gain status, and he started weaving a false history about his accomplishments. Both were obviously done to impress the impressionable. Donald had not traded on his father's wealth among his peers. When Fred Trump early on had his chauffeur drive him up to the military school one Sunday, Donald was so embarrassed he would not go to meet him.[48] But in his senior year he began to show off before his classmates with the most jaw-dropping, status-boosting, desperately desired trophies one could have at an all-boys military academy: beautiful girls. Most Sundays Fred and Mary Trump would arrive at the school with some attractive, smartly dressed young woman whom Donald would show around the grounds.[49] He was allowed to offer her his arm, but they could never be alone. Holding hands would have been punished by at least an hour of marching on penalty detail. Donald could take his date to the school canteen, which would have become packed with fellow students dying for a look at a "lovely" and a whiff of transporting perfume from Saks Fifth Avenue. But never, not ever, not even hardly ever, to his dorm. Every week brought a different girl, good-looking, and right out of *Vogue*. Donald was the envy of every boy in school. Which was exactly what he wanted. His classmates voted him Ladies' Man for the yearbook, not Baseball Star or Most Ambitious. They probably believed he was enormously successful with women, and that is why the beautiful girls flocked to him. What he was enormously successful at was looking enormously successful, whatever the truth. Then and now, in this way and many others, Donald Trump reeled in the gullible. Which so far as we know, he had never particularly done before. Who were these glamorous femmes? Perhaps acquaintances from wealthy families in Queens and Long Island whom Donald had dated during the previous summer. He was tall, fair-haired, good-looking, from a very wealthy family, and a bad boy, thus a combination that some immanent debutantes found irresistible. But some of them may never have known Donald before, but were sent by match-seeking parents on a chauffeured, chaperoned visit to an exclusive all-boys school and paraded before the scions of rich families. They were "princess for a day" at New York Military Academy, brought in to make the rest of the school envy him. None of the beautiful women on his arm was a girlfriend. Donald was not in love with any of them. No one, so far as we know, has ever mentioned Donald's falling in love in his youth, or meandering into it, or even ambling nearby. No one has ever mentioned him having even a steady date until he met his first wife when he was thirty. Trump's childhood friend and fellow student at NYMA, Sandy McIntosh, identified the major source of many men's attitudes toward women at the time: Hugh Hefner. McIntosh put it this way: "[The] biggest advice in our lives came from *Playboy* magazine . . . That's what we learned about women, so that was all [I had in] my adolescence. And that's why [learning to love after] getting out of military school was difficult. You had to realize that you couldn't just follow the Playboy philosophy. But I think that the things that we talked about at that time in 1964 really are very close to kind of the way Trump talks now, about women and minorities and people of different religions."[50]

Sandy McIntosh also informs us about Donald Trump's learning the value of legends in self-promotion at this time, even if they involved a tissue of lies. Trump had probably been blatantly lying since he was a child, giving the bully's standard, "No, I didn't" to charges that he had attacked others. But by the end of his senior year at the New York Military Academy, he began lying and getting other people to lie, too, for an altogether different reason: to make him look magnificent. "It was 1964, the year Donald graduated," McIntosh reported, "We were walking together near the baseball field where, he reminded me, he'd played exceptionally well. He demanded that I tell him the story of one of his greatest games. 'The bases were loaded,' I told him. 'We were losing by three. You hit the ball just over the third baseman's head. Neither the third baseman nor the left fielder could get to the ball in time. All four of our runs came in; we won the game.' 'No,' he said. 'That's not the way it happened. I want you to remember this: I hit the ball out of the ballpark! Remember that. I hit it out of the ballpark.' 'Ballpark?' I thought. 'We were talking about a high school practice field. There was no park to hit a ball out of. And anyway, his hit was a blooper the fielders very badly misplayed."[51] Thus, by age eighteen, Donald Trump was at work creating his legend. He wanted to look not just accomplished, but heroic. Fame's hook, cast his way through a headline in a local newspaper and set as he led a parade down the middle of Manhattan, had captured him for the rest of his life.[52]

DONALD'S CHARACTER DEVELOPMENT DURING YOUNG ADULTHOOD

All Trump's older siblings went to college, with the firstborn Maryanne shining brightest when she graduated cum laude from Mount Holyoke College in 1958. Donald therefore understood he would be heading for university in the fall of 1964. He decided to become a Hollywood producer and applied to the film school at the University of Southern California. (The idea also occurred to another Queens boy, Harvey Weinstein, a few years later.) But USC, which had the likes of George Lucas in its film school then, turned Trump down. Thus, he went to his "safe school," Fordham University in the Bronx. Donald did not have a madcap *Animal House* college experience at Fordham. He lived at home and spent his weekends working for his father in various outer borough building projects. His classmates remember him arriving on campus each day in a sports car, wearing suits and carrying a briefcase. He took up squash, a rich man's game, and made the university team because of his fast, hard-hitting play. Unlike his first year at NYMA, he made it clear to his teammates, and probably to everyone who knew him, that he was from a rich family. He had changed that much in four years. But Donald was unhappy at Fordham because it did not have a best-of-the-best reputation and by now he had set his eye on The Top.

By 1966 Donald had decided to become a builder like his father, only bigger and richer. His biographers agree that he was enthralled by the image of William Zeckendorf, a larger-than-life New York City property developer who hired a publicity agent to ensure his name was always in the news. Zeckendorf lived lavishly in Manhattan, where his Webb and Knapp realty company owned the Chrysler Building, the Hotel Astor, and the land where the United Nations Building was built. He made sure the media noticed his pursuit of the very best and announced sometimes fantastical real estate ventures to keep his name in the papers. He was also severely underfinanced, and his company went bankrupt in 1965, followed by his personal bankruptcy in 1968. Though he went down in flames, Zeckendorf's career inspired the young Donald Trump. In 1966, Trump applied to transfer to the undergraduate real estate major in the economics department at the Wharton School of Finance and Commerce at the University of Pennsylvania. His explanation in *The Art of the Deal*: "I decided that as long as I had to be in college, I might as well test myself against the best."[53] Trump wanted to graduate from an Ivy League university, and he thought a Wharton degree would impress financiers.

Donald Trump often implies he went to the highly ranked graduate business school at University of Pennsylvania, but he did not. He has a bachelor's degree from the Wharton undergraduate program, which is much less prestigious. He bases his frequent claim of being a "super genius" on his being admitted into the program, which he maintains was the hardest school in the world to get into. It was not—not at all. James Nolan, the admissions official who interviewed Trump, said the acceptance rate was better than 50 percent for transfer students.[54] Furthermore, Nolan was from Queens and had spent a good part of his youth in the Trump home playing with his friend, Freddy Trump. Fred Sr. even came along with Donald for his Penn interview to put an exclamation point to the wealthy family's desire that Son Number Two, the Heir Apparent, be allowed to transfer. Nolan recommended it happen, and it did.[55]

Trump's wish to be seen with attractive women continued at Penn. One fellow student recalls that, "Every time I saw [Donald] he had a pretty girl on his arm."[56] As at NYMA, the women may not have been as smitten with Donald as it seemed. Candice Bergen went on a date with him in her freshman year there. "He picked me up [at the women's dormitory]. He was wearing a burgundy three-piece suit with burgundy patent leather boots, and he was in a burgundy limousine, so it was very color-coordinated. I was home by nine. It was a very short dinner." Asked for her overall impression of him, she said, "He was a good-looking guy, and a douche."[57]

When Trump arrived at Penn he told other students he was going to be the next Bill Zeckendorf, only he would be bigger and better.[58] But although Trump probably knew more about some aspects of real estate operations and financing than any of his classmates, he betrayed no sign of wanting to "test himself against the best." Classmates remember his being disinterested in his studies. He spent a lot of time drawing and talking of the Manhattan skyline. Although he told many people afterward that he graduated first in his class at Wharton, he did not distinguish himself at all academically and was not even listed among the fifty-six students on the honor roll at graduation.[59] His marketing professor, William T. Kelly, remembers him well: "Donald Trump was the dumbest goddamn student I ever had!"[60] Like some other things we have seen, this assessment does not exactly coincide with Donald Trump's version of the facts. The discrepancies will grow ever greater as we consider his years between his university graduation and his becoming president.

CHAPTER THREE

TRUMP'S LIFE FROM 1968 TO 2016: ECSTASY, AGONY, FAKERY, FRAUD

What kind of person do you find President Trump? Here are some statements from another personality test. Do you think Trump would agree with them or disagree with them, if he were being completely truthful about his beliefs?

- "There really is no such thing as 'right' and 'wrong.' It all boils down to what you can get away with."
- "One of the most useful skills a person should develop is how to look someone straight in the eye and lie convincingly."
- "The best skill you can have is knowing the 'right move at the right time': when to 'soft-sell' someone, when to be tough, when to flatter, when to threaten, when to bribe, etc."
- "There's a sucker born every minute, and smart people learn how to take advantage of them."
- "It is more important to create a good image of yourself in the minds of others than to actually be the person others think you are."
- "One of the best ways to handle people is to tell them what they want to hear."

These statements come from the "Con Man Scale," which is presented in its entirety in Appendix II. Like the Power Mad Scale we considered at the beginning of Chapter 2, it was developed in 1996 to explore the thinking of people who might want to become authoritarian leaders. It tries to determine how amoral, manipulative, deceitful and exploitive someone is. It seemed these qualities would be found in power-mad individuals, since they make it so much easier to be a brute. And indeed, scores on the two tests did go along with each other very nicely.[1] The Con Man Scale was not developed with Donald Trump in mind, and of course we do not have his answers. But we invite you to keep its statements in the back of your mind as we cover Trump's life from college until he entered politics and see how much his behavior during this period speaks of someone who is amoral, manipulative, deceitful, and exploitive—in short, a con man.[2]

DONALD TRUMP: DRAFT-DODGER

When he graduated from Wharton, Donald moved back to Queens and went to work every day in his father's office in Brooklyn. He had never really left the office since he had hopped home most weekends to work on his father's projects. Now he was ready to accept his life's commission: master all aspects of the family business. But he had a problem. With his educational deferments gone, he was eligible for the draft, and in 1968 that usually meant heading to Vietnam. This, however, was not part of Fred Trump's grand plans, or his son's, either, for that matter. Donald had been given an army physical exam when he arrived at Wharton in 1966 and passed it with no problem. Yet, two years later, a physician said he had bone spurs on his heels, which would keep him from proper soldiering. That seems preposterous since he had been a star athlete in high school, regularly played squash, and bone spurs that severe would have been evident two years earlier. When asked about this later, Trump could not remember the name of the doctor who wrote the "very strong letter." *The New York Times* happily found him in December 2018.[3] He was the late Dr. Larry Braunstein, a podiatrist who rented his office in Queens from Donald's father. Braunstein told his daughters he wrote the letter "as a favor" to his landlord. Apparently Braunstein's rent did not go up later when other Trump-owned properties around his office did. A second podiatrist, Dr. Manny Weinstein, who rented an apartment from Fred Trump, may have served as a second opinion for the draft board. It is uncertain whether either man ever examined young Trump. (Bone spurs do not go away, so President Trump could show people his deferment was legit just by walking around barefoot some time.)

We do not know for certain that Donald wanted to dodge the draft, as his father pulled all the strings. But we do know the Donald wanted to out-Zeckendorf Zeckendorf. So he stayed at his father's side for quite a while, learning how the contracts were won, the kickbacks were kicked, the profits were hidden, professionals were corrupted, valuations were manipulated, federal requirements were ignored, Black tenants were systematically excluded, and the family fortune was siphoned off to its members with nary a penny going to the taxman. In his book *Surviving at the Top,* Trump heaps scorn on rich men who had simply inherited their wealth, calling them "The Lucky Sperm Club."[4] In counterpoint, Trump insists he got rich from his own effort and "smarts," except for a $1 million loan his father gave him early on, which he had to repay with interest.[5] Millions upon millions of people believe this tale of how Donald Trump made it on his own. But the story crashes on some shoals of facts dug up in the remarkable 2018 investigation by the *New York Times* of Fred Trump's financial records.[6] The Trump patriarch began shifting his wealth to trust funds for his children when they were young. Donald had received a million dollars by the time he was eight, and he kept getting more. After he finished college his father gave him a million dollars each year to live on, with no interest or repayment, nor were gift taxes paid. In short, it was a blatant tax fraud. Furthermore, as long as Fred Trump was alive, he helped bankroll all of Donald's major real estate deals in the form of loan guarantees, personal loans, and outright gifts. After he died, he left Donald assets worth hundreds of millions of dollars.[7] (As we will explain, Donald lost almost all of this rather quickly.)

DONALD TAKES MANHATTAN

Donald Trump lived in Queens for a few years after he graduated from Wharton, but by 1971, he had an apartment in Manhattan, the magical island that had first called to him as a thirteen-year-old. His father was unhappy that Donald wanted to "play" in the high-stakes real estate business, but he also realized that Son Number Two presented his only chance of maintaining and expanding the family's wealth. So, Donald commuted to his father's small Brooklyn office for a while longer, all the while remembering his goal of changing the Manhattan skyline. He drove around imagining deals he might swing to secure properties, sometimes accompanied by Louise Sunshine, his father's right-hand partner, who had myriad ties to the Democratic machine in the city. She helped Donald make friends at City Hall. Far from being a rags-to-riches Horatio Alger hero, Trump had much going for him when he arrived in Manhattan. He was from a wealthy family, personally had more money than almost any other twenty-five-year-old man alive, and had endless connections.

Socially Trump assumed the lifestyle of a prominent but unattainable playboy, the very stuff of Hugh Hefner's magazine. It took him several tries, but he bagged a membership in an exclusive lounge on Lexington Avenue called simply Le Club. Most of the regulars were rich and powerful men and, oddly enough, an endless array of beautiful women were also permitted on the premises. The membership committee, according to Donald, made him promise not to hit on other men's wives.[8]

It was at Le Club that Donald met the infamous "fixer" attorney Roy Cohn who had been chief pit bull to Senator Joseph McCarthy in the 1950s and shared in McCarthy's disgrace following the U.S. Army hearings in 1954. Post-McCarthy, he had returned home to New York City where his unprincipled and inflammatory legal tactics brought him many clients from the rich and powerful. Cohn took a special interest in the flashy playboy from Queens who was getting ink in the gossip columns and soon offered him some legal advice regarding a problem with the federal government. Fred Trump had discreetly discriminated against African American applications for homes in his federally financed housing projects for years, which led Woody Guthrie to write a song about it.[9] In 1973 the Justice Department hauled Trump Management Corporation into court. Donald, who was fully engaged in the discrimination by then, strongly denied the charge. But since the FBI had statements from some of his employees verifying the accusation, the firm's lawyer advised Fred and Donald to settle, which merely meant they would promise not to do it anymore. When Roy Cohn learned of the Trumps' problems with the Fair Housing Act of 1968, he advised Donald to fight it tooth and nail all the way. Donald hired him to help do so.

The essence of Cohn's approach to a lawsuit or a government investigation or a personal disagreement or a dropped gum wrapper on a sidewalk was to never admit or apologize for a wrongdoing, but instead use the media to deny everything. Cohn's five favorite tactics were rather simple: (1) Lie without hesitation whenever necessary, over and over, (2) threaten your opponent by counterattacking much harder than you were attacked, (3) be ruthless and get even with anyone who crosses you. (4) If you are undeniably in the wrong and guilty as sin, accuse your opponent of being ten times worse than you and put them on the defensive. Finally, (5) if after all this you still lose, claim you won, and move on. Journalist Marie Brenner says of Cohn: "Roy Cohn humiliated people. He made up things. He had no morals. You couldn't even say that he had the morals of a snake. He had no morals. He had no moral center."[9] Donald, who had received almost no moral instruction, found this tutorage and working with Cohn most agreeable, and instructive. Cohn's lessons amounted to graduate school in How to Be an Unprincipled Lying "Killer"—traits Donald had been developing instead of a conscience since childhood. He probably wanted to get as good as this master who had gone over to the Dark Side.

To combat the charge of racism at the Trump properties, Roy Cohn and Donald Trump called a showy news conference to announce a $100 million lawsuit against the federal government for damage done to the Trumps. Then Cohn phoned the Justice Department official supervising the investigation, Donna Goldstein, and screamed that he was going to use his contacts in the Republican Party (Nixon had been reelected in 1972) to get her fired if she did not immediately drop the case which, he assured her, she had no chance of winning.[10] Cohn then complained to the judge hearing the case that the FBI was using Gestapo tactics in its searching of Trump files for evidence. Cohn was bluffing up a storm, and it petered out miserably. Elliot Richardson was the attorney general, and Goldstein's job could not have been safer. The feds had all the evidence they needed to win in court. And the counter lawsuit was almost immediately dismissed by the judge. Donald and Fred Trump settled out of court in 1975 by promising not to discriminate in the future, which had been the original "penalty." And the agreement stipulated that the Urban League would have first dibs on placing Black tenants in many Trump apartments for the next two years. Donald, however, told the media the company had won because they had not discriminated in the first place, and he soon found all kinds of ways to renege on the Urban League agreement. Years later, he further lied, falsely claiming the Justice Department action had been brought against many landlords, not just the Trumps.[11]

Donald could be boyishly charming and friendly when he sensed that would pay off. He was never more successful than when he totally snookered *New York Times* "society writer" Judy Klemesrud in the fall of 1976. Donald took the reporter with him on a "typical day" around New York

City in his limousine wearing his favorite burgundy suit. Was she snowed? Boy was she ever! Her first words about him in her profile were, "He is tall, lean and blond, with dazzling white teeth, and he looks ever so much like Robert Redford."[12] She believed Donald when he said he was worth more than $200 million, that he was Swedish, and that he had graduated first in his class at the Wharton School of Finance. The biggest whopper he sold her was that he was publicity shy.[13] This *New York Times* piece by Klemesrud gave Donald credibility for the rest of his life, even though there is hardly a word of truth in it, and it has been debunked from beginning to end. The truth is still putting on its shoes, or pants, or whatever while Trump's early lies are still racing around the world forty-four years later, huffed and puffed by a man who has learned that lying works like magic with many people.

Wayne Barrett, the first of many investigative journalists who would become the bane of Trump's existence, proved more perceptive when he dug into the Trump family realty and tax records at City Hall. When he interviewed Donald, he was offered a better apartment for his growing family. But Barrett declined and kept digging. Next he was threatened by lawsuit after lawsuit filed by Roy Cohn. But Barrett still penned a critical two-part essay for the *Village Voice* in 1978.

ECSTASY: ONWARD AND UPWARD

Roy Cohn guided Donald Trump's first major deal in Manhattan, the purchase and redevelopment of Penn Central's decaying Commodore Hotel. Trump's role in this and many later deals was to propose a plan to people who had lots of money and convince them it would make them even more money. It helped a lot if the people you were trying to convince believed other people with money were going to invest. Despite his claim that he was worth $200 million, Donald Trump did not have much on his balance sheet beyond the proverbial collection of seashells. But, thanks to his father, he did have a $1 million per year income that made him look rich and his father was known to have dough. To pull off the Commodore deal, Donald needed someone to loan him the money to buy the hotel from the Penn Central Railroad. He needed someone to pay for the refurbishment of the hotel. And he needed someone of stature to promise to run the hotel when it was finished and make money for the financiers, and Trump. He maneuvered, pressured, lied, and threatened until he had pulled it all off. He told Penn Central he had a deal with Hyatt Hotels to add the hotel to its chain. He had no such deal, but he called a news conference to announce that he had a signed agreement with Penn Central to sell him the hotel. He had an "agreement," but it was signed only by him. The railroad was waiting for a $250,000 payment to show he really was a player. But he didn't have any money, so he was stymied. He tried using his father's political connections to get the new hotel declared exempt from real estate taxes. This would give it a significant advantage over every other hotel in the city. Trump went to an official who could grant the exemption under a new urban development program and demanded the tax break. When the official refused, Trump said, "I'm going to have you fired." The official stood his ground, but eventually by hook and crook—mostly a lot of crook, as uncovered by Wayne Barrett— and behind the scenes work by Roy Cohn, Trump got the tax exemption, and the pieces fell in place, ultimately creating the Grand Hyatt New York.[14] Afterward, Donald bragged to the media about how clever he had been. "They [city bureaucrats] only asked to see an agreement. They didn't say it had to be signed."[15] But the brash young man with drive and connections, the "new Zeckendorf," had produced in the heart of Manhattan.

Apparently, Trump learned three things from the Commodore con: Image matters more than reality. If you looked and acted like you had enormous wealth, people believed you did and behaved accordingly. Lying works even when it can be easily exposed. Few people bother to check. And overplaying your hand pays off.

For all his maneuvering and deceit, however, Donald could not have pulled off the Commodore Hotel deal without his father, who at a critical point guaranteed the bank loan needed to start construction.[16] And Roy Cohn got him the tax breaks, along with big media coverage that glorified Trump's play. But both those men preferred to work behind the scenes, allowing young Donald to take all the credit the newspapers gave him.

Resplendent in glorious publicity as a wunderkind savior of deteriorating Manhattan, Trump soared higher by building Trump Tower on Fifth Avenue between 56th and 57th streets. Greatly aided again by his father's money and connections, and more tax breaks cleverly arranged by Roy Cohn, he finished the skyscraping edifice to himself in 1983 and moved into its penthouse apartment as "king" of midtown Manhattan.[17] He had fulfilled, at age thirty-seven, his dreams of owning a piece of Fifth Avenue and changing the Manhattan skyline. And now his amazing success led to incredible ruin.

AGONY CREATED BY HUBRIS

Autocracy and personal glorification often travel together, and most authoritarian leaders feature their own magnificence in their movements. Making yourself famous and admired helps you win friends and influence people. Donald Trump did not learn this from his father, who preached "Be a killer," but not "Be famous for being a killer." But he knew something his father did not appreciate: fame not only felt good, it converted to power at better than par. Accordingly, he purposely created a lot of hype when he moved to Manhattan, the famous place where fame's hook had caught him earlier. Generating hype proved easy-peasy because the many media outlets and inlets there have a voracity for stories that demands feeding every twenty-four hours. Celebrities could get their names in print just by hitting the nightclubs where the gossip columnists hung out. Donald Trump knew this. As Tony Schwartz quoted him in *The Art of the Deal*, "One thing I've learned about the press is that they're always hungry for a good story, and the more sensational the better."[18] However, the pursuit of fame can turn into an insatiable lust that takes over your life, as many one-hit wonders in popular culture can tell you. Trump himself knew this, as he said in *Surviving at the Top* in 1990: "The more celebrities I meet, the more I realize that fame is a kind of drug, one that is way too powerful for most people to handle."[19] You dip your toe, you stick in a foot, both feet, and you discover you are in quicksand. Fame can be addictive. But one problem with needing gobs and gobs of attention from others is that other people have lives too. And while the media feast on celebrities, they especially like new celebrities, or new stories about old celebrities. There are newspapers, not oldspapers. The question would have arisen for Donald Trump as it does for any celebrity: What have you done lately that is more spectacular than everybody else's spectacle? If the answer is nothing, then you suffer withdrawal from this kind of drug and get a very painful attention deficit disorder. Donald's growing hubris was driving him toward a cliff without brakes.

TRUMP ALCHEMY: THE SADIM TOUCH*

Besides the inherent pleasure of being admired far and wide, and the power that fame would bring someone as power-hungry as Trump, there was another reason he had to keep on succeeding ad infinitum: his father's open-ended command to make all the money he possibly could. As a result, Donald Trump went gambling on gambling. New Jersey had recently legalized casinos, and Trump heard the betting businesses were making money faster than they could count it. As well, casinos became magnets for well-heeled celebrities and performers, whose very presence in your hotel and on

---

* "Sadim" is "Midas" spelled backwards. A Sadim touch turns everything gold into something base.

your stage lent luster to your name. Fred Trump was against making this move, pointing out that his son knew nothing about running a casino. But Donald had come to believe from his string of real estate victories in Manhattan that he had great instincts for making the right move, and he believed casinos would pay off for him in the most spectacular way possible.

In 1984 Trump borrowed a truckload of money from banks impressed with his track record to build a gambling spread in Atlantic City. In 1985 he borrowed more millions to buy a second Atlantic City casino without so much as inspecting the building. Then in 1986 he borrowed still more to buy stock in a third Atlantic City casino, still being built, the Taj Mahal, which was going to be bigger than his first two casinos. He had three glittering gaming houses in the seaside resort by 1987, which he had acquired by amassing mountains of debt. Donald was betting the suckers who came to his casinos would lose enough money to meet the interest payments he owed to the bigger suckers who had loaned him the money to get the casinos and still leave him big profits.

Had lenders known more of Donald's management style, they might have had second thoughts in lending him so much money. At this stage of his career, Donald's bullying behavior, which no one mentions noticing in his teens and early adulthood to this point, reappeared. According to John O'Donnell, once a Trump executive, Trump would make whirlwind tours of his first casino, the Trump Plaza, and "depending on his mood, a stray cigarette butt on the carpet or an employee's scuffed shoes could unleash in him a fearful tirade, always accompanied by a stream of expletives." Steve Hyde, O'Donnell's boss, told him that "our most important job might be to shield the Trump Plaza staff from Donald's volatile and unpredictable moods."[20] O'Donnell reported that midway through 1987 Trump decided to convert a space at the top of the Trump Plaza tower to an exclusive lounge for high rollers. But since the tower was already built and had pipes in the roof, the ceiling in the lounge had to be about a foot lower than usual to hide the infrastructure plumbing. But Donald liked high ceilings, so he swore mightily every time he visited the work site. After the reason for the low ceiling was explained to him, he said "Okay." Then he would explode the next time he visited the workplace. One day after the ceiling was finished Trump led a group of twenty executives and contractors on a tour of the new lounge. "Donald looked up at the ceiling as if it was the first time he had seen it; then he looked at Steve [Hyde]. 'What the fuck is this?' he said. 'Who said to make this ceiling so low?' 'You knew about this, Donald,' Steve replied. 'We talked about it, if you remember, and the plans—' Suddenly Donald leaped up and punched his fist through the ceiling. Then he turned on Steve in a rage. 'You cocksucker! Motherfucker! Where the fuck were you? Where was your fucking head?'"[21]

By many reports, numerous members of President Trump's staff have witnessed such a scene, right down to the seven-point Richter Scale outburst after Trump was reminded that he had previously approved the ceiling height. The truth was so unbearable that Trump humiliated his chief officer in his casino in front of other executives rather than take responsibility. Trump also ripped into his family, including his first wife, Ivana, who suffered protracted public humiliations. Donald made her president of the Trump Plaza because she was good at business, and he could trust her. Yet one night in the summer of 1987, when visiting her casino, he found a dice table that she had reserved for a high roller expected to show up later. "How could you close one of my tables on the busiest fucking night of the year!" he shouted at her on the casino floor. "I can't believe you could be so stupid. Do you know how much money I'm losing here? Stupid! You're costing me a fortune! This is the stupidest fucking thing I've ever seen!"[22]

By that time Trump had taken a mistress, Marla Maples. Ivana found out, and the marriage was falling apart fast. Ivana's biggest "sin" was apparently that she had gotten older and no longer made other men envy Donald. He wanted her out of Atlantic City, so he moved her to New York to manage the Park Plaza Hotel, which he had recently bought. She held a farewell cocktail party for some sixty of her casino managers and their partners and became emotional when she gave her farewell speech. "Donald then walked up to the microphone. 'Look at this,' he said, turning to her. 'I had to buy a $350 million hotel just to get her out of here and look at how she's crying. Now that's why I'm sending her back to New York. I don't need this, some woman crying. I need somebody strong in here to take care of this place.'"[23] That didn't make any sense. If Ivana was too emotional to run a hotel in one city, why would she be up to running one in another? Many in attendance appreciated the real reason Donald was running her out of town, and soon Trump made sure everyone knew as he publicly paraded his affair with Maples to humiliate Ivana when she would not go quietly into the night. Protected by various prenuptial agreements, he was intent on making Ivana suffer all the way to the divorce courts while their children watched.

We suspect Trump became so aggressive at this time because he had stuck his neck way, way out in Atlantic City, and his head was about to get chopped off. In October 1987, the stock market crashed on "Black Monday," and real estate values plummeted. Prudent investors cut their losses, but Trump, ignoring all warnings and believing completely in his instincts, energetically increased his debt load. Trump's investment strategy became more and more like someone losing his shirt at a roulette table. Each loss was interpreted as a sign his luck was about to turn. You just had to lose enough times to start winning again. Thus, in 1988, he bought a humongous yacht to anchor near one of his casinos. Then he bought a commuter airline. As mentioned, he bought the Park Plaza Hotel in New York. Next he acquired the Taj Mahal Hotel and made it (naturally) "the greatest casino in the world" for a mere billion dollars. Everything got named TRUMP, and objective analysts reported he showed no business acumen at all and recklessly overpaid for almost everything. When the banks around the world finally stopped climbing over one another to loan him money, he sold junk bonds that promised a return of 14 percent a year, or more. He spewed bold confidence in the future and in himself. It fooled many people in the late 1980s who had grown desperate in bad times. Most of all, he fooled himself as his "infallible instincts" led him to running hell's bells off a cliff. For a while he made his interest payments by selling assets given him years ago by his father, but these had run out.

Trump had no one to blame but himself for the way he had mangled his life. Not only were ceilings coming down on him, but the walls were closing in, so, in December 1990, he made a bold underhanded move that gave even his father considerable pause. Donald sent "The Bank of Dad" a twelve-page document that needed, he said, an immediate signature. As his eighty-five-year-old father worked his way through all the legal riga-maroles, supposedly aimed at protecting the family fortune from Ivana's divorce settlement, he saw that his son was sneakily trying to get him to change his last will and testament so that Donald would have vast powers over the family's wealth. Fred Trump realized the document was "an at-tempt to go behind his back and give his son total control over his affairs. He said he feared that Donald would sign over all his empire as collateral to rescue his failing businesses."[24] Fred Trump might have proudly thought to himself, the boy's a chip off the old block for trying to sneak a bad deal past him. But he had his own lawyers produce a different codicil that protected his fortune from Donald and from all the people to whom Donald owed money. However, he did give his son enough cash to meet an interest pay-ment due in just a few days. Always determined to cheat the government of gift taxes, he sent an intermediary to buy $3.35 million worth of gambling chips at one of Donald's casinos and not use them.

But most of Donald's showy and unwise investments kept losing money faster than one could count it. All three casinos closed and the Park Plaza Hotel declared bankruptcy in 1992. While Trump lost a whack of his own money, it was the various banks, buyers of his junk bonds, and hundreds of subcontractors who had built Trump's casinos who took the big hit.[25] Unlike William Zeckendorf, Donald Trump avoided personal bankruptcy thanks again to his father and to his siblings with whom Fred Trump had stashed large piles of assets. The junk bond holders found they held junk. Many of the subcontractors went out of business, ruined because they could not afford the long court cases Trump threw up to keep from paying them for the work they had done. There is no record of Trump's expressing regret for their losses. Tony Schwartz wrote, "I never saw any guilt or contrition about anything he'd done."[26] He observed that Trump "seems unconstrained by even the faintest hint of conscience. Trump feels no more shame over his most destructive behaviors than a male lion does killing the cubs of his predecessor when he takes over a pride."[27] The banks, whom Trump owed nearly $2 billion, decided at the end of 1990 not to call in their loans (which would have lost them most of that money) but instead negotiated with Trump and effectively took over most of his assets, which they hoped to sell off. They left Trump officially in charge of the operations in the belief his name added value to the properties. He was given a living allowance of $450,000 per *month* that enabled him to live a very extravagant lifestyle and convince others his name was still worth its weight in gold, not lead.[28]

Thus, Donald Trump continued to look rich as far as the public was concerned, but he was thoroughly shattered by the collapse of all his ventures. Trump's personal assistant Louise Sunshine said, "I think the downtime for him (in the 1990s) was really a shock, and he was not prepared for it. It caught him totally off guard. It was probably the biggest challenge of his life."[29] Trump himself tells the story that he was walking down Fifth Avenue in 1991 and across the street he saw a man in front of Tiffany's with a tin cup, and he said, "You know, right now that man is worth $900 million more than I am."[30] One of the bank negotiators told reporters later that at the last minute two Japanese lenders rejected the negotiated deal, saying Trump was getting off too easy. Trump was asked to phone them to try to change their minds. But instead, "Trump (sounded) miserable, dejected, as if he were almost crying. 'Why bother? There's no way this is getting done. It's all over.'"[31] It should have been. The *New York Times* published an account of Trump's finances from the years 1985 to 1994, based on copies of his 1040 tax forms it had obtained.[32] Over that decade, Trump lost $1.17 billion dollars, probably more than any other person in the country.

When all the banks finally agreed to let Trump continue to "look like a million dollars" so they could get the most for his former properties, Trump took heart and began to swagger once more. In 1995 he put his name and a few assets into a new company and enticed investors to put their money in a publicly traded stock identified on the ticker by "DJT."[33] Hundreds of millions of dollars poured in, a good deal of which Trump diverted into his own pockets as living expenses, salary, and bonuses. Then he had his company buy the two debt-ridden casinos in Atlantic City that he still owned, so his publicly owned company turned out to be a chute for channeling investors' cash directly into his pocket. As well he used investors' dough to open new casinos outside Atlantic City, all of which failed. Through such misguided maneuvers, DJT lost more than $1 billion by 2004 when it filed for bankruptcy. The investors as usual got almost nothing. Trump walked away much the richer.

The five bankruptcies he produced over this period showed what Trump did best as a businessman: crash and burn. Even though his father tried to help, Donald's mad spree in the 1980s ran up debts far beyond his family's ability to pay. His DJT reprise from 1995 to 2004 showed he had learned how to extract millions of dollars for himself despite his failures as a businessman. Image was more important than reality. But there is no denying that he failed time and again because of one bad judgment after another. Trump proudly claims he is the "King of Debt." But no one has ever called him the "King of Profit," and that, supposedly, is the idea.

EFFECT OF FAILURES ON TRUMP

How did Trump fail so spectacularly? He got himself into his messes by vastly overestimating his own inherent wisdom, relying on his instincts, and by believing his own publicity that he was a master dealmaker. The early failures should have thrown up a formidable challenge to his unbridled belief in himself. He might have concluded he was not as smart as he thought he was and hence become wiser. Instead, he blamed his setbacks on outside forces, such as the stock market crash of 1987, and especially on other people. He blamed his Atlantic City failures on three of his casino executives who had died in a helicopter crash in 1989. They had mismanaged the operations, not he. (This unjustified criticism of the dead men, along with the false narrative he gave to the media that he had come "this close" to being on the copter with them, creating the impression that fate was protecting him, so disgusted John O'Donnell that he quit in protest when Trump came after him too.[34])

Although it was his largest financial failure, Atlantic City was not the first time Trump had screwed up royally and blamed everyone but himself. Believing everything he touched turned to gold, he also bought the New Jersey Generals of the upstart United States Football League in 1984 and basked in the free publicity he got almost every day in the sports pages. The United States Football League scheduled its games in the spring to avoid competing with the NFL, but it had trouble drawing fans in months that meant baseball to Americans, not football. Trump convinced his co-owners to move to the fall in 1986, promising them a lucrative TV contract. When he could not deliver the league collapsed. But Donald had one more trick up his sleeve: the USFL would file an antitrust suit against the NFL and, he assured his co-owners, be awarded millions of dollars. It did file, and it won the case. And it was awarded $3.76![35] So whose fault was it? The other owners, Trump said. "If there was a single key miscalculation I made with the USFL, it was evaluating the strength of my fellow owners. In any partnership, you're only as strong as your weakest link."[36]

His business record indicated that in any enterprise involving Donald Trump, he was apt to be the weakest link. Yet he insisted, just as Roy Cohn would, that the opposite was true. "I win," he wrote. "I always win. In the end, I always win, whether it's in golf, whether it's in tennis, whether it's in life, I just always win.[37] And I tell people I always win, because I do."[38] But the facts tell an altogether different story. Going back at least to his days at New York Military Academy, when he failed despite his strong competitive drive to become the highest ranking cadet, to his being denied admission to University of Southern California, through his mediocre performance at Fordham and Wharton, to being caught (with his father) discriminating against Black renters in Brooklyn, to the monumental failures in Atlantic City followed by the loss of the Park Plaza Hotel in New York, the collapse of Trump Airlines, the failure of the New Jersey Generals, making DJT into a penny stock, the disgrace of the corrupt steal-from-the-poor Trump University, not to mention the numerous other lawsuits he lost or settled out of court because he was going to lose, Trump has been a loser over and over, much more often than he has won.

ROOTS OF TRUMP'S NARCISSISM

Donald Trump has wanted to be the center of attention since he was a child, but his need to be noticed remained relatively subdued and controlled prior to his arrival in Manhattan. Yes, he wanted to stand out as a ladies' man in high school; yes, he wanted to be remembered as a sports hero; yes, he drove a sports car to college and wore a business suit; yes, he was rich. But no one who knew him during those years mentions his being a braggart. If he was full of himself, he was at least not spilling over. And even when he "arrived" in Manhattan and cultivated the image of irresistible playboy and dynamic developer, he seemingly tried to keep the spotlight on him only for "instrumental" reasons—it was good for both business and pleasure. No one mentions his being an incredibly boring person, only able to talk about himself. But by 1986 Tony Schwartz noticed as he sat by Trump's desk for months on end that "he has no attention span . . . it's impossible to keep him focused on any topic, other than his own self-aggrandizement, for more than a few minutes."[39] And Schwartz discovered that Trump frequently lied in his storytelling to make himself look grander than he was. But why? By 1986, Trump had been living in the penthouse in Trump Tower for three years. He appeared to be the king of Atlantic City. He seemed to be fabulously rich. So why was he telling everyone how amazing he was? Most people probably already thought he was amazing. But we now know that at this time, when Trump seemingly began to go out of his way to tell everyone how smart he was as a businessman, he reported $68.7 million dollars in business losses on his taxes.[40] And Tony Schwartz was sitting there in Trump's office in the first place because Trump had hired him to write his self-glorifying biography since Trump felt he was not getting enough national exposure.[41] By all reports, Trump's drive for glory has only grown far more intense since then. It is not just that he talks about himself in the highest terms all the time, he cannot talk about anything else for long. That is a sure sign that he spends a considerable amount of the day thinking about his grandness. He had become a narcissist. He never sees a mirror he does not like, and he had fallen in love with fame and praise not just because they are addictive, as he himself noted, but because unending acclaim and adulation serve a deeper purpose in his personality. Donald's need for glory is so powerful, all the praise he gets from the world is not enough, and never can be enough. So he must keep piling it on himself.

Narcissism can have many causes, but if you feel unloved as a child and unlovable, you can protect yourself by developing an exaggerated sense of worth. Most of us are our own number one fans, but a narcissist builds an arena full of worshipers in his head who applaud everything he does. Donald Trump was short-changed in the loving parent department. His mother had little interest in him, and his father's affection was very conditional. By Donald's own account, Fred Trump's insistence that his sons follow in his footsteps and be "winners" was so intense that it drove Freddy Trump to alcoholism and an early death.[42] That is pressure. Fred Sr. demanded a lot from Donald, but he helped him out constantly in business. Donald is fond of saying he got rich the "old-fashioned way." Well, inherited wealth is old-fashioned. The *New York Times*'s October 2, 2018, investigation of Fred Trump's finances concluded that in every era of Donald Trump's life, his finances were deeply entwined with and dependent upon his father's wealth. If Donald had not had such a rich and well-connected father, he would have been a "loser" in all his business ventures up to the mid-1990s, including those that are counted as his successes. His father knew it and had warned his son from the beginning not to take the risks he did. Fred Trump surely expressed his disappointment as he wrote yet another check or shifted more millions to save his son one more time. We do not know that Fred ever directly told Donald that he was a loser, but nothing would have hurt Donald as much. He says his father always told him he was "the greatest." But if you watch Donald Trump long enough, you will learn that when he uses a superlative like "greatest," he is usually lying. We think he is lying to himself more than anyone else, and whenever he begins to have a doubt about a decision he made, whenever he imagines his father's voice telling him he is a loser, he immediately starts singing a song of praise to himself. And the more he fails, the louder the song.

We are hardly the first to offer this explanation of the man. Tony Schwartz told the *Guardian* in 2018, "There are two Trumps. The one he presents to the world is all bluster, bullying and certainty. The other, which I have long felt haunts his inner world, is the frightened child of a relentlessly critical and bullying father and a distant and disengaged mother who couldn't or wouldn't protect him."[43] In a sense, Donald Trump was set up to fail by his father. As we noted earlier, the contest to be the best never ended. Donald was told to run his heart out in a race that had no finish line. Being the absolute best can take over your life because there is always something more to be accomplished. Michael D'Antonio put it this way: "In his frenzied sprint through life, [Donald Trump] had continually sought to raise the bar in his own game, suggesting to the world that a successful man's trophies must be ever more glittering and impressive, lest he be judged a failure."[44] Therefore, each "win" makes you a loser if you cannot beat it. Trump can never get across the board to be crowned the king that Fred Trump told him he must be. Kings' Row moves away with each advance he makes.

FROM FAKING IT TO FRAUD

By 2004 when his publicly traded company DJT became bankrupt, Donald Trump again had more money than almost everyone, thanks to the salaries and bonuses he took out of DJT. But he had run out of bankers and brokers who would give him money for a new venture. He was down to his last and biggest asset, his name. He had, over the years, created an equivalence in many minds between *Trump* and *the best*. So, he figured (correctly) if someone had a product to sell, why not license his name with its implication that the product was the best that money could buy. The result was the TRUMP Hotel in Toronto and the TRUMP Resort in Indonesia, along with TRUMP steaks, wines, and so on, and he insisted always his name must be all capitalized. People assumed a shirt bearing his label would be just like the one he wore. What Trump surely liked best about selling his name was that people believed these were his projects and properties, not merely licensing deals, so he must own almost everything. Trump liked the optical illusion.

About the same time a TV producer named Mark Burnett was looking for a hook for a new reality show. Burnett had developed the successful *Survivor* series for CBS, which plopped assortments of interesting people on an island somewhere and gave them chances to eliminate one another (via a ballot box) until only one remained. Burnett lived in New York City, and it occurred to him, one day while filming on the Amazon River, that you could play Survivor on Manhattan Island too. Only instead of watching contestants sleep in the rain while their clothes got ratty and they plotted in dim lighting whom next to eliminate from the tribe, the TV audience could watch aspiring corporate executives screw one another over while trying to win the favor of the big corporate cheese. Burnett wanted someone swash-buckling and famous to be the big cheese. He found just the guy to say "You're fired!" every week living in Trump Tower. The show was produced by Burnett and Trump on a floor in Trump Tower that was converted to a boardroom and living quarters for the contestants. It was a big hit the first year and held a steady audience thereafter. Trump played the Major Domo for fourteen seasons—a very long run for this sort of thing. He featured his properties, his products, and his family all the time. He was making money by the truckload, and besides that, he was now more famous than ever. But the entire series was pure fakery.

A staff writer at the *New Yorker* peeled back the façade of *The Apprentice*. Patrick Radden Keefe explains that the series portrayed Trump not as the "skeezy hustler who huddles with local mobsters" that they found, rather "as a plutocrat with impeccable business instincts and unparalleled wealth—a ti-tan who always seemed to be climbing out of helicopters or into limousines." Those who created the television series told the *New Yorker* they "knew he was a fake," a man who had just gone through more bankruptcies than they could count, but they "made him out to be the most important person in the world. It was like making the court jester the king." One of the early produc-ers recalled when checking out Donald's Trump Tower offices, "We walked through the offices and saw chipped furniture. We saw a crumbling empire at every turn. Our job was to make it seem otherwise." Because Trump was never prepared for the largely unscripted show and occasionally fired the wrong person, the producers often shot three hundred hours of footage to get a one-hour show; by reverse engineering it, cutting it, and splicing it every which way, they were able to make a show in the editing room.[45]

After launching his reality TV career, Trump also created a multilevel marketing scheme called Trump University, which was Donald's most conspicuously fraudulent business undertaking and it targeted widows and retirees who could not afford to be scammed. The aftermath of the Trump University con was still ongoing when he announced his presidential candidacy in 2015. As Maria Konnikova wrote for the *New Yorker* during that campaign, the best evidence of Trump's potential con artistry comes from the lawsuit against his defunct university, a for-profit educational scam:

> That suit accuses Trump of actual fraud, or, as the decision [to continue the case] puts it, of the use of "deception, misrepresentation, concealment, suppression, false pretense, false promise or unconscionable contractual provisions" to "defraud." If, in the end, the ruling goes against Trump, we will be able to say, definitively, that he is a con artist—that he deliberately engaged in deception, using a wholly incidental platform to attain ends of money and influence.

The ruling did go against Trump, and the case was consolidated with an even larger class action California case, filed by former students, which not only laid out Trump's fraud, but charged him with criminal racketeering under the RICO law, for which there are civil penalties. The lawsuits spelled out the criminal con which Trump operated for several years. Under oath, his former employees admitted it was all a giant scam. For example, one employee who worked in Trump's office at 40 Wall Street, where Trump University was based, testified that "while Trump University claimed it wanted to help consumers make money in real estate, in fact, Trump University was only interested in selling every person the most expensive seminars they possibly could." The sworn statement concludes, "Based upon my personal experience and employment, I believe that Trump University was a fraudulent scheme, and that it preyed upon the elderly and uneducated to separate them from their money."[46] Trump University, now an open record of Donald's business practices, was closed down, and he paid $25 million to settle the lawsuits, a way to end his exposure without admitting guilt. So, as he always does, he moved on to another con, becoming president of the United States.

DONALD TRUMP AND WOMEN

We are about to move into Donald Trump's life as president, so this is a good place to consider his relationship with the part of the population that should least want him there: women. One of the female contestants on *The Apprentice* accused Donald Trump publicly in 2015 of sexually assaulting her in a hotel room one year at season's end. She was one of twenty-five women to come forward with such charges against Trump, which of course include the bombshell recording of Trump telling another man that he frequently kissed and groped women without their consent, and he had discovered that they would "let" him grab their genitalia if he wanted to.[47] Altogether about two dozen women have publicly asserted that Trump sexually assaulted or harassed them, with the severity ranging from unwanted kissing to rape. Trump denied all the charges and said in October 2016 he would sue these accusers. But he has not. Should we believe he has been wrongly accused? Bob Woodward reports the advice Trump gave a friend who had admitted some bad behavior toward women: "You've got to deny,

deny, deny, and push back on these women. If you admit to anything and any culpability, then you're dead. That was a big mistake you made. You didn't come out guns blazing and just challenge them. You showed weakness. You've got to be strong. You've got to be aggressive. You've got to push back hard. You've got to deny anything that's said about you. Never admit."[48] The friend he was advising had assaulted the women, but Trump was telling him that the facts had nothing to do with the situation. Just lie.

Donald Trump appears to place women into three categories: sex object, smart and talented, and the rest. He admits he lusts after beautiful young women and sometimes has trouble keeping his hands off them and kissing them.[49] The women who say Trump assaulted them almost uniformly describe what he calls kissing as an oral assault in which he jams his tongue in their mouth. It is about as romantic as a punch in the eye and seems to be done for the same reason: dominance. Trump sees women with a butcher shop mentality, most frequently referring to them as mere "pieces of ass." He told *Esquire* in 1991, "It really doesn't matter what [the media] write as long as you've got a young and beautiful piece of ass."[50] He told Howard Stern he could call his daughter Ivanka "a piece of ass."[51] In 1997, he told *New Yorker* reporter Mark Snyder that ideal company would be "a total piece of ass." And judging by Stormy Daniels's report, sex with Trump comes straight out of the "slam, bam, thank you ma'am" school of fast break coitus in which he displays no interest whatsoever in what the woman is experiencing.[52] To borrow from Thomas Hobbes, sexual intercourse with Donald Trump appears to be solitary, poor, nasty, brutish, and short. Beautiful women are sexual objects to Donald, useful for making other men envy him and for "relaxing" him, but otherwise unimportant and utterly interchangeable.

Trump once said, "Men are better than women, but a good woman is better than ten good men."[53] Category Two of Trump's view of women contains the few women whom Donald Trump has hired to do important jobs in his businesses and administration. Louise Sunshine, a Democratic Party operative, served as his first personal assistant in Manhattan. Barbara Res supervised the building of Trump Tower. And Ivana Trump, his first wife, became a true working partner in his real estate business for many years. Kellyanne Conway directed Trump's campaign to victory in 2016 and serves as counselor to the president. Hope Hicks was the White House communications director. Trump entrusted the job of defending him to the media to Sarah Sanders and then Kayleigh McEnany. Nikki Haley served as his ambassador to the United Nations from 2017 to 2018.

The last category of women, according to Trump—women in general— contains the remaining 90 percent or more, women who are not beautiful enough or competent enough for Trump. He thinks that women in general are awful and holds them in contempt, seeing them as sinister, aggressive, but clever manipulators who are out to exploit men. He is especially con- temptuous of accomplished women and women who stand up to him—as he has shown regularly in his press conferences. In 1992, he told Philip Johnson, a reporter for *New York Magazine*, that you " had to treat women like shit."[54] He also claims, "Women are really a lot different than por- trayed. They are far worse than men, far more aggressive. And boy, can they be smart."[55] But not as smart as he, because he understands (he thinks) what women are up to. And everything that goes wrong in a relationship is their fault. Thus, he endorses the classic blame-the-woman excuse for men's infidelity. It was Ivana's fault that he got a mistress because Ivana's beauty faded, and he lost interest in her. It was Hillary's fault that Bill Clinton wandered, as Trump made clear in a comment when he retweeted on April 16, 2015: "If Hillary Clinton can't satisfy her husband what makes her think she can satisfy America?"

As a president seeking re-election, Donald needs women. They can make the difference for him. But he has done little to win their allegiance; rather, he has offended even more as president.[56]

CHAPTER FOUR

TRUMP'S PAST AS PRESIDENTIAL PROLOGUE

The last two chapters hopefully provide a better understanding of Donald Trump than Americans had when they went to the polls in November 2016. His supporters thought he was a very successful entrepreneur whose business acumen made him worth, he claimed, about eight billion dollars. He was not. His detractors may have believed this too, but they saw him as vain, prejudiced, and uncouth. Still, few realized how deeply his ugly side was rooted in his personality and how it could cripple his presidency. Trump himself probably did not realize this, and that just as in his business career, as president he would keep making the same mistakes over and over. He is not half as brilliant as he tells himself and others. But why should he conclude this? He has been elected president of the United States. He is the most important and politically powerful person in the United States if not the world. Nevertheless, we submit that denying his behavioral proclivities has only made things worse as he careens through his presidency chasing a goal of universal adoration that will remain forever beyond his reach. As one of his former closest associates, Michael Cohen, told the House Oversight Committee on February 27, 2019: "Since taking office [Trump] has become the worst version of himself."[1]

Becoming president has traditionally been the highest goal one could have in the United States, and previous presidents have usually considered it the crowning achievement of their lives. But the day after his inauguration Trump claimed that the crowd attending his speech contained at least one million people and extended all the way to the Washington Monument. It did not. He asserted it was bigger than the crowd at President Obama's first inauguration. It was not. Then he claimed his victory in the Electoral College was the biggest since Ronald Reagan's, when it was the fourth largest out of seven. Then he claimed, at the hundred-day mark of his presidency that he had enacted more legislation and signed more executive orders than any other president in over a half century. He had signed a lot of executive orders, but Congress, not the president, enacts legislation, and despite Republican majorities in both houses of Congress, they had passed almost none of his campaign promises and most particularly failed on his promise to repeal Obamacare. And he proclaimed, over and over again, before the arrival of COVID-19, that the American economy was booming like never before, that he had been tougher on Russia than any president before him, that the United States was now respected around the world like never before, that America was safer than ever before, that he was making America great again like never before, that he was the least racist person anyone ever saw, and that no one respected women more than he did. Trump even stated that he had been more presidential than all his predecessors except Abraham Lincoln. None of this was true. But he has continued to make outlandish claims, and by his third year in office he declared himself the greatest president ever. Even that was not enough; he decided in August 2019 to declare that historically this period would be known as "the Age of Trump."[2]

These discharges of self-glorification that take your breath away tell us that reaching the highest office in the land was not enough for Donald.

He wants to be more loved than Obama; to have won his election more decisively than any modern president; to be better at getting his programs enacted than anyone since Lyndon Johnson; to be more presidential than anyone; to be greater and more successful than any American president has ever been, and to be such a towering historical figure that events of our time would be known by their association with him. You can wonder if Trump, like Caesar Augustus, wants to become a god. But suppose he did become one. He would want to become the number one god. We fear however that in the meanwhile he will try next for becoming president for life. If you look closely, Trump frequently claims a grandiose perch after a string of bad stories damage his image. Such stories started during his first days in office, and he has been writhing and floundering in a morass of recrimination since. Experienced diplomats in Washington noted the situation from the start. For example, the British ambassador witnessed the chaos in the administration and sent dispatches home that President Trump "radiates insecurity."[3] CNN reporter Jim Acosta reported that he was getting regular invites from foreign embassies for chats about Trump, where: "The conversations almost always boiled down to questions about Trump's mental state."[4] Many people could tell something was seriously wrong in the mind of the president. In fact, there is lots wrong, with lots of things.

This chapter will focus on and analyze the five most serious problems in Trump's mental behavior, all of which play essential roles in his drive to be an authoritarian leader: (1) his incessant lying, (2) his inability to think straight, (3) his reliance on his intuition, (4) his demand for loyalty, and (5) his growing aggressiveness. In each case we shall show how these failures led to, and exacerbated, the COVID-19 crisis that has so far killed more than one hundred thousand Americans, with ever growing body counts if the president gets his way.

LIES, LIES, AND MORE LIES.

Donald Trump plays whack-a-mole with the truth from morning to night. The most thankless, dreariest job in the world right now might be serving as a fact-checker on the president's public statements. He has to, as an authoritarian leader, to justify his lunges for increased power. The mistruths just keep coming with no end in sight, many monotonously repeated, showing it makes no difference to Trump that he has been found out. To a certain extent, lying comes with being a politician. *Politifact* lists seventy-two separate lies or misleading statements that Barack Obama made over his eight years in office.[5] But Donald Trump sometimes tops that in a single day. The "lie-brarians" at *The Washington Post*, headed by Glenn Kessler, have toted up more than sixteen thousand false or misleading claims that Trump made during his first three years in office.[6] It appears that an astounding twenty thousand, twenty-five thousand, or more is a sure thing by the end of his first term with an election coming up. Tony Schwartz wrote, "Lying is second nature to him. More than anyone else I have ever met, Trump has the ability to convince himself that whatever he is saying at any given moment is true, or sort of true, or at least ought to be true."[7]

Concocting a convincing lie about something takes much more energy than simply being truthful. Truth is interconnected, so lying creates discrepancies, for it tears the fabric of reality. A lie forces further lying to rearrange other things as well, requiring that you weave the proverbial tangled web. In fact, Donald Trump gave up trying to be convincing long ago. He just makes pronouncements and attacks those who ask for evidence. However, if you do this long enough you will eventually have trouble remembering the truth because your lies are not attached to a consistent, organized view of the world. The liar must ask: Did this really happen or did I make it up? His memory is a tattered lace doily of things barely hanging together. Trump lives in "Trump World," a mishmash of "alternate facts."[8] A place where "the truth isn't truth."[9] During Special Counsel Mueller's Russia connection investigation, Trump said he was willing to be interviewed, but his lawyers emphatically said no. They knew Trump would lie, lie, lie during any such inquiry, and perjury is a serious crime.[10] Trump's private counsel, Rudy Giuliani, claimed such an interview would be a perjury trap. Rudy did not say it, but for Trump, vast stretches of reality are perjury traps.

Trump's handling of the COVID-19 pandemic crisis provides a clear example of this because he has left such a tangled web of false assertions, no one can make a coherent narrative out of it. In the main, his statements after March 11 ("big problem") flatly contradicted the statements he made before that date ("no problem"). When pressed, he insisted that he did not change his tune, that he always knew there was a big problem. But he also lied when he said no one saw the crisis coming, his travel ban on China had been effective in keeping the virus out of the country, a vaccine would be available rapidly, everyone who wanted a test for the virus could get one, the virus was less dangerous than the flu, the medical professionals agree with his assessments of the situation, the virus would disappear by spring, and that he never said it would disappear by spring. Trump may believe he never said any of these things. He made them up on the spot to whack down an unpleasant fact that had come up. They were truth for a day. For history, however, all these conflicting statements were recorded.

Surely Trump knows he lies. Former White House Communications Director Anthony Scaramucci, who has known Trump for decades and worked briefly in the administration, says that lying has been part of Trump's act all his life. Pulitzer Prize winning investigative reporters Philip Rucker and Carol Leonnig relayed the following information from the Mooch: "People ask me if the president lies. Are you nuts? He's a fucking total liar," Scaramucci reported. "He lies all the time. Trump called me one night after I was on Bill Maher and he said, 'How come you always fucking figure me out?' I said, 'I've seen you around for twenty years. I know your act. I know when you're saying shit you don't really mean, and I know when you're saying bullshit.' He laughed." Scaramucci recalled that he then asked Trump, "'Are you an act?' Trump replied, 'I'm a total act and I don't understand why people don't get it.'"[11] We know this act, don't we? We first saw it in Trump's senior year at New York Military Academy with the "parade of lovelies" and the false memory of the "home run" that he tried to plant in a fellow student. It was certainly an act riding around in his limo when he snowed *New York Times* columnist Judy Klemesrud about graduating first at Wharton and being media-shy. Trump certainly knows he is lying about his academic record for he has threatened the living bejabbers out of his high school and colleges if they reveal his grades. Purposeful misrepresentation has always been a central feature of his business dealings: make 'em think you are much richer and smarter and better connected than you really are. The act can be summed up in one word: TRUMP—which was a lie he has franchised since 2004 to enable others to reel in suckers. And he often manipulates others into backing up his lies, such as the medical experts who are expected to "say nothing" as he touts the value of an untested cure for COVID-19, or the Chairman of the Joint Chiefs of Staff who was tricked into accompanying Trump on his shameless visit to the church across Pennsylvania Avenue during the Black Lives Matter protests.

We all try to shape how others perceive us, although with perhaps a millionth of the intensity that Donald Trump does. You start doing it each day when you comb your hair. But we think Trump sometimes lies to cancel out his failures in his own mind, not just in the minds of others. We believe this because of the volume of Trump lies, because he does it so automatically, and because he does it so stupidly. As for the volume problem, the whole point of lying is, uh, deception. You can fool some of the people all the time, and Trump will repeat a lie endlessly to convince his base that "the economy has never been so great" and that "there was no quid pro quo," and "two plus two equals five." He drummed out monotonous retweets of

"LAW AND ORDER" as his empty but completely predictable response to the Black Lives Matter demonstrations, as if saying it fifty times, like a penance after confession, would undo all the laws he, America's most unlawful president, broke or wanted to break.* But he really does not have to lie as much as he does to keep his base because they are not going anywhere. And if you lie profusely about almost everything and anything, the rest of the population is going to notice. Trump's ever climbing Pinocchio count has become a matter of amusement. It could someday be a Jeopardy! answer: "What was 24,197?" As a result of his behavior, sadly many people would not believe President Trump if he said water is wet. If his lips are moving (or his thumbs are tweeting), he is lying, most rightly conclude. So, the never-ending drumbeat of the man's lies has made them self-defeating for large parts of the world's population. Still, he keeps it up.

Trump spews so much hooey he may not always realize it. He just lies instinctively, and then dismisses his dishonesty so instantly when he is caught, the event has no time to register. To illustrate: Senator Lindsey Graham told Bob Woodward that Trump complained to him and Democratic Senator Dick Durbin on January 11, 2018, about immigrants coming to the United States from "shithole countries." Durbin told the press, and Graham confirmed the quote. When Trump learned this, he phoned Graham and said, "I didn't say some of the things that [Durbin] said I said. "Yeah, you did," Graham insisted. "Well, some people like what I said," replied Trump.[12] The fact that he had lied to Graham and been caught at it seemingly meant nothing to Trump. He did not even bother trying to justify it. Who cares, he might have said to himself as he changed the subject and moved on. You will notice that Trump was trying to convince someone who had heard him say "shithole countries" that he had never said

---

* It did not work very well. A You-Gov poll taken June 9-10 found that 52 percent of Americans believed by then that Trump was a racist, and only 34 percent thought he was not.

it. How smart is that? All he was doing by showing denial is that he is a bald-faced liar. Trump's efforts at deception are often so blatant and obvious to fact-checkers that we must wonder who he thinks believes him? Take the Sharpie incident. It started on September 1, 2019, as Hurricane Dorian was churning toward the United States, when Trump tweeted that Alabama "will most likely be hit harder than anticipated." Alabamans crashed the phone lines and the National Weather Service had to say, "No it won't." The president warned the National Weather Service not to contradict him and insisted he had seen a forecast showing Alabama was in the storm's path. Later he showed reporters a government map which he said predicted this. But the actual map did not extend into Alabama. Instead somebody had used a black felt tip pen to hand-draw an extension of the predicted path into a corner of southeastern Alabama. Trump consistently uses a black felt-tip Sharpie to sign everything. Again, how smart was that?

INABILITY TO THINK STRAIGHT

Anonymous, the high-ranking administration official who revealed the "stable state" in a *New York Times* op-ed essay on September 5, 2018, and later the book titled *A Warning*, wrote about Trump's thinking: "Normal people who spend any time with Donald Trump are uncomfortable by what they witness. He stumbles, slurs, gets confused, is easily irritated, and has trouble synthesizing information, not occasionally but with regularity . . . The president also can't remember what he's said or been told."[13] The inconsistency in Trump's thinking staggers into public view every time he reverses course, which is often. His disruptive policy U-turns often happen because he tends to announce things impulsively and then must backtrack when advisors explain the downsides of his rash decisions. As March became April in 2019, for example, he declared the Republicans would fight the 2020 election over repealing Obamacare, he would completely close the

Mexican border, the Mueller report should not be released to the public, and he no longer wanted his "firm" nominee for heading Immigration and Customs Enforcement to be his nominee. All of these were flip-flops from previous positions, sometimes within days, and he has again flop-flipped on most of these. Also, while he supported "very meaningful background checks" on people trying to buy firearms, despite the NRA's fear that it would be the first step on a slippery slope toward total gun control, he did not support them after all because the NRA was afraid it would be the first step on a slippery slope toward total gun control.[14]

Trump serially contradicts himself for the same reason he cannot keep track of his lies: he lacks an overall organizing scheme, in this case, principles, that would produce consistency in his policies. But like many authoritarian leaders before him, he is unprincipled, and his ad hoc decisions can be reversed instantly because, after all, his is the only mind that he thinks matters. That is why the nation has witnessed a president whose White House issued medically sound guidelines for reopening the economy once the COVID-19 virus was contained, and a president who, day after day, urges people to ignore those guidelines because he thinks following them will hamper his reelection. But even more troubling, Trump has trouble focusing on an issue and thinking it through to a logical conclusion. He cannot concentrate for long. His train of thought gets sidetracked all the time, not by telephone calls and tweets, but seemingly by other things going on in his head. He is a scatterbrain. This became evident in his first full Pentagon briefing in 2017. He quickly lost interest in reports on America's conflicts overseas and our state of preparedness. Instead he astonishingly attacked his generals for being incompetent cowards and switched the subject to how long and warmly the president of France had recently shaken his hand, and how grand it would be to have a big military parade in Washington. An observer noted that the president veered from one unrelated topic to another like a squirrel caught in traffic.[15] Readers of Chapter Three will recall that he repeatedly switched the conversation to events that spoke to his own grandeur.

Trump's grasp of international and domestic issues has remained shallow to molecular depth. He may be the least informed national leader in the world. Aides report he is only interested in the stock market, employment figures, and trade balances. He has often gone into meetings with heads of state and made a fool of himself because he had refused to learn anything about the topics on the agenda.[16] Former Staff Secretary Rob Porter learned that he had to present daily summaries of issues on single pieces of paper to get Trump to read them, and even that proved too much. His staff knows he will not open reports about what the United States should do regarding climate change or North Korea or NATO or almost anything. Trump would simply not be able to do what you are doing right now: read a book. Nor will he listen to briefings. Gary Cohn, Trump's chief economic advisor, reportedly told Rob Porter, "It's pointless to prepare a meaningful, substantive briefing for the president . . . Because you know he's never going to listen. We're never going to get through it. He's going to get through the first 10 minutes and then he's going to want to start talking about some other topic. And so we're going to be there for an hour, but we're never going to get through this briefing."[17]

Trump's unwillingness to learn something that does not inherently interest him is a serious deficit for someone who carries responsibilities that implicate the well-being of our nation and the world. The COVID-19 pandemic has cost tens upon tens of thousands of Americans their lives because he would not listen to the members of his staff who warned him in January and February 2020 about the great danger posed by the new coronavirus. He was not interested. He made it clear he did not want to be bothered. He did not actually sing "Na-na-na-na, I can't hear you" when a high-ranking official tried to tell him what would happen if he did nothing, but he might as well have.

The president's inability to concentrate means he frequently has trouble staying on message. Often he interrupts himself to go off topic, and it is instructive to notice the subjects he brings up when he barges in on his own presentation. For example, in the middle of a February 15, 2019, announcement about using emergency funding for his wall on the Mexican border, he stopped reading his notes and began talking instead about how well he was rebuilding the military. Then he patted himself on the back some more by talking about the stock market. Eventually he got back on topic, except he proceeded to completely undermine his message when he said, "I could do the wall over a longer period of time. I didn't need to do this." But that meant it was not really an emergency. He had destroyed the rationale for what he was announcing, an emergency. And he did not even notice it.[18]

Here's another example making the point. Bob Woodward openly recorded a phone discussion he had with Trump on August 14, 2018, shortly before the release of his book *Fear*. Trump called him because he wanted to know why Woodward had not spoken to him while writing this book, since he would have wanted to be interviewed. The conversation was recorded with the president's knowledge, and the transcript gives us an extended look at Trump's thinking processes.* When you look at the conversation, you notice four times Trump changed the subject and went off about his greatness. And every time it happened, the back-and-forth of the conversation had just reached the conclusion that Woodward had tried to call Trump but gotten nowhere. Thus, the failure to communicate was Trump's fault, not Woodward's. Furthermore, you will notice that when Trump could not find defendable ground on the "Why didn't you talk to me?" issue, he blamed other people for the problem, even blaming Woodward for not knowing what Trump knew about how to reach him. Well, Doctor, what is your clinical insight here? Is this a man who solidly believes in the amazing

---

* For transcript see https://nationalpost.com/news/world/trump-bob-woodward.

competence he claims to possess, who is so self-confident that he can easily admit inadequacies when they become apparent? There is room for doubt, is there not? This guy looks like a walking, talking, twenty-four-carat text-book-case "reaction formation."* His larger-than-life pose of Mr. Incredibly Successful must be serving a deep need since it breaks all the rules about social modesty. It could well be that at his core he believes he is a failure. And the instant he starts remembering past failures or realizes he has failed again; he must get a shot of praise. If no one else is there to give it, he rolls up his sleeve and gives it to himself.

RELIANCE ON HIS "INTUITION"

Authoritarian leaders usually believe they have great instincts for doing the right thing. It comes standard issue with megalomania. However, Donald Trump's instincts led him to his seismic failures in Atlantic City and thereafter. His "intuitive knowledge" and his prejudices have also produced a stream of reckless, false attacks. There was his demand, described in Chapter One, that the "Central Park Five" be put to death. Having learned nothing about looking before leaping, he led the charge in the national media that President Obama was not born in the United States. He asserted the government knew the 9/11 attack was coming. He said he saw thousands of Muslims in New Jersey celebrating the destruction of the World Trade Center in 2001. He claimed Ted Cruz's father helped assassinate John F. Kennedy. He "knew" that millions of illegal voters gave Hillary

---

* A "reaction formation" is described by American Psychological Association as "a defense mechanism in which unacceptable or threatening unconscious impulses are denied and are replaced in consciousness with their opposite. For example, to conceal an unconscious prejudice, an individual may preach tolerance; to deny feelings of rejection, a mother may be overindulgent toward her child. Through the symbolic relationship between the unconscious wish and its opposite, the outward behavior provides a disguised outlet for the tendencies it seems to oppose." See https://dictionary.apa.org/reaction-formation.

Clinton the popular vote victory in 2016. He repeatedly stated there was a link between vaccines and autism. He bought into the baseless theory that Supreme Court Justice Antonin Scalia had been murdered in 2016. He falsely claimed President Obama had the FBI tap his telephones in Trump Tower during the 2016 campaign. He endorsed an evidence-starved conspiracy theory that the Clintons were responsible for Jeffrey Epstein's death in prison in August 2019. You really must marvel that someone who has been so wrong so publicly so often can tell the world he has "great instincts."

Trump's worldview is based on conspiracy theories and uneducated beliefs. People embrace conspiracy theories for many reasons, but strong critical-thinking skills is not among them.[19] A wise person knows the danger of investing heavily in a belief that cannot be tested, which conspiracy theories cannot because any evidence against them is deemed evidence that the conspiracy exists. You are jumping off a cliff with a conspiracy theory if it is false since you can never find that out. But Trump appears to believe just about every quack-a-doodle-do conspiracy theory that comes down the road. His fateful telephone call to the president of Ukraine on July 25, 2019, was partly motivated by the conspiracy theory that the Russian interference in the 2016 election was really done by Ukraine, with Democratic Party and FBI complicity.[20] When the nation saw two Buffalo police officers push 75-year-old Martin Gugino backwards during a Black Lives Matter protest onto the sidewalk and marched by him as he lay bleeding from the head, Trump (who was trying pedal-to-the-metal to ally himself with the police) reached into the bottom of the stupidest conspiracy theories ever barrel and tweeted the man looked like an Antifa provocateur who fell harder than he was pushed. Mr. Gugino had long been a nonviolent peace activist.

As for uneducated beliefs, we observed earlier that nobody can know everything. But Trump's performance in school left him significantly less educated than he should have been, and he then concentrated so intensely on one thing—making money—that a great deal has remained outside his understanding. It is sad to say, but Donald Trump appears one-dimensional to some people because, to a significant extent, he is one-dimensional. If this were opposite land, a place in which Trump occasionally dwells, and they gave out merit badges for ignorance, the president would seemingly have them in all the physical sciences, the social sciences, history, philosophy, literature, and the arts. But he has often resented people who know more than he does, and that is probably why he blew his stack during that first military-diplomatic review at the Pentagon in 2017. He had no idea what the experts were talking about. He probably had not even heard of some of the countries and treaties being presented, So, he shut them up with Kaboom! and talked at length about how much the French president had liked him.

The great thing about believing in your own instincts is you do not have to learn anything to be right or be guided by people who do know more than you do—a tacit admission that you are inferior. Thus, when Trump was angry at a Federal Reserve decision to raise interest rates in 2018, he said, "They're making a mistake because I have a gut, and my gut tells me more sometimes than anybody else's brain can ever tell me."[21] Some of his early advisors may have concluded the gut involved was the colon. Former Secretary of Defense James Mattis told close associates that Donald Trump has the understanding of a fifth or sixth grader.[22] Former Secretary of State Rex Tillerson at various times called Trump a moron and an idiot.[23] One afternoon a senior White House official blurted out to a reporter, "The president's insane," adding Trump "did not understand the Constitution and what his powers were."[24] The former National Economic Council Chairman Gary Cohn discovered that Trump knew absolutely nothing about economics, of all things.[25]

Trump covers his far-flung ignorance by claiming widespread expertise. He publicly claims that he knows more about military matters than his generals do. He says he understands more about economics than virtually every economist in the world. He thinks he knows more about global warming than nearly every climate scientist. He has learned more about America's international relations than anyone in the State Department could possibly know and has many other areas of unmatched expertise.[26] In truth he knows astonishingly little. Consider the reason he gave for abandoning America's Kurdish allies in Syria in 2019: "They didn't help us in the Second World War, they didn't help us with Normandy."[27] His ignorance of who the Kurds are, World War II, and the invasion of Normandy revealed by that statement is so astounding, it hurts your hair.

Inevitably intuitions prove wrong some of the time, or racetracks would shut down.* And they can prove disastrous for a country helplessly in the grip of one-man rule. That is why authoritarianism so often leads to a nation's doom.[28] The greatest and most tragic example of President Trump's reliance on his intuition over the advice of experts was his handling of the COVID-19 virus infection in January and February 2020. "His gut" told him it posed no threat to America. He continued to believe this for well over a month, despite all the advice and pleading he got from public health experts who knew what they were talking about. During this critical period, when every case that went undetected could mean scores of cases farther down the road because of the exponential spread of the illness, the disease became established in the United States and began appearing everywhere airlines flew. Trump also ignored pleas for stockpiling supplies that would predictably start running out when the epidemic got rolling. He just had a hunch everybody else was wrong. Later he urged health authorities to use an antimalarial drug to treat the disease, without any clinical trials to determine if it would work when there was a chance it might make things

---

*   Daniel Kahneman, a psychologist who won the Nobel Prize in Economics, explores the working of intuitive thinking at great depth in his wonderful work *Thinking Fast and Slow* (New York: Farrar, Straus and Giroux, 2011). Suffice it to say that while intuitive thinking is fast, it is not as reliable as thinking slowly, systematically, and carefully.

worse. When asked why he pressured the medical community, he said he had a "good feeling" about it. Today, we know from highly sophisticated modeling that had he taken action one week earlier he could have saved more than 36,000 American lives, and two weeks earlier more than 50,000 American lives.[29] Trump's intuition has been deadly for Americans, and he alone is responsible for more ongoing mounting deaths still producing our nation's worst modern tragedy.

INCREASING DEMAND FOR LOYALTY

Presidents naturally expect a high degree of loyalty from their appointees, but how high, how wide, and how deep varies. Lyndon Johnson said of a potential appointee in 1967: "I don't want loyalty. I want LOYALTY. I want him to kiss my ass in Macy's window at high noon and tell me it smells like roses. I want his pecker in my pocket."[30] Johnson got extreme loyalty and total subservience in his administration, and America got the war in Vietnam. When you demand total loyalty from your staff, you take away your best chance to avoid blunders. You have built a car that can go top speed wherever the driver wants, but it has no brakes, so it is doomed to crash, probably quickly. The Donald made it clear over the decades that anyone who worked for him owed him great personal loyalty. While conspicuous incompetence may result in a humiliating, foul-mouthed callout, the loyal incompetent typically stayed on the payroll. Disloyalty however triggers Trump's favorite, power-asserting phrase, "You're fired!" Trump himself said in 2007, "I value loyalty above everything else—more than brains, more than drive, and more than energy."[31] Every authoritarian leader in history has probably felt the same way.

The first generation of advisors to serve under Trump likely thought their job was to advise the president. That is why they were called advisors. However, it quickly became clear that Trump dislikes getting advice and becomes angry when someone tries to explain something to him, for reasons we think lay deep in his personality. He was not interested in their opinions and saw them as mere implementers there to carry out his decisions. Nevertheless, some of them challenged Trump in private and even resisted his decisions in public, but they gave up or were forced to resign. They have been replaced, in almost every instance, by "Trump-pets," people who give the 45th president total support and loyalty.[32] They "let Trump be Trump" in the vernacular of these supplicants. Trump does not just want loyalty; he demands absolute fidelity and backing, with no exceptions, no matter the cost. Thus, he expected Ambassador Gordon Sondland to defy a congressional subpoena about the Ukraine Scandal, or lie if he did testify, and thereby sacrifice himself rather than tell the truth and reveal the president's underhandedness. As another example, during a December 2017 discussion about immigration, Trump said to Senator Lindsey Graham, "You're a middle-of-the-road guy. I want you to be 100 percent for Trump." Graham responded, "OK, what's the issue and I'll tell you whether I'm 100 percent for you or not." "You're like 82 percent," Trump continued. "Well, some days I'm 100 percent. Some days I may be zero," replied the senator from South Carolina. "I want you to be a 100 percent guy," said President Trump.[33]

It could not be clearer. Every day, in every way, on every issue, Trump now wanted all GOP senators to support what "Trump" (notice the third person) wanted. You will not find much wiggle room in 100 percent. Trump was asking these elected officials straight out to betray their oath of office, to give their highest loyalty to him, rather than the Constitution and those who had elected them. At that time Graham rightly refused, as did FBI Director James Comey, when Trump pressed him for such a commitment.[34] Today this is the standard, if unwritten, understanding to work in the Trump administration. But demanding total submission from appointees amounts to a confession of weakness. When someone asks you for total loyalty, he is not saying, "Promise to support me when I am right." He is saying, "You have

to promise to back me when I am wrong." Trump, who constantly tries to
sell himself as a strong leader, laid bare this fragility on October 21, 2019,
when he complained that the Republicans in the House of Representatives
were not fighting hard enough to save him from impeachment. He expected
total loyalty from all Republicans (whether they thought he was innocent
or guilty). He got it. The next day a group of Republican Representatives
presented him with a plan to swarm an impeachment hearing to protest its
being closed to the public, even though the action violated House rules.
Trump gave it his blessing, and the "action" took place.[35] Donnie was back
on the schoolyard again, and he said to his followers: If you want to be in
my gang, you have to show you're tough enough. Here is what you have to
do. And like a bully's followers in grade school, they did it.

Trump completely controls the Republican Party today. Its leaders have
sold out on most of the principles the GOP used to stand for, such as strict
interpretation of the Constitution, the separation of powers, accountability
in government, the rule of law, states' rights, small government, enmity
toward a hostile Russia, support of our allies, no deficit spending, reduc-
ing the national debt, strong backing of the military, FBI and intelligence
communities, free trade, even safeguarding the well-being of the citizens
by keeping as many Americans as possible alive during an epidemic. You
may wonder how much they ever believed in these things, given that one
maverick president could make them disappear so quickly. Real principles
stiffen your spine when someone pressures you to do evil. These look more
like talking points, in retrospect.

Dr. Anthony Fauci, the lead scientist in the nation's fight against
COVID-19, has shown more backbone than nearly every Republican in
Congress by refusing to endorse President Trump's absurd statements and
recommendations regarding the disease. Trump is visibly disturbed when
Fauci and Dr. Deborah Birx say the disease is not yet under control, inject-
ing bleach is not the answer, nor is taking an untested malarial drug, the

nation is not ready yet to be reopened, a vaccine will probably not be ready by December, and so on. The majority of the American public trusts the scientists more than they do Trump by a long shot.[36] Thus, they have not been fired the way four "disloyal" inspectors general have been. But it is probably just a matter of time, unless they bend to Trump's will.

Trump's demand for loyalty extends beyond his administration and Congress. During a campaign rally in Orlando, Florida, on March 5, 2016, he spontaneously asked the crowd to raise their right hands and pledge to vote for him. The "request" dripped with dominance and the crowd readily doubled down on its submissive union with the bridegroom. The scene immediately drew comparisons to the Nuremberg Rallies. Nevertheless, two nights later Trump asked for the pledge again in Concord, North Carolina. When criticism mounted, he replied that the crowd asked him to do it, and it had nothing to do with Nazis.[37] But it does, if in no other way than it signals yet again underlying anxiety. You can assume that people who come to your rallies and cheer your every word are going to vote for you. But if you want a loyalty oath on top of that, it shows you nonetheless have doubts about them, that you try to alleviate by making them promise to stand by you no matter what you do. Trump's behavior shows he worries that his staunchest supporters will abandon him. He is saying, "I know I'm going to screw up, but no matter how badly I do, promise you'll vote for me." How self-confident is that?

NOTICEABLE INCREASE IN AGGRESSION

If incessant lying, becoming scatterbrained, increasingly relying on the Hail Marys of intuition, and demanding unquestioning loyalty betray a mind fighting against its own grand inquisitor, frequent unjustified aggression may also flag that a person's mental life is collapsing under stress. Vicious combativeness is another hallmark of an authoritarian leader.

Where did the angry, hostile, combative, assaulting, vengeful, mean, taunting, scornful, nasty, victim-seeking, media-bashing Donald Trump come from? What sort of person wants to build a moat stocked with alligators and snakes in front of a border wall and wants undocumented immigrants shot in the legs "to slow them down?"[38] We know that was the kind of person Fred Trump raised, a son who was told over and over in his youth, "Be a killer." Donald learned from his father, just as he learned from Roy Cohn: attack, just attack, and double down as a basic rule of human interaction for winners. These influences produced a screaming boss on the casino floor; a temper-trantruming madman wrongly abusing his second-in-command over the height of a ceiling; a cheating husband publicly humiliating his wife in front of her friends and children because he no longer wants her; a man who drove small business owners in Atlantic City into bankruptcy when he refused to pay for the work they had done on his casinos; a man who defaults on his promise to pay 14 percent in interest on junk bonds that he sold to the gullible; a man who tried to trick his deteriorating father, the very author of his success, into signing over control of the family fortune so he could spend it on his failing casinos and other undertakings heading for bankruptcy; a man who bilked investors of millions of dollars in his DJT public company venture; a man who ran a multimillion-dollar scam called Trump University; and a heartless man who canceled the medical insurance on an infant with cerebral palsy to punish a relative who dared file a lawsuit against him. So, while Donald Trump has the con man's skill to impress people about what a charming, benevolent, sweet guy he can be, he has been a nasty piece of work since early childhood. And we cannot help but notice how he began losing control of his aggression in the late 1980s when his business operations collapsed. From that time, the lying, the inability to think straight, the inability to focus, the reliance on intuition, the demand for loyalty, and his hostility have ebbed and flowed—only to have all these traits grow out of control since seeking and becoming president.[39]

As a candidate and as president, there has been an increasing nastiness of Trump's attacks. If you are inclined to psychological explanations, you might notice that, besides women in general and successful women in particular and members of minority groups, he particularly goes after white men who have a lot more "class" than he has. Take Robert Mueller. The specter of the "shoot from the lip" Donald Trump, who is so often uninformed and blazingly wrong, slandering Robert Mueller for supposedly conducting a "witch hunt" strains the quality of justice to the breaking point. Mueller dedicated his career to being fair, thorough, and never making an avoidable mistake. He is widely considered an ultimate straight shooter in Washington.[40] Trump, by comparison, is a clueless president diving out of a plane without a parachute, landing in a minefield where he walks straight into a pit surrounded by billboards that read: "Danger. There's A Big Hole Here!" Often when shamelessly puffing himself up, vengefully attacking others, he seems such a little person compared with his targets like Robert Mueller and Barack Obama. Saying John McCain was not a hero, when as far as we know Trump has never done a single heroic thing in his life, shrunk him to the size of a flea. The worse he senses he compares against others, the more vicious his attacks. He openly fantasizes revenge: "I have an absolute right to know the identity of the 'whistleblower,'" and threatening the "traitor" on the White House staff who told the "whistleblower" about the July 25 phone call with President Zelensky. Trump wanted Adam Schiff, chairman of the House Intelligence Committee, arrested for treason after Schiff, to make a point, gave a parody interpretation of the Zelensky phone call at a committee hearing.[41] Trump claims House Speaker Nancy Pelosi "hates the United States of America" and attacked her in person in the White House, calling her a "third-grade politician."[42]

Maine Senator Susan Collins, in casting an acquittal vote for Trump in the impeachment trial, said she thought the president had learned his lesson. He certainly has, and it may go like this from Trump's point of view:

Nearly all the Republicans in Congress are total losers, I can do almost anything, and they will back me. Everybody who betrayed me is going to find out what a tough sonofabitch I am. It will be clear to the vast apparatus of federal officials that this is Trump's government. He has his foot on their neck and their only job is to do what he says, or else.

Trump's aggressiveness has markedly grown, quite predictably since he has always preached outsized retaliation against whoever attacks. He has threatened anyone who dares cross him in the future, saying his supporters would become violent if he were prosecuted for crimes he committed before or during his time in office, explaining threateningly: "I have the support of the police, the support of the military, the support of Bikers for Trump—I have tough people, but they don't play it tough until they go to a certain point and then it would be very, very bad."[43] It is Donny with his gang from grade school again throwing his weight around the nation's capital suggesting insurrection is not out of the question. We have never had a president as hostile and vicious as Trump. No previous president created the same level of fear in his subordinates, no president fired so many high officials, no president waged war with oversight committees and refused to comply with inspectors general, simply ignored the system of checks and balances, threatened so many governors, allies, and journalists, and watched so indifferently as his unjustifiable certainty in himself and determination to stay in power led to the unnecessary, tragic deaths of so many during a pandemic. What is the source of all his anger and hostility? Who is he most angry at? We believe the answer is very conspicuous and very simple: it is Donald himself.

Donald's biographical background tells us that he is not at all the person he pretends or claims to be. If he were the supremely self-assured, accomplished, insightful, reality-based, and focused genius he claims he is, we wonder if he would behave as he has while occupying the office of the president of the United States. His behavior reveals a mind fighting an epic battle within, a conflict that cannot be contained. It erupts constantly to the surface in self-defeating lying, alarming self-love, chaotic thinking, reliance on very faulty instincts, impulsive decision-making, fear of betrayal, and a barely controllable white-hot anger. We have offered our explanation of this war in terms of Trump's earlier experiences in life. We do not think that Donald Trump's psychological problems will inevitably lead to a mental collapse because he has had these challenges for most of his life and has managed to stay in the ring punching away at everything day after day. He has developed ways of handling his anxieties and reassuring himself of his magnificence, such as fawning media interviews, his rallies, and state visits abroad where foreign governments merrily engorge his vanity because they know that drawbridge is always down. But these good times keep getting swamped by his failures. We have the feeling that we are watching a five-act play that will end with a lot of bodies on the floor. On top of the ones already there.

We close with a few observations. Donald Trump does, in our view, have two exceptional skills not uncommon in authoritarian leaders: He is world-class at intimidating people and just as skilled at conning others. That is why we think he would score highly on the Power-Mad and Con-man Scales we used to introduce the previous chapters. In fact, he is a pro's pro at these things. In addition, Trump is a master at diverting attention, by changing the subject when he is in trouble. But this gambit is catching up to him for he has done this so many times people expect it as they do the sunrise. Thus, when his disastrous handling of the COVID-19 epidemic creates too much heat for him, he seeks a diversion. For example, in May 2020, he resurrected "Obamagate," which started as his long-discredited charge that the former president tapped his phones in Trump Tower during the 2016 election, and has grown to incorporate a number of right-wing conspiracy theories about the origins of the Russia investigation and the prosecution of former Trump national security adviser, Michael Flynn. But so far the bogus charge is just spinning a wheel in the mud. Everybody else knew it was just a distraction and frequently said so.[44] We only worry that he may feel he has to up the scale of the diversion to attract attention, and little short of nuclear war would divert attention from the COVID-19 pandemic—and we do not wish to go there.

Trump has used his con man skills to attack the principle of law and the Constitution. He is blundering into these actions when he discovers a legitimate presidential power, then the con in him quickly sees how he might use it illegitimately. He was passing out all kinds of money to foreign governments, why not get something in return, like a bogus investigation by Ukraine of his likely opponent Joe Biden and his son. This extortion scheme got him impeached but did not stop him. When he learned Michigan was going to use mail-in ballots in 2020, he threatened to withhold federal aid unless the Democratic governor halted the practice, which Donald feared could result in a fair election that he would lose. (This Michigan extortion scheme was simply ignored, as was a similar threat to withhold federal money from Nevada if the state adopted mail-in voting.)

After Trump first discovered the pardon power, he realized that he might use it to excuse his own criminal behavior. When he told the world that he would use it for himself, it got a rise.[45] The self-pardon was the first real evidence Trump was blatantly self-dealing. It took the country to a new place because no president had ever claimed this before in our 229-year history, not even Richard Nixon. While the Justice Department wondered, at the end of Watergate, if Nixon could pardon himself, they concluded he could not because of the fundamental legal principle that no one can be a judge in his own case, nor is any man above the law.[46] But Trump did not think that principle should apply to him.

For that matter, notwithstanding his oath to uphold the Constitution, he does not believe it applies to him. From the outset of his presidency he has ignored the Constitution's emoluments clause, which prohibits him

from directly accepting money from foreign governments. Yet he has refused to divest his interest in properties that are receiving significant money
from foreign governments. He correctly figures all this is too complex for
his supporters, so the lawsuit charging him with conspicuous violations of
the Constitution are simply ignored, as they have proceeded through the
federal courts.[47] Even some brazen violations of the Constitution, which
Trump often announces, do not trouble his base for they like them. For
example, on October 30, 2018, as the midterm election campaigns entered
the final week, Trump said he was preparing an executive order to override
the first clause of the Fourteenth Amendment to the Constitution.[48] This
clause grants American citizenship to anyone born or naturalized in the
United States who is subject to its jurisdiction. Children of illegal immigrants born in the United States have birthright citizenship, which Trump
does not like. The announcement stunned almost everyone. Politicians and
legal experts throughout the land said the president had no such power. If
he did, he could suspend any part of the Constitution he wished, thereby
giving himself the power for one-man rule that could continue for all his
life and be handed on to whomever he chose. It would make the Constitution meaningless. But Trump flatly asserted he had the power to override
the Constitution, and he refused to answer any further questions on the
subject.

The executive order was never issued, and Trump may just have been
trying to stir up his base for the midterm election. But if he was testing
the waters to see what would happen if he tried to overthrow the Constitution, say, to save his own skin, he would have noticed that nary a peep
came from either his base or the Republicans in Congress. The same thing
happened when Trump attacked Article I, Section 9 of the Constitution,
which gives Congress "sole power of the purse," by allocating money to a
project Congress had refused to support (Trump's border wall) from another project. Another extra-legal gambit appeared on May 22, when he

declared churches were essential services and should open for services in two days because if there was one thing America needed now, it was prayer and not more COVID-19 sheltering. (He did not mention that everything was not under control with the pandemic. Nor did he mention that prayer can be done anywhere by anyone and anytime outside of churches.) Rather, notwithstanding his lack of power to do so he declared that if governors would not open the churches in their states, he would "overrule" them. So far, Trump has not tried to enforce any of his powerless proclamations.

Trump has cast himself as an authoritarian figure as president, a tough guy, and a political strongman. But to do so he has engaged in incessant lying and self-aggrandizement, which has reduced further his ability to think straight. He may believe that tough guys have all the answers, right off the top, so he constantly relies on his uninformed intuition, which reveals his thinking is the swamp that most definitely plagues Washington now. He believes that strong leaders tolerate no dissent, and they do not want to be bothered with any information contrary to their view of the world, for they are infallible. Because at some level he understands he is deeply flawed he demands unquestioning loyalty from all, and total silence about what he is really like. Finally, as president he has become increasingly aggressive in attacking any who disagree with him. In brief, Trump's vision of the (his) presidency combines, however impossibly his being an admired king and a ruthless dictator. Nevertheless, he believes he must please his electoral base to get reelected. To date, these highly reliable supporters have been ostensibly oblivious to his distinctively unpresidential behavior, not to mention extraordinarily forgiving of his conspicuous incompetence. It is for this reason we turn our full focus over the next six chapters to understanding these astonishing believers, for they are source of Trump's political power. Without them, Donald Trump would be nothing but a Twitter troll.

CHAPTER FIVE

THE TRUMP BASE PART I—SOCIAL DOMINATORS

Although the deep twists of Donald Trump's motivation for becoming an authoritarian leader give our diagnostic skills a run for their money, on the surface it seems elementary. He wants power, the way all the other autocrats do. It is the supporters, the people trying to escape from freedom, who seem unfathomable. As Barack Obama observed in September 2018, Donald Trump is not the real problem, "he is a symptom, not the cause."[1] The very troubling vulnerability of our democracy to dictatorship lies with the startling number of Americans who made Trump president, despite his flaws and conspicuous lack of fitness for the job. Even Trump was amazed at his supporters' loyalty, which led to his infamous boast that if he openly murdered someone on Fifth Avenue it would not cost him a single vote.[2]

Altemeyer wrote in July 2016 that Trump's followers would stick with him to the end and that he could win in November 2016 through the zeal of his supporters.[3] This prediction was based on the accumulation of studies that as early as 1981 led to the conclusion that "there are so many people so genuinely submissive to established authority that they constitute a real threat to freedom in countries such as Canada and the United States."[4] By 1988 it was clear that "Wanna-be tyrants in a democracy are just comical figures on soap boxes when they have no followers."[5] So, the real threat lay in a large part of the population that was coiled like a tightly wound spring with enough pent-up energy to drive a dictator through all barriers into the White House. They needed but a demagogue to lead them and now they had one, leading thunderous legions in halls across the country chanting, "Make America Great Again." The steadfastness of Trump's supporters strikes even seasoned observers. As noted earlier, pollster and analyst Nate Silver charts the daily average of Trump's popularity-unpopularity ratings gathered by leading opinion polls.* The results among registered voters show that Trump has received on balance negative ratings (more disapproval than approval) since February 2017—not even a month into his presidency. His "presidential honeymoon" did not last two weeks. But despite everything that has followed, all the scandals and the convictions of cronies and government shutdowns and revelations of misconduct and bone-headed foreign policy decisions and betrayals that drove one disillusioned Trump appointee after another to leave his administration, and even after Trump's blatant attempts to subvert the Constitution, even after the impeachment and his allowing COVID-19 to spread throughout the United States killing more than a hundred thousand citizens and putting more than thirty million out of work, the needle on the approval rating has only flicked a bit. Trump has had a rock-solid 41 to 45 percent approval by likely voters. It almost always goes up and down within that range depending on independents (read: unaffiliated) who are temporarily affected by recent events. No previous president in the history of public opinion polling has enjoyed such consistently solid backing.[6] Trump is disliked by most Americans, but his base has kept the faith to a degree that seems to defy human understanding. That is the central focus in this book and set forth in the next six chapters.

But first we must say that Trump's supporters are entitled to back whomever they wish. Censoring their nonviolent messages, taking away

---

*   See https://projects.fivethirtyeight.com/trump-approval-ratings/voters.

their right to peacefully organize, restricting their right to vote would be an attack on the democracy one might claim to be protecting. You will find no appeal in this book to harass or intimidate the people who rushed to Donald Trump's ranks, or any suggestion that the appropriate exercise of their democratic rights should be limited. If our means to the end are mean, the ends become unjust. Democracy will prevail if those who want it vote against tyranny, but not if they create tyranny themselves. In short, "the Resistance" must win at the ballot box repeatedly if our democracy is to reach, say, its 250th birthday in 2037. If Trump loses in 2020 you can be certain that he, who has "fixed" more outcomes than the World Wrestling Federation and whose campaign for the presidency involved deception and lying from the start, will tell his followers the election was rigged, and they will believe him. And even if Trump accepts the will of the majority and the Electoral College and leaves the White House, his backers will remain a very powerful force, ready to give undying loyalty to him for as long as he wants, and then to the next dictator-in-waiting. And the next one will almost certainly be smarter than Donald Trump. You can be sure someone is watching Trump closely, planning to step into his place. Thus, if you want to remain free, you will probably have to outvote today's ardent Trump followers, not only in November 2020 but for some time in future elections. You may have heard that the price of freedom is eternal vigilance. It is true.

TRUMP'S BASE: THE SIZE OF THE PROBLEM

How many people voted for Donald? According to the final official tally, Hillary Clinton received 65,853,516 (48.2 percent) of the 136,669,237 votes for president in 2016, Trump was selected on 62,984,825 (46.1 percent) ballots, and various other candidates (including the ever-popular Mickey Mouse and "flesh-eating bacteria") received nearly eight million votes.[7] Trump triumphed in the Electoral College because he won some key states by small margins despite being enormously outspent there. Nothing the Democrats tried could get some traditional Democrats and independents to vote for Hillary Clinton.[8] In contrast, Trump's base:

- Showed up at his rallies and cheered at the top of their lungs.
- Ritualistically chanted "Build the wall" and "Lock her up" whenever Mexicans or Hillary Clinton were named.
- Vilified the media whenever Trump complained about its coverage.
- Proudly wore their MAGA hats everywhere.
- Gave the campaign as much as they could afford, and then some.
- Planted the lawn signs and attended local rallies.
- Talked up Trump at cafes and high school football games and churches.
- Faithfully followed Trump's Twitter output.
- Relayed stories they liked to fellow-enthusiasts faster than the latter could relay the same stories to them.

Then they voted for the man and spent the night of November 8, 2016 thinking, while tens of millions of other Americans sat stunned in confused agony, that at last the country would return to its golden past and everything was going to turn out right.[9]

Exit poll data (see Appendix III) indicate Trump got roughly 40,000,000 votes from Republicans, about 20,000,000 came from independents, and the remaining 3,000,000 were cast by self-described Democrats. Judging by the 2018 midterm election, virtually all the Republicans, some of the independents, and even some of the wandering Democrats have remained firmly committed to Trump. But not all. Many people voted for him even though they disliked him enormously. But they disliked Hillary Clinton enormously squared. A sizeable number of those who answered the exit polls (15 percent, or over 20 million voters) said neither of the candidates was qualified to be president, but they broke over 4 to 1 for Trump, giving him 12 million more votes than they gave Clinton.[10] Many Americans wanted to shake things up in Washington by electing a cage-rattling non-politician to "drain the swamp. "They had less commitment to Trump per se, and they apparently soured on him in the first two weeks of his presidency—turning his net approval rating in the polls into the net disapproval rating mentioned earlier. But some independents and even a few Democrats, who "somewhat-disapprove" of Trump, did swing temporarily into his column when he did something good, and they could help him win in 2020.

TRUMP SUPPORTERS VIEWED THROUGH PSYCHOLOGICAL RESEARCH ON AUTHORITARIANISM

The Hillary-haters and the anything-is-better-than-the-usual-thing voters would not seem to be money in the bank Trump backers. But Donald Trump appears to have developed a faithful base of about 50 million supporters in 2015–2016.[11] Who are they? We think most of them have one of the two authoritarian personalities that have been scientifically established, plus a unique group that combines these two. They are:

Social Dominators. People who believe in inequality between groups. Predictably, they usually believe their groups should be more prestigious and powerful than others. Some social dominators take their belief in inequality down to the personal level and are determined to gain power over people they know. Donald Trump, who wants to dominate everyone he meets and the rest of humanity by proxy, appears to be an extreme example of a social dominator. We shall look at other social dominators and why they are so attracted to Donald Trump in this chapter.

Authoritarian Followers. These people are submissive, fearful, and longing for a mighty leader who will protect them from life's threats. They divide the world into friend and foe, with the latter greatly outnumbering the former. Their ethnocentrism (partiality to one's own group) is often based on their religious training and they have been found to be highly self-righteous. Authoritarian followers have been studied for many decades and it will take three chapters to tie what we know about them to their passionate embrace of Donald Trump. This group includes the white evangelicals who support Trump more than anyone else—to the complete bewilderment of many. We shall uncover the rather amazing reason for their devotion in Chapter 8.

"*Double Highs.*" Some people score highly in both being a Social Dominator and being an Authoritarian Follower, which confuses one at first because it seems to make them dominating submissives. But this can happen in various ways. For example, dominating persons can strongly believe in other people submitting to authorities if they themselves are the authorities, or allied with them. Donald Trump would be a good example of such a Double High. He probably has not had a submissive inclination since his father died, but he obviously thinks other people should be submissive. Alternately, submissive people can come to endorse their group's superiority over others to protect themselves further. Double Highs usually combine the worst elements of the two authoritarian personalities in such a dangerous way that they are especially worrisome and merit separate examination (see Chapter 9).[12]

SOCIAL DOMINATORS: THE SDO SCALE

Research on social dominator personalities was inspired by a 1994 scholarly article by Felicia Pratto, Jim Sidanius, Lisa Stallworth, and Bert Malle, which presented the Social Dominance Orientation ("SDO") Scale for measuring this new personality variable.[13] The current version of the test comes in two parts. One part asks for reactions to the idea that certain groups should dominate others. It has statements such as, "Some groups of people must be kept in their place," and "It's probably a good thing that certain groups are at the top and other groups are at the bottom." The second part seeks responses to the idea that we should accept inequality between groups. For example, "We should not push for group equality" and "We shouldn't try to guarantee that every group has the same quality of life."

The Power-Mad and Con Man Scales, which we noted earlier fit Donald Trump's personality like a custom-made suit, were developed shortly after the SDO Scale appeared to (attempt to) flesh out Pratto et al.'s model. They and other surveys have produced the following list of attitudes and behaviors that studies have shown characterize social dominators in general. (This list was assembled by author Dean in 2005, long before he had any knowledge of Donald Trump.) The traits are:

men (typically)	faintly hedonistic
oppose equality	pitiless
dominating	intimidating and bullying
amoral	vengeful
desire personal power	exploitive
manipulative	dishonest
cheat to win	highly prejudiced (racist, sexist, homophobic)
mean-spirited	militant
nationalistic	tells others what they want to hear
takes advantage of suckers	specializes in creating false images to sell self
will pretend to be religious if they are not genuinely so	usually politically and economically conservative

Remember Thomas Jefferson's opening words in the Declaration of Independence: "We hold these truths to be self-evident, that all men are created equal . . ."? Studies have shown that the higher someone scores on the Social Dominance Orientation scale, the less likely he is to endorse this central tenet of our democracy. They do not believe in equality between individuals nor between groups. Social dominators want the people presently on top to stay on top, and the groups that presently dominate other groups to continue to do so. Everybody else should stay below, "in their place." They do not want "the losers" to become winners. SDOs not only oppose equality, but they also oppose giving people equal opportunity. They want the playing field tilted in their favor because that way they get more. People born with advantages of wealth, race, or gender deserve to keep them, they believe.[14]

Why would social dominators ever submit to someone else? Mostly because they got beat. A person driven to control others will eventually lose to someone in his world, unless he is fierce enough, endowed enough, and lucky enough to consistently become Number One. When social dominators meet their match, they can quit the game. But it is much more rewarding to claim a place in the hierarchy. Animals in many social species arrange themselves in "pecking orders" like this. Submitting to your superiors means you will be safer from further serious attacks by people who can hurt you. You are on their side. They will look down on you as a "loser" the way you look down on the people you have beaten. But that is better than suffering endless slings and arrows of outrageous misfortune. And you will probably get to share in exerting the power of your super-dominating betters, in however large or small a way as you can. In this way bullies build and keep their gangs. White social dominators prejudge and dislike almost every minority or disadvantaged group you can think of: Blacks, Jews, Mexicans, Latinos, Japanese, Chinese, homosexuals, Muslims, North American Indians, and women—to name ten. And they are often quite upfront and outspoken about it. When prejudiced people are given evidence of their prejudices, most deny it. "There must be some mistake," they say. But if they can get past that denial they wish it were not so. However, social dominators are likely to admit their discriminatory attitudes and even be proud of them. "Yeah, the Klingons stink. We should get rid of them all."

Social dominators, with their preference for keeping-things-as-they-are, might have generally preferred the Republican Party before 2008. But they probably began rushing pell-mell to the GOP banner when Barack Obama became the Democratic nominee in 2008. Trump's candidacy in 2016 just produced the final wave of a decades-long migration of social dominators and other authoritarians into the GOP camp as the party leaders who invited them in held the gates wide open.[15] You can see where this all led by considering the demographic profile of Donald Trump's supporters in the 2016 election. According to the exit polls, Trump received 57 percent of the ballots cast by whites. White men were especially likely to vote for him: 62 percent.[16] Take education into account, and Trump got 71 percent of the votes from (a) white (b) men (c) who did not have a college degree of any kind. Only one other group flocked to his movement in greater numbers: those white Christian "evangelicals" mentioned above.

"THE FORGOTTEN"

White "undereducated" voters might have chosen Trump for many reasons, but when asked in the exit polls how they were doing economically compared to four years ago, 27 percent said they were worse off now, and 77 percent of that group voted for Trump. That works out to nearly 29 million of the 63 million votes Trump received. Many blue-collar workers, especially in the "rust belt," had fallen on hard times. Their jobs had either left the country or immigrants were willing to do them for less pay. Americans who had lost income over the last four years could conclude they were being pushed down the greasy pole. But the politicians in Washington did not seem to care.

Ben Bradlee Jr.'s excellent book, *The Forgotten: How the People of One Pennsylvania County Elected Donald Trump and Changed America*, examined how Trump won "rust belt" Luzerne County in northwest Pennsylvania. Obama had won the county, 64,000+ to Mitt Romney's 58,000+ in 2012. But Hillary got only a little over 52,000 votes compared to Trump's 78,000+. So, nearly the same number of people voted in each election, and a 6,000 vote Democratic victory four years earlier turned into a crushing 26,000 vote loss. Clinton lost at least 12,000 previous Democratic votes to Trump. Those plus votes from people who had evidently not voted in 2012 produced Trump's big victory. Bradlee's interviews turned up lots of reasons why about 20 percent of the 2012 Democratic voters responded to Donald Trump's 2016 message, but loss of income—real or anticipated—came up most often. However, that by itself did not automatically cause a switch, because a solid majority (80 percent) of the Democratic voters seemingly saw through Trump's preposterous disguise as a nonpolitician devoted to helping the little guy. What then was different about the 20 percent who switched? We suspect Trump peeled off the most authoritarian of the traditional Democratic voters, including the social dominators who took their drop in status hardest.

Post-election surveys uncovered a second group who had not personally lost ground economically, but still believed white Americans were losing their dominance in the country.[17] They thought the newcomers were changing American culture, costing white people their privileges. Nearly half of them said they now felt like a stranger in their own country, it had changed so much. This anxiety about "cultural displacement" was especially prevalent in rural areas of midwestern states. Trump captured the mood of many white, undereducated voters who felt they were being left behind when he talked about "the forgotten," and their anger made them responsive to the enormous hostility that lathered his rhetoric. They wanted an "outsider" to bash Washington, and Trump had a sledgehammer of a mouth. Researchers predictably found a preference for an authoritarian leader among voters who felt their birthright was being stolen from them. For example, most (60 percent) of the white, working-class voters surveyed shortly after the election agreed that, "Because things have gotten so far off track in this country, we need a leader who is willing to break some rules if that's what it takes to set things right."[18]

You must feel compassion for many of Trump's supporters when you realize what they have gone through and when you see things through their eyes. The trouble is the anger aroused by their fear of being disinherited made them receptive to a political movement that will destroy the country if it goes unchecked. Trump's earnest supporters will end up much worse off than they are now, along with everybody else, if our democracy is destroyed. Furthermore, while you immediately sympathize with people who are struggling to feed their children, some of them felt they were more entitled to employment than others just because they were white. They believed in a stratified society in which "European types" prospered more than any other. They wanted non-whites laid off, and non-white children to go hungry, rather than their own, simply based on skin color. That is ten dimes out of a dollar short of an acceptable solution, and we should have no part of it.

PERSPECTIVE: TRUMP'S 2000 CAMPAIGN FOR PRESIDENT

To comprehend Trump's base, a brief flashback provides perspective because the Donald Trump of an earlier era would not have appealed at all to high SDOs. Trump wanted no part of a racist appeal in 2000 when he briefly sought the presidential nomination of Ross Perot's Reform Party. To the contrary, he charged his chief opponent, Patrick Buchanan, with being anti-immigrant, prejudiced against Blacks, gays, and Jews and called him a neo-Nazi "Hitler-lover" who was "having a love affair with Hitler."[19] Buchanan did not run an overtly racist campaign. Politicians traditionally appealed to prejudiced voters carefully, in subtle, wink-wink fashion, fearing a backlash if they called out minorities by name. George Wallace campaigned against civil rights, but said he was defending states' rights. George H. W. Bush just showed Willie Horton's mug shot without comment in the "Revolving Door" TV ad in 1988. Buchanan, the man who suggested "silent majority" to Richard Nixon in 1969, ran on a nudge-nudge, "America First" platform.

It was widely thought in 2000 that Trump had no intention of mounting a campaign and was only trying to advertise his brand through free publicity. He did make it difficult to take him seriously. For example, he criticized the Reform Party for not having a platform, and when he was immediately handed a copy of its platform he did not bother to read it. He had no platform himself, just assertions that he would renegotiate America's trade deals, eliminate the national debt (which he considered a very serious problem), and provide Americans with universal health care. (Yes, he did say that!) He kept any sign of understanding these issues strictly to himself. He went on television a lot, but his candidacy did not develop traction and he soon told his "exploratory committee" to stop exploring. He explained to the media that he could not make himself lie enough to be a successful politician.[20]

HOW TRUMP ROLLED UP THE SOCIAL DOMINATORS

By 2015 Trump was a nationally known star of an unreal reality TV show whose name stood for "the best!" He had as well been a frequent guest on "Fox and Friends," and was well known to conservative voters. He thundered onto the political scene as a take-charge tough guy promising to knock the hell out of everybody, Republicans and Democrats alike, who marginalized white voters. He drilled down into their deep-seated anger and it erupted through him, pervading and corrupting the election. People surged to Trump for lots of reasons, but you can see why his behavior and his slogan to make America great again would particularly appeal to social dominators for whom racial superiority meant a great deal. They believed he would make their lives great again. Trump promised to protect white, economically vulnerable, undereducated Americans against the non-white usurpers who they angrily thought were flooding the United States, living off their taxes, and rising in society at their expense. Trump unmistakably believes in social domination, so they could count on him cracking down on all the people who were not "real Americans." Furthermore, they would not have been offended by Trump's amoral behavior. Social dominators, scoring highly on the Con Man Scale, do not believe much in right and wrong. If lying, manipulating, and cheating gets you what you want, they say do it. "Go ahead, break some rules." Their man had entered the scene, stage right, and he was mustering a mob.

Did Trump know all this and cleverly tailor his message to capture the hearts and minds of these highly prejudiced Americans? Not likely. He did not have to tailor anything to corner the market on amoral prejudice, just reveal who he was, an industrial strength, world-class, thoroughly unprincipled social dominator. He clearly learned from the responses he got when he demanded the death penalty for the "Central Park Five" how many anti- "colored" votes were lying on the table that most politicians did not want to overtly pick up. He further discovered many Americans could barely control their hostility toward African Americans when he led the "birther movement," and chided President Obama to release his university grades. Trump understood that resentment seethed within many white Americans, especially among undereducated white men, over the increased immigration of non-whites to the United States and the perception that, in its efforts to give minorities a fairer chance at the American dream, the federal government was "against white people."

We believe the decisive moment in Trump's campaign came at the outset when he descended the escalator in Trump Tower on June 16, 2015 to announce his candidacy.[21] After congratulating himself on how well the event was being produced—it was staged right out of *The Apprentice*, so he knew it would work—he looked down at the speech placed for him on the podium, which had been prepared with his campaign manager, Corey Lewandowski. It was timed at seven-to-eight minutes, and it only took Trump forty minutes to deliver it.[22] The candidate started with "Our country is in serious trouble," a line that may take a seasoned reader back to the con-artist Professor Harold Hill in *The Music Man*. Then he played what he apparently thought was his strongest suit: the economy, specifically foreign trade—the same thing he led with in 2000. He named China, Japan, and Mexico as countries that had bested America, but blamed the American government for that. This drew weak, scattered applause, just as it had 15 years earlier, a deadly sound given the atrium had been sown with cheering supporters wearing TRUMP T-shirts provided for this "huge," televised event. Then Trump looked down at his speech again and apparently moved onto the next paragraph. "The U.S. has become a dumping ground for everybody else's problems," he said. This second point was perhaps an extension of the first, meant to illustrate how other countries were snookering the American government. Someone in the crowd shouted agreement. Trump said, "Thank you," and he got a noticeably louder round of applause. Whereupon he chuffed, probably because it was too inarticulate to have been prepared, "When Mexico sends its people, they're not sending their best. They're not sending you." (He gestured to someone in his audience.) "They're not sending you." (Another gesture.) "They're sending people that have lots of problems, and they're bringing their problems with them. They're bringing drugs, they're bringing crime, they're rapists." He went on to say that such people were also coming from South and Latin America, and probably from the Middle East too. "It's got to stop. It's got to stop," he concluded, and he got his biggest applause yet.

The "drugs, crime, rapists" sentence remains the most famous thing Trump ever said and it probably set the hook in social dominators across America as he dove headfirst into the dark side of American politics. Trump was not being politically correct. He was not pussyfooting around. He was not afraid of what anybody might call him. He was speaking his mind. The fact that he was not reading from a teleprompter, and his delivery was so choppy, and his ideas often ludicrous ("When did we beat Japan, at anything? . . . They beat us all the time.") told everybody he was saying whatever came into his head, and to hell with anybody who disagreed (or knew what he was talking about). When Trump "named names" he likely captured many prejudiced voters in one fell swoop because he was saying out loud what these Americans had been thinking for years but had been cowed into keeping to themselves. By now they were tired of "stifling" themselves, to use Archie Bunker's expression, for fear of being called politically incorrect. After "drugs, crime, rapists," two Trump supporters could meet, openly say what they believed, reinforce one another, and feel validated, empowered, refreshed. Trump liberated them as surely as Betty Friedan liberated women in the 1960s. He opened the floodgates on public racism that had been dammed in America for decades. Observers said he had "weaponized" prejudice.

The setting helped make Trump a champion of discrimination. The gorgeous building had marble walls. He was big and looked powerful. His wife was beautiful. His daughter was beautiful. Everything was "The Best." He seemed so honest, a straight shooter, not a politician. God knows he was not running for fame. He already had all of that anybody could want, they figured. He was not in it for money, for heaven's sake. He said he had billions upon billions of dollars and that he would pay for his whole campaign, so nobody could possibly "own" him. He obviously knew how to run things. NBC had made a TV show in which he played himself, a fabulously successful corporate executive. He was decisive; he fired someone every week on TV. And wonderfully, he was a WHITE MAN. He would be a great leader. This was one of the most exciting moments many social dominators had had in their adult lives, their epiphany. You can draw a straight line from this speech to the exit polls on November 8, 2016, when Trump's supporters, compared with Clinton's, said immigration and terrorism were the most important issues, and they were massively angry at the federal government.[23]

They did not know it, but they should also have been angry at Donald

Trump, because he had just massively conned them. The event was a TV show, even more staged than an episode of *The Apprentice*. Even the crowd was fake. Unable to find many people who would support his running for president, Trump had hired Extra-Mile Casting to provide actors to wear the Trump T-shirts and fill the atrium (which looked much bigger on TV than it really is) and celebrate the glorious news that The Donald was going to come down from on high and save the nation.[24] The pay was $50, and the campaign provided handmade signs that said things like, "People for a Stronger America." (They should have read, "Hire out-of-work actors trying to pay the rent."). It's possible that this whole nightmare we are living through, from the small child crying "Mama" in a Texas detention center to the bodies being stored in container trucks in some cities to the economy ricocheting between recession and depression, began when a "grassroots supporter" who was really Astroturf cheered at precisely the wrong time and set Trump after Mexican rapists.

THE 2015–16 CAMPAIGN

Trump quickly went from barely ticking in polls of Republican voters to front runner with a sonic boom of bombast no one could ignore.[25] He was more combative, abusive, assertive, and disruptive in the debates than anyone had ever been. He heaped scorn on the party he campaigned to lead. Republicans were as disgusting as Democrats, he said; all slimy denizens of the same swamp. He attacked everyone at his rallies who opposed him, and his crowds were bigger and louder than anyone else's, just as he was. And as he rained sarcasm and vitriol down on all the other candidates until their campaigns withered and died, most of their followers chose to support Trump, even though he had unconscionably insulted, ridiculed and smeared their first choices. He drove some voters out of the GOP, to be sure, but overall, the people who constituted the Republican Party in 2016 found him irresistible. As did many independents. A new American demagogue was born.

Over the course of the primaries, and during the campaign against Hillary Clinton, Trump received applause from his crowds when he touted his economic views, but the roof blew off when he attacked Mexicans, Muslims, and Obama. Wanting cheers more than anything else, getting drunk on them, Trump gave them more and more of what they came for. When he was criticized in the press for pandering to the most prejudiced people in American society, including the alt right, whose impulses he was locking and loading, and as the media pointed out the many falsehoods in his tweets and speeches, he began attacking the press too. Soon the media became his prime target, and he would point out the journalists at his rallies, sometimes naming them individually and calling them "dishonest" and "disgusting." The crowd would turn and shout at the reporters, whose social media accounts quickly filled up with "a bewildering mudslide of anger and abuse."[26]

Protestors, a staple of political campaigns, also got rough treatment. A Black Lives Matter demonstrator was beaten and choked after disrupting a Trump rally, and Trump said, "Maybe he should have been roughed up, because it was absolutely disgusting what he was doing."[27] At another time he said, as security was leading a protestor from the hall, "I'd like to punch him in the face. In the old days protestors would be carried out on stretchers."[28] Fearing that some demonstrator might throw tomatoes at him in Iowa, he told the crowd to "knock the crap" out of anyone who tried. "I promise you, I will pay the legal fees." When someone did blindside punch an African American protestor in North Carolina later, Trump said he would "look into" paying the attacker's fees. The attacker felt good afterwards about his assault, in which he hit the protestor in the face from behind. "You bet I liked it. Knocking the hell out of that big mouth . . . The next time we see him, we might have to kill him."[29] (There is no evidence Trump paid for a lawyer to defend the attacker.)[30]

Trump attacked foreigners night after night during his run for president. He continually described immigrants as freeloaders who want to suck up all the money in America's welfare system or take away the jobs hard-working taxpayers had had for years. Before you knew it, he said, his followers would be a minority controlled by hordes of immigrants the Democrats let infest the country so they could win elections. And foreign countries had been very unfair to America, he said, and that was why so many jobs were disappearing. Be angry. Be very angry. He also routinely reminded his audiences of grisly ISIS beheadings, violent gangs from Central America, and terrorist bombings wherever they occurred. Be afraid. Be very afraid.

The Trump supporters who cheered when he routinely debased his opponents with ugly nicknames as if they were in a schoolyard, and when he said he would have the families of terrorists killed, and that the form of torture known as waterboarding did not go far enough probably did not expect a dispassionate, rational analysis of anything at his rallies.[31] It was hard to tell them from the crowds at wrestling matches, a venue with which Donald is very familiar. Instead many of them came to release the anger and fear that the "Others" had aroused in them. An America dedicated to civil discourse, civil rights, and civility would give them no way to scream their anger. Then Donald Trump appeared and said, I am your voice. And they said, Oh, would you be? Lead us. Smite our enemies. Donald Trump's authoritarian-styled campaign let loose savagery in American politics, and it stunned his opponents who found it impossible to go as low as he went night after night. They perhaps recalled the old saying that there was no sense in wrestling with a pig; you will both get dirty and the pig will like it. Trump's viciousness emboldened his followers, some of whom had been waiting for years for a leader who would let them unleash a hatred that has long roiled within them. The target would be up to Trump. Accordingly, when he attacked the press someone posted the following on CNN's Jim Acosta's Facebook site: "I would love to be looking into your eyes as I choke the last fucking breath out of you."[32]

Some observers predicted Trump was opening the door to violence. But he brushed off the warnings as dismissively as the members of the Congressional gun lobby who say, after each massacre: This has nothing to do with us. We condemn it! When a series of mass shootings connectable to white supremacists broke out in the summer of 2019 Trump declared that "hate has no place in America." But he himself had ignited and legitimized hatred in every corner of the land. More than anyone in our lifetime Donald Trump promoted hatred in speech after speech, tweet after tweet, until it throbbed like your worst headache throughout our public life, spreading fear everywhere. When it showed up in Charlottesville, Virginia on August 11-12, 2017 as the Ku Klux Klan, neo-Nazis, and other members of the alt-right protested the removal of a statue of Robert E. Lee, President Trump had all kinds of trouble condemning these groups, even after a counter-demonstrator had been killed and many injured by an angry white supremacist. Trump's equivocation convinced many of the most prejudiced people in the United States that Donald Trump was indeed on their side, their secret leader, and that he thought of them as "his people" because he knew they supported him. They may have been right.

Social dominators have found their authoritarian leader, and we are witnessing the growing unfolding of authoritarianism in the United States. It is not attractive. It has not been our past and should not be our future. But if Trump—or any authoritarian leader—holds a post as powerful and pervasive as the American presidency, it will be our present, our way in the world. This is the reason it is so important that Americans appreciate that authoritarianism is on the ballot in the 2020 election, not to mention for many elections that will follow.

CHAPTER SIX

THE TRUMP BASE
PART II—AUTHORITARIAN
FOLLOWERS

We believe an even larger group of authoritarians (beside social dominators) swells the ranks of Donald Trump's supporters. They are *authoritarian followers*, and they are typically cut from altogether different cloth. Social dominators want to *control* other groups as much as they can, collectively as part of a superior group, and even individually on a person-to-person basis. In contrast, some other people want to *submit* to authority and authoritarian leaders, particularly to the powers that be (or ought to be, in their minds). Social scientists have been studying these people for more than forty years and have learned a great deal about them. These authoritarian followers show these three characteristics:

- a high degree of submission to the perceived established, legitimate authorities in society;
- high levels of aggression in the name of their authorities; and
- a high level of conventionalism, insisting that others follow the norms endorsed by their authorities.[1]

Because these followers submit to those they consider the established, legitimate authorities in society, they are called *right-wing authoritarians*.

The "right" in right-wing authoritarianism does not refer to conservatism as a political philosophy, but to the word's earlier use in Olde English, where *riht* (pronounced *writ*) meant lawful, proper, and correct. The established authorities involved may embrace any politico-economic position, even overwhelmingly "left-wing" views. Thus, when there was a Soviet Union, the people who gladly submitted to the Communist Party would be considered right-wing authoritarians, even though state-controlled socialism is anathema to conservatives in the United States. Right-wing authoritarianism, as used here, is a psychological variable, a trait. It is an aspect of a person's personality, like the need for achievement or emotional intelligence, not their economic philosophy or political beliefs.[2]

Nothing demonstrates right-wing authoritarians' submission to their leaders as clearly as Trump's supporters' acceptance of his pronouncements and guidance regarding COVID-19. Polls show they believed Trump's dismissal of the threat during January and February and up to March 11, 2020. Accordingly, they would have been more likely to ignore the advice coming from medical experts to socially distance themselves from others. Considerable numbers of them likely became infected and proceeded to infect others, including their loved ones. Trump's dramatic change in tune on March 11 should have made clear what he himself could never admit, namely that he had given them terrible, life-threatening advice for week after week. But their support continued unabated.[3] They did not blame him for leading them, as far as they knew, into the Valley of Death. And this insane willingness to follow Trump's advice and example has continued. Some of his followers began taking hydroxychloroquine because Trump said he did and urged people to try it, even though it was unproven as a treatment for COVID-19.[4] Some Trump followers insisted on not wearing face masks, and even cussed out people who did. Wearing a face mask (which protects others from getting the disease from you) was taken as a sign of disloyalty to the president. These startling behaviors provide a new version of his famous

"Fifth Avenue" boast. Trump can now say, "My followers are so loyal that if I mislead them and they all end up in hospital tents on Fifth Avenue to die, they will still vote for me."

THE RIGHT-WING AUTHORITARIANISM SCALE

Right-wing authoritarianism (RWA) is measured by a twenty-item personality test (which we made part of a survey the Monmouth University Polling Institute conducted for this book in late 2019). Here is an item from the scale that was written to tap submission to established authority, aggression in the name of that authority, and conventionalism: "Our country desperately needs a mighty leader who will do what has to be done to destroy the radical new ways and sinfulness that are ruining us." The person taking the test has nine ways to respond: −4 (very strong disagreement) to +4 (very strong agreement). 0 means "No opinion" or "Mind your own business."

You might immediately notice that this statement could appeal to some political and religious conservatives because it targets unconventional "radical new ways," and "sinfulness." Many of the other items on the RWA Scale raise issues or have phrases that would resonate with these groups even if their members are not authoritarian followers. Does that not show the test is biased to make such groups look like something they are not? It depends on whether these groups also want a mighty, tough leader (submission) charging around destroying (aggression) those who violate conventions. People can think that "new ways" and "sinfulness" are causing lots of problems, but also that they can be solved by better education, law enforcement, setting a good example, or prayer. Since each item is answered on a -4 to +4 basis, such a person could give a mild reaction, such as +1 or +2, to show their mixed feelings about the statement. Respondents are told to do this when they have different reactions to different parts of a statement. Conservatives who are not submissive and aggressive would probably not agree at all with the statement, much less very strongly agree. To score highly on the RWA Scale you must show all three of the attitudes in the definition of right-wing authoritarianism, compared to other people. If you are submissive and conventional, for example, but not aggressive, you will probably score higher than average on the scale, but not really high.

You may still suspect the RWA Scale basically measures political or religious conservatism. If you are right, then the research findings stretching out before you for the next three chapters apply basically to conservatives, or religious conservatives. Help yourself. But beware: You are choosing "Door A," and in a page or two when you see what RWA Scale scores correlate with you may wish you had said right-wing authoritarianism is different from conservatism, and chosen Door B instead.

WHY FACTS AND LOGIC DO NOT INFLUENCE TRUMP SUPPORTERS

Anyone who has had a serious "discussion" with a Trump supporter may have noticed that facts and logic often bounce right off them. Coherent arguments, even scientific studies, will not likely change the mind of a Trump supporter. Obstinate thinking has interested psychologists for decades. Their first explanation would involve cognitive dissonance, the anxiety produced when our thoughts conflict with one another. People classically reduce dissonance by reinforcing one idea or diminishing the importance of another. A lot of dissonance may lead them to change an idea entirely. High (and low) RWAs undoubtedly experience dissonance from ideas that do not fit together, but there ought to be so much conflict in high RWAs' thinking that they should be boiling over with anxiety. They have invested enormously in Donald Trump in their own minds and socially, yet every day he does something that shows he is unfit for office. That ought to produce so much dissonance—which after all is disruption in thinking just as it is in music—that the person can barely tie his shoes. So we think ardent Trump supporters necessarily use additional cognitive tactics to produce stability in their thinking—so much so that the stability becomes dogmatism.

Studies have found that persons who score highly on the RWA Scale, as a group, have (1) highly compartmentalized thinking; (2) they use a lot of double standards; (3) they believe many conflicting and even contradictory things; (4) they have a lot of trouble deciding what is sound evidence and what is not; (5) their thinking is highly ethnocentric; (6) they are decidedly prejudiced in what they believe about others; and (7) for all the difficulties they have getting their thinking cap on right, they are very dogmatic about what they believe, as we just noted. Because we think high RWAs tend to support Donald Trump, we believe it important to briefly examine each of these seven traits.

A note on the generalizations and relative differences revealed by the study of authoritarians: In this chapter and through chapter 9, we shall report dozens of social science findings about authoritarian followers. We have not cluttered the endnotes with every study involved, but you can find most of them at www.theauthoritarians.org or in *The Authoritarian Specter* by Bob Altemeyer, Harvard University Press, 1996. Beyond that, all of the findings reported are generalizations with exceptions, just like the statement "boys are taller than girls" is a generalization to which there are exceptions. It is important to guard against overgeneralizations. Every study had high RWAs who acted differently from the way most high RWAs did (and some low RWAs who were different from most lows). The social sciences can only offer relative differences. People, unlike hydrogen atoms, are much too complicated to be completely predictable. Furthermore, very few individuals will display all the traits found among a group of high RWAs in a study. Just as in baseball, center fielders often bat high in the lineup, have more infield hits, hit more triples, bounce into fewer double plays, make more shoestring catches, keep more home runs from clearing the fences, and a slew of other things. But very few center fielders do all these things on their team. The same occurs with the authoritarians studied by social science and the information revealed about them in the following chapters.

Another point may help avoid misunderstanding. The differences between low and high RWAs in a study are, obviously, relative. So if you want to know how many "high RWAs" there are in America, we have to ask back, "How many tall people are there, or heavy people?" We can measure all these things objectively, but the measurements do not have automatic boundary lines. We can just say some people, as a group, are more authoritarian, or taller, or heavier, than other people. In our studies we usually mean, by "low RWAs," the subjects who scored in the bottom 25% of the RWA Scale scores found in a study, and "high RWAs" scored in the top 25%. But those are arbitrary classifications.

1. HIGHLY COMPARTMENTALIZED THINKING

When you explore the minds of high RWAs you find yourself in a topsy-turvy maze of isolated compartments that contain unorganized slogans, cultural norms, "things 'they' say," rumored "well-established facts," and superstitions. It is all something of a muddle. Each idea is alive and well and living in its own safely deposited place, ready to be pulled out when it is useful, then returned to its compartment and shut tightly away again. They will say how great it is to live in a country that guarantees freedom of speech but then assert, "My country, love it or leave it," when somebody criticizes the nation. Their beliefs exist unorganized and all over the place, as independent as apartment dwellers in a high rise, except they do not even have a nodding acquaintance. Think of the vast box-filled warehouse at the end of the first Indiana Jones movie where the Ark of the Covenant is stored. We

all have some inconsistencies in our thinking, but if authoritarian supporters were on the starship *Enterprise*, they would frequently set their mouths
on Stun or even Stupefy with the inconsistency of their ideas.

The key to understanding the chaos in high RWA minds is that, compared to most people, they simply copied their ideas from trusted sources
and have never checked to see how well they all fit together. We all start
out with "hand-me-down truth," but most people have experiences that
challenge their preconceptions and start figuring things out for themselves.
Some people even go searching for other views (or have them brought emphatically to their attention—marriage can do this). And as new ideas crash
into the old ones, people try to make sense of what they have learned. Many
of us integrate. But high RWAs do not. They stick with the old truths, and
if a new learning contradicts an old one, it makes no difference because everything is in its own place and not to be disturbed. So even if you win the
argument, it is not likely to change their minds. Sound familiar?

This really is not their fault, at least not up to a point. High RWAs
were made to memorize "the truth" rather than discover it for themselves.
And those authorities very often were conscientiously passing on beliefs and
attitudes they believed were the best one could have. The problem is, any
set of beliefs can endure, even very evil ones, if examination is discouraged.
And you do not want to end up a case-in-point for Socrates when he said,
"The unexamined life is not worth living." But many authoritarian followers
learn at an early age that Submission 101 is a prerequisite to everything. Accordingly, they do not dare to critically examine the ideas their authorities
sticky-noted to their brains. It is just too scary a prospect.[5]

This came through clearly when university students were asked how
they reached their present beliefs about God. At some point, typically by
mid-adolescence, many children begin to have doubts about the religious
beliefs their parents and other social authorities have been teaching them all
their lives. Science can challenge such beliefs. New acquaintances from dif-

ferent backgrounds can confound them. Or maybe a loved one dies. A geno-
cide somewhere unforgettably hammers home the problem of evil. Many
things the child was taught seem under assault, even the existence of God.
"Is this just like Santa Claus?" the teen wonders. When asked what they did
when these doubts erupted, students scoring low on the RWA Scale said
they sought out evidence on both sides of the issue. They read Genesis *and*
they read about evolution. They talked to peers who were strong believers
and those who believed something else entirely. They read both Christian
apologists and Bertrand Russell. On the other hand, high RWA students,
more than anything else, said they went to their parents for guidance or
talked to friends from their own faith or prayed or consulted their clergy.
These one-sided searches show they were basically seeking reassurance, not
the truth, whatever it may be. Whereas some low RWAs modified or even
gave up their faiths, nearly all the highs stayed the course. They never resolved "evolution versus Genesis." They just compartmentalized the issue,
storing each explanation in a separate box, ignoring the implications each
one has for the other, and only opening one box at a time, as needed.[6]

Do we find examples of highly compartmentalized, unintegrated
thinking in Trump's base, just as we do in Trump himself? How many
dozens of examples would you like? We shall just bring up four major examples. The first example involves a particularly dangerous development.
Trump's supporters thought nothing when he promised his acting secretary
of Homeland Security that he would "fix" any legal problems if the secretary broke the law following his wishes by pardoning her.[7] Similarly, Trump
also urged officials building his wall to seize property and ignore environmental reviews, again promising presidential pardons if they were convicted
of breaking the law.[8] How do we know the base did not mind "your law and
order president's" cavalier attitude toward law and order? His support in the
polls did not meaningfully budge after these subterfuges were revealed.[9]
Trump's core supporters apparently did not grasp that if a president can

promise a pardon in advance for breaking the law, he can nullify any federal statute he wishes, a supremely dangerous power quite antithetical to the compartment marked The United States Constitution.

The second example shows how flimsily Trump's followers believe in America's values. When the immigration debate escalated in 2019 many people pointed out the contradiction between Trump's rejection of asylum seekers and the famous words displayed on the base of the Statue of Liberty: "Give me your tired, your poor, your huddled masses yearning to be free . . ." The words have been there for more than a century and proclaim America's noblest attitude toward newcomers. They tell the world, and us, who and what we are. This central belief ought to be connected to dozens of other principles and values firmly implanted in the American psyche. But when Stephen Miller, Trump's chief advisor on immigration, dismissed the inscription as merely the words of a poem that have nothing to do with the statue's purpose, no sign of disagreement arose in Trump's base.[10] Trump's authoritarian followers were silent because testing shows they have only a superficial belief in liberty and democracy. Like Trump, their thinking is highly compartmentalized because they do not have an underlying set of principles in which they believe. Thus, when authoritarians talk about how much they value freedom, they are talking about their own freedom. They do not give much thought to those who, in many ways, are still not "free at last." They do not grasp the principle that freedoms must be equally shared in a just society. Their point of view is well symbolized by the Gadsden flag you often see at Trump rallies—the one with the coiled rattlesnake on it and the inscription reading "Don't tread on me," not "Don't tread on us."

Our third example of compartmentalization in Trump's followers involves their most fervent cause, curtailing and/or outlawing abortion. They hold that a human soul is created at conception and any intentional termination of an embryo or a fetus means killing a human being. In short, they say they place great value on human life. But as the COVID-19 virus forced the American economy to lock down, Trump supporters (at his urging) began demanding that it be opened. Demonstrators and even governors such as Brian Kemp in Georgia acknowledged that permitting movie theaters, restaurants, beauty shops, and so forth to resume business would result in the death of people through "community spread." But it was worth it, they said, to get the economy back in business. In other words, while they greatly value the life of an unborn, it is all right to kill someone's grandparents or the poor or your next-door neighbor, if you get your job back a month or two sooner. What happened to the inviolate importance of human life?

A fourth example also centers on the reaction of Trump's base to his handling of the COVID-19 emergency. They believed him when he said it was a "nothing virus," and then they believed him when he said it was deadly serious, and then they believed him yet again when he began saying only days later that it was safe now to open up the economy, even though almost every medical expert in the world said, in essence, if stupid could fly, this idea would be a supersonic jet. And most of all, Trump's ardent followers believed him when he insisted the devastation COVID-19 had imposed on the United States vis-à-vis virtually every other country in the world, was not his fault. Why should they think it was? All his ignoring the danger and "it's just the flu" and "it will disappear in April" statements are neatly packed away, somewhere near the Covenant of the Ark.

2. DOUBLE-STANDARD JUDGMENTS

Because their thinking is so unintegrated, authoritarian followers often land on the Howling Hypocrites end of the integrity yardstick because they use so many double standards in their judgments. This has shown up many times in experiments where people are asked how much they want to punish a wrongdoer. In general, if high RWAs like the perpetrator, they go easy. They are especially likely to be lenient on authority figures who break the law. If they dislike the offender (say, because he is homosexual or Black), they are much more punitive. Low RWAs, on the other hand, are even-handed and, in general, punish the crime, not the criminal. An experiment run in the United States and the Soviet Union in the late 1980s shows high RWAs using double standards in their evaluations. In both nations the authoritarian followers thought their country was the "good guy" when it did something, such as interfering in the politics of another nation, that they condemned the other country for doing. So, high RWAs are in the box seats in the super-patriotic front row of their populations, loudly condemning their enemies. Ironically, these studies show if they had grown up to be the same kind of person (high RWA) in the other country, they would be in the front row on the other side, loudly condemning what they presently embrace and intensely believing what they presently find utterly repugnant.

Experiments have found that high RWAs seem to think with a "forked brain" in other areas of life as well. They thought unfair election practices were more serious when done by a liberal government than when done by a conservative one. They endorsed many traditional double standards regarding sex roles. They liked the idea of requiring public schools in North America to emphatically teach Christianity to all the students, but when asked how they would feel if they lived in a Muslim country and the government there insisted all the students in public schools be emphatically taught Islam, they thought that would definitely be wrong. In all these cases, low RWAs showed greater integrity.

For another example, take their ready acceptance of Trump's labeling Hillary Clinton as Crooked Hillary. How was she crooked? Trump alleged she required people who wanted access to her as secretary of state to contribute to the Clinton Foundation, a charity active on many fronts around the world. Were the "pay for play" accusations against Clinton true? Possibly. Some Clinton Foundation contributors seem to have benefited, and the perception may have been encouraged that a donation would open doors.[11] Certainly contributions to the foundation dropped like a rock after the 2016 election. But the FBI could not find evidence of influence peddling that would stand up in court, a story heard often about both sides during the 2016 election. It must also be said that the Clinton Foundation is recognized as one of the most efficient and beneficial charities in the world.[12] Meanwhile, an investigation spearheaded by David Fahrenthold of the *Washington Post* made it clear that Trump used the Donald J. Trump Foundation for years for numerous, wide-ranging activities that enriched him or his image.[13] The state of New York investigated numerous charges against the Trump Foundation, and they discovered he was running an illegal operation, using his charity to pay business and personal expenses, so they forced him to dissolve the charity in late 2018. His conduct was so illegal that the state has banned him from ever operating a charity in New York again.[14] Thus, there is no doubt about Trump being Crooked Donald, who has single-handedly given charity a bad name. Yet such stories, which we have seen go back to his earliest days as a real estate developer, were ignored by the crowds who cheered every time Trump referred to his Democratic opponent as being crooked.

Trump's supporters also show a double standard about Hillary Clinton and Donald Trump's truthfulness. They rightly made a great deal out of Clinton's, who claimed she never sent classified information in emails through her private server.[15] At the same time, they ignored the humongous number of lies Trump told before, during, and after the election campaign. The man lies while brushing his teeth. And after blasting Clinton for endangering national security through her emails, Trump's followers looked the other way when his daughter and husband were denied security clearances by the White House staff, but Trump awarded them anyway.[16]

3. CONFLICTING AND CONTRADICTORY IDEAS

Are the contradictory ideas in the compartmentalized minds of authoritarian followers truly so sealed off that even conspicuous inconsistency goes unnoticed? This was tested in a study in which subjects responded to ten statements at the bottom of a survey page, turned the page over, and then responded to ten other statements that were the opposites of the ones they had just answered. For example, "A government should allow total freedom of expression, even if it threatens law and order," and then on the next page, "A government should only allow freedom of expression so long as it does not threaten law and order." High RWAs showed a tendency to say "Yes" and "Yes," thus rejecting an idea they endorsed just a minute earlier. They had "turned the page," so to speak. Low RWAs were significantly more likely to answer consistently, such as answering "Yes" and "No."

As another example of this uncritical acceptance, authoritarian followers have a weakness for bombast that turns off careful thinkers.[17] This was demonstrated in a series of studies in which subjects were asked if a cited difficulty, such as the drug problem, qualified as the *most* serious problem facing the country. When the drug problem and the crime it causes was proposed, 74 percent of high RWAs agreed it was the country's number one problem. When another sample was asked about the "destruction" of the family, 84 percent said *that* was the biggest difficulty we faced. As did 72 percent in a third study about the loss of religion and commitment to God. Since they cannot all be our biggest problem, high RWAs appear easily excited. But maybe low RWAs would flare up just as indiscriminately if someone claimed various of their big worries pose our biggest threat. Accordingly, 66 percent of low RWAs did agree that the destruction of the environment was our biggest problem. But only 44 percent endorsed the destruction of individual freedom, and 35 percent agreed that poverty was the most serious threat in later studies. Low RWAs appear to be more careful thinkers, hence much less vulnerable to exaggeration. Demagogues would find them prickly and argumentative. (If people find you that way, it could be a good thing.)

Do Donald Trump's supporters accept contradictory statements from the "check back with us tomorrow" White House? That could be another chapter. NBC News counted thirty-two "new stances" on thirteen different issues during Trump's first six months in office.[18] (Unlike the *Washington Post's* running tab on Trump's lies, NBC did not continue counting.) The biggest early example involved Trump's firing of FBI Director James Comey on May 9, 2017. Trump said he acted after receiving a recommendation from the Department of Justice, then he said he had decided to fire Comey before he got the recommendation because of the FBI's investigation of Russian interference in the 2016 election. Then he said that investigation had nothing to do with the firing. Comey was fired because he had lost support among the rank-and-file of the bureau. When the FBI shouted from bottom to top that was not true, the White House settled on the following: Comey was not doing a good job, but do not ask us for any details, because we explained all that earlier.

For another example of Trump contradicting himself, consider the flip-flop-flip around the Mueller Report. For months, the president said the Mueller investigation on Russian interference in the 2016 election amounted to nothing more than a witch hunt and a hoax. Then on March 26, 2019, when Attorney General William Barr released his Trump-exonerating version of the Mueller Report, Trump ignored his previous aspersions and said Mueller had done a great job. Trump's counselor to the president Kellyanne Conway called Mueller's work "the gold standard" for such an investigation.[19] Then after more of the report became public and all the damaging material about obstruction of justice was revealed, Trump, on April 19, 2019, called it "crazy" and the work of "18 Angry Democrat Trump Haters" out to destroy him.[20]

How about bombast? Does Donald Trump occasionally blow things out of proportion? No, not occasionally. Almost always. It seems that for him, a properly formed sentence has to have a subject, a predicate, and an extreme exaggeration. Many people quickly notice this and learn to discount everything he says by something like ten-cents-to-the-dollar—a bankruptcy expression with which Trump is very familiar. But his base cheers wildly when his statements misrepresent wildly.

4. DIFFICULTY JUDGING EVIDENCE

In 1989 a woman named Mary Wegmann was performing her civic duty by sitting on a jury in Port Angeles, Washington. When the jury began deliberations, she wondered if some of her cohorts had attended a different trial than she had. They could not remember evidence she thought was vital, they invented evidence that did not exist, and they had a great deal of trouble inferring the logical conclusions from the facts that could be agreed on. It was a difficult experience for Wegmann, but it did give her, as a graduate student in psychology, a topic for her PhD dissertation. She ran experiments on RWA scores and the ability to think straight in samples drawn from the Port Angeles county jury pool and from a local college. And indeed, she found that high RWAs had trouble accurately remembering information they had just read and heard along with trouble reaching sensible conclusions from information presented.

Research has subsequently shown that high RWAs especially have trouble realizing a deduction is wrong. When asked to take a reasoning test, billed as such, that presented the syllogism, "All fish live in the sea. Sharks live in the sea. Therefore, sharks are fish," they said the conclusion logically followed. (It does not.) High RWAs are too used to saying yes, which the authorities in their lives likely taught them early on was the "right" answer when they did not know. This does not mean high RWAs agree with everything they hear. To the contrary, they carry around a long list of ideas and sources they will instantly doubt. But they do not disbelieve things because they have thought them through or learned from experience that they are wrong. Rather, their trusted authority figures have told them what to think. They were raised to believe what their raisers believed. For reasons easy to imagine, their authorities did not teach them to doubt what had been poured into their heads.

This shows up in their judgments regarding sufficiency of evidence: What proves an idea is right? Sometimes, for example, planes crash when their pilots' biorhythms (e.g. daily cycles of sleeping and waking) are out of sync. Does this prove biorhythms affect our lives? No, of course not. If biorhythms affected nothing at all, you would still find some crashes happened when the pilots were having a "low day" on their biorhythm charts, and some on "high days." Random events happen randomly, you know! Much better evidence is needed. Testing shows that across a broad range of issues, high RWAs are more likely than most to be swayed by inconclusive evidence. It is another example of their "yea-saying." And on some issues they show almost no capacity for critical thinking at all. They think the legends of big floods, which are found in many cultures, prove that the story of Noah and the Ark is true. They think a fallen wall found at Jericho proves the story of Joshua and the horns. They think the stories some people tell about going toward a "Being of Light" during near-death experiences proves there is an afterlife. They know what they want to be true, so it does not take much evidence to prove to them that they are right. Like the Queen of Hearts in *Alice in Wonderland* who said, "Sentence first, then the verdict," they effortlessly place the wagon in front of the horse. High RWAs are also unpersuaded by conclusive evidence when they do not like the conclusion. For example, they think that the scientific evidence showing the Shroud of Turin was created in the Middle Ages proves nothing, because they "know" it was wrapped around Jesus' body a thousand years earlier. They think the statistics on Black men killed while in custody by policemen prove nothing.

Trump's supporters show such biases frequently. With no evidence whatsoever, they believed Trump's claim that President Obama was not born in Hawaii and that Obama had placed listening devices on his phones in Trump Tower during the 2016 campaign. Many in Trump's legions similarly believe his assertion, as bereft of evidence as a newborn pig lacks a tuxedo, that he actually won the popular vote in 2016 if you take away the millions of illegal votes that Trump says Clinton received. With no evidence whatsoever, for Trump is unwilling to provide it, his supporters believe that the worst scandal in American history, far worse than Watergate, is "Obamagate." As we write, Trump is looking for anything he can use to validate his newly created "Obamagate" scandal.

Another outstanding example of Trump's supporters' dismissal of evidence lay in their persistent refusal to believe the Russians interfered in the 2016 election. (And the Russians are doing so again in 2020.) Despite the fact that all of the federal government's intelligence agencies publicly stated the Russians had, and Robert Mueller concluded they had, and a bipartisan report of the Republican-controlled Senate Intelligence Committee said they had, many Republicans in the U.S. House of Representatives, and almost all of Trump's base still believed that the Russians did not even try.[21] That is what Putin said, and Trump believes him, so it must be true. Imagine: Republicans, through Trump, believe Vladimir Putin over the FBI, CIA, and the National Security Agency. The tremor you feel in cemeteries around the nation is caused by deceased Republicans turning in their graves and hiding their faces in shame.

But the premier example of Trump's base refusing to accept science-based conclusions must be their belief that their president knows more about communicable viral diseases than the experts who have spent their lives studying them. Furthermore, everyone could see from the COVID-19 data what was happening in other countries, such as Italy and Spain, where a failure to implement the drastic social isolation measures (which had worked in Wuhan, China) resulted in the epidemic spreading very fast. But when Trump decided that the economy had to be revived, even if it did cost lives, the base was willing to stop taking precautions. And when epidemiologists observed there is not going to be any economy worth having if the medical system collapses in the middle of this pandemic, the base largely ignored them.

5. HIGHLY ETHNOCENTRIC

Studies have shown that high RWAs are usually very ethnocentric, strongly dividing the world into "Us" and "Them" categories, which has been called "tribalism" by some observers. This tendency comes close to being universally true of human beings, for we all do it to some extent. Look at how easily novelists and screenwriters get us to identify with their main characters' "Us" rather than the "Thems." But high RWAs have extra helpings of this naturally occurring tendency, so studies have explored when they got them. When RWA students were asked to recall the first time the world was described to them in terms of "people like us" and "people not like us," they reported it most often happened first, not about gender or race or nationality, but religion. Their distinctive identity was rooted more in their family's religious affiliation than anything else when they were growing up, and the home religion was stressed to high RWAs much more than it was stressed to low RWAs. That emphasis could have become a template for quick Us-versus-Them categorizations when they met people. Such an automatic drawing of distinctions can be laden with rejection of "Them" and a desire to isolate "the Other" from oneself. Accordingly, high RWA Christians score highly on a measure called the Religious Ethnocentrism Scale, where they agree with statements such as "non-Christian religions have a lot of weird beliefs and pagan ways that Christians should avoid having any contact with," and "If it were possible, I'd rather have a job where I worked with people with the same religious views I have rather than with people with different views."

Do Donald Trump's supporters draw distinctions between themselves and everyone else? Do they express a desire to keep people who are different away from them, even on a global scale? Would they say, "Since you don't agree with me, you're one of those people who hate America"? Do rhetorical questions have obvious answers? Consider them in the context of the issue of building The Wall: Against all odds and common sense history many state that the major issue within the United States from 2016 to 2018 was whether to build a high wall on its Mexican border. Once Trump's base got the Supreme Court justices they wanted, building this wall became their top priority, which was more than a little surprising because they had never thought of building the thing until Trump suggested it. And Trump only mentioned it by accident. In 2014 when Trump was exploring the notion of running for president, it became clear that illegal immigration could be a decisive issue among Republican voters and an effective, divisive wedge issue. But Trump, who cannot effectively read a speech from a teleprompter but has trouble remembering what he wants to say, kept forgetting to bring up immigration, leaving his seal-the-deal lines in his speaking notes. As a result, his advisors suggested that as he looked to the back of the room in which he was speaking, he visualize a wall along America's southern border to remind him that he wanted to stop illegal immigration. But no one in the campaign proposed building such a wall because it might win the prize for most incredibly stupid idea of the year, a superlative Trump did not want to claim. The "wall" was a mnemonic device, just a reminder to bring up immigration. Trump reportedly disliked the idea and dismissed it. But in January 2015, probably while confused about what he wanted to say next while addressing supporters in Iowa, he blurted out, "I will build a wall." And the crowd went crazy. He reflexively turned this into self-aggrandizement, saying nobody could build a wall like he could. The crowd cheered its brains out. Thus, it became a campaign slogan and promise, and eventually a chant at his rallies.[22] Trump probably had no idea what he was unleashing in his highly ethnocentric followers, who had spent their lives building walls between themselves and others. But his promise to build a wall did not merely strike a chord in their psyches, it sang an aria to their whole being. No matter who paid for it, no matter what the cost, including subverting the Constitution, no matter how completely and magnificently it would fail to solve the underlying problem, they had to have that wall!

It should surprise no one that Trump's approach to the COVID-19 pandemic was built on ethnocentrism, as was the reaction of his base. From the time he first ran for president in 2000, Donald Trump has promoted a nationalistic, America-first, isolationist outlook based on the belief that everybody else, friend and foe alike, was taking advantage of a patsy USA. It was us versus all others, whom we had to, according to Trump, keep at a distance. When he learned in January 2020 that a new disease had broken out in central China, his first thought was probably, "Good. That's going to hurt China," and the last thing he would have thought of was that it could reach the United States. So he did not give it a second thought. Even when he learned it was spreading elsewhere, and two cases had reached America, he took half-steps. He seemed to think that the in-group would be stronger, more resilient, "exceptional people" who would be an exclusion to the rule. This was remarkable because Trump has often acknowledged he is a germaphobe. But his behavior indicates he thought this disease was something foreigners got, not Americans. And the behavior of his followers mentioned earlier indicates they thought they were virus-proof too. Eventually the sign that you were a real Trump supporter was that you did not wear a mask. Divide, divide, divide, divide.

6. HIGHLY PREJUDICED

When ethnocentrism leads to prejudging others according to their being in the Out-group versus the In-group, it is prejudice. American authoritarians are not only prejudiced against Mexicans, Muslims, and migrants from many places, they also instantly judge most of their fellow citizens according to what racial, ethnic, religious, social class, et cetera group they belong to before they ever get to know them as individuals. Accordingly, a lot of people face an uphill battle if they are ever going to convince others to accept them. High RWAs, like high SDOs, take an awful lot of convincing. Forty years of research have established that, compared to most people, high RWAs think Black people are naturally violent, Jewish people cannot be trusted as much as other people, minority groups are spoiled and happy to live on welfare for the rest of their lives, various racial and ethnic groups are inherently promiscuous and irresponsible, homosexual people are sick, people who belong to a different religion are immoral, and women belong in the kitchen, barefoot and pregnant. You could say that because of their dislike of so many others, high RWAs are equal-opportunity discriminators. Studies show they dislike almost every group that is different, regardless of race, creed, color, or sexual orientation.

How strong are these prejudices? If a prejudice Olympics were held in North America some year, high RWAs would win either the bronze or the silver medal, with their fiercest competition coming from the social dominators discussed in chapter 5. (We will address the sure winner of the gold medal for prejudice in a later chapter.) We know this because of a trailblazing researcher at the University of Western Kentucky, Sam McFarland, and his collaborator Sherman Adelson. In 1996 they produced one of the most remarkable discoveries in the history of the social sciences that you never heard about. They "pitted" eighteen different personality tests against one another to see which could best predict prejudice against Black people,

women, and homosexual people. The personality measures were chosen because past studies indicated they could predict prejudice, however weakly.
The results could not have been clearer: Only two of the scales in the studies
climbed victoriously out of the pit: the Social Dominance Orientation Scale
and the Right-Wing Authoritarianism scale. The sixteen other tests could
add barely a penny to what these two tests revealed together when it came
to predicting prejudice. The results were quickly confirmed.[23] Furthermore,
the two tests could explain most of the prejudice against Black people,
women, and homosexual people. These results verified one of the earliest
discoveries in social psychology to a degree not previously seen, namely
that prejudice results mainly from the personalities of the discriminators,
not the behavior of the disliked group. But beyond that, only two kinds of
persons are notably involved: high social dominators and high authoritarian
followers, the very people occupying center stage in our narrative about authoritarianism in American politics today. If you want to know what aspect
of personality psychologically connects to social prejudice, discrimination,
ethnic cleansings, and Holocausts—and that is one hell of a question—the
answer is, more than anything else, authoritarianism!

Are Trump supporters highly prejudiced? Not all of them, of course.
But many studies concluded that prejudice was a major, or indeed *the* major
factor, leading white Americans to vote for Trump in 2016.[24] We suggested
in the last chapter that Trump's overtly prejudiced comments instantly attracted social dominators. "Mexican rapists" and his other racist remarks in
2015 and 2016 probably seemed too blatant at first to high RWAs, but they
would have resonated to the underlying rejection of the outsider. This leads
us to infer that *prejudice is a most common psychological denominator among
Trump's supporters*. It is the ugly foundation upon which he has built his
presidency, the glue that, more than anything else, binds most of Trump's
supporters to one another, and his base to him. Because of McFarland and

Adelson's now well-replicated findings, we conclude that when you attract the most prejudiced people in the country to a political movement, you can safely bet it will be packed with authoritarians.

As noted at the outset of this chapter, research reveals the differences between social dominators per se and authoritarian followers per se. Studies show both groups are angry and afraid. But the dominators' prejudices spring primarily from anger at how minorities are advancing, for example, whereas high RWAs' prejudices arise largely from fear (for their own safety, for instance), or of changes in their world that will result from cultural diversity. Also, as we said earlier, social dominators usually know they are prejudiced compared to most people, but they simply do not care. They embrace group inequality and take it home to meet mother. High RWAs, however, think they have normal levels of prejudice. They believe this because they associate principally with people like themselves. If their parents were anti-Semitic, if most of the people they associate with are anti-Semitic, they will think their own negative attitudes toward Jewish people are ordinary, free of any hint of prejudice, "just the truth." If you showed them how prejudiced they are compared to most people, they will say it simply could not be so. Conversely, social dominators will say, "Yeah, you're right. I hate Jews. So what?"

When Donald Trump flashes his prejudices, as he did when he reacted so divisively to the Black Lives Matter protests, upside-down Bible and all, it almost certainly encourages high RWAs to speak their prejudiced thoughts too and even act on them. Authoritarian leaders often use a divide-and-conquer strategy built on prejudice to gain control of a country. The reason is simple, as Pastor Martin Niemöller's famous statement reminds us: "First they came for the socialists, and I did not speak out—because I was not a socialist. Then they came for the trade unionists, and I did not speak out—because I was not a trade unionist. Then they came for the Jews, and I did not speak out—because I was not a Jew. Then they came for me—and there was no one left to speak for me."[25]

7. DOGMATISM

As biased and unintegrated as the beliefs of high RWAs may be, they are very difficult to change. Some things work, we shall see, but logic and evidence crash into a brick wall of dogmatism. The source of the dogmatism is obvious: People who have memorized rather than thought out their beliefs do not know why what they believe is true. They acquired their picture of the world on a since-you-say-so basis and are basically unable to defend their ideas against new information. But they have a keep in their redoubt against doubt, a last defense against arguments they cannot answer. Many readers may have slammed into it around the dinner table or in the carpool: dogmatism. True Believers simply refuse to change their views. They cannot explain why they are right, but they know they are.

High RWAs abound with dogmatism, agreeing with statements from a Dogmatism (DOG) scale such as, "The things I believe in are so completely true, I could never doubt them," and "There are no discoveries or facts that could possibly make me change my mind about the things that matter most in life." And they mean it. In one experiment students were asked if there were any inconsistencies or contradictions in the Bible. Most said yes; some said no, the Bible is perfectly consistent. Then the subjects were given the four Gospel accounts of Easter morning. If you look these up, you will find the Gospels agree on only one thing: Jesus's body was not in the tomb when someone went to it the Sunday after the crucifixion. Otherwise Mark, Matthew, Luke, and John have different—and, in places, flatly contradictory—accounts of what happened. After reading these accounts, subjects were asked again about inconsistent or contradictory material in the Bible. Students who (1) had earlier said there was none and (2) had scored highly on the DOG scale, who were almost all high RWAs, continued to say the Bible was perfectly consistent even though they had just read the clearest evidence imaginable that they were wrong. Furthermore, the explanation they most commonly gave for their steadfastness was that the evangelists were like witnesses at an automobile accident who saw things from different points of view. These faithful had likely been taught this analogy by their religious authorities, and you can tell they just memorized it rather than thought about it because it admits that inconsistencies and contradictions *do* exist and just tries to explain how they got there. These students were so committed to the oft-heard lesson that everything in the Bible is true that nothing, including the Bible itself, could change that.[26]

Do Trump's supporters show signs of dogmatism? They have an amazing capacity to believe Trump's position on things even when overwhelming evidence says he is wrong. Take the human role in climate change. After years of maintaining that the planet's climate was not changing, many deniers have retreated to agreeing it is, but not because of human activity. Or they now maintain increased carbon dioxide levels in the atmosphere are good. The vast majority of atmospheric scientists disagree with these defenses, well-funded by the extraction industries, and have concluded we are hurtling toward a catastrophe of planetary proportions far worse than COVID-19. But Trump believes that if you just say "It's a hoax" repeatedly (ad nauseam), a significant portion of the population will believe him. And indeed, most Republicans think human activity has nothing to do with the changes in our climate.[27]

Trump may change his tune on the human contribution to climate change someday as the damage to America mounts. You may eventually hear him say "use less gasoline" and "invest in wind power"—positions he totally rejects now—and say he was more concerned about climate change than anybody all along. Just as he knew all along that COVID-19 would produce a pandemic. Or for another example, Trump has completely flip-flopped on childhood vaccinations.[28] The outbreak of measles, a disease once all but eliminated, has produced a public health crisis so grave that Trump has cried out, "Get the shots!" He did not acknowledge that he had for years spread the totally refuted myth that the standard inoculations produced autism. Some children undoubtedly died because he did. (Does this sound a bit familiar?) And whenever he changes, you can be certain that his high RWA supporters will change too. They are dogmatic about defending the beliefs of their authorities.

Persons who have a lot of trouble submitting to others or who have difficulty accepting things without good reason might well wonder why high RWAs have not woken up and smelled the coffee. But it all comes easily to people who have a deep down, lifelong tendency to submit and who are terrified of what will happen if they stop believing what their authorities say is true. And if you understand this, you realize not only why Trump's supporters dogmatically stick to the party line, you realize that the worse the "news" is for their belief system, the greater the fear and the tighter they will cling to the system, when it seems it should be the other way around. Proving to them that they are wrong will usually backfire.

CHAPTER SEVEN

DISTURBING ATTITUDES OF AUTHORITARIAN FOLLOWERS

In this chapter we examine five disturbing aspects of authoritarian dispositions. First we examine how little these authoritarians value the great bequest from our ancestors who won the civil liberties we all enjoy. Then we explore why high RWAs are so aggressive and mean-spirited. Next we will consider evidence showing how they use social reinforcement to buttress their beliefs even though it makes them vulnerable to con man deception. Next we observe how susceptible they are to pressures to conform, and finally we look at their understanding of themselves. We undertake this further examination based on decades of study of high RWA authoritarian followers to further explain Donald Trump's core supporters.[*]

---

[*] Much of the earlier research addressed in this chapter has been replicated in later experiments. Experiments first undertaken in Canada have been largely later replicated in the United States. In relying upon these studies, we have no reason to believe they are not as valid today as when undertaken. This is the beauty of science. Others can examine these findings, and we hope they will do so given the importance of authoritarianism to contemporary American politics.

1. DISMISSAL OF CIVIL LIBERTIES

Many studies have shown that high RWAs would diminish the civil rights and liberties of others. For example, in the fall of 1974, students at the Universities of Virginia, Alabama, Indiana, and Wyoming, along with Penn State answered the RWA scale and also gave reactions to six instances in which government authorities had allegedly used high-handed and illegal methods to harass and prosecute various targets.[1] The test cases involved such things as illegal wiretaps, denial of the right to peacefully protest, and unwarranted searches and seizures. They were based on news reports of events in Canada and the United States, and the targets were usually small groups equally on the fringes of the left and right wings of the political spectrum. RWA scale scores strongly predicted acceptance of these injustices. High RWAs were not nearly as troubled by violations of other people's civil liberties as were low RWAs. They seem to have a "father knows best" view of authorities breaking the law, thus agreeing with statements like: "Since the authorities make the laws, they can decide whether the laws apply to them or not." These same students provided a vivid example of authoritarian submission and tolerance for authoritarian law-breaking when they gave their reactions to Watergate in the autumn of 1974. By then, unassailable evidence had emerged that President Nixon had authorized the Watergate cover-up from the beginning, he had been forced to resign when this evidence became public, and he had then accepted a pardon for the crimes he had committed. The students were given a timeline of developments in this saga and asked when they first seriously suspected, and then concluded, that Nixon was not telling the truth about Watergate. According to their responses, it took high RWAs much longer than most people to doubt the president and then to conclude he was guilty. Being a Democrat or a Republican mattered little compared to the person's level of authoritarianism. The high RWAs "stood by their man" until the end. And then, about one in six students, almost all high RWAs, still believed he had done nothing very wrong.[2]

How far does the authoritarian followers' acceptance of government injustice and disregard for liberty extend? All the way to the Constitution, it turns out. San Francisco State University students were asked in 1990 to react to a diatribe against the Bill of Rights and the Supreme Court. The attack began, "If a person stops to think about it, most of the problems we are having can be traced to the Bill of Rights, or more precisely, to the way it has been interpreted by the Supreme Court." The essay, based on late-night radio phone-in shows, went on to rage against freedom of speech rulings that had opened the door to pornographers and filth, freedom of religion decisions that meant children could not pray in public schools, right-to-happiness laws that meant women could have abortion after abortion, and so on. The hue and cry concluded, "The only thing we can do to make America the free, pure, safe, Christian nation that the founding fathers intended it to be, is to repeal the Bill of Rights." Most students rejected these claims and conclusion. But high RWAs thought the arguments sensible and agreed the Bill of Rights should be repealed.

Donald Trump's authoritarian followers appear to agree, as he has quietly undertaken a massive removal of civil liberties from significant numbers of people. If you are rich or middle class, you likely have not noticed it unless you use social media. If you are a person of color, an immigrant, a religious minority, a member of the LGBTQ community, or can barely make ends meet financially, you may have felt under constant siege. Several organizations have catalogued the Trump administration's harsh treatment of such groups. See, for example, the year-by-year listing of the administration's tampering with rights by the Leadership Conference on Civil and Human Rights.[3] From barring transgender military service to surveillance of American Muslims to revising the use of torture (a war crime), Trump's authoritarian supporters are not concerned, because these rights and liberties have been ripped primarily from *others, not themselves.*

Speaking of civil liberties, suppose the government decided to prosecute you because you belonged to some perfectly legal group they want to smash to smithereens. Who would defend you? Would high RWAs, who proclaim America as the land of the free? Better not count on it. In fact, it might not take much persuading by the government to get them to help persecute you. These bleak assertions are based on a series of experiments begun in 1982 called "Posse." In the first study Canadian university students were told: "Suppose the Canadian government, sometime in the future, passed a law outlawing the Communist Party in Canada.[4] Government officials then stated that the law would only be effective if it were vigorously enforced at the local level and appealed to every Canadian to aid in the fight against Communism." Students were then asked to indicate, on a −4 to +4 basis the extent to which they would (1) tell their friends and neighbors it was a good law, (2) tell the police about any Communist they knew, (3) help hunt down and arrest Communists if asked to do so by the police, (4) participate in attacks on Communist headquarters organized by the proper authorities, (5) support the use of physical force to make Communists reveal the identity of other Communists, and (6) support the execution of Communist leaders if the government insisted it was necessary to protect Canada. If you are one of the few Communists in Canada or the United States, you will be relieved to know that the students showed little support for these persecutions. But high RWAs did not object to them nearly as much as most. Low RWA subjects almost always answered −4 to everything but high RWAs were not so certain this would be wrong. They tended to mark −2, −1, Neutral, or even endorse the idea. A malevolent government would have no trouble organizing a mob to attack you the next time you and the other Communist in your county got together for coffee, not to mention torturing and killing you with their implicit blessing, if the government said it was necessary for the country's well-being. These same students were asked how they would react if the government decided to persecute homosexuals. Same basic finding. When parents of Canadian university students were asked the same two questions, the same results appeared. Researchers have collected corresponding data on American campuses.[5]

Experiments were run to see how far high RWAs might go. Generally, they were less willing to help persecute right-wing targets such as the KKK, and the mainstream Conservative Party of Canada, but still more willing than low RWAs who were against attacking anyone. Finally a sample of students was asked, "Suppose the Canadian government, sometime in the future, passed a law to eliminate right-wing authoritarians"< (defining them as people who are so submissive to authority, so authoritarian aggressive, and so conventional that they may pose a threat to democratic rule). In the experiment, government officials stated that "the law would only be effective if it were vigorously enforced at the local level and appealed to every Canadian to aid in the fight against right-wing authoritarianism." There appeared, once again, a positive connection between RWA Scale scores and willingness to get rid of those rascally right-wing authoritarians. It boggles the mind! It should have dawned on these authoritarians, if they had an ounce of insight, that by suppressing this group, they were doing the very thing that they were prosecuting their victims for doing. But if you remember the findings on compartmentalization you know these authoritarians do not always make obvious connections. Still, you must wonder at it all. If this posse realized what it was doing, they would get on their horses, ride over to the local hoosegow, march into the cells, lock themselves in, and throw away the keys.

Research reveals some authoritarian posses could target journalists. In 2006 a sample of parents of university students in Canada were asked Posse questions about "a law allowing [the government] to persecute journalists who had an 'antigovernment' slant to their news reports, columns, commentaries, and editorials." Most of the parents were appropriately appalled, but not all. Some high authoritarians showed nascent support for destroying freedom of the press.

When a sizable part of the population will accept the persecution of virtually anyone, it can signal a potential dictator to strike. When these submitters justify the persecution to others at the water fountain and the gym, they apply benediction to soul-destroying injustice. When they participate in the prosecution by betraying their friends and neighbors and go on raids to help round up the people being prosecuted, they give a despot the essential tools he needs to enforce a reign of terror across a nation. And when they approve of torturing and killing "enemies of the state" because their leader requires it, they have meekly given him everything he could want. Research has found many such people who, with just a little persuasion by their chosen authority, would apparently do all these things. So, the question about who would defend you if the government decided to persecute you could someday become suddenly very relevant.

2. ROOTS OF AUTHORITARIAN AGGRESSION AND BEING MEAN-SPIRITED

RWA scale scores correlate better with Posses going after disreputable targets than reputable ones mainly because "shameful" groups offend the authoritarian follower more. These connections lock into place in another example of authoritarian hostility, being mean-spirited. If you ask a group of people to remember their high school years, and, in particular, to recall fellow students who made serious mistakes and were punished for them (such as having a bad trip on drugs, getting pregnant, or having a car accident while drunk-driving), you will probably find that most people have some sympathy for the mistakes of youth. But high RWAs in a Canadian sample, later replicated by Creighton University researchers, proved more likely to say that such people "got exactly what they deserved." They also confessed to feeling a personal "secret pleasure" when they heard of the other person's misfortune.

Trump supporters at times show a lack of empathy that approaches inhumane coldheartedness. Probably no more gripping an example can be found than their reaction to the separation of children from their parents when the families crossed the Mexican border seeking asylum in the United States. The videos of these forced removals triggered memories of the Holocaust. The sound of young children calling out "Mama" from inside the detention centers, the sight of dozens of youngsters sleeping on mats on the floors of the overcrowded wire cages, the news that the American authorities could not (and still cannot) reunite parents with children in many cases—these are all seared in our memory and will not, should not, ever go away. We know from studies going back to the London blitz and the effects of the residential schools forced upon the indigenous peoples in Canada how terribly damaging such separations are to children, even when reunion finally occurs. If this is one of the underlying causes of Donald Trump's personal unhappiness in the world, he has multiplied it thousands and thousands of times. Some Hispanic parents understandably feared their children would be taken from them if they openly entered the United States claiming refugee status, so they tried to sneak across the border with their kids. Oscar Alberto Martinez and his daughter Valeria did. They were found floating face-down among reeds in the Rio Grande in June 2019.[6]

Not surprisingly, polls in 2018 found that Trump's "zero tolerance policy" on illegal entry was the most unpopular government act in recent American history.[7] But an Ipsos survey found 46 percent of Republicans approved of it, compared to 32 percent who did not. A Quinnipiac poll found even stronger support within Republican ranks for this plainly venomous policy.[8] Supporters usually told interviewers that the families were, after all, trying to enter the United States illegally. But that does not require separation after apprehension, which was plainly instituted to send the message: If you do this, we will take your children from you, and they will suffer. What kind of people make such threats and do such things? The dictators Trump admires, cold-blooded social dominators, a person who used the death of three associates in a helicopter crash to create the impression that he was a man of destiny, a President of the United States who would falsely charge a critical TV host with murder and force endless agony on the husband of the dead woman who died of natural causes. And Trump's supporters backed him up.

Why are authoritarian leaders and authoritarian followers so mean and aggressive? It does not take a lot of head-scratching to understand why social dominators aggress so much. They live in a "might makes right," law-of-the-jungle world, and generally believe hostility and intimidation will get them what they want. No one who understands social dominators can be surprised that Donald Trump wants a big military parade on the Fourth of July with him in the reviewing stand as the tanks roll by. Do you know any dictators who do not put on such shows? If these men feel their dominance is being threatened, they will lash out. Donald Trump, just as Roy Cohn taught him, doubles down on the slimmest slight. This, however, is not the cause of aggression in authoritarian followers, who usually have very little desire to dominate others. They seem to have a hoard of hostility stored up looking for a chance to hurt someone. If you ask people to act as "teachers" in a learning experiment in which they can give electric shocks to "learners," high RWAs will give stronger shocks than others.[9] And if you ask subjects in a "Sentence a Criminal" study why they gave out the long sentences they did, they will say it felt good to them and that they got pleasure from doing so.[10]

Psychologists have tried to understand and explain aggression in various ways. The approach that best unravels high RWA aggression was developed by Stanford University professor Albert Bandura, who postulated that hostile acts take place in two stages: something arouses an aggressive impulse, and then something releases it.[11] The instigator can be a particular event, or it can instead be a general emotional state. Anger can trigger volcanic aggression, and fear can produce fight-or-flight reactions. But an angry or scared person does not necessarily aggress. He may anticipate social condemnation, counterattack, arrest, self-reproach, and so on. The attack will only proceed, Bandura says, if something overcomes these inhibitions. Research shows that fear instigates high RWAs' aggression more than anything else. Authoritarian followers are noticeably more afraid of the world than other people are, and this is probably a big reason why they crave the protection of a strong hero and his militant group. Their level of fear, like the aggression found in social dominators, may be partly due to genetic factors. But we also know that, according to both themselves and their parents, high RWAs were taught to view the world as a dangerous place. They got a lot more indoctrination in the boogeyman than most children did. We do have to fear fear itself, as M. Brewster Smith, a psychologist involved in the research on authoritarianism from the very beginning, put it.[12] It can easily prime authoritarian followers to attack.

Donald Trump obviously believed he could draw throngs of voters by playing the fear card every day of the 2016 campaign. The exit polls found Trump voters were particularly worried about immigration and terrorism. Two years later he said the country was about to be invaded by a caravan of criminals, Arab terrorists, and Marxists closing in on the southern border. His supporters believed him despite continuous news reports that the caravan was almost entirely composed of poor families seeking open refugee entry into the United States for economic reasons. The threat from the caravan mysteriously disappeared after the election, but you can be sure abject fear and loathing will be spread again in some form during Trump's reelection campaign in 2020, which will not be difficult in a time of the COVID-19 pandemic.

What then releases the aggressive impulse that fear creates? Again, experiments reveal that high RWAs come fully charged with self-righteousness.[13] Feelings of moral superiority can brush aside inhibitions against attacking homosexual people, "radicals," high school classmates who got pregnant, and many racial and ethnic minorities. Experiments since 1985 have shown that if you have solid measures of fear of a dangerous world and self-righteousness, you can account for most of the authoritarian aggression shown by high RWAs. Most of high RWAs' self-righteousness appears rooted in their religious beliefs, especially in the fundamentalist beliefs proclaimed by a lot of Donald Trump's base. In their minds, their in-group of "respectable people" remains forever surrounded by debauchery, like Abraham's family in Sodom. They accordingly view themselves as God's designated hitters, smiting down evil whenever possible. The Bible (Romans 12:19) says they should leave the punishing to the Almighty, but just in case a problem crops up with the paperwork, high RWAs will punish while they still shuffle about this mortal coil.

3. USING SOCIAL REINFORCEMENT TO BUTTRESS BELIEFS

Individuals tend to connect with those who share their beliefs. We all do this, but high RWAs favor "birds of a feather" much more than others do because they rely more on the social support of like-feathered birds to tell them they are right about the world. This interlocking reinforcement was called consensual validation by the social psychologists who first studied it decades ago.[14] The resulting in-group operates as an echo chamber, in which others like you stamp your views as "correct," provided you validate their beliefs in return. As it goes in Gilbert and Sullivan's *The Mikado*, "I am right, and you are right, and everything is quite correct." The out-group—people and sources and forces and courses that might confront the authoritarian follower with how little he understands—is avoided as much as possible. Thus, when a group of university students and their best friends independently answered the RWA Scale, the two sets of scores correlated only modestly over the whole sample. But the high RWA students and their best friends showed over twice as much agreement between themselves as the lows and their pals did. While by no means perfect matches, highs shared a lot more plumage with their best friends than low RWAs did with their best buds. Highs probably screen potential friends for having the "right" beliefs appreciably more than lows do. Low RWAs, who often seem capable of starting an argument in an empty room (and without a telephone), might even enjoy people who challenge their opinions. Most high RWAs cannot risk steadily exposing themselves to conflicting views of the world.

Authoritarian followers restrict their sources of information in more ways than just choice of friends. Take news programming. A survey taken just before the 2018 midterm election found that 62 percent of Republicans watched Fox News.[15] And compared to the Republicans who did not, Fox-viewing Republicans took more extreme positions on a wide range of issues. In turn, Trump supporters' preference for political analysis on radio (e.g. Presidential Medal of Freedom holder Rush Limbaugh) and on the internet (e.g. Breitbart) is well known. While these outlets do not always endorse Trump's actions, they do support him far more than the mainstream media. To a considerable extent, Trump's frequent missteps, contradictions, and so forth make no negative impression on his supporters because either they do not hear about them, or if they do, they have often been homogenized by right-wing media to something barely recognizable.

In 2018 the Gallup Poll had more than three thousand Americans read several news reports and judge each for fairness. Half the sample was told the source of the report as they read it (e.g. *New York Times*), while the other half just got the report with no further information. Afterward each subject wrote down the news source he trusted most in the world. This last response let the pollsters separate the sample into groups of "CNN Trusters," "Fox Trusters," "PBS Trusters," and so on. They could then look at each group (e.g., CNN Trusters) to see how big a difference there was when such people rated an article blindly and when such people rated it knowing where it came from. This tells you how much the people in each group were swayed, not by the news itself or how it was presented, but merely by learning its source. Stated a bit differently: how biased they were, pro and con, toward news sources. Which group showed the least bias? That is, who judged the news reports on the reports' merits, not on who made the report? In order of excellence, the top five were PBS viewers, (least biased of all), readers of the *Wall Street Journal*, the *Economist*, viewers of CNN, and then viewers of BBC. Who were the most biased consumers? That is, who were most likely to boost the truthfulness of a report when they liked its source, but disparage a report because they did not like who said it? At the bottom of list, in descending order, followers of MSNBC, One America News, Fox News, Brietbart, and most biased of all, fans of Rush Limbaugh.[16] The MSNBC placement might indicate the choice of Trump opponents with a stronger than average news bias. But otherwise the results show that people who are probably Trump supporters are the most biased news consumers in the country. Like their choice of friends, they want news that tells them what they want to hear. They may complain about "fake news," and everybody has preferred sources of news, but Trump supporters have the biggest biases about who tells the truth and who does not. They really rely upon social support for their beliefs because, as we said in the last chapter, they do not have reasons why their beliefs are true, just somebody else's word for it.

High RWAs are also uniquely susceptible to a con man. Since they rely heavily on others to confirm their beliefs, they heartily welcome newcomers to their in-group who will tell them they are right. New arrivals, especially converts, provide highly valued confirmation. But this big payoff leads them to overlook reasons why someone might purposely look more agreeable than he or she really is so they can exploit the believers. As many a con man knows, some people are just "begging to be taken." A classic social psychology experiment shows how much authoritarian followers want to believe a stranger has the same opinion as they do. Students were shown an essay, supposedly written by another student, that was quite hostile to homosexual people. They were asked to judge how much the essay writer liked gay people. The answer was obvious: Do not invite this person to the next LBGTQ+ potluck! Some other students were shown the same essay, except they were told it was written for a philosophy course that taught you how to argue. The essay writer had been assigned to make the strongest put down of homosexual rights that he could argue, regardless of his own real feelings. So he did. Now, what do you think the essay writer's real attitude was toward gay people? You do not know, do you? You cannot know. The point of view was assigned, so low RWA students sensibly said they could not say. But high RWAs said this essay writer obviously disliked gays. Why would they say that? Because they did not like homosexual people, they think anybody who agrees with them is telling the truth, regardless of the circumstances involved. That is how eager they are to think others agree with them. In case you are wondering if low RWAs are similarly inclined to bend over backward to believe others agree with them, the experiment also used a pro-gay essay with which lows would agree. But they showed no tendency to believe an assigned positive essay on homosexual people told them anything about the writer's real feelings. They paid attention to the circumstances involved. These results have been affirmed in many other experiments.[17]

If you have encountered the stereotype that right-wingers suspect other people's intentions to the point of being paranoid, these experiments lead to a more sophisticated conclusion. High RWAs are indeed suspicious of their many out-groups, but they have hinges on their heels for someone they think shares their beliefs. They believe people on their own side to remarkable extents, blithely ignoring warning signs that they are being led down a primrose path and fleeced from nose to stern through their need for social confirmation. They Who Would Fleece found these marks a long time ago. So, suppose for the sake of argument that you are a power-hungry, manipulative, totally unethical slimeball who decides to enter politics. You do stand for a few things, but it is best for you that the public never finds out what exactly. You need an army of gullible followers who will believe you when you are lying, inside-out and upside-down and through your teeth. Turns out, large clusters of chumps exist; they are the authoritarian followers we have been addressing, and they will lift you on high if you tell them you devoutly believe whatever they devoutly believe. They will gladly ignore reasons why you might be less trustworthy, which are conspicuous to most people. Would a power-hungry, manipulative, and totally unethical person exploit such foolish people? Does the name "Trump" ring a bell? He was equally condemning of Republicans and Democrats, and he had been both before 2015. He had been a con man even longer, with a highly tuned antenna for suckers. He had seen for years how easily the GOP faithful let themselves be snookered.[18]

Richard Nixon would tell you if you are indeed "a crook," then volunteer to lead the most gullible people you can find. Members of high RWAs' in-group are automatically friends with benefits when it comes to credibility. Nixon's authoritarian followers stayed with him to the bitter end, with some trying after his disgraced departure from office to rewrite history. On the other hand, low RWAs are not so gullible, more inclined to critical thinking, and likely to be suspicious of a con from the start, watching if someone is trying to pull a fast one. Because low RWAs are relatively uninclined to submit to authority, they will even get snarky if their leader later offends them. Consider Nixon's predecessor, Lyndon B. Johnson, who was able to get the most progressive laws in the United States since the Civil War passed through Congress in the mid-1960s (e.g., the Civil Rights Act of 1964, the Voting Rights Act of 1965), only to be forced out of office by liberal Democrats in 1968, who turned on him over the war in Vietnam.

Today, research shows that high RWAs are concentrated in the Republican Party, and if you have ever wondered why there seem to be noticeably more crooked politicians in the GOP than among the Democrats, this is probably a big part of the reason why. The Republicans have been rounding up the highly gullible for decades.* "You can fool some of the people all of the time," George W. Bush joked at a Gridiron Club Dinner in 2001, adding "those are the ones you need to concentrate on."[19] Bush said he had been told this by a Democrat, but whether he was or not, this insight has long been a cornerstone of the thinking of authoritarian presidents. Richard Nixon was recorded as saying, when the dreadful truth about Watergate was tumbling out, "I think there's still a hell of a lot of people out there . . . [who] want to believe. That's the point, isn't it?" His chief of staff, H. R. Haldeman, responded, "Why sure, want to and do."[20]

However, taking advantage of the gullibility of authoritarian followers carries a hidden long-range danger for the manipulator. It was noted in 2006 that leaders of high RWAs can get seduced by how easy it is to just lie about things because their followers believe everything they say.[21] So after a while the leaders do not bother to even make the lies plausible. It takes too much effort to repair all the tears that lies make in the truth. If you lead masses of authoritarian followers long enough, you will forget to look like you care anymore what is true. As we noted earlier, Donald Trump increasingly does not bother to tell even semi-plausible lies anymore and he may have become blind to much of the truth. And the even greater danger follows just one step behind: you can no longer separate the truth from the lies, because you have lied so much they have become most of your story.

---

* These people were once spread among both parties, but as the Democrats became more progressive, conservative Southern Democrats became Republicans, bringing with them their authoritarian followers. Today, Southern Democrats are usually progressive and hold little appeal for authoritarians.

4. VULNERABILITY TO CONFORMITY

High RWAs' reliance on others to shore up their beliefs can create a sensitivity to what people think that leaves them uneasy when they stand markedly apart from the rest. While they would never believe what they have been explicitly told is wrong, they might show a greater tendency to avoid being too different from what is normal or average. Indeed, that has been found many times in a simple experiment. Suppose you answer the RWA scale in a study, beginning with its first item: "Our country desperately needs a mighty leader who will do what has to be done to destroy the radical new ways and sinfulness that are ruining us." Being a very low RWA, especially after Trump's first term, you answer −4 on the −4 to +4 response scale. Later you get feedback about the results of the study as follows: The experimenter hands out the survey again, except beside each item she has written down the average of the answers obtained from all participants in the sample. Let us say in the case of this first question, the median answer was 0, meaning as many people disagreed as agreed with it. Then the experimenter asks you to answer the items again, right on the feedback sheet, saying you may take the group average into account if you wish, or not. It would not be too surprising if you wrote down a −3 this time. However, a student two seats away wrote down a +4 the first time, and he writes down a +2 this time, twice as big a move toward the group average as you did.

That is what happens when you run this simple conformity experiment. On hot-button issues such as fear of a dangerous world, attitudes toward homosexuals, and even religious fundamentalism, high RWAs yield twice as much as lows to the pressure, as silent as gravity but in its own way just as powerful, to not be too different. It does not always happen. They will not budge an inch on abortion. But unless a position has been emphatically drilled into their minds, high RWAs seem quite reluctant to take independent stands, compared to low RWAs. They would much rather blend in than stand out, which is all rather remarkable. You can argue until you are blue in the face and get nowhere changing an authoritarian follower's mind. But if he finds he is outstandingly standing out, he will probably start inching back toward the crowd all by himself.

If you are relying heavily on others to confirm rather than confront your beliefs, you want a strongly bonded in-group. The whole mutual-support understanding depends on sticking together. A modified Group Cohesiveness Scale originally developed by the astute New Zealand researcher John Duckitt confirmed this fact. High RWAs agree with such sentiments as, "For any group to succeed, all its members have to give it their complete loyalty" and "There is nothing lower than a person who betrays his group or stirs up disagreement within it." One can see from these reactions a willingness by authoritarian followers to submerge themselves in a movement of like-minded persons. Everyone should bolster one another. You pledge allegiance not only to the group's leader, but to the other followers who are counting on you to agree with them. The pressure to say you believe what everybody expects you to believe can be overwhelming. But in return you get determined, steadfast support for your own opinions, and that is why you came to the party and will stay late.

The longing of authoritarian followers to belong to a powerful, strongly united movement helps explain why Trump's rallies have been noticeably more enthusiastic than anybody else's. First, every speech by Trump, who is seen by his supporters as a superfamous, superrich, supergenius, tells them their beliefs are right, a payoff less needed by supporters of other candidates who have done more of their own thinking on the issues. Second, every stranger's smile at a rally, every slogan-bearing T-shirt, every MAGA hat, communicates the subtext: you do not know me, but we are together. Have you noticed you see more personal testimonials at Trump events than other political gatherings? For the Trump crowd this is like bringing a casserole to the potluck. But the cheers and chants in the auditorium tell them they are home in a determined and united movement, which makes them yell as well in fellowship. The crowd frees high RWAs to shout things at the top of their lungs that they deeply feel but are too embarrassed to otherwise say, such as "Send her back, Send her back," in response to Trump's attack on Minnesota Congresswoman Ilhan Omar, a Somali American.[22] You get attached to people who yell your own hidden thoughts at the top of their lungs.

But it costs more to belong than you might think. When you have re-inforced other people's opinions in your family, neighborhood, workplace, and church, you are like a piece of a picture inside a jigsaw puzzle, locked in on all sides to the norm that everyone gives 100 percent support to Donald Trump. If evidence comes along that your leader is a crook, a fool, and he has been lying to you from the start, you might want to distance your-self from him. But you also believe "There is nothing lower than a person who betrays his group or stirs up disagreement within it," so you will likely keep your hesitations to yourself. Others in the group may also have second thoughts as well, but, like you, feel locked into the norm that they must support him no matter what he does. Thus, the next time Donald Trump does something truly horrendous, do not expect his supporters to waver. Partly, that is because even if they now realize how badly he is performing, he is still heading their movement and they owe it to their cause to say they strongly support him. They may also feel they owe it to their in-group, the birds of their feather who have strengthened their beliefs over time, to stand together. Most people do not realize the power of these social obligations to a group. But wounded soldiers do not leave hospitals during the night and return to the front lines because of their love of democracy or the Father-land or the Motherland. They usually go because they feel they owe it to their comrades to share their dangers. It can even make them accept certain death, as defenders who fight to the last man sometimes show. It could have been a factor at Jonestown.

Imagine that you are a seventeen-year-old who thinks Donald Trump is the greatest president of all time, and you went to West Palm Beach, Florida, to attend the Turning Point USA Conference on December 19–22, 2019, an annual event staged to increase enthusiasm among conservative youth. President Trump is speaking to the audience, and he has brought up (for ridicule) a liberal plan involving wind power for dealing with climate change. And he says whimsically: "We'll have an economy based on wind. I never understood wind. You know, I know windmills very much. I've studied it better than anybody. I know it's very expensive. They're made in China and Germany mostly—very few made here, almost none. But they're manufactured tremendous—if you're into this—tremendous fumes. Gases are spewing into the atmosphere. You know we have a world, right? So, the world is tiny compared to the universe. So tremendous, tremendous amount [sic] of fumes and everything. You talk about the carbon footprint—fumes are spewing into the air. Right? Spewing. Whether it's in China, Germany, it's going into the air. It's our air, their air, everything—right? So, they make these things and then they put them up."[*]

An eerie hush has fallen over the audience, which, a minute before, was cheering everything Trump said. It was as if a minister had stopped his sermon on the Faithful Centurion to shout out the names of the twelve tribes of Israel and then proceeded to explain where Samaria came from. No one knew what was going on, it was all terribly embarrassing, and everybody just froze. Trump went on to criticize windmills some more, especially because they kill birds. It's against the law to kill a bald eagle, he says, but windmills kill them all the time.

What are you going to do now? You have discovered the emperor has no clothes, that your leader not only has feet of clay, but a head of lead. He sounds like Grandpa jabbering away, making no sense at all anymore. Welcome to the most wrenching discovery of your life. And it is not fake news. You saw and felt it happen. Everybody did. Eventually Trump stopped talking, and for an instant no one did anything. Then people in the audience started standing and clapping. For all you knew these were "plants," put there in pure Trumpian style to make sure the president got a standing ovation. But as others around you rose to their feet, you quickly stood up too. You would not want to look less enthusiastic than everybody else. And that was how you handled the crisis in your confidence. Everyone just pretended "it" never happened.

What does this cost you? You cannot just disconnect a piece of reality and have everything fit together perfectly again. But beyond that, you are both a liar and a fool who makes himself believe the lie. You are stealing from your self-worth coming and going. The dogmatism of a true believer springs from a deep, self-inflicted wound.

---

* Philip Bump, "What Trump Was Talking about in His Baffling Rant about Wind Energy," *The Washington Post*, December 23, 2019, https://www.washingtonpost.com/politics/2019/12/23/what-trump-was-talking-about-his-baffling-rantabout-wind-energy/.

5. DO AUTHORITARIAN FOLLOWERS KNOW THEMSELVES?

The years of research have uncovered many disheartening and troubling things about authoritarian followers. Yet they themselves are not disheartened—far from it—because they realize almost none of their shortcomings. Therefore, if you ask them if a lot of their ideas are inconsistent and even contradict one another, they will likely think you are talking about somebody else. Ditto about employing double standards, tolerating government injustices, and being mean-spirited. You name it. Out of twenty well-established behaviors regularly found in high RWAs, they thought they were like everybody else, "You know, normal," in almost all instances. They did know they trusted authorities more than most people do and that they are more likely to help the government persecute vulnerable groups, and maybe have a touch of prejudice. But even then they had almost no grasp of how different they were compared to most people. Overall, they had practically zero insight into themselves. The person they thought they were did not exist.[23]

This discovery uncovering the remarkable lack of self-awareness in these authoritarian followers was complemented by a study in which students who had answered the RWA scale were given a forty-five-minute "feedback" lecture on what the test measured. After hearing much about the material we have been sharing about high RWAs, each student was given a sheet of paper with a chart showing the actual distribution of RWA scale scores in the class and asked to guess where he or she had landed on the scale. Low RWAs, by and large, correctly predicted they would score low. Most of the moderates, the students who formed the middle of the distribution on the scale, accurately thought they would be around the middle. But most of the high RWAs also thought they would place in the middle, "you know, normal." Like the students in the self-awareness research, they thought they would be average. So, if you have been thinking you were a low RWA as you read these findings, chances are you would score low on the test. If you consider yourself a moderate, you might be correct, although you could also be a high RWA. If you think you are a high RWA—well, almost nobody thinks that, so maybe you are a high social dominator. They do not care.

High RWAs positively yearn to be in the middle, normal in most respects. It's like they want to disappear. In another experiment students were again told what the RWA scale measures and then discreetly told they had scored highly on the test—a lie for everyone but the actual highs (which was confessed minutes later). The students were asked to mark where they wished they could be in the distribution. The lows wanted to be lows, as did many moderates. But interestingly, the highs generally wanted to be moderates, "normal," even though the feedback had made it clear that low scorers displayed strong integrity, careful thinking, low levels of prejudice, and other positive traits.

A DEEP TRIP INTO HIGH RWA MINDS

In last chapter's discussion of ethnocentrism, we offered one reason why authoritarian followers have so little self-insight. Their allegiance to their in-group keeps them traveling in such small circles that they think they are normal because so many of their friends act the way they do. But research shows they also simply cannot face up to their failings. That is, they are more defensive, more self-deceiving, more believing in a person they are not, than most people. They run away from, or avoid, the truth about themselves.

Assume again you are an Introduction to Psychology student answering a survey passed out in class, and you were told to leave the classroom and go to a private place of your choosing so you will be able to answer the questions with total honesty. The survey requests you write down two or three things that you are very reluctant to admit about yourself, but which are nonetheless true. Low RWAs disclosed nearly two ugly facts about themselves on the average, and highs revealed significantly fewer, mainly because a lot of them wrote down nothing. Later in the survey everyone was asked, "If you wrote down nothing, how come?" The highs almost always said there was nothing to write down because they squarely faced any shortcomings they might have. Were this true, and widespread in the population, a lot of clinical psychologists would have their afternoons free and drive cars in the price range that social psychologists can afford. But maybe these "non-responders" are kidding themselves. Maybe high RWAs collapse with fear when disturbing truths begin to flash before them, the way we think Donald Trump does, and they run away! run away! from any self-knowledge that hurts, including the fact that they run away.

While one cannot easily answer questions about "deep" and perhaps unconscious mental processes through the scientific method, this one was pursued in an experiment supposedly about self-esteem. Students answered a booklet of surveys including the RWA Scale and an obvious measure of self-esteem. Later the experimenter returned to their class to give them promised feedback. He praised the validity and power of the self esteem scale, saying studies had shown that high scorers got good grades at university, made lots of friends, and succeeded later in life, whereas low scorers were likely to drop out of school, be unpopular and got fired and divorced a lot later on. He then distributed a feedback sheet to the students and these sheets told them (supposedly) where they had had scored on the self-esteem scale. Half the students were told they had scored quite highly. You can guess what this evil experimenter told the others.

After the news had sunk in, the experimenter said he had prepared an easy-read summary of the research showing how great at prediction this self-esteem scale was, and he needed to know how many copies to print, "If you want a copy, write 'Yes' on the top of the feedback sheet; if not, write 'No.'" The sheets, which did not have the students names on them but which had been pre-coded to indicate whether the student was a low or high RWA, were then collected. At this point the experimenter told the class all the scores passed out had been fake, and when the booing had died down he revealed the true purpose of the study. (He used the opportunity to warn students about putting much credence in any single psychological test score, which is good advice.) A solid majority of the low RWAs asked for the evidence that the self-esteem scale was valid, and it did not matter whether they had gotten high or low self-esteem scores. Even more high RWAs who had gotten high self-esteem scores also wanted a copy of the validity evidence. But most of the "bad-news highs" did not. They "ran away, ran away."

In another experiment students were asked if they wanted to be told how they had scored on a prejudice scale. A solid majority of the low RWAs wanted to be told their score, whatever it was. So did the highs—*if the results showed they were unprejudiced.* But significantly fewer high RWAs wanted to be told evidence that they were prejudiced. So, again it seems that high RWAs have an appreciable reluctance to face up to bad news about themselves, and this defensiveness helps explain why many of them have so little self-awareness.

In summary, decades of research reveal that, as a group, authoritarian followers appear to have a lot of "hurt," which they are looking to lay on others. These impulses are triggered by fear of a dangerous world more than anything else, which are mainly released by their self-righteousness. When an authority approves the aggression, as in the very frightening Posse experiments, they find justification in attacking others. As we noted, research reveals these people have a deep need to belong to a powerful movement that they feel will safeguard them. These authoritarian followers are deeply dependent on others for social reinforcement of their beliefs, necessitated because they are more untethered and adrift than most people if they are forced to figure things out on their own. But this dependence makes them uniquely vulnerable to manipulators who know it is the open door to their allegiance and wallets. They have stronger drives to be normal, to conform more than most people do, and they relish being in movements that have a strong ethic of in-group loyalty, even though these can become crippling at time. These social psychological forces seem to give a protective shell to a weak ego that has difficulty facing up to shortcomings in its behavior. They would surely disagree, but these people do not know themselves very well, and, frankly, they do not want to if the insights are threatening. It has taken forty years of study, and given what has happened in the last four, we believe this research cannot be ignored.

CHAPTER EIGHT

SOLVING THE MYSTERY OF EVANGELICAL* SUPPORT OF DONALD TRUMP

Nothing in the 2016 presidential election stunned one more than Donald Trump's winning the votes of the "religious right."[1] Trump is the antithesis of most everything Christian ministers preach about the qualities of a good person and living a righteous life. His capturing the hearts and minds of the most active Christians in America appears almost a miracle of biblical proportions, and, indeed, some evangelicals believe he was sent by God. How did it happen?

A bit of backstory: Three men played significant roles in attracting millions of social conservatives to the Republican Party over the past forty years. Jerry Falwell took Richard Nixon's "Silent Majority" of 1972 an ethnocentric step further by organizing them into his "Moral Majority" in the late 1970s. Falwell fired up their latent, old-time religion zeal to advance right-wing religious views on abortion, homosexuality, pornography, and a host of other social issues. Soon, bumper stickers appeared declaring the Moral Majority was neither, yet by 1980 the faithful marched to the

---

* One must distinguish white from Black Evangelicals. The latter are sizeable in number but demographically and religiously quite different from the former. When we speak of Evangelicals in this chapter, assume we mean white Christians.

polls to send Ronald Reagan to the White House, a divorced and remarried Hollywood man about town whose attachment to Christianity was as relaxed as his smile. They chose Reagan over the devout, born-again, Sunday-school-teaching, and somewhat socially liberal Christian incumbent President Jimmy Carter. It foreshadowed how little the religious affiliations and behavior of a candidate mattered to social conservatives when you got down to issues such as abortion.

Ten years later, after the image of the Moral Majority was as shot full of holes as roadside signs in parts of America, television preacher and *700 Club* host Pat Robertson set out to take over the Republican Party by creating the Christian Coalition, an attempt to get God-fearing conservative Catholics as well as conservative Protestants involved in politics. Churches became hotbeds of political activity, and Robertson's followers began overwhelming "regular" Republicans in low-turnout primaries. By the end of the 1990s most of the Republican state committees had been taken over by the religious right at least once.[2] The GOP establishment was losing control of the party to a grassroots movement fighting them coast to coast in a "coup d'pew." The range of positions among Republican caucuses was being curtailed, compressed, squashed. Some Republican leaders reacted with alarm, notably the Republican Party's 1964 standard-bearer, Arizona Senator Barry Goldwater. "Goddamn it, John," he said to John Dean, "the Republicans are selling their souls to win elections. Mark my words. If and when these preachers get control of the party, and they're sure trying to do it, it's going to be a terrible damn problem."[3] Jimmy Carter noted as well that "fundamentalist movements are led by authoritarian males who consider themselves to be superior to others and, within religious groups, have an overwhelming commitment to subjugate women and to dominate their fellow believers."[4]

Such cries of alarm notwithstanding, George W. Bush's campaign director Karl Rove brought the Christian Coalition on board in 2000 with

promises of influence in the administration and strong action on the movement's biggest issues: abortion and homosexual rights. Millions more evangelicals moved to the Republican Party at no cost, it seemed. They brought
to the GOP tent dedication, evangelical zeal, and give-until-it-hurts donations, along with their thick social networks. Bush would not have come
close to winning his first term without them. He and Rove then forgot the
promise made to the religious leaders, who discovered they had no influence in Bush's White House. They were even quietly mocked.[5] Nonetheless, their leaders understood they controlled a mounting percentage of the
Republican rank-and-file, so they decided to endorse Bush for reelection
in 2004, given the lack of an alternative. Their growing influence in the
party drove some long-time members out the back of the tent, turning them
into independents longing to be Republicans again. But "the preachers"
did not weep at their departure. Goldwater observed that the newcomers,
convinced they were acting in the name of God, would not compromise as
they tore the stuffing out of the Grand Old Party and recast it into the sort
of state-church party that the nation's architects strove to avoid.[6] Following
the lead of Newt Gingrich, new Republican politicians made the capital
more divisive, and spread divisiveness throughout the country. Old Republicans were the enemy, too. Resistance was futile. Assimilate or scram.

The great migration of religious conservatives to the Republican Party
continued after Bush left the White House when the Democrats nominated
Barack Obama to be president in 2008, and John McCain selected Sarah
Palin to be his GOP running mate. By early 2015 the number of evangelicals in the Republican Party had risen to the point that they could easily
win primaries for national office in most states if their vote remained united.
The burgeoning strength of faith-based voters had encouraged many candidates with religious bona fides to step forward, and the boys in the back ves-
try knew that if they all recommended the same guy to their followers, they
would have a lock on the Republican nomination. Most of them liked Ted

Cruz. Almost no one endorsed Donald Trump. They probably thought his candidacy represented the latest tree ring girding a lifetime of ever-swelling self-promotion. (They were right. Trump referred to it among his advisors as the longest-running free infomercial ever.)

As Trump rose in strength for the 2016 GOP nomination, most religious leaders thought him too untrustworthy for serious consideration. On the national stage, only Franklin Graham, Billy Graham's hard-right son and successor, had words of praise for Trump.[7] He was an exception. Most thought like Bob Vander Plaats, CEO of the Family Leader, who stressed finding a candidate who could pass the character test he believed important to churchgoing voters. Some inmates incarcerated in America's penitentiaries would score higher on a character test than Donald Trump. He had been thunderously unfaithful to his first two wives and had loutishly bragged about his success at seducing women who, he said, found him irresistible. He was vain beyond belief, habitually deceitful, disgustingly foulmouthed, mean and demeaning to opponents, had a documented history of racial discrimination, and all the integrity of a five-star con artist. Which, again, he was. Of the seven deadly sins (lust, gluttony, greed, sloth, wrath, envy, and pride), Trump might get a pass on sloth if you count watching cable news as working. Otherwise, he had plainly reveled in sin for most of his life and delighted in it like a pig rolling in muck.

Furthermore, Trump did not have an inkling of Judeo-Christian beliefs, and every time he tried to pass as a Christian he put both feet in his mouth, sideways. His faux pas in referring to II Corinthians as "Two Corinthians" was the least of his gaffes. He insisted the Bible was his favorite book, that he was "with it all the way." But when asked by *New York Post* reporters in February 1990 if adultery was a sin, Trump showed amazing ignorance of the Ten Commandments by saying it was not.[8] When asked in August 2015 whether he preferred the Old Testament or the New Testament, he evasively (and ignorantly for a purported Christian) answered "equally." When asked for his favorite Bible verses, he said it was too personal to get into. (Translation: "There are verses in the Bible?") Given a second chance in April 2016, he mentioned: "An eye for an eye," holding aloft a principle of retaliation found indeed in Exodus and Leviticus, but one that Jesus had specifically repudiated in the Sermon on the Mount.[9] If cow pies were scattered widely in the field of religion, and Donald Trump was crossing the field, he would step in every one.

Trump's knowledge of the Bible parallels his knowledge of the US Constitution, which is to say he probably knows it usually has a black cover, that Eve made Adam eat the apple, Noah built an ark, and Delilah cut Sampson's hair. And not much else. Yet when confronted with his ignorance about the Bible, he gave a pure Trumpian response: "Nobody reads the Bible more than me."[10] (Translation: I know nothing about what I'm talking about, so I'll bluff.) When asked at the Family Leadership Summit in Ames, Iowa in July 2015 if he has ever asked God for forgiveness, Trump said no. He obviously had no idea of the significance of the question to evangelicals. When given a Mulligan later on that one too, he answered that he takes communion, and that for him was asking for forgiveness.[11] Which is definitely bass-ackward theology for a Christian, and it speaks volumes about his ignorance. In brief, evangelicals should have spotted Donald Trump from the start as an enormously phony Christian who moreover was stupidly lying to them about it the same stupid way he stupidly lies to everybody. They probably would have hooted from here to kingdom come on Judgment Day at any Democrat who made the same mistakes. But precious little condemnation rose from the Republican ranks as Trump almost instantly became a front-runner in the crowded field (probably because he appealed to social dominators from the moment he joined the race). By the middle of July 2015, a month after throwing his hat into the ring, he was in first place and stayed there for the rest of the campaign.[12]

MANY WERE CALLED, LOOK WHO WAS CHOSEN

Trump pulled ahead of the pack without saying much about what he would do as president. Mostly he just attacked, almost everybody: Mexicans, Muslims, Chinese, Japanese, NATO allies, Democrats, and his Republican opponents. He was selling aggression, and the Republican rank and file, shucked of moderates, was buying. One cannot tell from the polls how religious Republicans per se responded to Trump, but the surveys show that Cruz and the other religious candidates lost as much ground as anyone else while Trump climbed over them, which means some evangelicals were falling for his spiel and under his spell early on. And ascend he did during the runup to the primaries. Aided by a surprise endorsement by Jerry Falwell Jr., Trump finished a respectable second to Cruz in the leadoff Iowa primary on February 1, 2016.[13] Eight days later Trump won the New Hampshire primary and drew more support from evangelicals than Cruz did.

The hammer fell in the South Carolina primary on February 20, 2016. With two-thirds of the Republican voters being white evangelicals, everyone expected Cruz to run away with the delegates, and he worked the state hard. He ran a TV ad showing Trump's appearance on a "Meet the Press" program in 1999 in which he answered a question about abortion by asserting, "I am very pro-choice, in every respect." That should have totally cost Trump the evangelical vote everywhere. But Trump announced he had converted from being completely pro-choice to being completely pro-life, and he won not only the statewide vote, but the evangelical vote too. Trump captured nine of the eleven states that held Republican primaries on Super Tuesday, February 26, and in each of the nine he again chalked up more evangelical votes than Cruz.

On March 3, 2016, Mitt Romney, the Republican Party nominee for president in 2012, gave a speech in which he denounced Trump as "a fraud" and warned, "He's playing the American public for suckers." He warned Republicans not to vote for him.[14] But the leaders of the religious right began showing a jittery acceptance of candidate Trump as their followers increasingly wandered away from the fold to attend his energetic rallies, which he had started opening with a prayer. After Super Tuesday the de-flocked shepherds, scrambling to catch up to their runaways, grabbed hold of the bandwagon as it rumbled to the Republican convention. They were permitted to kiss Trump's ring, so to speak, by joining his one-thousand-member evangelical board.[15] The race effectively ended on May 3, 2016, when Trump won another evangelical-rich state, Indiana, although it would take a few more primaries for him to lock up a majority of the delegates.

In November, he most unexpectedly won the presidency. According to the exit polls, white voters who said they were born-again or evangelical Christians gave Donald Trump 80 percent of their votes, while only 16 percent went to Clinton.[16] That was five to one! Trump, who had spread sin like butter on toast, won massively among the religious right.* Furthermore, evangelicals crashed the voting centers more than any other group of Americans. They gave him nearly half (45 percent) of all the votes he received. They formed the solid, rebarred core of Trump's support in 2016—as they still do today.

So, while religious leaders (and the social psychologist composing this sentence) thought wild horses and Salome's dance could not get Evangelicals to vote for Trump, they instead carried him on their shoulders into the White House. How could such ethnocentric voters prefer an utterly reprehensible outsider, like Trump, to their long-established favorites on the religious right? The answer to the last part of the question appeared in the exit polls of the primaries, where most Republican voters said they felt betrayed by the Republican politicians they had voted for in the past. Their religious leaders had urged them to vote for these exploiters back then,

---

* As noted in chapter 5, white undereducated males, the other major component in Trump's base, only favored him by 71 percent to 23 percent, about three to one.

which they had done, and nothing had come of it. For all they knew, Ted Cruz was just the next George W. Bush: All talk and no effective action on their priorities. Trump ran as a nonpolitician who hated Republicans as much as he despised Democrats. That sounded good to people who felt the Republicans had repeatedly let them down. Enough was enough! Drain the whole darn swamp!

Like a lot of other Americans, Christian voters believed the myths Donald Trump had created about himself through fifty years of nonstop lying, and they thought he would be able to pull the plug and drain the capital. They figured a successful businessman such as he could straighten out the federal government, overlooking the fact that he had mainly promoted projects using other people's money and had no background whatsoever in government, not to mention abysmal management skills. They found Trump's inexperience in politics reassuring because politicians always lie. Like the social dominators who also packed Donald's rallies, the authoritarian followers believed he always told the truth because he said things they themselves believed but were afraid to say. This completely amoral person seemed, to them, a man of great conviction. And they believed that he could win—Ted Cruz, and others, could not.

The thousands of people whom Donald Trump cheated in business deals would not have been at all surprised if he had double-crossed his supporters after he was elected and become more moderate to guarantee his reelection. But since winning the presidency Trump has worked rabidly to keep his promises to the "hammerheads" (which was advisor Steve Bannon's nickname for Trump's die-hard supporters).[17] If there is an art to making a deal, Trump has sealed this one. After decades of being let down by presidents like George W. Bush, who took their votes and then ignored them because they were "too easy," the evangelicals finally found their champion. And Trump knows that if he keeps his base onside and energized, they will accept whatever he says and support him to the end, even though he often fails to get them what they want because of his inept-itude. He turned slam dunks into air balls during his first term, as when his insidious belittling of John McCain as "not a hero" saved Obamacare. His best chance to build The Wall came with a government shutdown looming in December 2018. Displaying the negotiating skills of a five-year-old, he proclaimed with bravado that he would "own" the government shutdown if he did not get his way. In fact, the Democrats let him own it, and he huffed, and he puffed, and he caved in.

DONALD TRUMP'S APPEAL TO EVANGELICALS

A great deal of research over the decades reveals that Evangelicals usually score quite highly on the RWA scale. Thus, when the Republican Party actively recruited religious conservatives, it was simultaneously filling it-self up with highly prejudiced authoritarian followers. Given that fact, one could predict from the outset that a dominating authoritarian leader like Donald Trump would appeal to Evangelicals.* High RWAs are search-ing for a strong authority to whom to submit. They crave that magnificent feeling of protection that children get from their parents. Also, Christian high RWAs are often looking for a mighty ruler like King David who will lead their nation forward, a messiah in the original sense. Pollster Steve Mitchell pointed out early in the 2016 primary season that evangelicals were attracted to Trump because he seemed so bold, dynamic, decisive, and strong.[18] He bowed to no one and seemed to expect others to bow to him. Physically he owned all the space around him. He looked commanding compared to the other Republican candidates. High RWAs, never wonder-ing why someone would act that way and never suspecting it was a big act

---

* What was not predicted was that this appeal would thoroughly overpower the many good reasons evangelicals had for rejecting Trump on religious grounds.

to cover a deep-seated fear of failure, thrilled to the show, and their ongoing need to submit to a protector helps explain why they support Trump no matter what he does.

Trump surely caught high RWAs' attention from the start when he brought up Chinese trade-cheaters, Mexican rapists, Muslim bombers, and so on. Submissive authoritarians run scared at the best of times, and Trump pushed the fear button harder and more often from June 2015 to November 2016 than any other presidential candidate in American history. Trump preached to the Choir Terrified, constantly scaring their pants off.[19] When his opponents rebuked Trump for recklessly exaggerating the danger, it convinced high RWAs that only he saw things clearly. Moreover, Trump's in-your-face racism and xenophobia meshed with the large amount of prejudice found among the high RWAs stocking the religious right and further told them that their destructive biases, based on lifelong training in ethnocentrism that began with their religious identification, were justified. Remember also how uncritically high RWAs accept someone when he tells them what they want to hear. And you can also see why Trump's promise of building The Wall meant so much to high RWAs, for they had been building ethnocentric walls between themselves and others for most of their lives. Here was Trump promising "a real, high, beautiful, concrete wall" (later, steel spikes) that said "Rejection!" almost as forcefully as cannon fire.

How could the evangelicals who screamed outrage at Bill Clinton for his extramarital affairs give Donald Trump a free pass for doing the same things? Not really a problem whatsoever if you have been using double standards all your life. Evangelicals may have been annoyed when Trump ripped into his opponents with schoolyard bullying tactics and vile insults. Trump was especially vicious to Ted Cruz, John McCain, and Mitt Romney. But recall that high RWAs, who very likely voted for these men in past elections, excel in compartmentalized thinking. They could easily have put their past votes into one compartment and Trump's insults and ugly comments into another, wrapping their Trump box with a bow saying it showed what a good fighter Trump was, and they wanted a good fighter. High RWAs have mind-boggling skill at mind-boggling rationalization. In this same context we know from several studies that high RWAs have a lot of aggressive impulses looking for an excuse to come out. Trump's hostility, evident in tweet after tweet, and speech after speech, when he broadsided refugees and the media at his rallies, or when he ordered security to rough up a heckler, probably made them clench their fists, wanting to throw the punch themselves. And remember, high RWAs have trouble realizing a claim is false, which made it easy for them to fall for Trump's absurd "most-this, worst-that" claims, which he drove like stampeding cattle through the debates. They did not find out the next day that most of what he said was claptrap, because they did not look.

Trump supporters have often said in interviews that they distinguished between the person Trump and his policies and voted for the latter, which is major-league compartmentalization again since they were saying Trump's personality did not matter. But if you think about it, you can come up with lots of good reasons why one should NOT make a power-mad, cheating, thoroughly dishonest, amoral man the leader of your country, even if you like his stand on various issues. Similarly, he said women who get abortions should be punished, and then the next day said no they should not. But these contradictions may not have bothered authoritarian followers whose own minds, we saw, endorse many contradictory beliefs. When Trump announced during the South Carolina primary that he had switched 180 degrees to being one hundred percent pro-life, most evangelical voters evidently believed him. This shows their vulnerability to "he agrees with me, therefore he believes what he's saying" self-deception. Few apparently stopped to think that views on abortion are harder to change than almost anything else. As far as we know, no one asked Trump what had caused this complete turnabout. It was enough that he had seen the light, high RWAs thought, and now wonderfully confirmed their beliefs.

Their well-learned non-learning of critical thinking led evangelicals to accept Trump's string of misrepresentations and outright lies about the United States's position in the world, its military strength, NATO's unpaid dues, trade imbalances, the failing economy, and other matters he invented out of thin air to dress up his claim that America needed to be made great again. His support took a temporary hit when the *Access Hollywood* tape revealed his boasting about numerous sexual assaults on women. But his supporters accepted his "locker-room talk" nondenial denial of having never done the things he bragged about doing, even though numerous women said Trump had indeed groped and even raped them. This acceptance fits right in with the finding that high RWAs have virtually impossible standards for evidence about something they do not want to believe. And in this case various religious leaders, jostling for a place on the bandwagon, chimed in with the (always selectively remembered) admission that we have all sinned, and who are we to judge, and God will forgive Trump, that Trump (age seventy) had to be seen as a "baby Christian," and whatever his faults, you had to admit he was God's instrument to save America.[20] Trump also denied he had sex with Stormy Daniels and paid her hush money, and then Michael Cohen made it clear "the Donald" had done both. Somehow this did not lead evangelicals to reconsider his earlier denials. (Or numerous later ones.)

Much of the negative information about Trump that emerged during the campaign never reached his authoritarian followers who, in pursuit of consensual validation, would have avoided news sources that would present him in a bad light. When damaging information did get through, they would readily dismiss it because of its supposed "fake-news" source, just as Fox viewers and Limbaugh listeners showed the greatest bias in the Gallup

Poll experiment. You might think that people who were bending over backward so much to make the unacceptable acceptable would realize how much they were fooling themselves. But a lot of evidence shows that high RWAs have little self-awareness. Just as high RWAs tend to run away from bad news about themselves, they almost certainly avoid information that places their preferred political leader in a bad light.

Another feature of the high RWA mind helped hesitant evangelicals eventually become devoted Trump followers: Evangelicals evangelize. As the primaries tumbled along in the first half of 2016 the evangelicals who favored a candidate very likely tried to convert others, especially their fellow Christians. Trump had more evangelicals onside than anyone else, from the New Hampshire primary on, and hence had an advantage appealing to people motivated to conform to what appears "normal," especially within the in-group. As Jeb Bush and Mike Huckabee and Marco Rubio dropped out, where were their followers most likely to go? Folks not as needy of group reinforcement probably cannot imagine how isolated an evangelical would have felt standing apart from the other members of her church, nor how welcomed she felt when she "crossed over the bridge." The pressure for group cohesion can be overpowering. Even many devoted supporters of Ted Cruz, whom Trump had most unfairly savaged in the campaign, swung over to Trump, and embraced their fellow evangelicals who had been preaching and praying furiously for them to do so.

Year in, year out, evangelicals bring potential converts to their church services where they can see for themselves their wonderful faith and congregation. Similarly, many Trump supporters said that attending a local rally had been their road to Damascus. As described earlier, two powerful bonds unite the people at the rallies. They would have been attracted to Trump himself, a man who thinks the sun comes up every morning so it can look at him, and who also knows how to stage an event to make him look grand. They would have completely misattributed his motives and thought this supposedly talented and successful man was generously giving up his perfect life to help them, when actually he was running to make Donald Trump feel great again. The least they could do was be grateful and supremely loyal to their "voice." As well, high RWAs would have been thrilled at being in a rocking hall filled to the rafters with people who all seemed to believe the same thing. The chance they could stand apart from that crowd and assess the reality of the situation equaled a snowflake's chance at a Fourth of July picnic in Paducah. If the newcomer felt exposed and vulnerable in the outside world that Trump agreeably portrayed as a fearful, terrifying place, they felt safe, nay powerful, in this crowd of like-minded supporters who would fight alongside the newcomers with all their might. All they had to do was join in.

This application of the research findings from Chapters 6 and 7 shows why Trump's *appeal* to evangelicals would have been much greater than anticipated. In many respects high RWAs were built from the ground up to fall for someone like him. The reader may also appreciate the irony in how the religious authorities in evangelicals' lives, by encouraging compartmentalization, teaching double standards, rewarding memorization over critical thinking, promoting ethnocentrism, et cetera, made it easy for Donald Trump to steal their flocks. They were the unwitting architects of their own decline. Some evangelical leaders went so far as to say they came to support Trump because they realized he had been sent by God to save America. That certainly endeared them to The Donald. If Trump now has a Messiah complex on top of everything else he got the idea from these preachers. When he told reporters on August 21, 2019, that he was "the Chosen One," he was just saying what various prominent religious leaders such as Robert Jeffress of Dallas had told both him and the parishioners in their mega-churches.[21] And not missing a trick, Trump has a full-time spiritual adviser on his staff, Paula White, who has declared that Trump speaks God's word.[22]

THE OTHER HALF OF THE MYSTERY

Research on authoritarian followers explains why evangelicals have been attracted to Donald Trump, but it does not explain how they can simply dismiss all his sinfulness given their openly declared religious beliefs? Why did that not instantly disqualify him? After all, by several different measures, evangelicals rank as about the most religious people in America. When tested on the RWA scale they consistently say atheists and others who have rebelled against the established religions cannot be as good as those who go to church regularly. When tested on some prejudice scales they say that religions such as Buddhism, Islam, and Hinduism do not produce as much "good behavior" as Christianity, and that people cannot lead the best life unless they belong to the Christian religion. In short, with their faith guiding them, they should never have accepted someone as obviously immoral and un-Christ-like as Donald Trump as their political lord and savior. So how could they have?

Well, a large stack of research findings shows that evangelicals' religious beliefs do not make *them* particularly moral. For example, in a series of experiments run over a span of years, it appeared to some university students that through a clerical error they were going to get a higher grade than they deserved in a course. The professor handed out individual feedback sheets showing his record of the students' test scores and their total. But the professor purposely made calculation errors on an equal number of low and high RWA students' feedback. Some students would have gotten lower grades than they deserved, and others higher ones. Virtually all the students who were "short-changed" brought the error to the professor's attention, and virtually all of those who got an undeserved bonus did not. So high RWAs proved just as likely as everyone else to take the undeserved better mark and run. Over the years the amount of the error was increased from a trivial one percent to a grade-changing ten percent, and the results remained the same. This professor could also identify some students who had cheated on the first test in the course, before they learned that different versions of the multiple-choice test were systematically distributed in the densely seated lecture hall. If someone copied a neighbor's correct answers, he would get a very low score. Cheaters' poor marks would then go up appreciably on the second test, unlike students who got disastrously low marks the old-fashioned way. Cheaters were just as likely to be high RWAs as lows. It was also possible to tell at times that students had filled in surveys themselves that were supposed to be filled out by parents or friends. High RWAs were just as likely to cheat in this way as lows.

One can dismiss all these findings as trivial, since the worst of them would only change, say, a C to a B in one course. But Ronald J. Sider, a theologian at Eastern Baptist Theological Seminary, observed that despite Jesus's unequivocal stand on the permanence of marriage, evangelical Christians divorce as often as others do.[23] The number of unmarried couples living together, he noted, jumped more in the Bible Belt in the 1990s than in the USA as a whole. And 88 percent of the evangelical youth who took an oath to remain virgins until they married broke it. "Saved" men used pornography and physically abused their wives as much as "unsaved" men. And churchgoing Christian women were about as likely to end an unwanted pregnancy with an abortion as other women.[24] Obviously, evangelicals are very good at disengaging their religion when need arises. They look just as immoral, in terms of their own ethical system, as the people they condemn as worse. Which raises the question, what good is their religion doing them? For which there is an answer: authoritarian followers give more to charities than low RWAs do. But if one adds in the various moral shortcomings that highs display in abundance, such as prejudice, ethical superiority seems untenable.

Nevertheless, high RWAs have shown a streak of self-righteousness since they began joining the Moral Majority in the 1970s, and we saw in Chapter 7 that it plays a key role in their aggression. How can we untwist the incongruity in the finding that some of the most self-proclaimed religious people among us tend to be, in some ways, morally among the worst, and yet they think they are better? The answer lay in the cloaked circuit-closing connection between sin and self-righteousness. Let us say you have sinned against your neighbor. Maybe you stole something, or started a malicious rumor, or bedded a coveted wife or husband. Now this bothers you. You have a guilty conscience. What do you do? When given a list of possible reactions to guilt, high RWAs were very likely to say they ask God for forgiveness. They did not check off things like "I discuss what I did with those who may have suffered and make it up to them" or "I talk to someone close, such as a good friend or relative, about what I did." Low RWAs did those sorts of things but received little relief. They still felt crummy afterward, maybe because they had seen firsthand the damage they had done or knew knowledge of their misdeed had now spread. But authoritarian followers felt almost completely forgiven by God. They had applied divine White-Out, which was far less messy than admitting to the wounded person that they had done the wounding. Once again they ran away. Fearful people are not very courageous. Final Guilt Scores are: low RWAs—lots of guilt, high RWAs—nearly zero. The highs win, but society loses. The authoritarians have taken instant guilt-be-gone, and as a result they do not have to stifle a nagging conscience still reminding them on Saturday night what happened last Saturday night. Their religion has taken the guilt out of guilt. As a result, when the impulse next arises to stick it to someone, they have no trouble sugarcoating the point on their spear with self-righteousness and firing away. And if later they feel guilty about letting their prejudices and hatreds get the better of them, no problem. They will just wipe the slate clean again with a prayer for forgiveness and get back to feeling good about themselves, thus reloading for future aggression. Easy forgiveness makes sin more likely to recur. Given the guilt-evaporating belief that God will forgive everything you confess, why wouldn't you sin when temptation arose, with such easy-off, easy-on ramps to holiness continually available as you travel through life? You can have your cake and go to heaven too.

Being "religious" can particularly lead to sin if one is exposed to the pernicious theology that detractors call "cheap grace." Some pastors preach that once you have accepted Jesus as your personal savior, which typically involves a one-time verbal commitment, it just doesn't matter if you are in the Klan, cheat on your spouse, or push drugs in schoolyards. You are going to heaven no matter what you do. Being good is not a prerequisite for salvation. You are already, now and forever, among The Saved. Good little boys and girls do not necessarily go to heaven, this doctrine says, only The Saved do. And one can join The Saved in less time than it takes to pay your credit card bill online. You can do it in twenty words or less, there is nothing to sign, and nobody's going to look up your moral credit rating. It is obvious why persons up to no good in their lives are attracted to pastors who use this hymnbook. Once evildoers have said the magic words, it seems, they can lie, cheat, and steal as much as they want without jeopardizing in the least their reserved seat in the heavenly choir. They have acquired a "get out of hell free" card. They do not even have to apologize to fellow beings or to God. Accepting this point of view, they could think, means never having to say you are sorry. The theologian Dietrich Bonhoeffer coined the phrase "cheap grace" to denigrate this obscene interpretation of the New Testament.[25] But the notion of cheap grace appeals to many. A large sample of university student parents were asked to react to, "If we have faith in Jesus, accepting him as our personal savior and asking forgiveness of our sins, we will be saved, no matter what kind of life we live afterwards." Forty-two percent of the evangelicals in the sample agreed. That is a lot.

HOW IMPORTANT IS THEIR RELIGION
TO EVANGELICALS?

Evangelicals believe the Bible is the revealed word of God, the supernatu-
ral being who created the vast universe and who is going to decide one day
whether they will henceforth have an eternity of happiness or the joylessness
of the dark side. And the Bible is the place where God has written down
what you need to know to go to heaven, so you could know how to get there.
It follows that evangelicals would read the Bible. In fact, they would read
it over and over, looking for things they might have missed and reminding
themselves of things they had forgotten. You can see why they might never
read anything else, but instead always be cramming for "the final" that could
come at any time, if they believe the Bible is what they tell everybody it is.
But consider what happened when a large sample of Canadian parents was
given a list of the 66 Books in the King James Bible and asked how many of
them they had read from beginning to end. Only one out of five high RWA
parents said they had read them all. (We tip our hats in awe to anyone who
plowed his way through the first nine chapters of Chronicles I.) Just as many
had not read any of the Books. On average, evangelicals had only read about
a third of them. Given what they should be doing, can anyone seriously say
that most of them really believed the Bible is God's all-important message
to them? Most of them had never read it even once.

Perhaps one can better gauge the importance of their religion to evangelicals by toting up how much their lives reflect the teachings of Jesus.
Let us consider ten possibilities: (1) People who take Jesus' story of the
Good Samaritan to heart should be among the least prejudiced around. (2)
Those who understand Jesus's forgiveness should be less mean-spirited than
average. (3) Readers of the Gospels should realize how much hypocrites in-
furiated Jesus and so would demonstrate outstanding integrity.[26] (4) People
who realize Jesus's love for social outcasts would be terrifically accepting of
those who are different. (5) How many walls did Jesus build to keep "un-

desirables" away? (6) People who realize the extraordinary extent to which Jesus was "his own man" would be less conforming than most. (7) Bible readers who know Jesus's words about how hard it is for a rich man to get to heaven would have no interest in becoming wealthy. (8) Those who follow Jesus would not submit to unjust authority but challenge it. (9) Familiarity with the Gospels would inform one that Jesus had absolutely no time for big showy displays of virtue and self-righteousness. And (10) people devoted to Jesus would not join "Posses" like the one that came to Gethsemane to arrest him. Does it seem, by this accounting, that many Evangelicals have accepted Jesus's invitation, "Come follow me?"

There may be a deep, deep, reason why many evangelicals find it hard to make a commitment to the message of the Gospels. Although they will deny it, deny it a second time, and then a third, many of them do not really, totally, believe in God. Altemeyer studied this using an analogy from research on hypnosis involving a Hidden Observer—a fictional alterego who admits that one's public statements when hypnotized (e.g., "I am a chicken") are just pretend. He asked his students in a very private survey to let their Hidden Observers say whether they had doubts about the existence of God. A third of the high RWA students checked an alternative that read, "Yes, (s)he has secret doubts which (s)he has kept strictly to herself/himself that this is really true." Another 20 percent said they had such doubts, but at least one other person knew about them. That adds up to 53 percent of the high RWAs, almost all of whom would have been "highly religious." But you would never guess these doubts existed from what they almost always publicly proclaim about their beliefs.

THE SOLUTION TO THE MYSTERY

So why did the greater religiousness of evangelicals not keep them from embracing Donald Trump? Because for a great many of them, despite all the fuss and bother and appearances, their religion is simply not important. Their religious commitment, like the person they think they are, does not exist in significant ways. When Donald Trump came along, resplendent in moral shortcomings but promising the moon, evangelicals had little difficulty setting aside their supposed beliefs and supporting him. In fact, this was their S.O.P. They had been setting those beliefs aside 167 hours a week for most of their lives. Con men know that the easiest people to fool are the people who persistently fool themselves. This reality is an amazingly simple answer, yet when you stand back from it, it also is simply amazing. Luke 4 says that old Devil offered Jesus the deal of a lifetime if Jesus would just fall down and worship him. The man from Galilee reportedly replied, "Get thee behind me, Satan." In contrast, when Donald Trump, a man wallowing in the Biblical cardinal sins, made evangelicals the same offer for the same low, low price, millions of them fell to their knees.

However, let us extend some charity to these high RWAs who are bowed down to Donald Trump. Remember, they are frightened, and they have been frightened for most of their lives, notwithstanding their efforts to hide that fear. Living in fear can deeply affect how you perceive the world. Furthermore, they were raised to copy the beliefs of the "proper authorities" in their lives. Independent thinking may have been punished, so they are not very good at it. Like many animals that are prey for carnivores, they find safety by being in a herd whose prime directives are follow the leader and stick together. If you, the reader, realize the world is not as dangerous a place as some see it, if you are good at figuring things out on your own, if you can stand alone when your conscience says you have to, please realize how lucky you are. And before you fall into the trap of self-righteousness that is always just one step away, realize also that a lot of research shows you and almost everyone else can still be made to do hideous things in the wrong situation.[27]

CHAPTER NINE

"DOUBLE HIGH" AUTHORITARIANS

At the outset, we introduced three kinds of authoritarians. You have met two: social dominators and authoritarian followers, and we have explained their different reasons for helping a demagogue seize total power in a democracy. Now we turn to the third group of authoritarian supporters, persons who score highly on both the Social Dominance Orientation Scale and the Right-Wing Authoritarianism Scale whom we call "Double Highs." You will see in this chapter why these people threaten our democracy more than any other group we have studied.

Persons who score highly on these two measures of authoritarianism would seem to have impulses to both dominate and submit, and be mightily confused. But there are ways it sensibly happens. Someone driven by social dominance could endorse RWA Scale statements like, "Our country desperately needs a mighty leader who will do what has to be done to destroy the radical new ways and sinfulness that are ruining us," by thinking of himself as the mighty leader involved. We think Donald Trump would be a Double High if he honestly answered the two tests, but he is not a dominating submissive, a walking oxymoron. As we have shown, Trump is a very strong dominator who believes in submission by others to him. Other social dominators who have been beaten by the alpha can similarly endorse submission. They have power as the leader's lieutenants and sergeants and enjoy exerting it. It is in their interest that everybody else submit, so they score highly on the RWA Scale as well.

High RWAs in turn may have little desire for personal domination, but they and social dominators who also have little personal power may identify with a group that does. These numerous foot soldiers can believe strongly in their group's dominance in society and at the same time believe that they, along with almost everybody else, should submit to the leaders of their group. While these different paths to becoming a Double High exist, not many people seem to have walked down them as such folks have been hard to find in past research.[1] Only forty-two turned up in a large (N=638) 2005 Canadian parent study, which fits in well with previous American rates. But as unusual as Double Highs were, you could not help noticing them. For one thing, they uniquely bundled the worst traits of the two kinds of authoritarians. Take dogmatism, which high RWAs have by the bucketful, while high SDOs can carry theirs in a cup because they do not care about creeds and philosophies enough to be dogmatic about them. But Double Highs need a bucket. High RWAs, in turn, are not power-mad or amoral deceitful manipulators, but high SDOs are and so are Double Highs. High SDOs do not effervesce with religious fundamentalism and religious ethnocentrism, but Double Highs tend to, like high RWAs. So, like an unfortunate child who has his father's alligator skin and bowlegs plus his mother's bad hearing and poor digestion, Double Highs generally carry with them the worst features of high SDOs and high RWAs. You can say about high RWAs, for example, they may be dogmatic, but at least they are not power-mad. But with Double Highs, they tend to be both. And this spells real trouble.

And it gets worse. If both high SDOs and high RWAs have the same tendency, Double Highs have it supersized. Thus, we noted in previous chapters that both high SDOs and high RWAs piled up big scores on prejudice scales. But Double Highs racked up the biggest numbers of all in study after study. They apparently have the social dominator's desire to have white people rule an unfair society and fear of "the other" and self-righteous-ness found in high RWAs. These two helpings of prejudice steroids shoot them faster, higher, and stronger when it comes to prejudging others than you find with any other group studied so far, placing them atop the med-als podium in the Prejudice Olympics. Double Highs also combine SDO and RWA tendencies; when it comes to political party preference, they are hard right conservatives.[2] Similarly, both high SDOs and high RWAs score highly on a Militia Scale developed after the Oklahoma City bombing that measures belief in the conspiracy theory that the country is being taken over by Jews and Communists through the United Nations. But Double Highs score highest of all and agree that armed resistance will probably be needed to fight plots to take away citizens' firearms.

You may now be thinking, "Thank God there aren't very many of these power-mad, raging, fearful, self-righteous, dominating, amoral, dogmatic discriminators around!" But like certain spices in a stew, a little Double High goes a long way in a crowd of authoritarian followers, which became clear in a series of simulation experiments designed to see what happened when authoritarians ruled the earth.

THE GLOBAL CHANGE GAME EXPERIMENTS

What would happen if everyone in the world was a low RWA? Or if the planet were stocked with only high RWAs? These questions were pursued in a 1994 experiment using Canadian university students participating in an environmental awareness exercise called the Global Change Game. The game places the fate of the earth in the hands of about sixty participants for the next forty years.[3] The players are assigned to different sections of the world on a big map that covers a gym floor, according to the real population of their region. There are only a handful of North American citizens and a lot of Chinese citizens. Each region has its own set of economic, health, and environmental problems to deal with, and a leader who becomes such simply by volunteering for the job at the beginning of the exercise. The leaders can leave their region and meet with other leaders to make deals, try to solve global problems together, and make threats if they so wish that can lead to war. Back home, the citizens of each region study their situation and make recommendations about how to use their resources to improve their lives. The problems and assets given the players in each region are realistic. Some regions are much more blessed than others, but they are all riding on the same rock around the sun.

The Low RWA World. One evening, sixty-seven low RWAs, drawn from more than twenty sections of their university's introductory psychology course in which they had earlier answered the RWA scale, played the game for three hours. They had been invited to participate, they were told, through a random draw of more than twenty-six hundred intro students. They were assigned to ten different regions within the constraint that there be about as many women as men in each region. Seven men and three women stood up and volunteered to be leaders when the simulation began. Right away, the leader of the Pacific Rim called a meeting of all the "elites" on the "Island Paradise of Tasmania," where they agreed to meet again any time there was a global problem that needed cooperative action. Meanwhile most of the regions independently reduced their military spending and invested in health, education, and economic development. Elites negotiated mutually beneficial deals, and most of the regions made headway solving their problems in sustainable ways. An hour into the simulation, its administrators announced that the ozone layer was seriously diminished and some of the players were in danger of "dying" from skin cancer. It would affect everyone and would take a lot of money to fix. The elites met on Tasmania and successfully negotiated how much each region would pay, with the richest paying the most, and the crisis was averted.

It became clear however that the Third World regions would not be able to solve their problems without a lot of help. Europe gave some assistance, but the four North American players literally turned their backs on the rest of the world as they sat on the gym floor. A global summit was called to increase aid, which the North American elite declined to attend until he was dragged to Tasmania by other elites. Even then, he would not contribute to save players in Africa and India who were about to die. The students tried to control population growth, but their efforts fell short. After forty years had passed and the exercise ended, 8.7 billion people inhabited the earth (up from 5.5 billion at the start). But the Lows were able to provide for almost all through international cooperation, demilitarizing, and sustainable economic development. There had been no wars or threats of war. The North American elite raised the subject of attacking other regions, but his fellow North Americans told him to forget it. The Third World lost some 400 million citizens to starvation and disease—no laughing matter. But the administrators of the simulation—who were not told how the students had been picked or the purpose of the experiment—agreed it was one of the most successful runs they had seen over several years.

The High RWA World. The next night, sixty-eight high RWAs played the same game in the same place, run by the same administrators in exactly the same manner with the same rules and procedures that had been used with the low RWAs. On this night, however, only males rose to their feet and made themselves elites. The game had hardly started when the elite from the Middle East tried to double the price of oil. Then Russia began beating its ploughshares into swords, built a strong conventional army, and invaded North America. North America launched nuclear weapons to repel the invaders, and a full nuclear exchange ensued. The administrators turned out most of the lights in the gym and explained the probable consequences of a nuclear holocaust. All of the human population (7.4 billion by that point) was declared dead, along with most other forms of life. They then gave the players a second chance, restarting the game two years before the war broke out. But the Russia region rebuilt its large army, attacked China, and 400 million died in the war that followed. The Middle East elite called for a "United Nations" meeting to handle this and future crises, but the response was underwhelming.

The ozone layer crisis was announced but inspired only piecemeal reactions. Europe lowered its atmospheric emissions and loaned money to underdeveloped regions to do the same. But no one else did anything, and the ozone layer was largely destroyed with subsequent loss of life for the rest of the simulation. Meanwhile the earth's population was growing by leaps and bounds because the high RWAs were unwilling to invest in birth control measures. They also pursued fast-buck economic goals that cost them dearly in the long run, such as planting just one kind of tree because it was (temporarily) very profitable. Catastrophe overwhelmed the Third World, with hundreds of millions dying from inadequate food supplies and poor medical treatment. But their elites gave their regions' meager resources to the leader of the Middle East to be included in a confederacy he was organizing. Other regions formed a competing confederacy, and the two camps increased their arms and threatened each other with war. Realizing what a nuclear war would produce, both sides settled for an uneasy stalemate. By the end of the forty-year simulation, 1.7 billion people had died from starvation and disease. Add in the 400 million who perished in the Russia-China war, and the death toll rose to 2.1 billion. Recalling that the whole population of the earth had already died once during the nuclear war, you must give the high RWAs an F in world management. Maybe an F minus.[4]

The 1998 Global Change Game: Participants in the 1994 Global Change Game experiment had been chosen by their scores on the RWA Scale. The SDO Scale was not used in the selection process because it was still under development at Stanford. But once its significance became apparent one could see that social dominance might have played a big role in the disastrous high RWA game in 1994, as some of the sixty-eight high RWAs might have been Double Highs. Thus, the high RWA part of the experiment was repeated in 1998, with the world being inhabited entirely by persons who had scored highly on the Right-Wing Authoritarianism Scale.[5] However manipulation of the sign-up booklets for the "randomly chosen" students for the first night kept out everybody who had scored highly on the Social Dominance Orientation Scale. On the second night, however, there were seven Double Highs in the mix.

A World of Just High RWAs. When the simulation with no Double Highs began, none of the fifty-three players (divided into eight regions) wanted to be an Elite. Eventually eight students (including three females) stood up, sometimes being forced up by others more determined than they to be followers. But when the simulation began, the elites stayed with their groups, instead of roaming the planet looking for deals that would bring their regions resources they needed. The three women elites went to the man serving as elite in rich North America and tried to get some aid from him. He refused, and that was the end of interregion bargaining for the night. The students sat on eight "islands" and tried to solve their problems in isolation from the rest of the world. Sometimes when a "foreigner" (as they called her) came over to talk with a region, they told her to "Go away."

Then, when the ozone layer crisis occurred, a couple of the players looked over their shoulders and asked players on a nearby "island" if they had any ideas. Nobody did, however, and it was concluded the problem was too big to be solved. Skin cancer began to kill millions, then scores of millions around the planet. The regions tried very hard to solve their problems but could not make any headway. They struck the administrators as earnest but unimaginative. As well they did nothing about birth control and became swamped by the next generation whom they could not feed, much less find jobs and medical care for. Europe and North America made charitable contributions to the Third World regions, but it was not enough. A thick fog of gloom and despair covered most of the earth as the players sat on the gym floor, glumly resigned to failure. Disaster ravaged the earth in the form of two of the Four Horsemen of the Apocalypse: Famine and Death. What about the other two horsemen, War and Conquest? They never got out of the paddock. No one uttered the slightest threat. But almost all the regions kept the military forces they had been given at the start of the simulation. They seemed to have a "You don't bother us, and we won't bother you" attitude toward the rest of the world, but they husbanded some of their desperately needed resources for weapons and armies because of fear someone might sometime bother them. By the time forty years had passed, 1.9 billion people had died, which the facilitators thought was a record for a non-war version of the game. It was startling to watch. Here were dozens of high RWAs, divided arbitrarily into groups but surrounded by people just like themselves, and in every group the profound ethnocentrism of the members made them turn their backs on everyone else. Each one of them—thus all—had built a wall.

High RWAs Including a Few Double Highs. The next night, fifty-five new high RWAs showed up for their appointment with destiny. Seven of them, all males, had also placed in the upper quarter of the SDO Scale distribution, and they were assigned to different regions of the earth. Care was taken to always have at least one other man in each region so none of the Double Highs would become leader just because he was the only male in a group of high RWA females who wanted no part of leadership. Four of the seven Double Highs leapt to their feet when the facilitators asked for volunteers to be elites. Two of the remaining three found ways to take over their groups on the sly. One made himself his elite's assistant, and the other elites quickly found he was the person they had to negotiate with. The other Double High led a rebellion "at home," which required their elite to bring all proposed moves to them for approval. The seventh elite, located in Latin America, was as quiet as a mouse during the exercise. When the simulation started it was as if the bell had opened a trading session on the New York Stock Exchange floor, as one of the administrators put it. A constant buzz of negotiations could be heard as elites visited one another, sometimes in groups of two or three, trying to get the best deals they could with the resources they controlled. The winners enhanced their regions, and the losers lost ground.

When the ozone layer crisis was announced, the elites met to deal with it. They understood the problem required a worldwide fix, but the rich regions (who were identified as causing most of the ozone problem) refused to pay as much as the poor nations thought appropriate, and nobody put in a penny. Instead, some of the regions began building up their armies, and military threats became part of economic negotiations. A lot of bullying appeared. The Oceania elite bought nuclear weapons and declared war on vastly out-gunned India. Getting no help from others, India surrendered and gave most of its resources to Oceania as tribute. The victorious elite, who had not asked his region-aires if they wanted to venture down this path, brought home the bacon and used it to sell the slogan that "War is good." Few of his cohorts wanted to continue with this approach, but none of them took the lead in stopping him. So, he declared war on Africa and Latin America. At this point, the North American elite offered protection from Oceania to anyone who would pay for it, and the earth divided into two camps that bought tons of nuclear weapons. The facilitators expected an all-out nuclear war to begin just as the forty-year time limit for the simulation expired. The ozone layer was destroyed once again, and for a third time, the high RWAs had done nothing about population control. The bullying of weaker regions and the militarization of the world toward the end of the simulation also took their tolls. Altogether 1.6 billion people died. And everybody might have died had there been another year.

Overall, the three simulations that used high RWA subjects showed how badly they perform as stewards of the earth. They appeared ill-equipped to act cooperatively to solve problems, even with people just like themselves. Once they were given a specific identity, their ethnocentrism seemed to surge through their bones, and they wanted as little to do with "foreigners" as possible. In a world that rewarded intergroup cooperation, their "nationalism" locked them into solitary confinement and threw away the key. It was especially ironic because while they probably assumed the people in the other groups would be different from them in important ways, the gym was full of other high RWAs.

These simulations provide no comfort regarding the democratic skills of high SDOs, high RWAs, and Double Highs, and two other simulation experiments support this conclusion. Canadian researchers led by Leanne S. Son Hing put high and low SDO and high and low RWA students on two-person teams (one a boss, the other her subordinate) tasked with making a corporate decision that could inflict severe damage on the environment. High SDO bosses usually wanted a high profit outcome even if it damaged the environment. Low RWA subordinates usually fought this decision, but high RWA subordinates went along with it and ever praised their boss to the administrators. The researchers called the combination of a high SDO superior and a high RWA underling "the lethal union" because it was most likely to act unethically.[6]

The other simulation sprang from the creative mind of Gerry Sande of the University of Manitoba, who designed a 1987 experiment in which five-man teams of low RWAs and five-man teams of high RWAs played the role of NATO in a European war-games setting.[7] The simulation opened with the Warsaw Pact making a couple of ambiguous moves (e.g., withdrawing troops from border regions, which appears to be a peaceful gesture, but, it was pointed out, could be masking a redeployment for an imminent invasion). Unbeknownst to the subjects, the administrator played the opposing Warsaw Pact, and whatever NATO did, the Warsaw Pact did back double. So, if NATO made a threatening move in response to the opening scenario, the "dirty Commies" answered with military threats twice as powerful. But if NATO made a peaceful move, the Warsaw Pact disarmed twice as much. Each NATO team, fighting itself in a mirror, created its future. The high RWA teams almost always thought the opening moves signaled evil intent, and so made threats in response. High RWAs scare easily. When the Warsaw Pact responded with twice as much threat, that confirmed the highs' interpretation, and off they went precipitating a major crisis. By the time the simulation ended the world was usually on the brink of all-out nuclear war. Low RWAs almost always reacted calmly to the ambiguous opening, and when nothing happened, they often made a peaceful move, which was reciprocated by the Warsaw Pact, and large-scale disarmament followed.

The study predated the Social Dominance Scale, so it is unknown if a Double High sometimes landed in a high RWA group and channeled the fear within them into aggressiveness. But the occasional presence of Double Highs can explain the results of a follow-up experiment. This time the NATO teams were told they had a perfect "Star Wars" missile defense system that would guarantee them victory in any nuclear war, and the Warsaw Pact knew it. So, if push came to shove came to firing off the ICBMs, they couldn't get hurt. You would think that high RWAs would be less inclined to make threats when they had nothing to fear, and about half the high RWA groups showed almost no aggression at all—in contrast to the previous study. But the other high RWA groups became belligerent right from the start. "We wanted them to realize we could wipe them out at any time," wrote one bellicose student afterward. "We had all the power, and we wanted them to kiss our asses," wrote another. That smacks of "Double High talk." Since the Warsaw Pact met big threats with even bigger threats in this second experiment, things quickly got out of hand.[8]

RWA SCALE SCORES AMONG STATE LAWMAKERS

Almost all the research on the RWA Scale reported up to now was conducted on North American university students and their parents.[*] A

---

[*]   This is not to say these are the only studies relating to RWAs. Study of RWAs, not to mention SDOs and other scales we have mentioned, have been conducted widely in the United States, and elsewhere in the world, and affirm the findings presented.

quite different population was sampled beginning in 1983 when North American lawmakers were asked to complete surveys "on a variety of social issues." These studies help explain another perplexing mystery of Trump's presidency: why nearly all the Republicans in Congress have at best done nothing, and in a few cases (for example, Senate Majority Leader Mitch McConnell) jumped in with both feet to help Donald Trump stomp American democracy to death. This first American legislator study was undertaken in 1986 when state Senate members in California, Connecticut, Minnesota, and Mississippi were asked, through mailings to the state capitols, to anonymously answer the RWA scale.[8] No Connecticut Democrat and only one Mississippi Republican replied. In the two states where returns proved more substantial, California and Minnesota, Republicans scored higher than Democrats.[9]

SUBMISSIVE LAWMAKERS?

Some of the senators posted very high marks on the RWA Scale, which raises the question: Why would legislators score highly on a measure of authoritarian submission? Are they not among the established authorities that high RWAs are supposed to be yearning to submit to? Yes. But suppose you became a lawmaker in the first place because you are a high social dominator dedicating yourself to, hmmm, yourself by becoming one of the most powerful people in society. If you are asked in a variety of ways on a survey, "Should people submit to the established authorities?" would you not strongly agree that they should, not because you intend to do much submitting yourself, but because, as was presented earlier with Double Highs, you want people to submit to you? If so, a lawmaker's high score on the RWA Scale would probably reflect a social dominance orientation, not necessarily that of an authoritarian follower. Later evidence upholds this interpretation.

Between 1990 and 1993 legislators in nearly all the other states answered the RWA Scale and other material in eight different studies.[10] Altogether, 4,741 lawmakers were approached, and 1,233 of them (26 percent) responded. This is eight to ten times the response rate that nationwide polls typically obtain, but the self-selection rate still means the results might be biased. However, the findings were strongest in the legislatures that had the highest response rates, so the results would likely have been a bit brawnier, not weaker, had more politicians answered. The lawmakers answered anonymously, except at the end they were asked whether they were Democrats or Republicans. The surveys were discreetly coded to indicate whether they had been sent to a Democrat or Republican, and in every case but one self-identification matched this designation.

LEVELS OF RWA SCALE SCORES IN THE STATE CAPITALS

An astounding picture appeared as the answers were tabulated, as you can see in Figure 1 below. Republicans in every legislature save one scored higher on the RWA Scale as a group than did Democrats. The averages of the scores obtained are shown in Figure 1, which graphically illustrates the clustering of Democrats as low RWAs and Republicans as high RWAs. You can immediately see that the Democrats produced an enormous range of caucus scores, thanks to outliers in Southern states, but in general they landed below the midpoint (100) on the scale. The Republicans, with two exceptions (the Connecticut House and Senate) laid down much higher scores, above 100, and showed much greater uniformity.

Figure 1. Mean Scores on the RWA Scale by Various State Caucuses

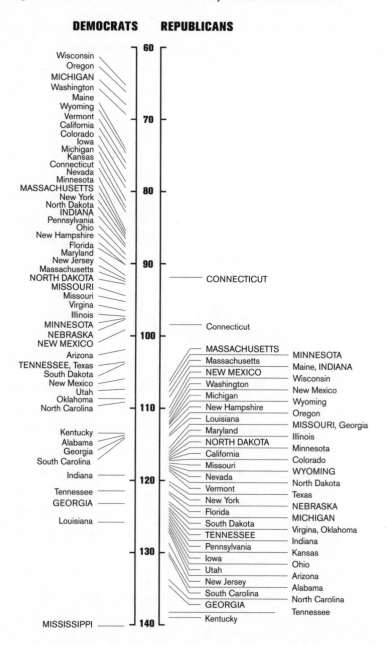

The sample includes 549 Republican legislators and 682 Democrats. Scores from upper chambers are presented in larger print (e.g., CONNECTICUT versus Connecticut). No Connecticut Democratic senator and only one Mississippi Republican and one Wyoming Democratic senator answered, and hence no scores are given for those caucuses.

Even though this is another study you probably never heard of, it would appear to be a rather revealing investigation of extremely important people in our country. The lawmakers were not making a speech, endorsing a proposal, or casting a vote. They were answering anonymously a survey on social attitudes, which they probably did not know measures a politically important aspect of their personality, namely how strongly they embraced democracy, or were ready to sell it out to some autocrat. They were personally anonymous, completely hidden while answering the items, and their unmassaged answers probably give us a clearer view of who they are than you are going to get in any other way—unless you work for one of them. When else have you ever gotten that straight a look at who these politicians are? Well, take a good look.

ADDITIONAL FINDINGS AMONG THE LEGISLATORS

In each of these studies, the RWA Scale was followed by a small number of other statements measuring other things. It was found that, compared to low RWA lawmakers, high RWAs:

- Considered equality an unimportant value in guiding the country.
- Rejected a law raising taxes on the rich while lowering them on the poor.
- Favored extending capital punishment to more crimes.
- Wanted to forbid news programs broadcasting from cities (such as Baghdad) that the United States was bombing.

- Opposed gun control laws.
- Favored teaching Christianity in public schools.
- Scored high in dogmatism.
- Opposed affirmative action laws.
- Favored giving police more power to search, arrest, and interrogate suspects.
- Favored outlawing the Communist Party.
- Opposed the Equal Rights Amendment.
- Favored placing more restrictions on abortion than Roe vs. Wade.
- Had conservative economic philosophies.
- Favored restricting anti-war protests so they would have little impact.
- Saw the USA as uniformly the good guys and the USSR as the bad guys.
- Opposed laws guaranteeing equal rights for homosexual people.
- Showed racial and ethnic prejudice.

None of these findings is going to knock you off your horse if you have been paying any attention to the goings-on down at the state capitol, but almost every one of them connects to material in chapters Five through Eight, from the dissing of equality through the "Government Injustices" and "Posse" experiments to the findings about double standards and prejudice. They show that the stark truth about authoritarianism displayed in Figure 1 runs much deeper and wider in the legislatures within the United States than the answers to a personality test. A good many of the people in America elected to write our laws have very little commitment to the form of government they are entrusted to protect. If it were not for the Constitution and the safeguard of the judicial system and other politicians who value freedom and equality, who knows what our laws would be?

LACK OF SOCIAL DOMINANCE DATA ON THE LAWMAKERS

These American lawmaker studies did not collect answers to the Social Dominance Orientation Scale because that test was still being developed at the time. But at least half a dozen of the issues above involve equality, and from poo-pooing equality as a goal of democracy to soul-crushing prejudices it seems clear the high RWA lawmakers would also have scored highly on the SDO Scale. This, in fact, was indicated in two Canadian studies. Members of the Conservative Party in the Alberta Legislature scored highly on SDO items at the end of the survey, as did members of Parliament who belonged to the conservative Reform Party in the national House of Commons. The latter also scored highly on a series of items written to measure prejudice.[11] All of the evidence thus agrees that the caucuses of "conservative" parties in North American legislatures are not only thick with persons who score highly on the Right-Wing Authoritarianism Scale, but also that many if not most of these lawmakers are also high Social Dominators. That makes them the super authoritarian, super prejudiced, super dangerous people this chapter is about: Double Highs.

Reflect on what this information about state lawmakers means. These people write our laws. Think what they would do if they had no constitutional restrictions enforced by the courts. Consider for example one of the items from the RWA Scale that the 1,233 American lawmakers encountered: "Once our government leaders and the authorities condemn the dangerous elements in our society, it will be the duty of every patriotic citizen to help stomp out the rot that is poisoning our country from within." It is a preposterous statement. It is practically a Nazi cheer. It is the six Posse questions rolled into one. You should be pleased to learn that most (66 percent) of the responding legislators disagreed with this sentiment, usually strongly and some very strongly. Yet 8 percent said they were neutral or did not answer it. Strikingly, the other 26 percent, nearly all of them Republicans, said they agreed with the notion that the public should help destroy whatever "dangerous element" they, the lawmakers, decided to get rid of. That is halfway to a majority.

WHAT HAS HAPPENED TO THE REPUBLICAN PARTY?

One can conclude, with the backing of this study of more than five hundred of the highest-ranking leaders of the GOP, that the Republican Party had become the Authoritarian Party by the mid-1990s. They scored highly on the RWA Scale, looked like they would be social dominators, and in every respect that was tested showed beliefs and attitudes associated with authoritarians. And the label fit coast to coast; there weren't any pockets of low RWA Republican legislators anywhere in the United States outside Connecticut.[12] That seems to be a terrifically damning conclusion. Perhaps it would be worse if they turned out to be drug kingpins or spies for foreign powers. To any student of authoritarianism, however, this is very, very bad.

If you worked for a Republican public relations firm, what is the first thing you would say about super-embarrassing Figure 1? Probably, "These studies are terribly outdated. The Republican Party has changed a lot since then." Yes, it has, but it has almost certainly gotten *more* authoritarian over time, not less. When these surveys were answered, to reprise material from chapter 8, the Christian Coalition had been working for (and on) the Republican Party for a decade. In the years after these studies Pat Robertson's grassroots organizations took over most of the state GOP committees and had hundreds of their favorites elected to office. Moderate Republican office holders began disappearing across America. This abandonment-of-the-middle gained momentum in 1994 when Newt Gingrich ended the tradition of bipartisan cooperation between Republicans and Democrats in the House of Representatives. He had long advocated polarizing politics, telling a group of young Republican hopefuls in 1978, "One of the great problems we have in the Republican Party is that we don't encourage you to be nasty. If Republicans were to rise from the ashes, they would have to learn to 'raise hell,' to stop being so 'nice,' to realize that politics was, above all, a cut-throat 'war for power'—and to start acting like it."[13] Gingrich led his kind of Republicans, Double Highs being sent to Washington by an increasingly authoritarian GOP base, in partisan wars and obstructionism that have made Americans sick of Congress and led presidents to assuming greater powers.[14] Karl Rove then enticed religious leaders to bring millions of white Evangelicals into the fold in 2000. These Republicans, far less religious than they might be, brought not just social conservative views on abortion and gay rights with them, but also a great deal of authoritarianism and its ugly sidecar companion, prejudice. When joined by "the forgotten" in 2016, the transformation of the GOP from a conservative political party to an authoritarian one with precious little connection to its past was complete. So one can readily believe that if one collected authoritarianism scores today in state legislatures, the Congress, the Republican National Committee, and the White House, the Republicans would be squeezed together even further to the right on Figure 1, crowded together toward the end of the political diving board, getting ready to plunge into the deep, dark waters below, taking the nation down with them.

CHAPTER TEN

NATIONAL SURVEY ON AUTHORITARIANISM

While we know only what others have revealed about Donald Trump's background, we believe the material set forth in Chapters 2 through 4 explains his authoritarianism. We furthermore believe that most of the people in his "impossible to understand" base can be understood, given the research on authoritarian supporters that has accumulated over the years. However, almost all these studies used samples drawn from limited populations, most of them not even American. Accordingly, you may rightly wonder: What's the evidence that these 'theories' apply to American voters the way these fellows say it does? It's a good question. We wondered about it too. Now we have the answer. Solid evidence says the explanations are correct.

In 2018 Patrick Murray, the director of the Monmouth University Polling Institute in West Long Branch, New Jersey, offered to assist us with this project by collecting answers to our tests from a nationwide sample of American voters.[1] Given the professionalism and reputation of the Monmouth operation, we were delighted.[2] A survey using so many complete scales and ancillary items had never been conducted with a national sample before.[3] In synopsis, after a trial run with a sample of New Jersey residents in May 2019, nearly a thousand registered voters across America answered five personality tests in late October and early November online, also providing information about themselves and their political preferences. Besides the Social Dominance Orientation and Right-Wing Authoritarianism Scales, they were asked the four child-rearing questions described in appendix I and the Religious Fundamentalism Scale mentioned in chapter 8. In addition, they responded to twenty-four statements (also found in appendix V) designed to measure ethnocentric prejudice among whites against racial and ethnic minorities, as well as belief in white supremacy. For example, we sought −4 to +4 responses to statements such as: "There are entirely too many people from the wrong places getting into the United States now." "White people are the major victims of discrimination in the United States. The government is on everybody else's side but theirs." "There's no way a religion like Islam that produces so many terrorists is as good a religion as Christianity is." "Instead of complaining and protesting all the time, African Americans should be grateful for how good they have it compared to where they came from." And, "Certain races of people do NOT have the natural intelligence and 'get up and go' of the white race."

A fair-minded person could argue that items like "too many people from the wrong places" come directly out of Donald Trump's speeches and may not reflect personal prejudice but rather a general support of the president. But that statement comes from a prejudice scale developed in 1979 to measure ethnocentrism in Canada. Xenophobia has long been an aspect of prejudice, found around the world. And many of the prejudice items in our survey included classic stereotypes that were part of prejudiced thinking before any of us was born, such as black people are naturally violent; Jews secretly control the world's economy; and Latinxs are lazy, promiscuous, and irresponsible. If participants who agreed with "too many people from the wrong places" also agreed with these well-known indicators of prejudice (and they do), the label of "prejudiced" is accurate.

We purposely included in our Monmouth sample more people who had voted Republican in the past than was indicated by census data because those were the people we were trying to understand.[4] Nevertheless, most of our 990 respondents, which included independents as well as Democrats and Republicans, had a negative opinion of Trump's performance as president, which has been true in almost every poll taken since Trump took office. The people who dislike him nowadays almost always loathe him, that is, they "strongly disapprove" of him rather than "somewhat disapprove." This proved true in the Monmouth sample too. Past Republican supporters, we found, usually loved Trump but his overall support has gotten softer over time, with many of his backers these days merely "Somewhat" rather than "Strongly" approving of him. We also found that very few people had no opinion of the man, which you can discover for yourself just by walking into a saloon or a quilting bee and shouting out, "What about President Trump?" Go ahead, see what happens.

We put our key conclusions about Trump's base to the acid test in this survey, hoping it would tell us if we were wrong about six key load-bearing issues, namely (1) are Trump's supporters highly authoritarian, (2) are they highly prejudiced, (3) how deeply embedded is authoritarianism in the United States today, (4) can most prejudice be explained by just authoritarianism, (5) are there many Double High authoritarians in the United States, and (6) have we correctly identified the two pillars of Trump's base? In the following pages we have provided the six clear answers that emerged with the Monmouth Institute survey.

QUESTION ONE: Are Trump's Supporters Highly Authoritarian? ANSWER: Are They Ever!

Happily, for our explanation, but most unhappily for the country, the poll said yes. As predicted, the more people supported Donald Trump, the more they were likely to be high RWAs. Figure 1 shows the findings with the RWA Scale. (The results for the Social Dominance Orientation Scale are quite similar, just a little less dramatic.) Figure 1 breaks down this relationship. The overwhelming majority of low RWAs disapproved of Trump, almost always "strongly." He is anathema to low RWAs. On the other hand, high RWAs simply cannot get enough of the guy. Almost all of them approved of his performance, usually strongly.

Figure 1. How Authoritarian Are Donald Trump's Supporters?

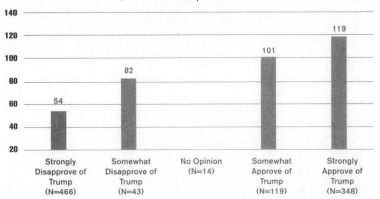

(N = All 990 Respondent)

Note: The items were scored on a 1–9 basis, and there are 20 items. So, the lowest possible score is 20, and the highest is 180. Actual scores ran from 20 to 176. The mean for "No Opinion" is not shown because so few people chose that category.

QUESTION TWO: Are Trump's Supporters Highly Prejudiced?
ANSWER: Very Much So.

Figure 2 displays the prejudice scores compiled by the white people in our survey in terms of their support of President Trump. You can see that it greatly resembles Figure 1. Compared with other Americans, Trump's white supporters are, as a group, highly prejudiced. The difference naturally sizzled most on items that reflect Trump's rhetoric, but it showed up on every single statement in the twenty-four-item inquiry. Trump supporters were prejudiced from A to Z. With a great deal of preliminary help from the Republican Party, and as predicted in chapters 5 and 6, Trump has attracted the most prejudiced white people in America like a magnet attracts metal filings. Furthermore, no one can whitewash the relationship by claiming it involves only a few rotten apples who are making everybody else look bad. Nearly the whole barrel is significantly more prejudiced than average. And the people who support Trump the strongest, the people who likely attended his rallies and are most active on his behalf, tend to be the most prejudiced of all. White voters who oppose him, on the other hand, are much less prejudiced than average, especially those who strongly oppose him. They would, by and large, probably be the white Americans who joined Black Americans in protesting George Floyd's murder in Minneapolis in late May 2020.

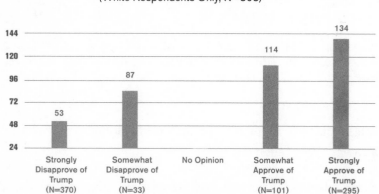

Figure 2. How Prejudiced Are Donald Trump's Supporters?

(White Respondents Only, N=808)

Note: The items were scored on a 1–9 basis, and there are 24 items. So, the lowest possible score is 24, and the highest is 216. Actual scores ran from 24 to 214. The mean for "No Opinion" is not shown because so few people chose that category.

QUESTION THREE: Can Most Prejudice Be Explained by
Authoritarianism?
ANSWER: Yes, Almost Totally.

Figures 1 and 2 show that whether you are talking about the levels of
authoritarianism, or prejudice, found among Trump's detractors and
supporters, the picture barely flickers. Which, as far as our explanation
goes, amounts to a grand slam homer that clears the bases. The connection
between prejudice and authoritarianism lay at the heart of our analysis of
Trump's supporters, and the survey strongly supported it. How strongly?
The correlation between RWA Scale scores and prejudice equalled .856,
which is as close to perfection (1.00) as you are likely to ever see in social
science. To put it another way, suppose you decided to hold a dance for the
100 most prejudiced white people in your community, along with the 100
most authoritarian ones. (Who knows why you would want to? We do not.)
Would you need to print 200 invitations? No, about 120 should do it, since
most of the people who are one will also be the other. There is about an 80
percent overlap.

Monmouth's polling for us confirms to an incredible degree the earlier
finding by McFarland and Adelson, that "most amazing discovery you never
heard of," that you can explain most prejudice in terms of authoritarianism.[5]
So social scientists have not been crying wolf for all these years. There truly
is a big, very bad wolf at our collective doors, and this metaphoric evil snarls
such intolerance, discrimination, and victimization that it not only injures
its immediate victims, but also shakes our democratic society to its core.
Knowingly or unknowingly, prejudiced people bring into the voting booth
something of even greater danger to everyone's freedom and our country's
very existence: authoritarianism. As we explained in our earlier chapters,
the most prejudiced people in America were likely drawn to Trump because
he told them their prejudices were justified. But they connected with him
and with one another on more than their attitudes toward minorities, for

the showman at the rallies was a megalomaniac and demagogue driven to dominate everyone in the world. He did not campaign on a platform of overthrowing democracy, obviously, but he did sanctify prejudice. And the crowd that responded to his evil message was full of authoritarian supporters yearning for a mighty leader to fight their enemies and protect them.

QUESTION FOUR: How Deeply Embedded is Authoritarianism in America?
ANSWER: It is Deep. And Thick.

Decades of study have established the validity of both the RWA and SDO Scales as measures of authoritarianism. But we wondered, does authoritarianism, so defined, exist *strongly* in the United States? Is it a highly organized, interlocking, cohesive system of attitudes that would show great resistance to change if challenged? Or is it a hit-and-miss, loosely assembled superficial rattletrap of beliefs that would fall apart if at all challenged? The poll answered, "Sisters and brothers, this is almost an *ideology* and will probably survive no matter who calls it out and how often they do so." Responses to the RWA Scale's items went together to a degree never seen in previous studies of ordinary people.[6] The same was true for the SDO measures. The RWA Scale's result particularly caught one's eye because its items are much more diverse. But respondents' beliefs about all its issues proved almost as highly organized as the beliefs in a religion's statement of faith such as the Apostles' Creed, which some people actually do memorize. Nobody emphatically teaches all the specific elements of right-wing authoritarianism to Americans, but many people come to embrace the whole deal, bit for bit, pound for pound. The desire to submit to a strong leader, aggress in his name, and insist that everyone follow your rules is dialed up to intense in some people while being almost totally absent in others. So also, to nearly the same extent, is the belief in one group dominating others, as measured by the SDO Scales.[7]

QUESTION FIVE: Are There Many Double Highs in America? ANSWER: Far More than Anticipated.

The especially troublesome and frightening Double Highs from chapter 9 have been rare in previous social science research because High RWAs have seldom scored highly on the SDO Scale, and vice versa. But they abounded, strikingly, in the survey undertaken by Monmouth for this book. Fourteen percent of the white subjects in the sample—far more than usual—proved to be Double Highs. Maybe so many have always roosted in the United States but remained previously undiscovered. But it could instead be that some people who would have been just social dominators in the past are now scoring high on the RWA measure as well, and some authoritarian submitters are now scoring high on the SDO test. We think both things happened, for the reason Dean exclaimed when he learned of this result: "Trump brings out the worst in people!" Trump has made submission to his mighty leadership more acceptable to some of "the forgotten," who believe he is their ticket to greater dominance. And he has convinced some evangelicals, who basically want to submit to a powerful leader, that they deserve to be superior too. These two kinds of authoritarians have seemingly interacted with each other in cafes and cheered for one another's goals so much at Trump rallies that they have become more alike.

This leads us to the Prejudice Olympics, where Double Highs have always captured the gold in previous studies. They flew to the top of the podium once again in this survey, outpointing the others as the most prejudiced group you could find in the poll. Of the 114 Double Highs, a staggering 112 of them support Trump's performance as president. When we say Donald Trump has largely cornered the market not just on typical authoritarians, but also (and especially) on the particularly dangerous Double Highs, we are making a generalization that has exceptions. In this case two exceptions, out of 114 cases.

Figure 3. "Prejudice Olympics" in Terms of Authoritarianism Scores (White Respondents Only; N=805)

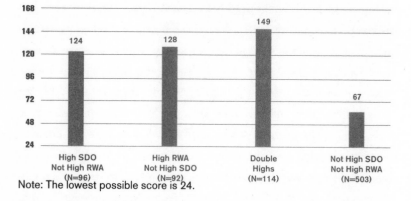

Note: The lowest possible score is 24.

QUESTION SIX: Are the Pillars of Trump's Base Prejudiced Authoritarians?
ANSWER: Definitely.

We have described the pillars of Trump's base as those authoritarians that abound among "the forgotten," and white evangelicals. The Monmouth survey confirmed this explanation.

As we observed in chapter 5, a solid majority (71 percent) of white males with less than a four-year college degree voted for Trump. We proposed these men would tend to be social dominators who believed Trump would champion their collective right, as they saw things, to rule the country. In our poll 73 percent of 157 such men approved of Trump's performance. As a group they were highly prejudiced and highly authoritarian. But contrary to our prediction, there were slightly more high RWAs than high SDOs (45 to 43 percent).

White evangelicals, the other and even larger pillar of Trump's base, comprised 26 percent of the exit poll in 2016 and gave him 80 percent of their votes, which amounted to nearly half of the ballots marked for Trump. We concluded in chapter 8 that Trump appealed to them because he is a prejudiced authoritarian leader, and they are prejudiced authoritarian followers, and in fact, their religion means little to them. The Monmouth Institute survey asked respondents if they would describe themselves as "born-again," "evangelical," or "both." Twenty-six percent of our white participants clicked evangelical, and then 80 percent of these subjects said they approved of Trump's performance (just like the 2016 exit poll had done). These religious Trump supporters are, as predicted, well supplied with both authoritarianism and prejudice, even more so than "the forgotten." Most of the evangelicals are high RWAs, considerably outnumbering the high SDOs in their ranks.

We also had a few "forgotten evangelicals." More specifically, 51 of the men in our survey had a foot in both pillars, so to speak. That is, they were white, undereducated, and said they were evangelical. As you might predict based on past findings on double-pumped authoritarians, they landed among the highest scorers in each group in terms of authoritarianism and prejudice. Nearly half were Double Highs as well, and all supported Trump. This sub-sub-sub-subgroup formed the crème de la hardest crème of Trump's base.

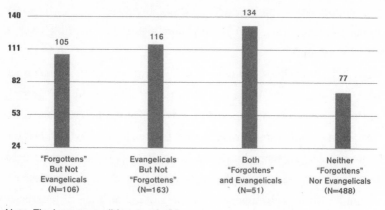

Figure 4. How Prejudiced Are the Pillars of Trump's Base?
(White Respondents Only N=808)

Note: The lowest possible score is 24.

SUMMARY OF FINDINGS ON THE SIX KEY HYPOTHESES

We have charged Trump's political movement as being driven by authoritarianism and prejudice and tested the central issues by requesting the Monmouth University Polling Institute in a completely independent, nationwide survey of registered voters to collect data bearing on the subjects. The verdicts are in. (1) Donald Trump's supporters are, as a group, highly authoritarian compared to most Americans. (2) They are also highly prejudiced compared to most Americans. (3) You can explain the prejudice in Trump's supporters almost entirely by their authoritarianism. (4) Authoritarianism is a strongly organized set of attitudes in America that will prove very difficult to reduce and control. (5) Far more, particularly dangerous, Double High authoritarians exist in the United States than we imagined, with most of them now affiliated with the Republican Party. (6) The pillars of Trump's base, white evangelicals and white undereducated males are highly authoritarian and prejudiced. But even this pithy summary does not really do justice to the survey's major findings, which amount to much more than a line score of going six for six wih six runs scored and six RBIs. (For those of us who still remember, in 2021, what that refers to.) The connections among prejudice, authoritarianism and support for Donald Trump are so strong that no other independent factor can be as important in supporting his reelection.[8] There just is not much left to be explained, which is a highly unusual situation in the social sciences, but that is where the data have taken us. Ask a very complicated question: Who are Trump's staunch supporters? Get a very simple answer: Prejudiced authoritarians, and a few others. How often does that happen?

OTHER IMPORTANT FINDINGS

In addition to the key issues summarized above, we sought to elicit other related information in the Monmouth survey.

Stomping out the rot. Remember what might be called the "Nazi Cheer" mentioned in the study of state legislators in chapter 9? It went like this: "Once our government leaders and the authorities condemn the dangerous elements in our society, it will be the duty of every patriotic citizen to help stomp out the rot that is poisoning our country from within." You will re-call that a third of the lawmakers, overwhelmingly Republicans, agreed with this statement or said they were neutral. We included this item in the Monmouth survey right after the RWA Scale, and most (52 percent) of Trump's supporters said they agreed with it, with another 14 percent saying they were neutral. So, millions of Americans are seemingly primed and waiting for the word to start stomping out "the rot." It will be their duty, they say, to help persecute whomever a vengeful Trump decides to stomp out. We realize it takes some time to get your head around this, because this is not the America people think they live in. But these results tell us most

Trump supporters, willingly or unwittingly, are ready to be part of an East German Stasi-type operation by spying on their neighbors and helping the government oppress whomever it wishes. It appears that if President Trump wanted his very loyal supporters to betray whomever he wanted to persecute he would not have to order it. He would only have to ask, or, more likely, merely suggest it.

Refusing to Accept a 2020 Defeat. Much has been written about the possibility of Trump refusing to accept a loss in 2020. For that reason, we raised the issue in our survey, inquiring about a nightmare scenario that we hope never materializes but which we address further in chapter 12. We asked, "If Donald Trump is defeated in November 2020, (should he) continue to be president if he declares the election was fixed and crooked?" Trump's opponents answered with one voice: "No!" But Trump's supporters proved less likely to side with the Constitution. Only two-thirds of them said no. Fourteen percent outright agreed Trump should declare the election null and void, if he wished, and 19 percent said they were unsure. We believe that Trump could get strong support from his base to stay in power, even if he made even an obviously false claim of electoral wrongdoing.[9]

Ignoring the Constitution. Giving oneself another term in office after losing the election would clearly violate the Constitution and end American democracy. Another item on the survey bluntly posed the issue of overthrowing the legal foundation of our country. It read: "The U.S. Constitution gets in the way of things too much nowadays and should just be ignored when it interferes with taking action on some issue." Based on previous studies on abolishing the Bill of Rights and solid support of Trump when he did try to violate the Constitution, we expected many of Trump's supporters might agree with this. Fortunately, we were wrong. Virtually everyone in the survey sample disagreed with this sentiment, including 96 percent of Trump supporters. So, on this we misjudged Trump's base. But it may just be a case of compartmentalized thinking. In Box A, one finds, "The Constitution must always be followed." But in Box B dwells, "The Constitution can be ignored if that gets you something you really want." We do know that authoritarian followers' thinking is highly compartmentalized and rife with contradictory principles, and they will believe whatever is convenient at the moment. So, we may not be as wrong as we hope we are.

A Trump Self-Pardon. As you would expect, 96 percent of those who have a negative view of Trump's presidency said he could not pardon himself. But most of Trump's supporters said either they were neutral on the issue (32 percent), or that Trump could pardon himself (24 percent). Since that would permanently place him above the law, we can again wonder how many of Trump's supporters really believe the Constitution must be inviolate.

News Sources Preferred by Trump Supporters. We asked our sample to indicate which news source they relied on most from more than thirty possibilities. Forty-six percent of Trump's supporters said it was Fox News, and in second place came One America News at a meager 5 percent. Rupert Murdoch's news network is undoubtedly the loudest voice in the echo chamber that tells Trump's followers almost everything he does is right. Trump's opponents do not have such a dominant influence: 22 percent favored MSNBC, 16 percent relied on CNN, and 13 percent followed the news on NPR.

Where the Independents Stand. The American electorate divides itself into three groups of roughly equal size: Democrats, Republicans, and self-described independents. Unless one of the parties stumbles badly in getting its vote out, independents who go to the polls in 2020 will decide who becomes president, as they did in 2016. In our sample of 990 registered voters, 349 said they were independents. As pollsters often do, we asked them if they leaned more Democrat, more Republican, or neither. A third of them (115) leaned to the left, more (146) leaned to the right, and only 88 said they were straight-up-and-down Independents. The leaners turned out to be almost indistinguishable from those who identified with their preferred party. For example, 98 percent of the left-leaners disapproved of Trump's performance as president, and 95 percent of those disapproved of him strongly. Eighty-four percent of those who leaned Republican approved of Trump, with 67 percent strongly. These match closely the responses of the out-and-out Democrats and Republicans. It therefore seems to us that most people who call themselves independents are significantly attached to the Democrats or the Republicans but prefer to be disassociated for various reasons. Pollsters who combine Democrats with "Lean Democrat" in making their predictions and Republicans with "Lean GOP" seem to be well justified, as they doubtless know from experience.

Figure 5 shows the mean prejudice scores among the white respondents broken down by political party preference, including the differentiation among independents.[10] You will notice that Republicans outnumber Democrats; again, that is because Republicans were oversampled. You will also notice that non-leaning independent-registered voters amount to only a small fraction of the sample. Although small in number, true independents can determine who wins a close election, and their presidential choice is probably more moveable than anybody else's. They likely constitute a sizable chunk of the undecided voters who lead pollsters to an early grave because they make up their minds on election day. And to the extent that the TV ads, et cetera, that we all get sick of during a campaign are intended to persuade voters, they are targeting this small group of straight-up-and-down independents. (Their level of prejudice places them closer to the Republicans than to the Democrats, but remember we oversampled Trump supporters.)

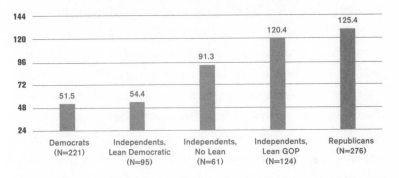

Figure 5. Average Prejudice Scores of Democrats, Independents, and Republicans (White Respondents Only; N=777)

Note: There were 808 white respondents in the sample, but 29 said they favored "another party," and two did not answer the prejudice items.

Comparison with the New Jersey Pilot Study. As we mentioned at the beginning of this chapter, the Monmouth University Polling Institute ran an online pilot study of our survey for us in May 2019 using a sample of 478 New Jersey adults who had participated in an earlier poll for them. The Institute was chiefly testing whether our questions could be asked in an internet setting or if we would get lots of non-responses, skipped scales, and sloppy answering when there was not a human being on the other end of the line recording the responses and available for clarification. The test run, obviously, said "Go ahead. This works very well." Because the May and autumn survey instruments were very similar, we can determine the extent to which the first one "replicated" the second. The overall answer was: "Very strongly." The scales had the same head-banging psychometric properties that showed up in the fall, extremely strong correlations fell in our laps, our expectations about the importance of various factors proved way too understated, a large number of Double Highs, nearly all of them Republicans, turned up as it would later, and so on.

Long-Term Confirmations. The data collected for us by Monmouth confirms and greatly extends the RWA Scale findings of the Libertarian Party quota sample of American adults conducted in 2005[11], as it does previous results with the Social Dominance Scale, as it does the large survey of legislators in nearly all of the states in the United States reported in chapter 9, as it does some forty years of research using diverse samples from Manitoba to Moscow. One got used to trudging through thoroughgoing consistency over the years, but nothing approaches the power to measure and the clarity (and simplicity) of explanation found in these latest results. Without exception, this nationwide study confirmed *every previous finding* put to the test, usually with bust-a-gut, *ffff* exuberance.[12] We also had some expectations about what would happen when we sailed into previously unexplored waters, and these too were usually supported. Still, other hunches have not been put to the real test yet (such as whether high RWAs will back up Trump if he loses the 2020 election and tries to stay in office). We did hypothesize that low RWAs would be better informed than high RWAs about the Ukraine scandal, and that proved wrong.[13] But if all one's predictions about the future turn out to be correct, you probably have not ventured very far or been very imaginative.

CHAPTER ELEVEN

TRUMP'S AUTHORITARIAN ENABLERS

Donald Trump has led an enabled life.* We noted it started with his father Fred, who gave him millions of dollars, bequeathing it faster than Donald could lose it. While Donald takes credit for all his real estate successes, when examined closely there was always someone like a Roy Cohn working behind the scenes getting (or finagling) the tax break or piece of property or solving the union problem that made them happen. It was Mark Burnett who came along after Trump's career-ending string of bankruptcies and created *The Apprentice*, reviving Donald's fading persona into the image of the wildly successful New York real estate mogul that he was not, allowing him to flush out his authoritarian nature for reality television. Successfully playing an authoritarian personality on television appears to have made it easy for Trump to make it his public personality as well. His former enabler and fixer, the attorney who took care of nasty problems (like mistresses who might talk), Michael Cohen, explained under oath to the U.S. Congress that Trump had become the worst version of himself, and reported the reason Trump sought

---

* Note: These enablers are composed of social dominators, authoritarian followers, and Double Highs. Because we have tested none, we cannot say with certainty, but at this point in the book you should be able to have a fair estimation of where each these personalities might fall if they were tested.

the presidency:

> Donald Trump is a man who ran for office to make his brand
> great, not to make our country great. He had no desire or in-
> tention to lead this nation – only to market himself and to
> build his wealth and power. Mr. Trump would often say this
> campaign was going to be the "greatest infomercial in politi-
> cal history." He never expected to win the primary. He never
> expected to win the general election. The campaign – for him
> – was always a marketing opportunity.[1]

When Trump decided to run, he had no staff capable of mounting a national
presidential campaign. All who knew him figured the undertaking would
be nothing but a publicity foray. Trump himself appears to have viewed the
race as a no-lose situation, where if he lost the race, he would have spread
the word about the Trump brand, but if he happened to win, he would only
enhance his brand further as president of the United States. Donald being
all about Donald, always overestimating his talents, he thought it would be
easy to be president, if that happened. The idea of preparing to be president,
or surrounding himself with knowledgeable people, never occurred to him.
It seems no one told him that most presidential candidates are building
their future presidency with their campaign team, most of whom simply
moved on to the White House if they win.

ENABLING THE 2016 PRESIDENTIAL RACE

The remarkable aspect of Trump's presidential campaign, given the fact
he won, was the people he attracted to join his undertaking, his early
political enablers. To say that his campaign team was third-rate would be
a vast overstatement of their qualifications. It was a collection of oddballs

and misfits. All of the qualified people had gone to work for the sixteen candidates Trump would face in the Republican primaries.[*] As these Republican candidates dropped out of the race, many because they were defeated by Trump, none of the campaign professionals associated with these campaigns had any interest in going to work for Trump for two reasons: First, Trump did not reach out to any of them because he did not believe they could be loyal to him and loyalty is his only hiring criteria.[2] Secondly, professionals were not interested in working for Trump because the word had gone out that they would forever be blacklisted by other Republicans if they worked for Trump, so it was a career-ending move if he lost.[3]

Trump turned to his two trusted political advisers, men with whom he had a long association. Trump had worked with Roger Stone since 1980 and David Bossie since 2010. Both Stone and Bossie were well known in political circles as bottom-dwelling political creatures, the worst among the we-play-dirty types. Stone and Bossie were not associated with each other; rather, each had separate relationships with Trump. With a political team which began with Stone and Bossie, Trump telegraphed to the political world he would not be playing by Queensberry Rules.

Roger Stone is a consummate sycophant, something of a dandy in dress, and like Trump he wears a face bronzer. He is a self-proclaimed "political dirty trickster," who at nineteen years of age volunteered in 1972 to do dirty tricks for Nixon's Committee to Re-elect the President and would later work for Nixon after he had resigned from office. Roger wears a tattoo of Nixon between his shoulder blades on his back.[4] Roger joined his college friend Paul Manafort to form a lobbying firm, which worked for

---

[*]   (Listed alphabetically his primary opponents were:) Jeb Bush, Ben Carson, Chris Christie, Ted Cruz, Carly Fiorina, Jim Gilmore, Lindsey Graham, Mike Huckabee, Bobby Jindal, John Kasich, George Pataki, Rand Paul, Rick Perry, Marco Rubio, Rick Santorum and Scott Walker.

many less-than-respectable clients. In recent years, Roger has morphed into a huckster for conspiracy theories, selling ghost-written books to the fools who buy them. His most recent distinction is his conviction for federal felonies of lying to Congress about the Trump campaign's connections with WikiLeaks and threatening to kill another witness for telling the truth, for which he was convicted for lying to, and obstruction of, Congress. At present, Trump has tweeted – in a conspicuously corrupt and criminal fashion if he actually does it – assurances to Stone that he will not go to prison.[5]

Trump's other early political adviser, David Bossie, is a college dropout and a former volunteer fireman, who became notorious as the pit bull of the "vast right-wing conspiracy" that sought to destroy the Clinton presidency, a label which Bossie embraces.[6] Bossie was so over-the-top in his investigation of the Clintons (for example, he doctored evidence) it resulted in his being fired by Speaker Newt Gingrich as a congressional investigator. After his short-lived career with Congress, Bossie went to work as an intern at the uber-conservative Citizens United,* producing dubious documentary films about the Clintons and others, all protected by the First Amendment. His ruthlessness took him to the top of Citizens United, where as the organization's president he has played hardball conservative-based politics for decades. Bossie met Trump in 2010 through Las Vegas casino mogul Steve Wynn, who had supported a charity Bossie started for a children's hospital in Washington, DC after his son survived infant heart and brain surgeries. Trump, who aided Bossie's charity, discovered that Bossie knew his way around Washington. They did not have serious political conversations until June 2011, when Mitt Romney announced he was running for

---

* Citizens United claims to be an organization dedicated to restoring our government to citizens' control. Through a combination of education, advocacy, and grassroots organization, Citizens United's mission is to reassert the traditional American values of limited government, freedom of enterprise, strong families, and national sovereignty and security. See http://www.citizensunited.org/who-we-are.aspx.

the GOP nomination in 2012. Trump thought Romney a terrible potential candidate. "Do you want to run?" Bossie asked Trump, and when Donald hedged, Bossie volunteered to do some unofficial exploration and run a poll. With *The Apprentice* in its tenth season, the poll revealed Trump's name recognition was "off the charts," voters thought more highly of Trump as a businessman than they did Romney, and the poll showed Trump defeating Romney in several head-to-head contests. But there was a big negative: Voters did not believe he would run. Bossie claims his 2011 polling "was perhaps the first documented evidence that Donald J. Trump would be a formidable candidate."[7] In the end, Trump endorsed Romney in 2012. By 2014, Bossie and Trump had developed a relatively close relationship. Part of Bossie's business was setting up gatherings for conservatives around the country, and he was planning his first Freedom Summit in New Hampshire, in 2014. To assist with this event he turned to Corey Lewandowski, a fellow he met on Capitol Hill who was then based in New Hampshire. David and Corey attracted several big names to the New Hampshire Freedom Summit, including former House Speaker Newt Gingrich, Governor Mike Huckabee, Senators Ted Cruz, Rand Paul, and Kelly Ayotte along with a few other GOP luminaries. But the surprise celebrity for the packed conference (roughly a thousand paying fans attending) was Donald Trump, the reality TV star, who walked on stage to Frank Sinatra's "New York, New York." Speaking extemporaneously, Trump ranted about trade and the economy, which got little reaction from the crowd. What did catch the crowd's attention was his xenophobic attacks on immigrants, with his biggest applause line coming with a call for "border fencing," (he had not yet stumbled into his wall), followed by a half-serious, half-absurd eight-minute riff on why politicians should not be allowed to use teleprompters.

Roger Stone became a paid political consultant for Trump in 2015, when Donald realized if he was going to run for president he needed a campaign team. Trump also hired one of Stone's associates, Sam Nunberg.

They were looking in earnest for a person qualified to run Trump's presidential race. We will never know how many feelers and inquiries they put out looking for an experienced campaign manager, but no qualified person wanted the job. Trump was also talking to Bossie about a campaign manager for the 2016 race. Bossie would later write there were two problems in finding an experienced professional: "Few would be willing to take a chance on something that might dry up in a few weeks or months," and the person had to be "the right personality to work with Trump." Bossie added, he "knew [Trump] could be abrasive, to say the least." Plus, he recognized that "Trump would not fit into a traditional campaign strategy or get along with a traditional political handler. That's when Corey Lewandowski came to mind."[8] Bossie suggested Lewandowski to Stone and Nunberg. Neither knew him but checked him out and found him suitable.

Lewandowski spent his hardscrabble youth in Lowell, Massachusetts, and after two tries graduated cum laude in 1995 from the University of Massachusetts, Lowell, with a BA in political science. After graduation he worked in Washington, DC as an aide for Massachusetts Republican Congressman Peter G. Torkildsen, while doing graduate work in political science at American University in Washington, DC. Torkildsen, a conservative, was voted out in 1997 and Lewandowski went to work for Ohio Republican Congressman Bob Ney, where he worked from December 1997 until February 2001. Ney would later plead guilty and be sentenced to thirty months in prison for being a beneficiary of Jack Abramoff's scandalous lobbying (read: bribery), which occurred while Lewandowski worked for Ney. The facts of the Ney case suggest that Lewandowski learned how to avoid getting in personal trouble while working for a corrupt politician and remaining on their good side in the process – a skill that would later help him with Donald Trump.[9] Lewandowski went to work for the Koch brothers-funded advocacy group Americans for Prosperity, which is where Sam Nunberg found him, when Trump wanted to meet him. Corey and

Sam arranged to meet at the Starbucks in the atrium of Trump Towers. While Nunberg vaped during the elevator ride to the twenty-fourth floor, he explained how he had recently been fired and rehired by Trump. Corey was ushered into Trump's office. Corey found the experience surreal, "like something out of the opening of *The Apprentice*," he later recounted.[10] After Trump finished his call he immediately launched into the fact he had "the greatest air force in the world, I've got a 757, I've got a Citation X, and I've got three helicopters." The unprovoked bragging continued with all the houses he owed, plus "seventeen golf courses." Lewandowski had no idea why Trump was telling him all this, but we do. It is Trump's deep insecurity and need to impress and dominate everyone he meets, as in, "Hi. I'm Donald Trump. How many planes you got?" Corey was hired, with Nunberg telling Corey it happened because "Roger Stone said you could."[11] So Trump's initial campaign team consisted of Sam Nunberg, Roger Stone and Corey Lewandowski, with David Bossie offering occasional advice.

Corey decided to only offer advice to Trump when specifically sought and otherwise: "Let Trump Be Trump." After Trump's rocky performance during the first Republican debate, run by Fox News on August 6, 2015, both Nunberg and Stone were gone from the campaign. They had "prepared" him. Lewandowski became a one-man show and did a remarkable job as a rookie of getting Trump to the best venues at the right time. Trump's celebrity and unorthodoxy attracted outsized news media coverage, so media was not a concern. Lewandowski knew what had to be done to get him in the game, getting him on the ballots and establishing local offices when necessary, and he did it. Trump came in second in Iowa and went on to win New Hampshire and South Carolina. By mid-March, the only GOP candidates in play were Trump, Texas Senator Ted Cruz, and Ohio Governor John Kasich. Trump was on his way to win the nomination, and Lewandowski had done all the heavy lifting.

Paul Manafort, who lived in Trump Tower, had been watching Trump

bumble and fumble his way to the front of the pack, and saw an opportunity – a candidate who could win the presidency, with Manafort getting
credit for taking him across the finishing line. Manafort made his move in
March 2016, which Lewandowski learned when Trump asked him to set
up a meeting with Manafort. Corey had heard the name, but he did not
know Manafort, only that he had been a partner in a once hot Washington
lobbying firm with Roger Stone. Corey knew Manafort had not been active
in presidential campaigns in decades. For Manafort, Trump was a potential godsend. By February 2016, when Manafort realized that Trump was
a viable candidate, he went to Trump's long-time friend Thomas Barrack
Jr., the head of Colony Capital, a multi-billion dollar hedge fund based in
California, to sell Barrack on going to his friend Donald Trump and telling
him he needed a seasoned professional like Manafort to get him the GOP
nomination, and then for winning the general election. Manafort certainly
did not tell Barrack the financial mess he was in and why he was willing to
work for free for Trump.* More remarkable is that Barrack, without checking, passed along the request to meet with Trump, for Paul Manafort had
baggage bulging with dirty laundry, including an active FBI investigation
that had started in 2014. Anyone in the Washington GOP political establishment could have told Trump that Manafort was a disaster waiting to
happen, but Trump was attacking the GOP establishment as incompetent
fools, so they merely watched him as bemused spectators. None believed
Trump would ever become president of the United States.

Those who knew Manafort knew he was in dire condition, and so were

---

* We know about Manafort's dire financial circumstance because he was later indicted and
convicted for bank fraud during the time he was associated with Trump, promising jobs in
the Trump administration to obtain a multimillion-dollar loan. In addition, Manafort was
also being pursued by a Russian oligarch, Oleg Deripaska, for a $10 million loan. He was
not in a position to work for free, but he must have figured if Trump won, he might get away
with his frauds.

surprised when he stepped into the limelight of Trump's campaign. In the 1980s and 1990s Manafort's lobbying clients were those no one else would represent. By 2004 Manafort was representing Oleg Deripaska, a Russian oligarch, and Viktor Yanukovych, who was seeking the presidency in Ukraine through his Party of Regions. Manafort became deeply involved with Deripaska and Yanukovych, both personas non grata in the United States. It is not known how much money Manafort made or stole from these people, employing offshore shell companies and numbered bank accounts, but it is known it was multi-millions. When Manafort joined the Trump campaign, Lewandowski quickly realized Manafort was a leaker, and "he knew that the addition of Manafort to the [Trump campaign] team was not going to turn out well. Especially for him."[12] Corey was correct, and within weeks Manafort was taking over the campaign from the rookie who had positioned Trump to win the nomination. Manafort's method was to befriend Trump's kids, who had largely been spectators on the sidelines. Manafort convinced them their father could win with a professional like him running to campaign. On June 20, 2016 Trump's son, Don Jr., fired Corey, who was not told why, although he knew Manafort had formed an alliance with the kids. Corey Lewandowski, even when fired, remained loyal. He found Donald Trump to be a figure he greatly admired, and as campaign manager, and after, he remained submissive to Trump, aggressive on Trump's behalf, and got on with his otherwise conventional life. Corey hit all the touchstones of a high RWA.

Paul Manafort, who was out for only Paul Manafort, made a fatal error. While Manafort was turning the knife in Corey's back, falsely telling reporters that Corey had stolen money from the Trump campaign—which was not possible—he began telling television producers that he, Manafort, would go on television while Trump would stay quiet. When Trump learned of Manafort's action it was like a starving man being told he would never again eat. Trump exploded, verbally eviscerating Manafort, and never trusting his judgement thereafter.[13] The last straw for Manafort with the campaign followed a *New York Times* story on August 13, 2016, reporting that the adults in the Trump campaign were trying to get Donald to act more presidential.[14] It appeared a conspicuous leak from Manafort and clearly the effort failed. Trump was down double digits to Hillary in the polling and there were only eighty-six days to Election Day. Trump's campaign was falling apart. But as so often happens in Donald's life, a new enabler came to his rescue, resulting in a pivot point for his campaign.

The definitive history of Trump's 2016 presidential campaign cannot be written without understanding the significant role of the little-known players who had great influence – billionaire Robert Mercer and his daughter Rebekah. But getting the full story will be difficult because Robert Mercer is a reclusive figure. Indeed, because Trump won, it resulted in media attention being focused on Mercer and his daughter, so he has withdrawn some of his financial support from conservative Republican causes.[15] Initially, the Mercers supported Trump's chief rival, Texas Senator Ted Cruz. When Cruz dropped out and Trump won the nomination in July 2016, the billionaire turned his attention to Trump; not because he was enamored of Trump, but because he was motivated to defeat Hillary Clinton. Mercer and his daughter were much like others who turned to Trump only slowly, but soon forgetting what they disliked about him. Notwithstanding Mercer's brilliance as a mathematician and computer engineer, a man who developed stock trading algorithms that made him (and others) billions, he believes in many conspiracy theories, particularly about Hillary, along with other extreme libertarian ideas.[16] While supporting Cruz, the Mercers had assembled the rudiments of the kind of organizations needed to win the general election, namely Steve Bannon, Kellyanne Conway, and Cambridge Analytica. The Mercer money and team were sitting on the sidelines when Trump's struggling campaign was collapsing in mid-August at the outset of the general election contest.

By August 14, 2016, the rumors of Paul Manafort's nefarious past surfaced on the front page of the *New York Times*, which published information about an off-the-books ledger showing Manafort had received $12.7 million in illegal and undisclosed cash payments from a pro-Russian political party in Ukraine. Trump's reaction was on the mark: "I've got a crook running my campaign."[17] Moving behind the scenes were Bob Mercer and daughter Rebekah. Rebekah spoke to Steve Bannon, who was running the Breitbart news platform for the Mercers and was also on the board of directors of Cambridge Analytica, which the Mercer money funded. Earlier Bannon had told Rebekah that Trump would win the nomination and could win the presidency, but "the way Manafort was running the campaign sickened him."[18] Bannon had watched Manafort on *Meet the Press* wearing a yachting outfit, being interviewed from Southampton, New York, which he told Rebekah were all wrong signals for Trump's "populist, nationalist" campaign. Rebekah told Bannon major GOP donors were going to jump ship, Senator Majority Leader Mitch McConnell was going to focus on the Senate and walk from Trump, and GOP Super PAC money was going to be redirected down-ballot. Bannon told Rebekah he thought he could help, however.

Minutes later, Rebekah's father, the silent Mercer, was on the phone with Bannon, listening to his ideas: make Kellyanne Conway campaign manager, put her on television as the face of the campaign, and put Bannon in charge of the day-to-day operations. They would rely on the Cambridge Analytica data and bring in David Bossie, who Mercer knew for he had contributed to Citizens United – Bossie knew more about Hillary Clinton's life than Hillary Clinton knew. Trump, who realized his campaign was falling apart, agreed to meet with the Mercers at an event on Long Island. Not surprisingly, Trump loved the plan: he was drowning and had just been tossed a lifeline. He only wanted to add Roger Ailes as an adviser. Ailes had just been fired from Fox News, the organization he created, for sexually harassing women, behavior that has never been offensive to Donald

Trump. Plus, no one could deny that Ailes was a political genius, having once helped Richard Nixon get elected and re-elected. Trump announced his campaign shakeup on August 17, 2016.[19] He did not fire Manafort, he simply restructured his campaign without him. On August 19, 2016 Manafort, realizing he was irrelevant and in legal trouble, announced his resignation from the campaign. (Manafort also tried unsuccessfully to get a $5 million advertising buy before he departed, which in hindsight looks like he wanted to pocket some severance pay, but it did not work.) Trump's statement was blunt: "This morning Paul Manafort offered, and I accepted, his resignation from the campaign." Trump said in the statement, "I am very appreciative for his great work in helping to get us where we are today, and . . . I wish him the greatest success."[20]

Thanks to the Mercers, Trump had saved his foundering campaign. Trump understood there was no Republican Party establishment he could turn to, for he had attacked what did exist. Soon he would discover that with Bannon and Ailes, he had a direct pipeline to the authoritarian voters most interested in his campaign, the readers of Breitbart News and the viewers of Fox News. Both Bannon and Kellyanne were of the "Let Trump Be Trump" school of campaigning, realizing that his demagogic and authoritarian style was key to his appeal, and Bannon loved his populist message. Both Bannon and Kellyanne knew the importance of data, Bannon as a board member of Cambridge Analytica and Kellyanne as a veteran of the polling business. They knew how to use the information Cambridge Analytica was providing, and to develop a campaign strategy that would give their candidate a win in the Electoral College.[21] None of these people held Donald Trump in any esteem whatsoever, for they knew he was a fool with no grasp of how to lead anyone anywhere; rather, they were fixated on Hillary Clinton not becoming president of the United States, for she could lead in a fashion they did not want. Mercer and Bannon are ideologues, radicals who want to keep white elites like themselves in control, with power.

Unwittingly Trump had assembled a campaign team that provided media and messaging links to the authoritarian base of the Republican Party plus independent voters with such leanings. He had not planned it, but once they stumbled into his voters, they recognized them. But Trump's staffing was a fluke, a gift from the Mercers, as his entire campaign was a series of flukes: the drip, drip, drip of Hillary's emails in October,[22] the Russian intervention on his behalf,[23] and Comey's public flip-flopping, all of which damaged Hillary Clinton's campaign.[24] All gifts, all flukes. But most importantly, Trump stumbled into a base of support which was far wider and deeper than he suspected when he started, and with which he could do no wrong. In Chapters 5 through 10 we have explained why his base was not troubled by his troubling past, so they sent him to the White House where he would enjoy the same immunity from his base. Trump did not find these authoritarian followers, they found him, and put him in the White House, and with time he had found a core cadre of enablers who have facilitated his presidency, and his effort to get reelected.

ALL THE PRESIDENT'S ENABLERS

When Trump arrived in the White House on January 20, 2017, he did not hire a seasoned White House staff. We pass over Trump hiring his daughter and son-in-law as senior White House aides, notwithstanding their having no knowledge or experience whatsoever in the workings of the federal government. To understand this relationship it is only necessary to be familiar with the dynamics of a mafia-like family, as portrayed in the "Godfather" films. Trump is clearly comfortable with his family for he controls them. He is conspicuously uncomfortable with people who know more about being president of the United States than he does. This means Trump is intimidated by all types of people most presidents would hire. In spite of himself, initially he did call on some able and qualified people to work in his White House and Cabinet, but the turnover at the top has been extraordinary, the highest turnover of any modern presidency, according to the nonpartisan Brookings Institute.[25] It is spinning turnstile-type turnover, fast enough to amaze even veteran observers. "It's historic, it's unprecedented, it's off the charts," said the author of the non-partisan Brookings Institute study, who told NBC News, "I've never seen this kind of turnover before." In just thirty-two months, Trump's rate of change surpassed "all of his predecessors who served four-year terms." Thus, even when Trump has been able to get good people he has been unable to keep them.[26]

If you do not play by Trump's rules, or lack thereof, and if you are not a totally subservient follower, he does not want you on his team. Thus, the high turnover at the top. Given this turnover it is not surprising that former appointees have openly leaked information about Trump to journalists and writers, so we have a good understanding of the constant chaos and disruptive processes that have dominated Trump's presidency. But it is not just turnover at the top that has made the Trump administration less than competent. It is also Trump's refusal to fill many mid-level appointees, often relying on an "acting" official to run the operations across the government, or simply leaving it vacant, and removing offices and operations he believes non-essential. So abnormal is Trump's refusal to fill key posts, including Cabinet secretaries, their deputy and assistants, general counsels, agency heads, and ambassadorships, that the *Washington Post*, along with the non-profit Partnership for Public Service, began tracking some 700 key positions.[27]

Of much greater interest are those who have pledged allegiance to President Trump, those who have emerged over the first thousand plus days of his presidency to be his key enablers, and without whom his presidency would have collapsed long ago. Lest there be any doubt about whom we are talking allow us to name names of the heavies, because they typify the president's enablers throughout the Executive Branch: Vice President Mike Pence, Secretary of State Mike Pompeo, and Attorney General William Barr. Note, none of these men were enamored with candidate Trump. Indiana Governor Mike Pence had been openly critical of Trump's call to ban Muslims, declaring it "offensive and unconstitutional."[28] But the moment he became Trump's potential pick for vice president, he banished his negative thoughts. Kansas Congressman Mike Pompeo supported Marco Rubio's presidential campaign and actively tried to block Trump from prevailing in the 2016 GOP primaries. Pompeo told the Kansas caucus-goers Trump would be "an authoritarian President who ignored our Constitution," suggesting Trump would order American soldiers "to do things that are inconsistent with our Constitution." Pompeo warned: "It's time to turn down the lights on the circus," calling Trump a "kook" and a "cancer."[29] According to news reports, Bill Barr turned down Donald Trump's efforts to hire him as a defense attorney on two occasions, before later openly seeking to become attorney general, a post he held under President George H. W. Bush.[30] Ironically, what these three leading Trump enablers have in common is that they all are hard-right religious conservatives. As Trump entered the final year of his first term as president, Mike Pence, Mike Pompeo, and Bill Barr have become his go-to guys.

At the time of his selection, Governor Mike Pence was facing a difficult reelection contest in Indiana so the opportunity to become vice president of the United States placed his life in an entirely different dimension. Trump was interested in Pence because his campaign manager Paul Manafort explained that Pence was free of scandal; he could bring essential evangelical voters, along with the rust belt voters – all necessary for Trump to win. Trump type-casts all his appointees (how will they look on television) and the gray-haired Pence looked like a vice president. Trump discovered that Pence is a natural-born groveler, always a smooth sycophant, because Mike believes God has a greater plan for him.[31] Mike Pompeo, who had graduated at the top of his class at West Point, and later Harvard Law, was a failed businessman, who had then served three terms as a Kansas Congressman nobody had ever heard of before Trump selected him, at the suggestion of Mike Pence, to head the CIA, and later as secretary of state. Both Mikes got their jobs using Hoover-vacuum-level sucking-up to Trump. Pence is conspicuous and public, he panders like a puppy who has fallen in love. Pompeo operates behind closed doors, where one official who observed Pompeo with Trump reports he is "among the most sycophantic and obsequious people around Trump," or more pointedly, "He's like a heat-seeking missile for Trump's ass."[32] Notwithstanding turning Trump down as a client, on June 8, 2018 Bill Barr sent an unusual memo to the leadership of the Justice Department, outlining his unsolicited analysis of the Mueller inquiry based on uninformed assumption and made-up facts.[33] It was a conspicuous audition by a former attorney general (who held the post from 1991 to 1993) who wanted to be attorney general again, and he was telling Trump he would not let Special Counsel Mueller nail him for obstruction of justice.[34]

The motives of Pence and Pompeo in becoming Trump's top sycophants is at one level obvious. Both men have big-time political ambitions – they see themselves as future presidents of the United States – yet neither man can succeed on their own, so by becoming Donald's courtiers, they are looking for a chance to propel themselves onward and upward. That is the best-case scenario, for there appears to be more going on with Pence and Pompeo than meets the eye. They are operating on another level which can be easily overlooked. Pence may have recommended Pompeo because both men are deeply devout evangelicals. Pence wears his religiosity in his unctuous manner, not to mention his openly pious behavior (e.g., he refuses to eat alone with women not his wife or attend events with alcohol unless his wife is present).[35] Pompeo sends his message by leaving an open Bible on his desk, with a Swiss Army knife marking the end of the Book on Queen

Esther.[36] Pompeo told a *New York Times* reporter that the Bible informs everything he does.[37] And he says "it's possible that God raised up Trump as a modern Queen Esther, the Biblical figure who convinced the King of Persia to spare the Jewish people."[38] Whoa, just a minute. This is "End Times" talk for Christian fundamentalists, meaning "the Rapture" is not far behind. Without getting all theological about it and broadly stated, the Rapture in Christian teachings holds that both living and dead believers will ascend into heaven to meet Jesus Christ at the Second Coming. For evangelicals, the Rapture will be preceded by a horrific war in the Middle East (e.g. Iran attacking Israel), which they do not encourage but certainly do not fear. Hold this thought about End Times.

Bill Barr does not appear interested in higher office, but it is not difficult to discern why he wanted to return to the post of Attorney General of the United States, one of the most powerful of the cabinet offices.[39] If you look closely at Bill Barr you will find a committed Republican partisan, a deep believer in maximum presidential power (for Republican presidents, anyway), and an unpretentious religious zealot. Given Barr's thinking, it is not difficult to believe that he realized Donald Trump was, in fact, the weakest man to ever become a modern president: a blank slate with no understanding of the office, a person with authoritarian instincts who could be easily manipulated with flattery and from whom Barr could gain eternal gratitude by keeping him in office, notwithstanding his propensity and disposition to engage in criminal behavior. Surely it occurred to Barr that he could gain Trump's eternal gratitude by being his Roy Cohn. In doing so, Barr could accomplish his own goals of expanding presidential powers, assist the Senate Republicans in packing the federal judiciary with conservative judges, and use the Department of Justice to reshape religion in American.

Let us look closer. Katherine Stewart and Caroline Fredrickson write that "no understanding of William Barr can be complete without taking into account his views of the role of religion in society." More specifically, they report:

> Mr. Barr has embraced wholesale the "religious liberty" rhetoric of today's Christian nationalist movement. When religious nationalists invoke "religious freedom," it is typically code for religious privilege. The freedom they have in mind is the freedom of people of certain conservative and authoritarian varieties of religion to discriminate against those of whom they disapprove or over whom they wish to exert power. This form of "religious liberty" seeks to foment the sense of persecution and paranoia of a collection of conservative religious groups that see themselves as on the cusp of losing their rightful position of dominance over American culture.[40]

The journalist and historian Anne Applebaum, a scholar deeply familiar with authoritarianism past and present, has published a revealing analysis of these three Trump enablers. Ms. Applebaum finds historical parallels for Trump's Republican stalwarts. She calls them "collaborators," but not in the neutral or positive sense of the word. Applebaum uses "collaborator" in the sense of "someone who works with the enemy, with the occupying power, with the dictatorial regime" -- more akin to "collusion," "complicity," and "connivance." She explains this negative meaning gained currency during the Second World War "to describe Europeans who cooperate with Nazi occupiers." She hastens to add: "The point is not to compare Trump to Hitler or Stalin; the point is to compare the experiences of high-ranking members of the American Republican Party, especially those who work most closely with the White House, to the experiences" of those who collaborated during WWII because they were "forced to accept an alien ideology or a set of values that are in sharp conflict with their own."[41] In elaborating on her essay on NPR, Ms. Applebaum explains, "from the outset it was clear Trump was bringing a very different ideology to the White House, a completely different set of values, which bore no relation to anything that we've known in American history for the last hundred years. He was seeking to use the presidency for his own personal and political gain, for his own psychological gain. He was seeking to game the system." And she added, "to go around bureaucracies, to have secret policies, to deploy people throughout the system in order to undermine it."[42]

When addressing her overriding question of "why have Republican leaders abandoned their principles in support of an immoral and dangerous president," Ms. Applebaum found six historical rationales employed by enablers of authoritarian regimes, which we summarize: "We can use this moment to achieve great things," using an example of an unnamed Trump official who appears to have convinced himself Trump is helping the Uighurs in China, when the opposite is the case; "We can protect the country from the president," using Gary Cohn's noisy departure and Anonymous's revealing accounts, plus former Defense Secretary James Mattis (who had not yet spoken out); "I, personally, will benefit," using Secretary of Agriculture Sonny Perdue, who has refused to comply with conflicts of interest laws and appears to be profiting from his post; "LOL nothing matters," referring to the many on Trump's team who are engaging in cynicism, nihilism, relativism, amorality, irony, sarcasm, boredom, and amusement as their reasons for collaborating; "I am afraid to speak out," noting all those who refused to testify when Trump instructed his aides not to do so; and "My side might be flawed, but the political opposition is much worse," which was the rationale of the Vichy government in Nazi-occupied France during WWII. The Vichy regime, Applebaum explains, felt that the real enemy was not the Nazis but French parliamentarians, socialists, anarchists, Jews, and other leftists and democrats.[43] With this rationale she focuses on Mike Pence, Mike Pompeo, and Bill Barr – given their importance in Trump's cabinet. She notes: "All three are clever enough to understand what Trumpism really means, that it has nothing to do with God or faith, that it is self-serving, greedy, and unpatriotic." A former insider told Ms. Applebaum "that both Pence and Pompeo have convinced themselves that they are in a biblical moment." All of the things they care about—outlawing abortion and same-sex marriage, and (though this is never said out loud) maintaining a white majority in America—are under threat. Time is growing short. They believe that "we are approaching the Rapture, and this is a moment of deep religious significance." She notes that Barr, a conservative Catholic, believes "militant secularists" are destroying America and that "irreligion and secular values are being forced on people of faith." She concludes: "Whatever evil Trump does, whatever he damages or destroys, at least he enables Barr, Pence, and Pompeo to save America from a far worse fate. If you are convinced we are living in the End Times, then anything the president does can be forgiven."[44]

It is a thoughtful analysis, and history may prove her correct. Of only one thing are we certain: Donald Trump has managed to remove all checks on his behavior from his advisers. They all appear afraid of him. Ms. Applebaum's explanation is as good as we have found, and there is no question that conservative Catholics and evangelical Christians are present in unusually high numbers in his cabinet and subcabinet posts.[45] We do not, however, anticipate the Rapture while Trump is president, but if he remains in the White House for a second term it will be pure hell.

REPUBLICANS TOLERATE TRUMP'S OUTRAGEOUS BEHAVIOR

Trump became president without any true legislative agenda, other than to repeal Obamacare, which he was unable to do even when Republicans controlled the Congress, thanks to Senator John McCain, who was dying of brain cancer as he voted against Trump's effort to kill medical assistance to Americans. Congress did enact, and Trump supported, the GOP's long-simmering tax cut legislation, because it benefitted those with wealth like Trump. In addition, because it pleased his evangelical base, Trump has given Senate Majority Leader Mitch McConnell free reign to select federal judges, men and woman typically recommended by the Federal Society, the uber-conservative breeding ground for judges and lawyers, which has produced a remarkable number of unqualified candidates that McConnell has forced the GOP Senate to approve, giving them lifetime appointments. Thanks to McConnell, Trump is approaching a record for judicial appointments in a four-year term, which could exceed 200 judges.[46] This is pure partisan court-packing and could affect the federal judiciary for decades.* Trump, of course, takes credit for the appointment of Supreme Court justices, and federal judges, but he actually has little to do with the process.

Trump's presidency, accurately described by Ms. Applebaum as operating for "his own personal and political gain, for his own psychological gain," while toying with authoritarianism, has been without objection of Republicans, save Utah Senator Mitt Romney. Trump can literally do most anything without GOP criticism. Yet these people were apoplectic when (seriously!) accusing President Barack Obama of defiling his high office for wearing a tan suit and later for occasionally tossing a football in the Oval Office. That's right: wearing a khaki-colored suit.[47] And throwing a football in the Oval was unacceptable conduct for an American president.[48] This prompted the *New York Times* editorial board to collect hundreds of examples of Trump's norm-busting conduct as president, which they labelled the

---

* To balance the increasingly GOP federal judiciary, when Democrats gain control of the House, Senate, and White House, they must enact legislation adding more judgeships to the federal judiciary, which needs more judges from top to bottom because of increased business. Congress controls the number of judges. Such an expansion can check this Republican effort to control the federal courts.

new Republican presidential etiquette. After three-plus years there are literally thousands of these examples.[49] We know from Chapters 5 through 10 why Trump's very unpresidential behavior – even criminal conduct – does not bother Republicans.

In the mid-term election of 2018, American voters decidedly rejected Trump's behavior. American voters gave Democrats control of House in 2018. (There were not sufficient Republican Senate seats up in 2018 to turn control of the Senate to the Democrats.) The House, once under the control of the Democrats—men and women who are not submissive to Donald Trump—began addressing Trump's abuses of power. But in 2018 Democrats did not campaign for Congress exclusively by running against Trump's performance as president, or his behavior that ranges between that of a juvenile delinquent and a mafia boss; rather, they ran on issues like Republican efforts to abolish the Affordable Care Act (Obamacare), making healthcare the biggest issue, followed by criminal justice law reforms, comprehensive immigration law reform, increases in the minimum wage, and other bread and butter matters. Yet the exit polls showed the election was very much a referendum on Donald Trump. Nonetheless, future Democratic Speaker of the House of Representatives Nancy Pelosi announced just before the big election win, at a meeting with Democratic donors and strategists, that there was a line she would not cross: "Attempting to impeach Mr. Trump, she said, was not on the agenda."[50] Historically, such undertakings had been a disaster.[51] Speaker Pelosi understood that a bungled impeachment could backfire.

The first half of Trump's presidency had been dominated by Special Counsel Robert Mueller's investigation of the role Russia played in the 2016 presidential campaign, along with the Trump campaign's connections with these Russian efforts to defeat Hillary Clinton. The twenty-two-month special counsel investigation started on May 17, 2017 and ended on March 22, 2019, when former FBI Director Mueller sent his report to

Attorney General William P. Barr. Two days later, the wily Bill Barr sent a four-page letter to the chairmen and ranking members of the House and Senate Judiciary Committees, which have oversight of the Justice Department. The letter, which Barr knew would leak, bent the facts in Mueller's report to make them favorable to Trump. Barr summarized the report as finding no coordination between the Trump campaign and Russia, but the attorney general also found no obstruction of justice. Not surprisingly, Trump claimed total exoneration – "No collusion, no obstruction" – and with the report unavailable no one was the wiser. In fact, Attorney General Barr had perpetrated what a seasoned federal judge, Reggie B. Walton, who was appointed to the bench by President George W. Bush, later described as a "distorted" and "misleading" account of Mueller's finding in a Freedom of Information Act lawsuit seeking to remove the redacted parts of the report.[52]

Mueller's Report raised the issue of impeachable behavior, based on Trump's abuses of power, not to mention Barr's behavior in twisting the information, and abusing his office as well. But Speaker Pelosi quickly put the kibosh on talk of impeachment hearings before the House Judiciary Committee, where the impeachment process begins. On April 26, 2019, about a month after Attorney General Barr exonerated Trump, author Dean had occasion to visit with Speaker Pelosi at a small private event. Having been a commentator for MSNBC during the Clinton impeachment debacle, author Dean praised the Speaker's wisdom of not allowing the impeachment process to commence, given the thin although deeply troubling findings of the Mueller Report, which Barr had largely blunted. But author Dean was well into this project studying Donald Trump's behavior, along with that of his authoritarian followers, so he shared with Speaker Pelosi his thinking: "Madam Speaker, Donald Trump is a public version of the private Richard Nixon. These men are authoritarian personalities. You can count on Trump engaging in worse behavior than that Mueller reported, and that behavior may call out for impeachment, which will be appropriate." Author Dean had no idea how prophetic his words would be, for at the very time they were talking Donald Trump was already running a scheme with former New York Mayor Rudy Giuliani to extort the newly elected president of Ukraine to agree to announce a bogus investigation of former Vice President Biden, and his son Hunter Biden, who had sat on the board of directors of a Ukrainian company while his father was vice president. (A bad decision by Hunter Biden, but there is not a scintilla of evidence of any wrongdoing by Hunter or his father, notwithstanding the appearance of a conflict of interest, which should have been avoided.) In addition, Trump's scheme also included having Ukraine buy into a debunked conspiracy theory and take blame for the Russian hacking/leaking interference in the 2016 presidential election in the United States, thus absolving Russia. This, of course, would discredit the Mueller investigation. To force the new Ukrainian president, Volodymyr Zelensky, to undertake these actions, Trump was withholding a much sought-after meeting at the White House by Zelensky and threatened to withhold $400 million in appropriated aide to Ukraine, a country at war with Russia. We would soon learn Trump personally transmitted his request to President Zelensky in a July 25, 2019 monitored telephone call.

The Ukraine scandal jumped to the front of the news in mid-August 2019 when a whistleblower complaint was filed with the Inspector General (IG) for the intelligence community, in which the anonymous complainant asserted: "In the course of my official duties, I have received information from multiple U.S. Government officials that the President of the United States is using the power of his office to solicit interference from a foreign country in the 2020 U.S. election. This interference includes, among other things, pressuring a foreign country to investigate one of the President's main domestic political rivals."[53] The IG investigated and found the complaint accurate. Because such a complaint had never been filed against a president of the United States, the IG went to the U.S. Department of Justice for guidance, where they tried to kill the complaint and prevent it from being sent to Congress as required by law. The House Intelligence Committee got wind of what was occurring, and subpoenaed the IG to testify, and the whistleblower's complaint was revealed. The focus of the complaint was the July 25, 2019 call by Trump to President Zelensky, trying to impose his scheme to help win the 2020 election by getting Zelensky to do dirty deeds in exchange for American assistance. It was also hinted that much more than one telephone call was involved in implementing the plot, because Trump referred to his personal attorney Rudy Giuliani and Attorney General Bill Barr.

All presidents prepare transcripts of their conversations with foreign heads of state by allowing select staff of the National Security Council to listen and make notes of the call as it is taking place. (It is possible the foreign government electronically records such calls, and some presidents have recorded, while others use note takers.) The note takers compare their notes after the call and prepare an agreed upon transcript of the conversation. One or more of the persons listening to the call obviously expressed their concern to the person who later became the whistleblower (a person whose identity remains anonymous, but he or she is believed to be an experienced intelligence officer with the CIA). Given the fact there was a record of the call there was instant Congressional and public clamor, which forced Trump to release the White House transcript. On September 24, 2019 the president declassified the call.* Trump, who has endlessly described this

---

* The call was classified SECRET/ORCON/NOFORN. Not the highest classification, but the transcript was stored on a computer that placed it with the highest classified documents, thus severely restricting access. *Top Secret* means unauthorized disclosure would likely cause "exceptionally grave" injury to our national interest, whereas *Secret* means it would cause "serious" injury. *ORCON* an acronym for "originator control" gives the person classifying the document control of its dissemination. And *NOFORN* means no foreign country should see the document.

call as "perfect," reveals his New York wheeler-and-dealer disposition, for he has probably extorted and bribed many folks on a regular basis, far more bluntly. Here, however, he knew others were listening, so he is proud of the nuance he employed in framing his actual message, which we would paraphrase as, "If you don't announce you're investigating Hunter and Joe Biden, not only are you never coming to the White House, you won't get another f**king penny from the United States."

The July 25, 2019 call was a mafia-like shakedown by Trump to get a foreign country to help with his reelection. If anyone other than the President of the United States had made the call and it had become public, they would have been arrested and indicted for soliciting a foreign contribution (52 USC 30121 and 18 USC 3571), bribery (18 USC 201), extortion (18 USC 1951), possibly obstruction of justice (18 USC 1503), and conspiracy (18 USC 371).[54] The transcript of Trump's telephone conversation is about as conspicuously corrupt as anyone has ever seen by an American president. It is way beyond Nixon-level behavior, who we know from his secret recordings always had others do this sort of thing for him, so he would have deniability. Trump's conversation represented precisely the kind of self-interested corrupt behavior the nation's founders had in mind when they added the provisions for impeachment and removal.[55]

First privately, then publicly, Speaker Pelosi saw Trump's scheme for what it was, a plan to use his presidential powers to "cheat" to win reelection, by illegally withholding foreign aid already appropriated by Congress, along with withholding a meeting sought by President Zelensky at the White House to show the Russians that he had the backing of the United States. All of this was intended to tilt the 2020 contest in Trump's favor by creating a bogus investigation against his most likely opponent Joe Biden, and legitimizing a debunked conspiracy theory that it was Ukraine not Russia that helped Trump win his last election. Plainly, Trump was using the powers of the presidency corruptly. He was abusing power entrusted to him, and by cheating in an election, doing injury to society and the election processes. Because the Justice Department had passed on any investigation of the whistleblower's charges, Speaker Pelosi turned to the House Intelligence Committee, which had jurisdiction over the matter, and whose chairman, Adam Schiff, had the skills to undertake such a preliminary investigation. If they found impeachable conduct – "Treason, Bribery, or other high crimes and misdemeanors" – they would refer their findings to the House Judiciary Committee, which has jurisdiction over impeachment.

IMPEACHMENT OF TRUMP: WHY DID THE REPUBLICAN SENATE SAVE HIM?

At first Republicans denied any wrongdoing by Trump, and Trump tried to block all witnesses in the executive branch from testifying. He wanted them to defy Congressional subpoenas, claiming they have absolute immunity.* Some did defy subpoenas. Others did not. Nonetheless, the House Intelligence Committee was able to develop overwhelming evidence that Trump had schemed to cheat in the 2020 election by forcing Ukraine to do his bidding. When the facts were established Republicans changed their defense to "so what if he did it, it does not rise to the level of an impeachable offense." With the greatly increased authoritarianism of the Republican base and the consequent greater ethnocentrism and authoritarianism of the people they elect, the Republican House caucus predictably voted against impeaching Trump over the Ukraine scandal, but the Democratic majority sent two articles of impeachment to "the greatest deliberative body in the

---

* This issue, slowed by the coronavirus, is working its way to the U.S. Supreme Court. The trial court said no, Trump is not a king with absolute immunity. A three-judge panel of the District of Columbia U.S. Court of Appeals said the U.S. House of Representatives could not use the federal courts to enforce their subpoenas. The House has requested the full Court of Appeals rule on the issue, and whoever loses will likely take the question to the U.S. Supreme Court.

world," the Senate, which held its Constitutionally authorized trial in January 2020. (It only requires a simple majority to impeach a president in the House of Representatives, but it requires a two-thirds super-majority —67 votes if all 100 senators are present—to convict, which result in automatic removal from office. A simple majority of the Senate can then vote to disqualify the convicted president from holding any federal office in the future.)

Trump was never in danger of being removed from office, but he fought hard to keep further evidence of his misdeeds from being revealed and considered in the trial. For example, it was learned that John Bolton, who lasted only seventeen months before Trump fired him as his National Security Adviser in early September 2019, was privy to many of the events that had surfaced during the inquiry by the House Intelligence Committee. Bolton had advised several National Security Council personnel to report what they had learned about Trump's behavior with President Zelensky to the White House Counsel. Bolton told others he did not want any part of the "drug deal," his disparaging moniker for Trump's activities. Bolton, who has written a book about his 519 days in the Trump White House, offered to testify during the Senate trial, if he was subpoenaed by the Senate, but the GOP-controlled Senate did not want more facts, nor for the public to learn anything more.

Polls found that 70 to 75 percent of the American public wanted new witnesses called, although the hard-core Republican base was against it. On the crucial vote to hear new witnesses, two GOP senators, Susan Collins from Maine and Mitt Romney from Utah, broke ranks and said the extremely pertinent evidence newly available should be heard. But the other 51 Republican senators said "No," and that was that. A few days later Trump was acquitted, 52–48, on the charge of abuse of power, with Mitt Romney voting to convict. The vote was 53–47 on obstructing Congress – a straight party line vote. The GOP rationales for excusing Trump's corrupt behavior were dubious and weak, not to mention evolving over time. In the House they insisted Trump had not withheld military aid from Ukraine to force that government to help smear Joe Biden. As the details of Trump's campaign to coerce Ukraine became known, the GOP stuck to a steadily deteriorating position that there was no proof of a "quid pro quo" and passed this dead duck of a baton to their colleagues in the Upper Chamber. Eventually this defense became so untenable that individual senators came up with their own excuses for exonerating the president, such as the attempted extortion was not a high crime or misdemeanor, and there was no point in removing a president when he would be up for re-election at the end of the year, this was just a partisan effort to undo the 2016 election, and Trump still insisted he had done nothing wrong, so who could say he did? Some Republicans conceded the president had acted "improperly," but it was not so serious a matter that he should be removed from office.

Congress knew everything you know about Donald Trump, if not more. They surely knew that Trump despised them. They were part of "the swamp" in Washington that he had promised to drain when he campaigned against the GOP establishment in 2015–6. They knew he had autocratic beliefs about himself, that he had no understanding of the Constitution and certainly no respect for it, that he had told appointees to break the law and he would pardon them if they were convicted, that he could pardon himself if he were ever convicted in a federal court of a crime, that he was a terrible administrator whose White House was chaotic, that he had lost all persons of character from his Cabinet and White House staff and replaced them with "royal favorites" whose main task was not to keep him from doing unlawful things, but to lie for him when he did. Senators knew from personal experience that he was vain beyond description, ignorant and confused, nearly out of control on occasions, a pathological liar and an amoral megalomaniac who believed he could get away with anything. And they must have known that if he indeed got away with demanding foreign help to destroy his main opponent in the 2020 election, it would convince him that he really could get away with anything.

Why did the Republicans acquit Trump in so perfunctory a fashion, punting away the chance for Congressional restraint of an authoritarian president running wild and giving him every reason to conclude that he is free to do whatever he wants? Stated a bit differently, why did they become his ultimate enablers? Look back at Figure 1 in Chapter 9. Look at the RWA Scale scores of the Republican legislators and recall the evidence that these high RWAs were also high SDOs. The authoritarian constituencies that sent these Double High lawmakers to their state legislatures in the 1990s are the same people who elected Republican senators to Congress over the next two decades, only more so. Tons of Republican office-holders got nominated and elected because they are highly authoritarian themselves. They knew what Donald Trump is—a yet more dominating version of themselves—and frankly they do not care about the Constitution. These are probably not your father's Republicans, and certainly not your grandfather's. As we have seen, they have abandoned many of the principles that used to guide their party. They talk all the time about American freedom, but they rank among its biggest enemies. Donald Trump does not have to threaten most of them one bit to get them to sell out America. Trump truly was acquitted by a jury of his peers.[56]

CHAPTER TWELVE

THE NOVEMBER 2020 ELECTION WILL DECIDE THE FATE OF AMERICA'S DEMOCRACY

For millions of Americans stunned with disbelief on November 8, 2016, and totally appalled by what Donald Trump has done since, November 3, 2020 could not come soon enough. Many wondered if we would live to see the day, because we have been forced to endure almost daily doses of rampant incompetence over the past three plus years, not to mention endless assaults on our democratic institutions. As we finished this book, America was still crippled by the COVID-19 virus and was agonizing over police brutality against our African American citizens. Nothing has become clearer than the realization that Donald Trump is no part of the solution to our nation's problems, but instead in very large measure the cause of them. No matter how many people die, he is jamming "open the economy" down the nation's throat while the plague remains viral, and fanning violence in our cities to get himself reelected. He may succeed. Although public polling shows large numbers of Americans want to take back their government from Trump and yearn to "Make America Sane Again," we must caution that November 2020 could result instead in another stunning Trump victory. If that happens, we believe it will be the end of our democracy, but no reader of this book should be greatly surprised if that happens. A large number of Americans stand ready to give Trump all the power he wants.

HOW TRUMP COULD AND SHOULD LOSE IN 2020

If it will restore your faith in a just world, no sitting president has ever given his opponent so many damaging statements or so much non-presidential behavior to remind voters how awful he has been, as has Donald Trump. The people putting together the campaign ads for the Democrats may have trouble agreeing on the top fifty best-of-the-worst sound bites, there are so many. To a considerable extent Trump has chained himself to a doghouse with most of the American electorate through a never-ending stream of ill-advised and transparently stupid decisions. In particular, he has lost the support of independent voters, who gave him 46 percent of their votes and Clinton 42 percent in 2016. Just two years later independents favored Democrats over Republicans by 12 percent in the midterm election. That dramatic switch gave Democrats control of the House of Representatives.[1] Since the midterms, independents have on balance disapproved of Trump's performance by roughly seven percent, most of them "strongly." As almost all Republicans support the president and almost all the Democrats find him repugnant, independents provide most of the net disapproval we find in the national polls and, barring a truly cataclysmic turn of events (Have we room for another one?), they will decide the 2020 election.

When things are relatively quiet on the domestic scene, independents start drifting ever so slowly back to the president. But such lulls last days, never weeks, for almost as if he is pre-programed to self-destruct, Trump does something very off-putting and loses his recent gains. "The Donald" has alienated a huge number of American voters; over 40 percent of the registered voters in the April and May 2020 polls strongly disapproved of his performance. People that mad might walk barefooted over broken glass and stand in line for hours to vote against him in November. He has very little chance of changing their minds. A Pew poll conducted in late April and early May even detected a perceptible slip in evangelicals' support for the president over the COVID-19 crisis. This reportedly matched GOP internal polling,[2] and set off various transparent moves to shore up Trump's support among conservative Christians, such as declaring places of worship to be essential services, visiting the shrine of Pope John Paul II, and saying prayer was the answer to the pandemic. Unfavorability ratings however do not mean lost votes. As became painfully clear to Democrats in 2016, it also depends on how unfavorably the electorate holds Trump's opponent. The Biden vs. Trump matchups in the polls always show a closer race than the difference in favourability ratings. Biden usually comes out on top, but you would not want to live off the difference. It will come down to the independent voters in the swing states, and how many Democrat supporters (get to) vote. But Trump's path through the Electoral College seems problematic in June.

TRUMP'S 2020 REELECTION PLAYBOOK

President Trump planned to campaign for reelection on a strong economy. That plan has come crashing down, thanks to his own blundering, and now he has pinned his hopes on the callous calculation that Americans will care more about increased job numbers because of an economy he is forcing open than the increased COVID-19 deaths this will cause as well. Trump and his campaign staff are busy developing other stratagems he will probably pursue regardless.

SECTION ONE: FEAR AND LOATHING. The first tactic in his re-election playbook will almost certainly be, "Scare them out of their minds."* He

---

* While the playbook we envision may not have been written out, you never know. The Nixon knows fear worked in 2016 with "Mexican rapists . . ." and he updated it in 2018 with "the caravan" of murderers, rapists, and terrorists about to invade the United States from Latin America. He has undoubtedly been searching for a new threat since then to directly engage his base's prejudices. Then on May 25, 2020, a Minneapolis police officer named Derek Chauvin changed everything when he casually murdered George Floyd in broad daylight, in public, and on camera. When the Black community and many others took to the streets in protest, the president positioned himself as the protector of white Americans against violent Blacks and radical left-wingers out to loot and burn down our cities and then head for the suburbs to rape and pillage.

If you sense that lots of white Americans would rush to back Trump if the ghettos in our cities exploded with violence, scientific evidence as well as a lot of history supports your intuition. When people were asked to answer the RWA Scale as they imagined they would when a violent left-wing movement was shaking the country, scores shot up.[3] That is, people became much more inclined toward authoritarianism, wanting a strong leader to protect them. This effect was called "the Nixon trap," a label named after the way support for Nixon escalated in 1968 following the riots at the Democratic National Convention in Chicago. Trump saw the Black Lives Matter demonstrations as a golden escalator to high poll numbers and he jumped right on. His reaction to the Floyd murder barely mentioned Floyd, or that tens of thousands of people were peacefully protesting racism and police brutality. Instead, he lambasted the very few in the crowds who were violent and ignored the underlying problem of systemic prejudice that was tearing the nation apart. Mr. "Death Penalty for the Central Park Five" wanted the story to be about left-wing radicals, looters, and those who fought with the police being steadfastly opposed by him, a powerful, dominating, violence-threat-

---

Committee to Reelect the President (CREEP) inexplicably prepared many such materials one would not think would be written out.

ening, hooligan-bashing, force-is-the-answer, law-and order-president. (He, by any evidentiary standard is the most unlawful president of all time.)

But it turned out the President's intuition had once again misled him and he had jumped on the "Down Escalator." Polls from CBS News, Emerson College, Reuters/Ipsos and Monmouth University all showed most Americans disapproved of his response to the demonstrations.[4] And for good reason. The experiments that highlighted the "Nixon trap" also found a situation which made people less authoritarian: when authorities attacked peaceful demonstrators. That was called the "Gandhi Trap," and the police and soldiers who fired tear gas and rubber bullets at, and rode horses through, peaceful demonstrators reminded people of films they had seen of Selma, an event that made many white Americans sick of the racism that runs so deeply throughout our nation's history. And if Trump had stayed up all night thinking about it, we doubt he could have made a more self-defeating threat than to turn "vicious dogs" on demonstrators who entered the White House grounds. And had he spent a week planning his next move, he could hardly have come up with anything more heinous than clearing away peaceful demonstrators with more tear gas and rubber bullets so he could walk across Pennsylvania Avenue and hold a Bible (upside down) in front of a church. Condemnation rained down on the White House because the photo-op was so incredibly hypocritical you felt slimed just seeing it. The mayor of Washington, DC, Muriel Bowser, joined a growing chorus of officials condemning the action, and had "Black Lives Matter" painted in big yellow letters over three blocks on the street leading directly to the White House. She out-trumped Trump by memorializing and making a monument of his folly.

Peaceful protests spread across the nation and remained surprisingly nonviolent as organizers condemned aggression, knowing that was just what the president wanted. The Black Lives Matter protestors knew all about the Gandhi Trap, just as Martin Luther King, Jr. had, and they must have been delighted when Donald Trump charged into it at full speed. Trump tried to paint radical left-wingers and antifa as the cause of the early violence. But he failed. Minnesota officials reported that white supremacists had traveled to Minneapolis to instigate violence. The FBI in Las Vegas arrested three members of the right-wing Boogaloo Boys extremist movement and charged them with planning to use firearms and explosives to create violence within a peaceful protest against police brutality.[5]

The fact that demonstrators are peaceful, not attacking police and looting stores, is a problem for Trump, particularly if this continues as the November 3 election nears. What do you think he will do to "fix" that? Uh-huh. We doubt he or his campaign are so stupid as to write out instructions on sabotaging a demo on a little card for their agents, but his supporters know what to do. So, if you are participating in a peaceful demonstration against a presidential policy this fall and the person next to you tries to get you to throw a bottle at the police, you might ask, as you are photographing him, and pointing him or her out to people around you, if he is being paid directly by the Trump campaign or through an intermediary.

SECTION TWO: SMEAR BIDEN TACTICS. Trump's reelection playbook surely involves any way he can think of to bring down Joe Biden's popularity. Biden's numbers have already fallen, probably because of his son's sweet deal serving on the board of a Ukrainian energy corporation and an accusation of sexual assault. But the attacks and smear tactics will get worse. A string of dramatic anti-Biden stories are likely lined up in the thoroughly pro-Trump *National Enquirer*, the slim sheet designed to catch shoppers' eyes as they wait to buy their groceries. They will be as misleading as the bogus stories about Hillary Clinton in 2016 that led some people to vote against her.[6] Remember: "24 Years of Cover-ups and Crimes Exposed: Hillary Hitman Tells All" or "Hillary Fails FBI Lie Test." The US intelligence community had determined by February 2020 that the Russian government was again trying to affect our election in various ways. Since Putin worked hard to get Trump elected last time, and has been handsomely rewarded for his effort, it would not be surprising if he is at it again. Russian propagandists will no doubt produce their own pile of anti-Biden stories and postings, soon to arrive on a screen near you. Does anyone believe Trump has any limit on how low and dirty he will go to win?

SECTION THREE: CREATE DEMOCRATIC DISARRAY. Trump can win by keeping Democrats from uniting. Parties typically lick their primary wounds and unite for the general election once the standard-bearer is chosen. The GOP did, to the astonishment of many, in 2016 after a particularly vicious run-up to the convention, and they united behind the person who had attacked the other candidates the most! So, Bernie Sanders's passionate supporters could join Biden's campaign in the fall and work for their joint interests, despite their honest differences on many matters. Sanders has said many times that above all else, Trump must be defeated. But Trump's re-election team, having learned in the 2016 campaign that some of Bernie's supporters only support Bernie, will do everything possible to keep them from voting for Biden in November. Trump has already pronounced, with his usual empty bucket of evidence, that the Democratic Party rigged the nomination against Bernie. You can be sure social media will be full of inflammatory stories and accusations against Biden's campaign for the nomination, many of them written by Republican graduates of the Roger Stone School of Dirty Tricks. If the GOP can get 20 percent of Sanders's faithful to stay home on November 3, 2020 in key states, it could tip the balance to Trump. Do not think for a moment that every vote does not matter.

Politics ain't beanball, the saying goes, and both Democrats and Republicans will misrepresent one another's positions and cite the most trumped-up, irrelevant statistics you can imagine to make points that are baseless. Fact checkers will be exhausted by early November. But we have no doubt which side will stretch the truth the most and stoop the lowest. Author Dean remembers when Democrats were at least as bad as Republicans. But lately, perhaps because demographic changes have put the GOP increasingly at a disadvantage, the Republicans have metamorphized into the party of foul play, and thankfully the remaining Democrats did not fully reciprocate. Witness "Willie Horton-ing," "Brooks Brothers Rioting," "Swift-boating," and "Benghazi-ing."

With Donald Trump for inspiration, a president who has broken norm after norm and openly engaged in illegal behavior, the GOP campaign will likely be governed by no rules whatsoever. Monstrous misrepresentations and fabrications will be commonplace. A good example of this occurred when Joe Biden was asked a question on December 30, 2019 about domestic violence. In responding he reminded everyone that for a long time our society shamefully tolerated husbands beating their wives, and this acceptance came from European culture and was included in British jurisprudence. But a 17-second video clip of his answer made it look like Biden believed in white supremacy: "Our culture is not imported from some African nation, or some Asian nation. It's our English jurisprudential culture. Our European culture."[10] "It's almost like Joe Biden is prejudiced," someone tweeted while spreading the distortion. Factcheckers will compile a very large portfolio of lies, overwhelmingly by Republicans is our bet. There are two reasons why Republicans lie so much: The truth makes them look bad, and lying works especially well with their followers, as we have seen.

Some of the dirty work is already underway as the conservative media tries to portray Joe Biden as suffering from mental and physical health problems. That is, of course, one of Roy Cohn's chief tactics: If you have a vulnerability, tell everybody your opponent reeks of it. As we have seen repeatedly in this book, Donald Trump has great trouble thinking straight. The problem is so severe that he often cannot control his thinking when he is making formal statements. His train of thought goes zip-zap-zup all over the place. Joe Biden, in comparison, occasionally misremembers names and his syntax can be worse than Sylvester Stallone's Rocky Balboa. But when he gets up after he has stumbled, he does express himself clearly. Trump often cannot do that, because usually there is no "clear" there. He cannot find what he is trying to say. He left that track four zip zaps back. And there is the added monumental difference that when Joe makes a mistake, he usually comes back and corrects it. Whereas if Trump does manage to say what he wanted to say, it is apt to be a lie, which just remains forever uncorrected by him and his allies. As for physical fitness for the job, we will pay $1000 to watch Trump and Biden do sit-ups, push-ups, or run a mile. We are not sure Donald Trump can even throw a baseball with any authority anymore. Anyone who drives a golf cart on the green to putt is unusually averse to exercise.

SECTION FOUR: VOTE SUPPRESSION. Few tools have become more important in the Republican election playbook than vote suppression. Withholding the franchise is as old as our republic, which at its birth did not let men without property, women, Blacks, and others vote. It took a series of constitutional amendments to enfranchise most of these groups. But some of these reforms were stymied at the state level, particularly through Jim Crow laws aimed at disenfranchising Black citizens. Thankfully, the Voting Rights Act of 1965 ended Jim Crow laws, bogus redistricting practices, and the array of other tactics that had been employed by white supremacists for decades to prevent minorities, particularly in the south, from voting. The act changed America and the political parties. It drove southern conservatives from the Democratic Party, where they had blocked such civil rights laws for decades, to the Republican Party, which went from the party of Abraham Lincoln to the party of an open racist, Strom Thurmond. Republicans have been attacking the Voting Rights Act for decades, but it remained largely intact until 2013, when the conservatives on the U.S. Supreme Court gutted the law by asserting that racism was in America's past.

Since the High Court eviscerated the Voting Rights Act, Republicans have joyfully adopted all manner of ways in states they control to make it difficult if not impossible for racial minorities, the poor, and the young to vote, if they are deemed likely to vote Democratic. All these suppression tactics are justified, supposedly, to control widespread voter fraud, which no one has yet shown even exists. The argument against voting by mail, for example, rests on several studies that show the list of voters who could receive ballots indeed do have numerous deceased and non-resident names on it, opening the door to systematic fraud. But no one has ever shown that such fraud has occurred. The real reason for making it harder, rather than easier, for targeted groups was stated by Donald Trump on a Fox TV show: Republicans would never be elected again if it were easier to vote.[7]

Additionally, Republican legislators have passed ID requirements to suppress votes from poor people. They have also cut the number of days for advanced voting, penalizing persons whose jobs or locations make it difficult for them to vote on election day. Some states have closed hundreds of polling stations. A shortage of voting machines may produce long line-ups and keep people with small windows for voting from exercising their right. Do not be surprised if voting machines fail a lot in certain places. Texas began checking immigrant registrations against citizenship, which made naturalized citizens afraid to register simply because they did not want to develop a file with ICE. Some states have removed citizens from the voting list if they have not voted in recent elections, which affects discouraged, disadvantaged groups more should they now try to have their say. Tennessee passed a law that held persons who conducted registration drives criminally responsible if some of the forms they turned in were incomplete. Georgia had prosecuted a dozen African Americans who conducted voter registration drives in Brooks County (the "Quitman 10+2") for such acts as carrying absentee ballots to registrars after voters had signed them.* Florida unsuccessfully tried to stop convicted felons from being able to vote after they had served their sentences. These and other moves to keep American citizens from casting a ballot have almost certainly decided recent elections. The Florida and Georgia gubernatorial races in 2018, for example, were won by Republicans by razor-thin margins, and those governors and their wink-wink, nod-nod legislatures will set up the 2020 voting system. COVID-19 will be exploited by the Republicans to suppress voting, on that you can be certain.[8]

SECTION FIVE: INVOLVE THE UNINVOLVED. In 2016, only 61.4 percent of the eligible voters cast a ballot for president, while four years earlier it was 61.8 percent. Obviously, if either party can win the affection of the stay-at-homes, it could run away with the election. You can bet that both parties have tried to corral their vote in the past, and mostly failed. Persons eighteen to thirty years of age vote less than any other age group, but they are also the most liberal, so the Trump campaign will not expend much effort wooing them. Instead, Trump will try to persuade older non-voters and intermittent voters to go to the polls. But it will be a hard sell. Pollsters find these people are alienated from the political process, feeling it does not matter who wins an election. Also, they are distrustful of others in general.[9] They will not likely vote unless something vitally important to them is at stake.

And now something is, namely, COVID-19. Even though Trump caused its dire impact on the United States more than anybody else, he went up in the polls when he looked like a President during his daily news

---

* Yahoo! News editorial staff, "The Quitman 10 + 2: How a Georgia voter fraud case set the stage for suppression," MSNBC News (Aug. 6, 2019) at https://www.msn.com/en-us/weather/other/the-quitman-10plus2-how-a-georgia-voter-fraud-case-set-the-stage-for-suppression/vp-AAFpKOi.

conferences with the scientists and doctors. Then, and we would say inevitably because Trump's inner problems which we uncovered in Chapters 2, 3, and 4 make him such a "loser," he blew it with hydroxychloroquine, re-open the economy now, injecting disinfectants, a vaccine very soon, no face mask, defunding the World Health Organization, fighting with the Center for Disease Control, demands that governors appreciate him, freezing out states from federal aid because their leaders criticized him, and so on. He squandered the sure path to re-election that fate had given him.

SECTION SIX: GO FOR THE UNDECIDEDS. Almost all registered voters in America have decided whether they want Trump removed from office or returned, but a few, most of them unaffiliated independents, have not. Last quadrennial election, FBI Director James Comey reintroduced the Hillary-emails issue on October 28, 2016, and that undoubtedly helped Trump win most of the voters who decided in the last week of the campaign. Since every vote will count in 2020, the Trump campaign will surely make a special effort to identify the undecideds, find out what they want, give them highly customized literature drops, invite them to coffee chats with other (supposedly undecided) voters, and so on. Thus, this is a vote to watch, and potential ground for the well funded Trump campaign.

SECTION SEVEN: THE OCTOBER SURPRISE. As if all this were not enough, we have not even touched upon every president's ace in the hole. When a president wants something, he can make things happen like nobody else. Even things that did not happen, such as North Vietnam's attacks on American destroyers in the Gulf of Tonkin in 1964 that Lyndon Johnson used to escalate the war. Trump is almost certain to pull off an "October surprise." It can be good news, such as China will (supposedly) give America everything it wants in a new trade deal, thanks to Master Negotiator Trump.

Or he will announce peace in Syria thanks to the same guy. Or a vaccine against COVID-19 will be available in just a day or two. Or the just-before-the-election surprise can be scary as all hell, our weakened nation is now vulnerable to a terrorist attack made possible by Democratic governors, or our overleveraged economy is pushing Social Security to the verge of bankruptcy because the Democrats have let too many "undeserving folks" onto the rolls. There usually is not enough time with an October surprise to fully check it out. That is why there aren't many September surprises. But once the election is over and won, nothing happens and the thoroughly snookered do not care. Did anyone who voted Republican in 2018 because the "caravan" was about to crash through the gates ask afterwards, "Hey, what happened to that caravan?"

SECTION EIGHT: VOTES ARE NOT ALWAYS COUNTED. If Democratic voters do make their way through the thickets and mazes that have been thrown up to keep them from voting, their vote may still not be counted. America's intelligence communities concluded that Russia launched cyber-attacks against the voting systems in all fifty states in 2016, and they are still at it. Other hackers, domestic as well as foreign, may have tried as well. For example, about 100,000 votes for Lieutenant Governor in Georgia, predominantly from African American polling places, simply disappeared without explanation in 2018. The state used outdated touchscreen voting machines that are easy to hack and leave no paper trail for a recount. The machines used in 2020 in Georgia will hopefully be better, but they failed so badly in June 2020 primaries that nobody knew the next day who had won. Some of the best hackers in the world will be trying intensely to affect the American election, and in the United States the leader of one of the major parties is known for "fixing" things and not minding in the least if Russia will fix things for him.

SECTION NINE: FLAGRANT BREAKING OF THE ELECTION LAWS. If as election day draws near and all the president's horses and all the president's men cannot guarantee Trump a victory, should anyone doubt he will try to steal the election? The authoritarian Republican Party's apparatus might instruct its loyal supporters to "vote early and vote often." Polling places in anti-Trump districts might be closed at mid-day because of "technical problems with the voting machines" or reports of gas leaks or COVID-19 advisories. Or voting machines might be directly corrupted, with every eighth Democratic vote converted to a Republican one. Tallies might be wildly wrong. Paper trails could be destroyed. Officials could be bribed. Would the people on the ground who carried out these instructions think they could someday be punished? Trump has already told civil servants in less crucial matters that if they break the law carrying out his wishes, he will grant them a pardon, and they may believe he can and will. With a lawless president, there is no way to predict what he might authorize, but those who want him out of the White House must brace for anything and everything.

AND WHAT WOULD TRUMP'S SECOND TERM BE LIKE?

If Trump wins the popular vote, then a majority of Americans will have endorsed an amoral authoritarian leader who could now do whatever he wanted. The question is not what would he do in his second term, but rather what would he not do? We would have given a man-child, stuck in "terrible two" tantrums, the keys to a tank and told him he can do whatever he wants. We will have a raging, utterly self-centered, "I want what I want when I want it" demagogue, who would be Commander in Chief of the mightiest military on the planet, who believes the American people have elected him king.

What about the Congress, you ask. Even if Congress were controlled by the Democrats, impeachment and removal would be impossible unless Trump was caught selling all of America's military and intelligence secrets to Russia for a hotel on Kremlin Square. While Democrats could again impeach, it is not likely they could muster the two-thirds vote in the Senate to remove. Or even override presidential vetoes on ordinary bills. Would not this most powerful president ever, with his long history of extracting revenge against everyone who ever crossed him, carpet bomb his mile-long Enemies List? Especially since he knows that a ruthless "settling of accounts" will intimidate future dissenters and carry him, pulverizing like a tornado, toward absolute control? With these ruined lives on display, like heads on London Bridge during the reign of the strikingly analogous Henry VIII, few if any would stand up to him when the inextinguishable fear within him made him expand his power over and over again for the rest of his days.

Could the courts stop him? Trump has never shown any respect for the judiciary, and his immediate response to any unfavorable ruling has usually been, "Get rid of the judge(s)." And if Republicans continue to control the Senate he would have the opportunity to replace and enlarge the "conservative" majority on the Supreme Court that already is willing to give him far more power than any president previously held. There is no previous ruling that this precedent-ignoring majority could not overturn. Everything you assume is legal, everything you believe is against the law, every freedom you think you have will be at risk. Four more years of President Trump will see the destruction of the Constitution as the foundation of our country. He and his authoritarian Republican cohorts and their authoritarian supporters will have undercut and overpowered the protections against absolute rule that George Washington, Benjamin Franklin, Thomas Jefferson, James Madison, Alexander Hamilton, and the other founders of the United States fought for. It was their overriding goal to keep the country from ever having a king. Yet a re-elected Donald Trump in 2021 would feel as powerful as James I, who believed he was appointed by God, or Louis XIV, who simply said, "I am the State." We pray we are wrong, but fear we are correct.

WHAT IF TRUMP LOSES IN 2020

Everyone knows Donald Trump is a sore loser, and the final precept of Roy Cohn's Machiavellian instructions was, "If you lose, say you won." So if Trump loses in November he will probably claim it was a rigged election, and he will try to get it overturned. But a sufficiently overwhelming outpouring by Democrats, and Democratic-leaning independents, can send him packing and bring moving vans to the South Portico of the White House on January 20, 2021. Trump's wretched mishandling of the COVID-19 and George Floyd tragedies has moved, perhaps only temporarily, some undecided voters into the Democratic camp, and even a handful of Trump's base appear (as of early June) shaken by how badly he has responded to these crises. The matter can be decided without a doubt by young voters, who are the least prejudiced age group in the United States and strongly oppose Trump on numerous grounds. Historically, persons eighteen to thirty years old vote less but they make up a majority of the crowds peacefully protesting against prejudice after George Floyd's murder. If the Democrats run good registration campaigns among the young, and if Biden supporters can overcome all the vote-suppression barriers the Republicans will throw at them, and if Bernie Sanders's supporters can settle for half of what they want in order to have a certain chance to get the rest later on, rather than no chance at all if Trump wins, Democrats can win the White House and both Houses of Congress in November.

Let us say that happens. The election is close, but even in the Electoral College the Democrats post a winning total. Nonetheless Trump claims there was colossal fraud, and the election should not count. "It was a hoax," he claims for the umpteenth time. "It has to be fair!" he says, and his base takes to the street shouting support for Trump. No one should be surprised if Trump loses and refuses to leave. Michael Cohen, Trump's in-house attorney for many years who knows the man much better than most, said under oath on February 27, 2019, "Given my experience working for Mr. Trump, I fear that if he loses the election in 2020 that there will never be a peaceful transition of power."[10] Trump's high-level staffer known as Anonymous for his/her *New York Times* OpEd and book, *A Warning*, says Trump "will not exit quietly – or easily," suggesting a "'civil war' in the offing."[11] Speaker Nancy Pelosi told the *New York Times* in May 2019 that Trump's refusal to accept defeat in 2020 was something that concerned her, adding, "We have to inoculate against that, we have to be prepared for that."[12]

Even if he loses the election, Trump will remain president until noon on January 20, 2021. He can try to stay in power lots of ways during that interval, even though no previous president has defied the wishes of the voters.[13] He could call his attorney general, William Barr, on November 4 and have him order federal attorneys in every state which the Democrats won to contest the election results in the courts. The states must by law resolve any controversies over appointment of electors by December 8, 2020. If recounts are underway in states the Democrats narrowly won, and Trump is ahead when the counting ends on December 8, the state's electoral votes could be awarded to him. George W. Bush won the election in 2000 because the Supreme Court held, 5–4, that this requirement had to be met, so the Florida recount was halted with many votes left to be examined. There are yet further opportunities for "putting a thumb on the scale" in later activities of the bizarre Electoral College system, and you can bet that "fixer" Trump has dozens of sycophants burrowing through the rules and procedures searching for ways to subvert them.

Donald Trump faces indictment on numerous crimes once he leaves office, and he has probably spent more time worrying about how to escape criminal prosecution than he has on containing COVID-19. He thinks he can pardon himself. Whether he can would be decided by the Supreme Court.[14] His surest path to staying out of jail would be to remain president—the American voters, the Electoral College, and the Constitution be damned. Thus, Trump, like many deposed demagogues before him, may well use his supporters' willingness to die for him to bargain an escape from ever standing trial. He would in effect be saying to his successor, "Don't you dare try to punish me for breaking the law. I will ignite a civil war and ruin the country if you do." This is how authoritarians usually try to escape when the jig is up. It is all about them to the last minute. But Trump faces more than potential federal charges, for we know he is an unindicted co-conspirator in New York, in the case that sent Michael Cohen to prison. Maybe he will go to Russia, where Putin will refuse to extradite him back to New York.

Or he might just boldly assert he has the right as president to stay in office "until the whole mess is cleared up" and see who dares oppose him. Donald Trump has probably developed one key insight during his first term as president: He can get away with almost anything. His base is massive and remarkably cohesive. They will believe and do almost anything he wishes. So too will almost all the Republicans in Congress, on almost all issues. They are at least "99 percenters," and anyway most of them would probably really like one-party rule with them forming the backbone of the new TRUMP Party. But we doubt the FBI, federal marshals, and the military would readily fall in line. All their members take an oath to defend the Constitution, and unlike Trump they place the highest emphasis, a John McCain-type emphasis, on personal honor, integrity, and self-sacrifice.

There is thankfully a "Deep State" in the American government, but it is not the subversive one Trump and his followers howl about. To the contrary, it consists of career public servants such as (listed alphabetically) Christopher Anderson, Michael Atkinson, Laura Cooper, Catherine Croft, David

Hale, David Holmes, George Kent, Michael McKinley, Robert Mueller, Philip Reeker, Mark Sandy, Bill Taylor, Alexander Vindman, Jennifer Williams, and Marie Yovanovitch – to use examples of people who testified before Congress notwithstanding Trump's instruction to not testify. There are surely countless others, like the "Whistleblower," who are deeply committed to the ideals of America. They have placed their country's interests ahead of their own and ahead of any despicable loyalty to the kind of power-seeking usurper George Washington warned about in his Farewell Address: "cunning, ambitious, and unprincipled men" who would "usurp for themselves the reins of government; destroying afterwards the very engines, which have lifted them to unjust dominion." These true public servants know an illegal act and an illegal order when they see one, and the federal law and the Constitution are quite clear about presidential succession.

COMING TOGETHER

Even if Trump leaves office peacefully in 2021 his base will remain intact and be available to him to hobble his successor as it did his predecessor; should Trump slip inexorably, that base is available to whoever can capture it for themselves. Someone smarter than Trump and championed by Fox News and the right-wing media echo chamber, could pose a much greater threat down the road. You can bet that various Double Highs have already begun thinking how to get incarnated as the next messiah. You can also bet the "king-makers" are studying the field right now too, including the leaders of the religious right who might sense Trump losing a bit of his hold on their believers.

Given the authoritarian base that abounds in America, unease lies ahead. Polarization will remain. Many Americans, perhaps heeding the words of Abraham Lincoln, and Matthew 12, understand that a house divided against itself cannot stand. Many are as well exhausted with the strife that American politics have become, and they yearn for a reconciliation of our sharply divided people. It cannot be done, however, by a saw-off such as "You guys become less prejudiced and authoritarian and we'll become more so." If there is one thing the weeks of "Black Lives Matter" demonstrations and the polls made clear, it is that America is sick and tired of being sick and tired. Our levels of prejudice and authoritarianism must go down. Fortunately, that can be done, by the high RWAs at least. Most of them, we know from studies, have no idea how afflicted they are with these traits compared with the rest of the American population. They think they have "normal" levels of prejudice, for example, and you can be sure Republican spokespersons will tell them they are not prejudiced at all, "just normal, you know." But you can be both prejudiced and normal and will definitely be both in a society that practices systematic discrimination. Calling high RWAs and evangelicals "bigots" will only make them dig in. But the data revealed in Chapter 10 shows how relatively prejudiced Trump's supporters proved to be in a straight-up-and-down poll. And that ought to lead to some serious soul-searching by those people.

The change will last if it comes from within them, from a desire to do better with their lives, from a realization that following their religious beliefs should make them the least prejudiced and least authoritarian people in society, not lead them to falling face-down before a world class false prophet. It will not be easy for them. They are afraid, and unaccustomed to such self-searching. In a real sense, *they* have been denied the blessings of liberty to which they are entitled in a democracy. They were raised more to be copies than originals. They did not have the freedom to decide their beliefs that others had. They were reared in a way that made them vulnerable to a con man like Trump, just as he was raised to become the deeply unconfident social dominator he has been since an early age. These people have not yet claimed their birthright as Americans. But if they realize that, they can choose for themselves.

It is possible, and we certainly hope, that some of the social dominators also might change. Competitiveness is as baked into Americana as apple pie. We ritualistically celebrate winners every year from the Golden Globes awards to the Best Float in the Rose Bowl Parade, including shelves of sports trophies, school awards, and blue ribbons from the county fair for such things as Best Pickled Beets. We realized long ago what every jogger knows from day one: That you perform better when somebody else is with you, even if it is not a race. And you will likely post your personal best if it is a race. The problem with social dominators is not their desire to excel, nor to win per se. It is their craving for the power that comes from besting, the difference between a need for achievement and a need for dominance. It is that craving that leads to cheating. If competitiveness is baked into Americana, it has been understood that the competition must be fair and square, it must abide by the rules that everyone has agreed upon. Golf is difficult because of the rules, so when you cheat you are not playing golf. When you have someone in the dugout banging on a barrel so your batter will know that the next pitch will be a fastball, that's not apple pie. Donald Trump has never played by the rules, has always instead tried to gain advantage over others by gaming the system, bribing, or intimidating officials, lying about anything, hiring people to be what they are not, and insisting on always having it his way. People who want to win because they are genuinely better will not want to follow his example. It leads to momentary triumph and a lifetime of disgrace. Think Tonya Harding or Lance Armstrong. There are many far better women and men to emulate.

If in January 2021 Donald Trump becomes a one-term president, his successor will inherit a deeply damaged country, in even worse shape than the one Barack Obama had to get out of the ditch in 2009. The COVID-19 pandemic will likely be unresolved unless (and until) a vaccine and therapeutic treatment are widely available, and the world economy will still be reeling from it all, if not in deep recession or depression. Our allies will have every reason to distrust our loyalty and the shelf-life of our commitments, not to mention the value of our word. How can they trust that we will not elect another Donald Trump in four or eight or twelve years? America will still be bleeding from outbursts of racism and other violence from coast to coast, border to border. Often when a populist authoritarian government has been voted out of office in a democracy, the country just careens toward a different form of dictatorship. The institutions of government have been corrupted, the principle of rule by law has been tortured by a thousand cuts, and the guardrails have all been kicked away.[15] Social dominators can be chameleons, adopting whatever beliefs and disguise will enrich them, and they grow mightily in a culture of chaos. Eternal vigilance. Remember, no one said democracy would be easy.

CLOSING THE BOOK . . .

Donald John Trump is way out of his league playing a clever usurper of power. If it appears that we have been hard on him, listen to the people who do. As human beings go, he is a sorry specimen. His driveway has not reached the main road for a long, long time. He is incapable of fixing his own life, which is deeply scarred by escarpments of chutzpah and pitted with bottomless potholes of ignorance and self-deception, so he is incapable of repairing the damage he has done. If he becomes a monarch, we can brag that it did not take us generations of inbreeding to produce an imbecile king. We shall have started with one. Even sadder, Trump might be made dictator by a distinct minority of the country. Most Americans will not have voted for him; they simply did not vote. In short, we could lose what our forebearers fought for and won and preserved and rightly celebrated because most of us would not even go to the polls in 2020 to keep them.

If there is one thing Trump opponents can do to win back the country, besides voting in large numbers in November, it is to help a non-voter become a voter too. Making personal contact, pointing out how their future depends on who gets elected, facilitating registration and getting them to the polls—even from a minimum distance of six feet—will probably be a lot more effective than giving a campaign money. So will participating in registration drives. The largest group that can save America from authoritarianism are young American adults, who also will lose the most if the United States becomes a dictatorship. The rest of their lives figure to be a lot longer than the time left for a couple of old duffers like your authors. We understand that it is a lot to ask of young people, those in their late teens, 20s, and 30s to add politics to their list of concerns as they try to lay down the foundations of their lives in a world as economically screwed up as this one is. But their country truly needs them, now! They are the least prejudiced, best educated, most technically savvy part of our society. They recognize the danger of global warming, which has become a most unwelcome part of their inheritance, and are most aware of the role the United States must play in containing the climate disaster ahead. They are also the group most likely to come out of the COVID-19 pandemic alive. They are the people who can and do reach out and embrace one another across the racial splits and close our hemorrhaging wounds.

We would like to make a closing plea to these young people, starting with those we know: Molly, Sally, Franny, Sean, Camryn, Ollie, Caleb and Carter. The planet needs another greatest generation. It is all going to come down to you. Many young people believe becoming politically active will make no difference, because no one pays any attention to them. Well, that comes straight out of the box of instant self-fulfilling prophecies. Nobody will pay attention to you if you do not vote. But we promise you the obvious: When you start voting in big numbers, everybody will pay attention to what you want. Pull up a chair to the table where your future is being decided.

In the end the hope for healing America depends on the same thing as the hope for preserving America as a nation: Defeating Donald Trump at the polls in enough states to give us a new president. And a new Congress would be invaluable as well. This November 2020 is the biggest election of your authors' lives. Nothing much is at stake, you know: just the Constitution, the rule of law, and American democracy. America has not stood so clearly at a fork in the road since the 1860s. The route laid out by our nation's founders is clearly marked. The other road, of which they warned, has danger signs flashing all along the way, and yet many Americans are tugging at the steering wheel to yank us in that dangerous direction. They must be outvoted. It is trite but true: We have a rendezvous with destiny once again to see if our government of all the people, by all the people, and for all the people shall perish from the earth.

AFTERWORD

THE JANUARY 6TH INSURRECTION AND THE AUTHORITARIAN REPUBLICAN PARTY

JOHN W. DEAN

Today, the Republican Party is authoritarian from bottom to top, with the exception of a few dreamers who hope the party will come to its senses and return to its less autocratic ways of old. That is not going to happen. We provide the hard evidence for this GOP transition to authoritarianism in Chapters Nine and Eleven, information confirmed by the national survey on authoritarianism undertaken for this book by the Monmouth University Polling Institute in late 2020 and reported in Chapter Ten. The information was reconfirmed post–2020 election by a supplemental survey by Monmouth taken from a subset of the same panel initially examined before the election. We are all witnessing, and too often on the daily news, what this means for American politics, as the anti-democratic ways of authoritarian Republicans play out in current affairs.

One of the questions our Monmouth survey asked (see page 224) was whether Trump supporters would tolerate his declaring the 2020 election "fixed and crooked," making the "election results null and void," so he might remain as president: 14 percent were okay with this, and 19 percent were unsure. Stated a bit differently, 33 percent said they would tolerate such a ploy, which was remarkably strong. On the other hand, 96 percent of his supporters were opposed to his ignoring the Constitution, which surprised us, causing us to wonder if the survey reflected "a case of compartmentalized thinking," such as stating support for the Constitution being merely a visceral response, for when Trump actually ignored the Constitution it became another matter. Turns out we were correct in questioning this response on our survey. Trump has not given his supporters any reason to ignore the Constitution, yet that is what he is doing, and they fully support him.

When the Monmouth team returned to the field after the election it contacted 303 participants from the prior study to quiz them about the results of the election. While these findings are not projectable to a larger population, Monmouth explains, the data is certainly revealing about Trump's dyed-in-the-wool authoritarian followers.[1] Monmouth looked at those who scored high on the Right Wing Authoritarian (RWA) scale and on the Social Dominance (SD) scale, which included those who tested high on both, the "Double Highs." In releasing these findings, Patrick Murray, who heads the Monmouth Polling Institute, noted, "Research on authoritarianism suggests that a fairly consistent proportion of the public has anti-democratic inclinations," and, more importantly, added that the "extent to which we see these authoritarian tendencies play out in public life depends on whether those views are given credibility by society, particularly by its leaders."[2] I would add to Dr. Murray's observation that Donald Trump followers have displayed their anti-democratic inclinations during the past four years, and he invited them, after he lost the 2020 election, to double down, which provided a spectacle for all to witness. It was, in fact, the most profound authoritarian nightmare Americans have ever experienced.

Shamelessly, and with absolutely no evidence, Donald Trump claims that he won the 2020 reelection—in a landslide, no less—and says that he is not serving his second term because the election was "stolen." The fact that he has no evidence to back up this claim is irrelevant; when Trump declares an allegation true, it becomes fact for him. Appropriately, the news media has labeled Trump's bogus claim that he won in 2020 election as "The Big Lie."[3] Establishing a new low for gullibility of American authoritarians, compartmentalization, and the embrace of dystopian beliefs, Trump has sold The Big Lie to a stunning number of his followers, such as his Vice President Mike Pence,[4] no less than eight Republican US Senators,[5] most Republican Members of the US House of Representatives including the top leadership (sans Liz Cheney),[6] and the overwhelming majority of Republican state attorneys general,[7] not to mention 76 percent of all self-declared Republicans.[8] As we indicated, authoritarians are not particularly interested in the truth, nor inclined toward critical thinking. Who are these people? From the vantage point of social science no doubt most of these elected GOP officials are Social Dominators, if not Double Highs. As the post-election Monmouth survey revealed, probably most of those self-declared Republicans, those who are buying into Trump's Big Lie, are likely RWAs. For example, among those people Monmouth identified as High RWA Trump voters, 93 percent believe the "Deep State" was definitely trying to hurt Trump and 91 percent agreed that voter fraud changed the 2020 election outcome, with 62 percent of them not believing Republican officials who say there was NO fraud, rather, these people are covering up evidence.[9]

Trump's post-election behavior has not been without consequences, for he has created an attitude wave of distrust that continues to influence government and public affairs. Because he claimed the election was stolen, Trump largely refused to participate in some seventy days of transition from his administration to his successor's, President Joe Biden. Even more troubling, he was not interested in a *peaceful* transfer of power—a hallmark of American democracy. Trump's behavior made it far more difficult for the Biden administration to distribute the desperately needed COVID-19 vaccines that had been developed with no plans for distribution. Trump's dismantling of immigration processes at America's southern border produced a humanitarian crisis when undocumented children seeking to escape violence and poverty at their homes made what has become an annual spring pilgrimage to the United States of generational dimensions. Trump left America's foreign policy in shambles, with Republicans now admiring Russia's Vladimir Vladimirovich Putin—a pure authoritarian—more than President Joe Biden—a classic (small d) democrat. But for the grace of God and a strong military (which Trump did not have time to destroy), the Biden administration has made clear to the world that "America is back." Trump clutched to the power of his office not because he understood it, or even knew how to employ it, but rather because it provided a shield from the world awaiting him when the presidency no longer will protect him from his corruption. Clearly, had the office of presidency not departed him, Trump would have never let go of it. But Trump's presidency ended at noon on January 20, 2021 by the terms of the US Constitution, notwithstanding his escalating efforts to continue as president, endeavors which culminated with nothing less than an unimaginable but thankfully failed insurrection on January 6, 2021—actions which will forever scar American democracy. Trump's call for insurrection was every bit the "High Crime" for which he would be impeached a second time, on January 13, 2021, just as the office was leaving him.

The Twentieth Amendment to the Constitution states that a president's term ends "at noon on the 20th day of January," and the term of a successor "shall then begin." For a president to have a second term, needless to say, he or she must be reelected. To be reelected Trump had to be certified as the winner of the electoral college by the vice president, Mike Pence, who, pursuant to a long-standing statute (the Electoral Count Act of 1887) reports the results, alphabetically and state by state, at a Joint Session of Congress on January 6th. The vice president's role is purely ceremonial—his job is to announce what has already been certified by the laws of each state. If a member of the House, joined by a member of the Senate, objects to any state's certified vote, the matter is returned to each chamber for debate and resolution. It takes a majority vote of both House and Senate to reject the certified electoral vote of any state.[10] If for any reason no president is named as a result of this process, the speaker of the House of Representatives becomes the "Acting President," until it is resolved. This has long been the law, and it has never been clear how Trump believed he could reverse the results of the November 3, 2020 election either before, during, or after the Congressional proceedings on January 6, 2021. But planning, or even rudimentary understanding of our government, has never been Trump's strong suit. At the end Trump appears to have lost the aid and assistance of those who had tired of pleasing the naked emperor, a thankless man, and without them he was at best a bumbling demagogue without the knowledge or skills to engineer the coup of his dreams.

Within three days of the election it was clear that Trump had lost, conspicuously so. The projected results were announced on November 6, 2020, first by CNN, and followed soon by NBC, CBS, MSNBC, and ABC, all finding Biden the winner with even Trump's news organization of choice, Fox News, joining the Biden projection. By November 7, it was reported by virtually all print and electronic news media that Trump had received 232 electoral votes, and Biden had received 306 electoral votes. (Biden had won by the exact same electoral college total as Trump had when he defeated Hillary Clinton in 2016 and claimed himself a landslide winner.) On November 8, Trump made his first public statement regarding his projected loss, when he tweeted, "this was a stolen election."[11] Trump's loss could not have been a surprise to him because public polling, and surely his own campaign's internal polling, showed him losing throughout the 2020 campaign. Correspondingly, whenever he was asked by a reporter if he would accept the election results, Trump evaded or refused to respond. Rather than commit to a peaceful transfer of power, he said, "We're going to have to see what happens." Even after the early returns went against him, Trump tweeted on November 4, "We are up BIG, but they are trying to STEAL the Election." Then, following the November 8 projected loss, Trump began promoting his new mantra to his supporters: "Stop the Steal!" Just as he never made clear how he planned to reverse the election results, he never made clear who had stolen the election. Trump was also vague about how he would reverse the election because there was no legal way to do so. And he could not identify how the election had been stolen because, in fact, it had not been.

Trump's lawyers filed dubious lawsuit after dubious lawsuit, which is something court rules everywhere prohibit, yet they succeeded without being sanctioned by judges or bar associations.[12] Meanwhile, Trump was running a private and brazenly illegal effort to use the powers of his high office to overturn the results in a sufficient number of these elections to pick up the 38 electoral votes he needed.[13]

It is a felony in every state in the United States to corruptly interfere with the election process, and when this activity involves a federal election, as here, there are also applicable federal laws prohibiting interference in the election processes.[14] Because Trump was leaning on Republican officials and his friends in high places in seven states, only a little has been reported of his illicit efforts, and only one state, Georgia, has initiated a formal investigation into his activities (as this is being written.) Nonetheless, there is considerable public information about Trump's conspicuously corrupt if not criminal behavior in seeking to overturn the election results in several states. For example, public reports indicate that Trump focused his effort to overturn the results by bullying election officials in three states: Michigan, Pennsylvania, and Georgia.

On November 18, 2020 Trump falsely tweeted "Democrats cheated big time" in Michigan, and he personally lobbied two members of the board of canvassers for Wayne County, Michigan, to rescind their prior votes certi-

fying the election results.[15] He next flew Michigan's top Republican legislative officials to Washington for a meeting at the White House.[16] Because
the news media got wind of these activities, state officials became less than
willing to openly break the law for the president of the United States, who
wanted them to overthrow the election in Michigan, which he had lost by
over 150,000 votes.* Trump moved next to Pennsylvania, where he openly
(and probably covertly, as well) attacked the election results. His Pennsylvania lawsuits, in both federal and state courts, were going nowhere. So
Trump focused on corrupting the Pennsylvania state legislature.[17] When
the Republican legislative leaders refused to travel to the White House and
entertain Trump's efforts to change the vote, nothing came of the session
with the legislators who had gone to the White House.

Trump worked particularly hard to overturn Georgia's election results.†
While most of the states that Trump leaned on to reverse the results, including many in Georgia, were and are friendly to him, so willing to ignore
his attacks. But even Republican officials in Georgia who had voted for him
were sufficiently leery of his blatantly criminal behavior that they took pre-

---

* The reports of Trump's planned efforts to get states officials to have their legislatures to ap-
point Trump electors contrary to state laws (which required the electors be awarded to the
winner of popular vote) appears to be a remnant of a grand scheme conceived by Trump's
2020 campaign team to ignore (overthrow) existing election laws openly and illegally in 26
states where Republicans control the legislatures. This scheme was revealed, and the plans
were apparently disrupted, by Barton Gellman's report of September 23 for *The Atlantic*, "The
Election That Could Break America: If the vote is close, Donald Trump could easily throw
the election into chaos and subvert the results. Who will stop him?" The pitiless spotlight of
publicity appears to have killed the scheme.

† Trump also had others doing his dirty work, as well. South Carolina Republican Senator
Lindsey Graham called at least three states to sway their vote totals, including Georgia. In
late November 2020 Graham called Georgia Secretary of State Raffensperger and requested
he throw out all mail in ballots, while threatening Raffensperger. When his illegal behavior
became public, Graham denied it. This appears to have prompted Georgia officials to start
recording their calls with Trump and his enablers, so there is no doubt who said what. Because Georgia is investigating these activities, we should all learn more, but this summary
will suffice to illustrate how authoritarians operate.

cautions. They had witnesses on the telephone calls, which they recorded. Authoritarian followers are not stupid, nor are they automatically blindly loyal. Most Social Dominators and Double Highs are thinking and looking out for themselves. So while they may have voted for him, they were not interested in going to jail for him. For example, on December 23, 2020, during the official inquiry into whether there were any voting irregularities in Georgia, Trump, who was the only person claiming irregularities without hard evidence, called Georgia's lead elections investigator, Frances Watson, to encourage her to scrutinize ballots in Fulton County, claiming she would find "dishonesty there." Trump also told this state-level investigator that she had "the most important job in the country right now," as he clearly sought to corrupt her efforts to find the truth.[18]

If that were not sufficiently outrageous (and illegal) behavior Trump's next attacks on Georgia's Secretary of State Brad Raffensperger—also a staunch Trump supporter—was ruthless, as he employed the full powers of his bully pulpit against a defenseless state official. The House impeachment managers described the situation for the Senate:

> On November 11, while Georgia's vote count was in progress, Republican Secretary of State Brad Raffensperger publicly stated that there was no evidence of widespread voter fraud and that ballots were being accurately counted. President Trump then tweeted about Raffensperger seventeen times between November 11 and the date on which Georgia finally certified its election results. On Thanksgiving Day, he declared Raffensperger an "enemy of the people" for insisting upon the integrity of Georgia's election. Reflecting an ominous pattern that would recur many times over the weeks that followed, President Trump's attacks on Raffensperger sparked threats of death and violence; one such message warned that

"the Raffenspergers [sic] should be put on trial for treason and face execution." Nonetheless, President Trump continued his assault on Raffensperger. President Trump's attacks [on Georgia officials] were so concerning that Gabriel Sterling, another Republican election official in Georgia, publicly warned: "Mr. President . . . Stop inspiring people to commit potential acts of violence. Someone's going to get hurt, someone's going to get shot, someone's going to get killed."[19]

Trump remained intent on Raffensperger with no interest in backing off. On January 2, 2021, his chief of staff, Mark Meadows, assembled a call with four Trump attorneys on the line when he spoke to Raffensperger. Four attorneys listened as Trump badgered the top election official of Georgia to change the vote. On that call was former law professor and dean of Chapman Law School John Eastman, who knew election laws, for he had run for attorney general of California, and Rudy Giuliani, a former high-level official at the Department of Justice and US Attorney of the Southern District of New York. Rudy had to know harassing a state election official was potentially a violation of federal and state law. Also on Trump's side of the call were lawyers Cleta Mitchell, a conservative gadfly and election law expert who should have known this call was out of bounds, and real estate law expert Kurt Hilbert, who shows how far Trump had fallen to find lawyers. It is not clear why all these lawyers were on this call, but it certainly was not to prevent Trump from violating the law, for none of them intervened to blunt Trump's behavior. Eastman, Giuliani, Mitchell and Hilbert appear to be classic Double Highs—they are going along because they want to please the most powerful client they have ever had, and man they may have assumed would protect them if this all went south. In times past, I watched spines dissolve like this before a president, and it is never pretty.

During the Raffensperger call, Trump focused mostly on Fulton County, the largest political subdivision in Georgia and where most of the city of Atlanta is located. Over a million people live in Fulton County with about 44 percent of them white while 44 percent of them are black or African American. Trump lost in Fulton County heavily: 137,240 for Trump and 381,144 for Biden. Fulton County comes up sixteen times during this conversation.[20] Trump bullied, browbeat, and belittled as he worked to intimidate Georgia's top election official into changing the vote. At one point he told Raffensperger to "find" 11,780 votes—one more vote than Trump needed to win Georgia, which Biden had carried by 11,779 votes. Trump falsely accused Raffensperger of criminal misconduct and accused (former and future candidate for governor of Georgia) Stacey Abrams of dishonesty and unconstitutional behavior (both unspecified) in his efforts to mislead Raffensperger. This was typical Trump behavior—and not unlike most authoritarian leaders who do not care about the law. We do not know if his lawyers advised him that both federal and Georgia law prohibit interference with the election process. Appropriately, Raffensperger, who recorded the call, referred it to Fulton County District Attorney Fani Wills, who is investigating Trump's behavior, which soon got worse, as often happens when authoritarians do not get their way.

It would be difficult to find a nastier example of contemporary authoritarian politics playing out than Trump's effort to incite an insurrection on January 6, 2021, when the Congress was tasked by law to count the electoral college votes and declare a winner. His efforts at the state and local levels had failed. So he attacked the US Congress, a coequal branch of the government he wanted to control. Trump viewed Congress as his last chance to keep the presidency and overturn the election. If Congress could not declare a winner he thought he would be the winner. (He never explained how he would get around the law making the Speaker the acting president, but Donald does not do details.)

As early as December 2020, Trump was eyeing January 6, 2021 as his backup solution to dealing with the election he had lost. He started telling supporters on Twitter to show up for the "big protest" at the Capitol on January 6th. For example, on December 19, 2020 he included in a tweet: "Statistically impossible to have lost the 2020 Election. Big protest in D.C. on January 6th. Be there, will be wild!" On December 27th he tweeted: "See you in Washington, DC, on January 6th. Don't miss it. Information to follow!" By January 1, his tweets were getting more specific: "The BIG Protest Rally in Washington, D.C., will take place at 11.00 A.M. on January 6th. Locational details to follow. StopTheSteal!" A few days later he told supporters the January 6 rally in Washington would start on the Ellipse, which adjoins the White House grounds. (This is a venue that can be used only with the permission of the White House, meaning the president.) As January 6 approached, he pushed his supporters, as he rallied them on January 4 in Georgia "to fight like hell."

On January 6, when Trump addressed his supporters on the Ellipse after warmup speakers like Rudy Giuliani and Don Trump Jr. had stoked the crowd, he continued this belligerent tone, calling for a fight to stop the steal. It was clear he wanted his supporters to believe what was occurring at the Capitol was illegal—and notwithstanding the fact he was commander in chief of the most powerful government in the world, he needed his motley crowed to protect his election. As the House Impeachment Managers described his hour-long harangue of his supporters:

> President Trump repeatedly reiterated his claim that Democrats had "stolen" the election. He described vote tranches that favored President Biden as "explosions of bullshit." He exhorted the crowd to "fight much harder" to "stop the steal" and "take back our country." He also demanded again that Vice President Pence illegally interfere with the work of the

Joint Session—a position that the vice president rejected even as President Trump spoke. Time and again, President Trump declared that the future of the country was on the line and that only the crowd assembled before him could stop the massive fraud taking place at the Capitol.[21]

The House managers also noted that "At numerous points during the rally, President Trump urged the crowd toward the Capitol . . ."[22]

Like millions of television viewers I witnessed what happened at the Capitol Building on January 6, 2021 with utter horror. Having studied authoritarian personalities over a decade and collaborated on this book with a foremost expert on these people, I was not surprised by their behavior. Rather the revulsion came from the president of the United States encouraging and then unleashing these people to disrupt the culmination of his defeat which occurred with the official count of the electoral votes. In fact, this coup attempt was pathetic, typical of the incompetence Trump has shown at everything he does. The disgust came from the spineless and sniveling Republicans who believe Trump is powerful because he conned millions of unsophisticated and gullible Americans into voting for him. It was the Republicans in the House and Senate who had joined his cabal by claiming the Big Lie was true, so they opposed the certification. House members objected to certification in Arizona, Georgia, Michigan, Nevada, and Pennsylvania. These objections were joined by Senators in only Arizona and Pennsylvania, after being interrupted for hours during the insurrection riot, they were voted down in both House and Senate after being debated. There was no fraud or voting irregularities anywhere. Who were these elected officials that played along with Trump? The marquee players were Senator Josh Hawley of Missouri and Senator Ted Cruz of Texas, both of whom want to inherit Trump's base—and to do so believe they must sink lower than him. All of those who joined Trump's insurrection, both those elected and unelected, were conspicuous Double Highs, the authoritarian personality that brings forth some of the nastiest of traits in humans.

The Trump January 6, 2021 insurrection will live in infamy. Accompanying it is the travesty of the 43 Senate Republicans who spinelessly refused to hold Trump accountable, after he was impeached by the House of Representatives, for inciting the insurrection at the Capitol. Virtually all of these Republicans are Double Highs, who undoubtedly could envision themselves doing what Trump had done and trying to overturn an election by sending supporters to attack Congress—although few would admit embracing such un-American behavior. The January 6 insurrection and its aftermath are the unfortunate but illustrative capstone of all we have warned about in this book. Trump's Big Lie failed to overturn the 2020 election, but Republicans are using it at the state and local level to rewrite election laws to suppress potentially Democratic voters, specifically people of color and college students, who tend to vote against Republicans. Republican officials have introduced hundreds of proposals to suppress voting. Authoritarians will employ whatever tactics they can find to win, and they are ruthless. The world knows this is a revival of the infamous and disgraceful Jim Crow tactics that followed the Civil War and Reconstruction era. But Republicans cannot be shamed into democratic behavior. What worries me is that I am not sure Democrats can or will match them, so Republican authoritarianism will grow and become even more ruthless.

As I see it, it will not get better; rather, it will get worse. The Republican Party has declared open and unabashed war on American democracy— they want to disenfranchise any and all whom they believe will stand in their way. They fear all who do not look and think like they do. Republicans no longer offer a governing philosophy; rather they tout personalities and cultural bromides as they seek return to a time when white men controlled women and all who were not white.

These people have always been amongst us, and always will be. Maintaining democracy, and a democratic republic such as ours, is a never-ending struggle. Authoritarians do not necessarily want an autocracy or dictatorship, but rather control and dominance, and they might settle for minority rule, since they will always be a minority. But please remember if you give authoritarians the control they seek they will not take us to a more prefect union. Rather these personalities will never accept others unlike themselves, and the threat they believe others unlike them pose. They are not naturals for democratic government where the will of the majority must prevail.

So what is the answer? Vigilance. Understand who these people are and what they want, including more scholars and social scientists examining and explaining these Americans.[23] Never stop challenging them. They can be outvoted as occurred in 2020, albeit by a thin margin. They can be outvoted by larger margins if more non- and low-authoritarians vote and participate in their government. Remember this: There are more of us than there are of them, and if the majority rules, America can and will move toward a more perfect union. If the authoritarians rule, government will be for the few not the many, and we will regress as a nation as we have during every period when modern Republicans have ruled in Washington, and in the red states they control. The best thing that could happen in the coming few years is for the Republican Party, now controlled by authoritarians and increasingly dysfunctional, to collapse. And there is more chance of that occurring than their succeeding in making America the autocracy they believe would solve their problems.

ACKNOWLEDGMENTS

My thanks to Valerie Merians, Dennis Johnson, Mike Lindgren, Tim McCall, Cassie Gutman, and the team at Melville House for going beyond the call of duty to make this book happen.

JOHN W. DEAN

I want to thank John Dean for inviting me along on this interesting venture.

My good friend and eminent personality researcher Lew Goldberg read the first draft of "AN." He provided one powerful criticism of our presentation, but otherwise thought it was a good show.

Most of the research reported in Chapter Eight was done with the late Bruce Hunsberger, who died of leukemia in 2003. Bruce was a great teacher, administrator, and a brilliant investigator. He won the William James Award given by the American Psychological Association's Division on the Psychology of Religion.

BOB ALTEMEYER

APPENDIX I

"FLUIDS" VERSUS "FIXEDS"

Hetherington and Weiler's explanation of the stark polarization in America is based on a four-item questionnaire that was invented by Stanley Feldman and inserted into the American National Election Survey (ANES) in 1992. (This is a big landmark poll taken before and after each presidential election by the University of Michigan and Stanford University.) The four questions seek out preferences in child-rearing.

- Please tell me which one you think is more important for a child to have: independence or *respect for elders*?
- Please tell me which one you think is more important for a child to have: obedience or *self-reliance*?
- Please tell me which one you think is more important for a child to have: to be considerate or to be *well-behaved*?
- Please tell me which one you think is more important for a child to have: curiosity or *good manners*?

Feldman believed the italicized choices (which were not italicized in the survey) indicated a preference for conforming to old values. He thought this was the essence of authoritarianism. The alternatives in the four items indicated a desire to challenge old values, he believed.[*]

The questions were used in subsequent "ANESs." Hetherington and Weiler studied these results and believed they demonstrated how different levels of authoritarianism had produced the great polarization in American politics.[†] But nine years later

---

[*] Stanley Feldman, "Enforcing social conformity: A theory of authoritarianism," *Political Psychology* (Vol. 24, No. 1, 2003), 41-74.

[†] Marc J. Hetherington & Jonathan D. Weiler, *Authoritarianism and Polarization in American Politics* (New York: Cambridge University Press, 2009).

they said the four questions did not measure authoritarianism after all, but instead how "fluid" or "fixed" people were. "Fluids" do not see the world as dangerous and endorse letting people find their own way in life. "Fixeds" think the world is dangerous and prefer clear and unwavering rules to help them navigate all the threats.[*]

If you want to see how "Fixed" you are, count the number of italicized alternatives you favor in the four questions. Zero makes you totally unFixed but so fluid you could be a soft drink. A score of four makes you as Fixed as a beam driven into the ground by a pile driver. The gist of Hetherington and Weiler's approach is that when you compare the "Zeros" with the "Fours," in the ANES surveys and other studies, the two extremes have starkly different opinions on many issues. In 2016, 71 percent of the Zeros were Democrats and 60% of the Fours were Republicans.

HOWEVER, MISGIVINGS

American public opinion is so polarized now one can easily find a slew of beliefs on which people are sharply divided, with Democrats and Republicans dominating opposite extremes. Religion, economics, immigration, sex roles, welfare, the environment, civil rights, American Exceptionalism, you name it. You could do this with *one* simple question about abortion, capital punishment, the right to protest, gun control, voter registration, Rush Limbaugh, country music, or the Academy Awards program. The fact that Democrats and Republicans tend to dominate opposing extremes on child-rearing preferences does not, by itself, mean it can *explain* "America's great divide." That requires a lot more evidence. Speaking of which: If Fixeds, more than anything else, see the world as being much more dangerous than Fluids do, that should be demonstrated by a "pitting" experiment in which scores on the Four Questions show they correlate better with perceived threat than other conceivable explanations do. Those, and other comparative studies one might require before accepting the authors' conclusions, do not appear to have been done.

Beyond that, the conceptual framework could be more convincing. Preferences for different kinds of children are open to many interpretations. Feldman thought the italicized choices showed a wish/need to conform to old values. Hethrington and Weiler (2009) thought they showed "authoritarianism." Then they said, No they don't. They show how fixed you are in wanting clear and unwavering rules (determined by how threatened you feel). You could say instead the four questions show how much you believe children should be seen and not heard, or how much one wants a well-ordered life. One can as well opine that people who want respectful, obedient, well-behaved kids with good manners simply want effortless, minimally involving parenting (LOL, by the

---

[*] Marc J. Hetherington & Jonathan D. Weiler, *Prius or Pickup? How the Answers to Four Simple Questions Explain America's Great Divide* (New York: Cambridge University Press, 2018), 17.

way) or the admiration of their neighbors. All these interpretations may be related, but they are all different as well. It boils down to this: The "four simple questions" cannot explain anything if we do not know what they measure. And in this regard, we also do not know how highly the four preferences correlated among themselves, which would show how much they are indeed tapping the same underlying dimension.

Analyzing the difference between *just the extremes* on a measure also produces hesitations. Did the percent of Democrats and Republicans who scored One, Two, and Three go down steadily, and the Republicans go up steadily, as the scores went from 0 to 4? We do not know. The analysis just reports on the 13 percent who scored zero and the 16 percent who scored four. That means 71 percent of the data was ignored. (Sometimes the rest are lumped together as "Mixeds.") You could however use all the data and simply compute the correlation between party affiliation and Fixed-ness (which varies from 0 to 4), and then compare the extremes for further insight. But that does not seem to have happened.

THE POWER MAD SCALE
AND THE CON MAN SCALE

THE POWER MAD SCALE

Instructions:

Write down a -4 if you very strongly disagree with the statement.

-3 if you strongly disagree with the statement.

-2 if you moderately disagree with the statement.

-1 if you slightly disagree with the statement,

Write down a +1 if you slightly agree with the statement.

+2 if you moderately agree with the statement.

+3 if you strongly agree with the statement.

+4 if you very strongly agree with the statement.

If you feel exactly and precisely neutral about a statement, write down a "0."

- It's a mistake to interfere with the "law of the jungle." Some people were meant to dominate others.
- Would you like to be a kind and helpful person to those in need? *
- "Winning is not the first thing; it's the only thing."
- The best way to lead a group under your supervision is to show them kindness, consideration, and treat them as fellow workers, not as inferiors. *
- If you have power in a situation, you should use it however you have to, to get your way.
- Would you be cold-blooded and vengeful, if that's what it took to reach your goals?
- Life is NOT governed by the "survival of the fittest." We should let compassion and moral laws be our guide. *
- Do money, wealth, and luxuries mean a lot to you?
- It is much better to be loved than to be feared. *

- Do you enjoy having the power to hurt people when they anger or disappoint you?
- It is much more important in life to have integrity in your dealings with others than to have money and power. *
- It's a dog-eat-dog world where you have to be ruthless at times.
- Charity (i.e. giving somebody something for nothing) is admirable, not stupid. *
- Would you like to be known as a gentle and forgiving person? *
- Do you enjoy taking charge of things and making people do things your way?
- Would it bother you if other people thought you were mean and pitiless? *
- Do you like other people to be afraid of you?
- Do you hate to play practical jokes that can sometimes really hurt people? *
- It would bother me if I intimidated people, and they worried about what I might do next.*
- I will do my best to destroy anyone who deliberately blocks my plans and goals.

The responses are scored as follows. If the statement is not followed by an asterisk, -4=1, -3=2, -2=3, -1=4, 0=5, +1=6, +2=7, +3=8, and +4=9. If the statement is followed by an asterisk, it is a "contrait" item, meaning it taps the opposite of being power mad. In that case, the scoring key is reversed: -4=9, -3=8, and so on until +4=1. A person's score on the test is the sum of the 20 item-scores and can vary from 20 to 180. We think

Donald Trump would score a 180.

THE CON MAN SCALE

(Same instructions for responding.)
- One of the most useful skills a person should develop is how to look someone straight in the eye and lie convincingly.
- All in all, it is better to be humble and honest than important and dishonest.*
- There is really no such thing as "right" and "wrong." It all boils down to what you can get away with.
- Do unto others as you would have them do unto you, and never do anything unfair to someone else.*
- Deceit and cheating are justified when they get you what you really want.
- Basically, people are objects to be quietly and coolly manipulated for your own benefit.
- It gains a person nothing if he uses deceit and treachery to get power and riches.*
- The best skill one can have is knowing the "right move at the right time":

when to "soft-sell" someone, when to be tough, when to flatter, when to threaten, when to bribe, etc.

- One should give others the benefit of the doubt. Most people are trustworthy if you have faith in them.*
- You know that most people are out to "screw" you, so you have to get them first when you get the chance.
- Honesty is the best policy in all cases.*
- The best reason for belonging to a church is to project a good image and have contact with some of the important people in your community.
- No one should do evil acts, even when they can "get away with them" and make lots of money.*
- There's a sucker born every minute, and smart people learn how to take advantage of them.
- The end does NOT justify the means. If you can only get something by unfairness, lying, or hurting others, then give up trying.*
- Our lives should be governed by high ethical principles and religious morals, not by power and greed.*
- It is more important to create a good image of yourself in the minds of others than to actually be the person others think you are.
- There's no excuse for lying to someone else.*
- One of the best ways to handle people is to tell them what they want to hear.
- The truly smart person knows that honesty is the best policy, not manipulation and deceit.*

Scoring is done the same way as for the Power Mad Scale. Scores can vary from 20 to 180. We again think Donald Trump would score a perfect 180.

APPENDIX III

EXIT POLLS

For a while each major news outlet in the United States did its own survey of how voters felt during presidential campaigns. Then in 2003 AP, ABC, CBS, CNN, FOX, and NBC formed the National Election Pool and hired Edison Media Research of Somerville, New Jersey to conduct exit polls of American voters in each federal election. These surveys were taken on election day and used that night to help predict winners and explain how they won. Then the data would be mined and beaten to a pulp by political parties and social scientists to determine Who voted for Whom and Why.

Here's how the exit polls worked. The news organizations would decide which states to concentrate on, and how much data they wanted (i.e., how much $$$ to spend) in each case. Then Edison would pick the precincts that it thought had the most predictive clout. Trained "interviewers" would be stationed at polling places in these precincts and approach (say) every fourth person leaving the poll. She would identify her mission and ask if the voter would fill out a questionnaire on a clipboard about the election. She would note the gender, race, and approximate age of those who declined. Edison reports that about 45 percent agreed to participate in 2016—which is enormously better than the ~3 percent response rate polling firms typically get for the public opinion surveys you read about in the paper.

Still, most people said no to the exit pollster, and that means the results she obtained could be tainted by a self-selection bias. Whether they are or not, even if everyone who was asked complied, the sample still would not exactly match the demographic breakdown of everyone who voted at that poll that day. Just by luck you could get too many men in the random sample, too few white folks, and so on. Even if the exit polls magically matched the demographic background of everyone who voted at the station, it could still be misleading because so many people vote before election day now. If old people tend to vote Republican, and also tend to vote at advance polls or by mail because each is more convenient, the exit poll will overestimate the Democratic vote. Edison tries to figure in the pre-vote vote, but it is difficult.

Back to the Exit Polls: Voters who accepted a questionnaire as they left the voting station marked their answers to twenty or so questions on the survey, folded it, and placed it in a "ballot box." Three times a day the interviewer phoned in all the answers she had received thus far, which were combined with other polling stations and trends spotted. Edison compensates for a low turnout in some demographic categories by giving extra "weight" to the answers received thus far by, say, old African-Americans. Virtually all polling organizations do this sort of thing all the time because, as just noted, the randomness of even a good sampling procedure is going to underrepresent somebody. But you do have to be smart enough to know what percentage of the actual voters in a precinct should be, say, old African-Americans. Pollsters develop computer models to guide them in this. Different models give different estimates.

Edison says that in 2016 28,558 voters answered its national exit poll; the basic results are available online, e.g. https://www.cnn.com/election/2016/results/exit-polls. However, the highly respected Pew Research Center compared the composition of those respondents with its own collection of over 3000 verified voters. While one would think the results from a much larger sample would be more trustworthy, nothing is as important in polling as getting a representative sample and a lot hinges on how the polling firm adjusts its actual results to match what it *estimates* are the true demographics of the population. On that score, the Pew respondents were members of a nationally representative (based on probability sampling) "panel" of Americans who answered monthly online surveys on various topics for Pew: https://www.people-press. org/2018/08/09/an-examination-of-the-2016-electorate-based-on-validated-voters/. That's a pretty impressive sample.

Pew concluded that the exit polls seriously underestimated the number of white non-college graduates who voted (which comprised 34 percent in the exit polls versus 44 percent of the Pew sample). This led to erroneous early predictions on election night that Clinton would win crucial states because female non-graduates were known to favor Trump but a lot of them seemingly did not vote. But they actually did, for Trump, and he won, and the exit polls had egg on their faces. The Associated Press and Fox News left the consortium as a result of this "mislead" and contracted with the National Opinion Research Center at the University of Chicago to develop alternate polling techniques for predicting elections. Those are currently underway and use online sampling rather than exit polls.

The difference between the results gathered by the exit polls and the Pew sample may not, however, lay in sampling techniques or demographic weighting, but rather in one of the classic bugaboos of survey research: Presenting inadequate answers to the question you asked. The 2016 exit poll apparently gave respondents four possible answers to its question about education: "High school or less," "Some college," "College graduate," and "Postgraduate." Suppose you graduated from a two-year community college or a junior college? Are you not a "college graduate"? The Pew survey was clearer: "non-college" meant "all those who did not have a degree from a four-year college or university." If you think community college graduates would consider themselves "college graduates, you can see why the exit polls might have 10% more "college graduates" than Pew, why Edison would think this supposed increase in well-educated female voters and decrease in less educated women would boost Clinton's chances, and how the "mislead" occurred.

This is only speculation from afar, but Edison changed its education answers for the 2018 midterm exit polls to "High school or less," "Some College," "Associate degree," "Bachelor's degree," and "Advanced degree." Eleven percent of the voters said they had Associate degrees, which come from community and junior colleges. That's just about right, right?

This also explains why Trump did unexpectedly well among "college graduates" in 2016. Graduates of 2-year post-secondary programs probably voted for him more than graduates from a four-year college. Whether this satisfactorily explains the discrepancy or not, at this point we have to use the exit polls in this book to analyze Who voted for Whom and Why in 2016. Nothing else provides the same history for comparisons. But we shall handle the conclusions involving education with care. Exit poll data in 2016 almost certainly underestimated Trump's support in the working class and overestimated his appeal to holders of four-year college degrees.

APPENDIX IV

"RIGHT" VERSUS "LEFT"

BOB ALTEMEYER

The original meaning of "right" and "left" in English probably referred to the hand with which one did most one-handed tasks. Since about 90 percent of humans are "right-handed," the word "right" naturally acquired second meanings of "preferred" and "trusted." It may not have taken long for the usage to create such expressions as "sitting at the right hand of God,' as in Psalm 110 and many other places in the Bible. As "right" gathered a broader meaning of "blessed," it easily came to mean "correct" and "good" as well. At the same time "left" was left (don't you know) with the dregs. It gathered a connotation of "un-preferred" that broadened to "unwanted" (as in "left-overs," "left out," and "left behind") to "wrong" and "evil." Similarly the Italian word "sinistra" which means "on the left" gave us "sinister" in English.

Ironically our right hands are controlled by the left hemisphere of our brains, and most people are right-handed because the left half of their cerebral cortex dominates the right half when it comes to using our hands. If people in ancient times could see what was going on in their brains, which as it happened they could not, the tribal chief's right-hand man would have been seated to his left. And The Powers That Be would have absconded with the word "left" to describe their exalted place in society. The best people would consider themselves "in the left," where "moral leftness" was. The first ten amendments to the U.S. Constitution would be called the Bill of Lefts. People would be self-leftious. British motorists would still drive on the left, and Americans would think there was something not left about that. Left? Left-on, bro.

Politically the phrase "being on the right" in English goes back to 1548 when Edward VI let the House of Commons meet in St. Steven's Chapel in Westminister Palace. The benches were set up in the choir stalls to the sides of the altar, facing each other rather than facing the altar. In the late 1600s when political parties were formed it became customary for the party with the largest number of seats to sit (naturally) on the right hand of the person running the meeting. You can see this on the BBC News tonight, and you will notice that Members bow slightly when entering and leaving the House. They're not kowtowing to the Speaker, they're genuflecting, sort of, before the altar (which was removed centuries ago).

But the terms "Right-wing" and "Left-wing" themselves arose in France in 1789 during the French Revolution, when delegates to the newly formed National Assembly sat to one side or the other of the President of the Parliament as they did in England.

But where you sat depended on what you stood for. The nobility, called the Second Estate, sat to the right (of course) of the President, and the Liberal Deputies (the Third Estate) sat to the left. (They said they wanted to, thumbing their noses at the nobility's craving to have language as well as the angels on their side.) The phrases "right-wing" and "left-wing" did not enter British politics for a long time, until the late 1930s. They seemingly first appeared in the United States during McCarthyism when the Senator from Wisconsin, who knew a thing or three about casting malicious aspersions, termed Democrats "leftists."

MONMOUTH UNIVERSITY POLLING INSTITUTE SURVEY SPRING & AUTUMN 2019

BOB ALTEMEYER

Chapter Ten of this book, especially Endnote 2, explains how the highly reputable Monmouth University Polling Institute came to conduct the first nation-wide survey of responses to the full versions of our various authoritarianism scales, other personality tests, and sundry related measures. But I doubted the traditional person-to-person telephone poll would work all that well. The RWA Scale in particular, with its long and complicated items, would be plagued by error variance when people had to hear and remember multi-part statements. A brief test in January supported this apprehension and Patrick Murray obligingly set his staff to developing an on-line platform which came much closer to producing the traditional testing circumstances in personality research: a test whose items subjects read at their own pace, repeatedly if they wished, and then marked down their response on a "page" with the other items on that scale. I also thought that since no one was listening to the responses and writing them down, as in a telephone poll, an Internet survey would lessen impression management effects.

The Institute conducted a pilot study in May 2019 by sending our survey to about 13,000 New Jersey adults who had participated in an earlier Monmouth poll. (We gave everyone contacted three chances to join in the fun.) Because of this earlier connection, about 7 percent of the people contacted by Internet—more than twice as high as usual—opened the email when it arrived. About a third of those 937 took a look and clicked our beautiful survey away into little bits of nothingness. (Patrick thought this was because the survey started off with questions about religion, at my insistence, against his advice.) (It took a lot of work on my part, but I finally convinced Murray that he, knew a helluva lot more about public opinion polling than I did.) Another sixth of those who opened the email started answering, but gave up after a while. This left us with 478 more or less complete sets of answers, representing 3.6 percent of the people contacted. This was a sharp decline from my Canadian studies where over 90 percent of the students and about 80 percent of their parent filled out surveys for the tiny incentive of 1-2 percent of the students' grade in a course. It took Murray's fine citizens of the Garden State a median 18 minutes to answer the 96 items on the questionnaire.

Emboldened by the Institute's skill at developing and implementing such a fine way of administering the personality tests, I began trying to insert all the scales I could into the "money" questionnaire being designed for the autumn. Meanwhile Monmouth University Polling Institute purchased email addresses of registered voters from Aristotle International, a Dallas-based firm that has assembled addresses and relevant information on about 30% of the registered voters in the USA. The poll was administered over the Internet in two waves on October 28 and November 17, 2019. The first wave deliberately oversampled Republicans because we were more interested in understanding them. The second wave was sent on its way after 569 sets of answers had come in and it tried to sculp the sample to fit national demographic values better. Altogether appeals were made to 223,138 voters, but only 5,138 opened the email which asked them to answer a 25-35 minute survey for the Monmouth University Poll "about social attitudes, values, and issues facing the country today." Only 1,618 clicked through to see the survey, however, and of these, 990 completed all, or nearly all, of the 131 items involved, in a median time of 30.5 minutes. These 990[1] represented 0.44 percent of the 200,000+ who were invited to participate. There is no known "norm" for response rates for a long, out-of-the-blue online survey like this, The telephone polls you hear about today have a response rate of about 3 percent. (How often do you give up eating dinner to answer one?)

A guy who has been rejected by 97 percent of the women he asks out on a date (1) is asking a lot of women for a date, and (2) might find it small comfort, but he is still better off than a fellow shot down 99.56 percent of the time. However, we should not feel too downhearted. We are not trying to determine within a percentage point or two how much of the population likes Donald Trump—the regular polls do that—but rather what his fans are like compared to those who can't stand him. So, we did not need a close fit to the population. The sample we collected proved typical of cell-phone survey samples (more likely to be male, white, older, and college educated). Patrick Murray did not think there were any notable distortions beyond those four just mentioned.

THE SURVEY USED

The survey is given below as it would have appeared on the screens of our participants. Highlighted material has been inserted here to document what was going on as the poll progressed.

Survey Invitation

Subject: The Monmouth University Poll wants your opinion
Body: [MUPI logo]
Dear [FIRSTNAME],
Monmouth University is conducting a public opinion survey about social attitudes, values, and issues facing the country today.

Your participation is very important because only a few hundred people have been randomly selected for this survey and your views will represent many people throughout the country.

Please help with this important project by completing this online survey **before November XX**. It will take about **25 to 35 minutes** of your time and **your opinion will really count**.

We are not selling anything or asking for money. All your answers are completely confidential.

This project is conducted by the Monmouth University Polling Institute. For more information, visit: www.monmouth.edu/polling

SOCIAL ISSUES AND ATTITUDES SURVEY

This survey asks for your opinion on a variety of issues. This includes your views on current events as well as your reaction to a number of statements that some people might make about society in general. Some statements may be strongly worded and we ask that you gauge your response to them as they are presented, even though you may not hear such statements in your own daily life.

Note: The numbering of the items (e.g., "A0" below) did not appear on the survey itself.

A0.   **Would you say things in the country are going in the right direction, or have they gotten off on the wrong track?** (.664) [Numbers in parentheses after an item show correlation with Approval of Trump's performance, with Strong or Somewhat Disapproval coded as "0" and Somewhat or Strong Approval coded as "1."]

                    Definitely in the right direction
                    Probably in the right direction
                    Probably on the wrong track
                    Definitely on the wrong track
                    Not sure

A1.   **Thinking about your current financial situation, would you say you are struggling to remain where you are financially, basically stable in your current financial situation, or is your financial situation improving?** (.227) [Those for whom things have improved support Trump a bit more.]

                    Struggling
                    Stable
                    Improving
                    Not sure

A2.   **Recent indicators have shown that the U.S. economy has been growing, including lower unemployment and higher productivity. How much has your family benefitted from this economic upturn?** (.468) [Those who have benefitted more support Trump more than most]

Great deal
Some
Not much
Not at all
Not sure

A3.   **Thinking about today, how would you say that peop le like you are doing now in American society?** (.459) [People who think they are getting ahead support Trump more.]

People like me are getting left behind by a lot
People like me are getting left behind by a little
People like me are doing no better or worse than others
People like me are getting ahead by a little
People like me are getting ahead by a lot

Respondents were notified when they asked for the next page if they had left items on the present page unanswered. They could go back and answer, or continue, as they wished.

The following pages contain different statements. For each one, please indicate how much you <u>disagree</u> or <u>agree</u> with each using this scale:

Very strongly disagree (-4)
Strongly disagree (-3)
Moderately disagree (-2)
Slightly disagree (-1)
Neither disagree nor agree (0)
Slightly agree (+1)
Moderately agree (+2)
Strongly agree (+3)
Very strongly agree (+4)

It is important that you try to answer every question. If you have different reactions to different parts of a statement, select an average response that indicates how you feel on balance.

RWA Scale

RX1.   We need more marches and demonstrations to protest how badly minorities are treated in America. [This item is not part of the RWA Scale, but was put in to give participants a little practice with the nine-point response scale.]

RWA1.   Our country desperately needs a mighty leader who will do what has to be done to destroy the radical new ways and sinfulness that are ruining us. [Beginning of the RWA Scale. A "-4" was scored as a 1, a "-3" was scored as a 2, etcetera, up to "+4" being scored a 9. "0" was scored as a 5.]

RWA2.   Gays and lesbians are just as healthy and moral as anybody else.* [Note: Statements marked with an asterisk are worded in the con-trait direction. That means the scoring key is reversed when the response is scored. The asterisk did not appear on the survey, of course.]

RWA3.   It is always better to trust the judgment of the proper authorities in government and religion than to listen to the noisy rabble-rousers in our society who are trying to create doubt in people's minds

RWA4.   Atheists and others who have rebelled against the established religions are no doubt every bit as good and virtuous as those who attend church regularly.*

RWA5.   The only way our country can get through the crisis ahead is to get back to our traditional values, put some tough leaders in power, and silence the troublemakers spreading bad ideas.

RWA6.   There is absolutely nothing wrong with nudist camps.*

RWA7.   Our country <u>needs</u> free thinkers who have the courage to defy traditional ways, even if this upsets many people.*

RWA8.   Our country will be destroyed someday if we do not smash the perversions eating away at our moral fiber and traditional beliefs.

RWA9.   Everyone should have their own lifestyle, religious beliefs, and sexual preferences, even if it makes them different from everyone else.*

RWA10. The "old-fashioned ways" and the "old-fashioned values" still show the best way to live.

RWA11. You have to admire those who challenged the law and the majority's view by protesting for women's abortion rights, for animal rights, or to abolish school prayer.*

RWA12. What our country really needs is a strong, determined leader who will crush evil, and take us back to our true path.

RWA13. Some of the best people in our country are those who are challenging our government, criticizing religion, and ignoring the "normal way things are supposed to be done." *

RWA14. God's laws about abortion, pornography and marriage must be strictly followed before it is too late, and those who break them must be strongly punished.

RWA15. There are many radical, immoral people in our country today, who are trying to ruin it for their own godless purposes, whom the authorities should put out of action.

RWA16. A "woman's place" should be wherever she wants to be. The days when women are submissive to their husbands and social conventions belong strictly in the past.*

RWA17. Our country will be great if we honour the ways of our forefathers, do what the authorities tell us to do, and get rid of the "rotten apples" who are ruining everything.

RWA18. There is no "ONE right way" to live life; everybody has to create their <u>own</u> way.*

RWA19. Homosexuals and feminists should be praised for being brave enough to defy "traditional family values."*

RWA20. This country would work a lot better if certain groups of troublemakers would just shut up and accept their group's traditional place in society. [End of the RWA Scale]

RX2. Once our government leaders and the authorities condemn the dangerous elements in our society, it will be the duty of every patriotic citizen to help stomp out the rot that is poisoning our country from within. (.50)

RX3. The U.S. Constitution gets in the way of things too much nowadays and should just be ignored when it interferes with taking action on some issue. (-.15)

RX4. It is more important for a leader to be able to arouse the deep passions of the common man than to offer well-reasoned arguments for policies. (.31)

For the next set of statements, please indicate how much you <u>oppose</u> or <u>favor</u> each using this scale:
   Very strongly oppose (-4)
   Strongly oppose (-3)
   Moderately oppose (-2)
   Slightly oppose (-1)
   Neither oppose nor favor (0)
   Slightly favor (+1)
   Moderately favor (+2)
   Strongly favor (+3)
   Very strongly favor (+4)

You can work quickly. Your first reaction is generally best. Please try to answer every question.

Social Dominance Scale

SD1. Some groups of people must be kept in their place. [Beginning of the 8-item Dominance SDO Scale]

SD2.   It's probably a good thing that certain groups are at the top and other groups are at the bottom.

SD3.   An ideal society requires some groups to be on top and others to be on the bottom.

SD4.   Some groups of people are simply inferior to other groups.

SD5.   Groups at the bottom are just as deserving as groups at the top.*

SD6.   No one group should dominate in society.*

SD7.   Groups at the bottom should not have to stay in their place.*

SD8.   Group dominance is a poor principle.*

SD9.   We should not push for group equality. [Beginning of the 8-item Anti-Equality SDO Scale]

SD10.   We shouldn't try to guarantee that every group has the same quality of life.

SD11.   It is unjust to make groups equal.

SD12.   Group equality should not be our primary goal.

SD13.   We should work to give all groups an equal chance to succeed.*

SD14.   We should do what we can to equalize conditions for different groups.*

SD15.   No matter how much effort it takes, we ought to strive to ensure that all groups have the same chance in life.*

SD16.   Group equality should be our ideal.*

"Child Rearing" Scale

Although there are a number of qualities that people feel children should have, every person thinks that some are more important than others. For each of the following pairs of desirable qualities, **please select the one you think is** *more* **important for a child to have**.

CR1.   **It is more important for a child to have:**
                1. Independence   2. Respect for Elders (.413)

CR2.   **It is more important for a child to show:***
                1. Obedience   2. Self-reliance (.350)

CR3.   **It is more important for a child to have:**
                1. Curiosity   2. Good Manners (.349)

CR4.   **It is more important for a child to be:**
                1. Considerate   2. Well-behaved (.269)

For the next set of statements, please indicate how much you disagree or agree with each using this scale:

Very strongly disagree (-4)
Strongly disagree (-3)
Moderately disagree (-2)
Slightly disagree (-1)
Neither disagree nor agree (0)
Slightly agree (+1)
Moderately agree (+2)
Strongly agree (+3)
Very strongly agree (+4)

It is important that you try to answer every question. If you have different reactions to different parts of a statement, select an average response that indicates how you feel on balance.

24 Prejudice items

PR1. There are entirely too many people from the wrong places getting into the United States now.

PR2. Muslims bring a valuable new element to American society and should be welcomed.*

PR3. White people are the major victims of discrimination in the United States. The government is on everybody else's side but theirs.

PR4. The more diverse America becomes, with different people with different religions and heritages from everywhere else in the world, the stronger it will be.*

PR5. Black Americans continue to get less than their fair share of our country's wealth because of discrimination.*

R6. Latin Americans are naturally lazy, promiscuous, and irresponsible.

PR7. We should tear down the walls that keep people from different cultures away from us, rather than build new ones. *

PR8. Two really bad things about the Jews is that they killed Jesus, and they secretly control the world's banks and economy.

PR9. Racial minorities have had it good for years in the United States because of all the government programs that help them get ahead of white people.

PR10. It will be great if someday America has become such a mixture of different people that white persons are in a minority like everybody else.*

PR11. Instead of complaining and protesting all the time, African-Americans should be grateful for how good they have it here compared to where they came from.

PR12. Religions like Islam, Hinduism, and Buddhism are just as true as Christianity, and produce as much good behavior.*

PR13. Every person we let into the country as a "refugee" means another American won't be able to find a job, or another foreigner will go on welfare here.

PR14. Overall the white race has mainly brought exploitation and suffering to the other peoples of the world.*

PR15. America should stop giving foreign aid to backward countries. They made their mess by themselves, so let them clean it up.

PR16. Black people are just naturally more violent than white people.

PR17. Christianity has very unjustly persecuted the Jews over the centuries.*

PR18. Most minorities on welfare would rather work, but they can't get jobs that pay a living wage.*

PR19. There's no way a religion like Islam that produces so many terrorists is as good a religion as Christianity is.

PR20. Latin-Americans are as hard-working, law-abiding, and responsible as any other group of Americans.*

PR21. Certain races of people clearly do NOT have the natural intelligence and "get up and go" of the white race.

PR22. Americans are NOT exceptionally noble compared to the rest of the world. "American Exceptionalism" is just another ugly "master race" theory.*

PR23. The immigrants from the Caribbean and Africa who have come to America have mainly brought disease, ignorance, and violence with them.

PR24. It is good to live in a country where there are so many minority groups present, such as African-Americans, Hispanics, and Asians.*

Topical Questions

The next set of questions ask about some current events.

A4. **How much interest do you have in the 2020 election for President?** (-.02)
>> A lot of interest
>> Some interest
>> Only a little interest
>> No interest

A5. **How likely are you to vote in the November 2020 general election for President?** (-.02)
>> Definitely will vote
>> Probably will vote
>> Probably will not vote
>> Definitely will not vote
>> Not sure

A6.   **As of right now, how would you vote in the November 2020 presidential election?** (.927)

> Definitely vote to re-elect Donald Trump
> Probably vote to re-elect Donald Trump
> Lean <u>toward</u> voting to re-elect Donald Trump
> Completely undecided, do not lean either way
> Lean <u>against</u> voting to re-elect Donald Trump
> Probably vote against re-electing Donald Trump
> Definitely vote against re-electing Donald Trump
> Will not vote in 2020

A7.   **What type of candidate would it be better for the Democrats to nominate?**

> Definitely prefer an experienced candidate who knows how to get things done
> Probably prefer an experienced candidate who knows how to get things done
> Probably prefer an outsider candidate who can shake up the system
> Definitely prefer an outsider candidate who can shake up the system
> Not sure
> Does not matter to me

A8.   **Which candidate would you prefer to see the Democrats to nominate?**[2]
(See Endnote 2)

> Joe Biden
> Pete Buttigieg
> Kamala Harris
> Bernie Sanders
> Elizabeth Warren
> Someone else, specify: [Amy Klubuchar]
> Someone else, specify: [Andrew Yang]
> Someone else, specify: [Tulsi Gabbard]
> Someone else, specify: [Mike Bloomberg]
> Someone else, specify: [all others]
> Not sure
> No one, does not matter to me

A9.   **Who did you vote for in the 2016 election for president?**

> Hillary Clinton
> Donald Trump
> Other candidate

Do not remember

Did not vote

A10.   **Do you approve or disapprove of the job Donald Trump is doing as president?**

Strongly approve

Somewhat approve

Somewhat disapprove

Strongly disapprove

Not sure

A11.   **Do you support or oppose impeaching and removing Donald Trump from office before the 2020 election?** (-.799)

Strongly support

Somewhat support

Somewhat oppose

Strongly oppose

Not sure

For the next set of statements, please indicate how much you disagree or agree with each using this scale:

Very strongly disagree (-4)

Strongly disagree (-3)

Moderately disagree (-2)

Slightly disagree (-1)

Neither disagree nor agree (0)

Slightly agree (+1)

Moderately agree (+2)

Strongly agree (+3)

Very strongly agree (+4)

A12.   If Donald Trump is defeated in November 2020, he should continue to be president if he declares the election was fixed and crooked. (.466)

A13.   If the impeachment inquiry turns up information about potential criminal activity by Donald Trump, it would be fair to investigate him for possible prosecution of those activities once he is out of office. (-.638)

A14.   Donald Trump has the right to give himself a presidential pardon before he leaves office for any crimes he could be investigated for. (.628)

A15.   If Donald Trump is impeached and removed from office, he should be put on trial for any crimes he may have committed while in office. (-.711)

A16.   If Donald Trump resigns from office before his term is up, he   should
be put on trial for any crimes he may have committed while in office. (-.732)

A17.   If Donald Trump is defeated for re-election in 2020, he should be put on
trial for any crimes he may have committed while in office. (-.741)

Demographics

These questions are for grouping purposes only.

D1.   **What is your gender?**
Male (54%)
Female (45%)
Other

D2.   **What was your age in years on your last birthday?**
_____ [ENTER NUMBER]
(Mean = 60.7 years; r=.137)

D3.   **What was the last grade in school you completed?**
8th grade or less   (00%)
High school incomplete (Grades 9, 10 and 11)   (01%)
High school complete (Grade 12)   (07%)
Vocational/technical school   (06%)
Some college, but no degree   (16%)
Junior College graduate (2 year, Associate Degree) (08%)
4-year college graduate (Bachelor's Degree)   (27%)
Attended graduate school   (06%)
Completed graduate school (Masters, Law, Medical
degree, etc.) (29%)

D4.   **Do you have any children under the age of 18?**
No   Yes

D5.   **In politics today, do you consider yourself a Republican, Democrat,
independent, or something else?**
Republican   (N=301)
Democrat   (N=286)
Independent   (N=349)
Another party, please specify: _____

D5A.   **If you are an Independent, do you lean more toward the Republican Party
or more toward the Democratic Party?**

Lean more Republican   (N=146)
Lean more Democrat   (N=115)
Neither   (N=88)

D6.   **In general, would you describe your political views as liberal, moderate, or conservative?** (.661)

Very liberal   (N=098)
Somewhat liberal   (N=193)
Moderate   (N=288)
Somewhat conservative   (N=222)
Very conservative   (N=176)

D7.   **Are you of Latino or Hispanic origin?**

Yes (06%)
No

D8.   **Are you white, black or of Asian origin?**

White   (82%)
Black   (06%)
Asian   (02%)
Hispanic (white)   (06%)
Other, specify: [Mixed race]
Other, specify: [other]

D9.   **How often do you attend religious or worship services, not including weddings or funerals?**

More than once a week   (08%)
Once a week   (21%)
Once or twice a month   10%)
A few times a year   (15%)
Seldom   (22%)
Never   (22%)

D10.   **What is your religious affiliation?**

Protestant   (34%)
Catholic   (21%)
Other Christian   (18%)
Jewish   (03%)
Hindu
Muslim
Other, specify: [Buddhist]
Other, specify: [other]
None [D10A = Believe in God] (5%)

None [D10A = Agnostic]   (7%)
None [D10A = Atheist   (6%)

D10A.   **If your religious affiliation is "None," Which of the following best describes you:**
        Atheist. I believe there is no God.
        Agnostic. I do not believe, or disbelieve, in God. I do not know.
        I believe in God, but do not belong to or identify with any religion.
        Other, describe: ___

D11.   **If you belong to a specific religious denomination, please enter it here:**
        _____

D12.   **Would you describe yourself as a born-again or an evangelical Christian?**
        Yes, Born-again, but not evangelical
        Yes, Evangelical, but not born-again
        Yes, both born-again and evangelical
        No, neither of these

D13.   **So that we can group all answers, what is your total annual family income before taxes? Your answers are recorded confidentially.**
        Under $25,000   (07%)
        $25,000 to just under $50,000   (15%)
        $50,000 to just under $75,000   (18%)
        $75,000 to just under $100,000   (18%)
        $100,000 to just under $150,000   (19%)
        $150,000 to just under $200,000   (09%)
        $200,000 or more   (13%)

N1.   **Which ONE of the following is the news source you use most often to find out what is going on in the country and the world?** *[Please choose only one]*
        ABC News
        Breitbart News
        CBS News
        CNN
        Drudge Report
        Facebook
        Fox News Channel
        Huffington Post
        Los Angeles Times
        MSNBC

NBC News
NPR/National Public Radio
Newsmax
New York Post
New York Times
One America News
PBS News
Politico
Reddit
Reuters
RT
Rush Limbaugh
Twitter
USA Today
Wall Street Journal
Washington Post
Yahoo News
YouTube
Other, specify: [BBC]
Other, specify: [Google or Apple news feeds]
Other, specify: [Internet, non-specific]
Other, specify: [Talk radio, non-specific]
Other, specify: [other]
Other, specify: [Multiple sources, non-specific]
Other, specify: [None, no sources used]

We are nearly to the end of the survey. Your opinions are extremely valuable. There are a few more questions left that will really help with this research project.

U1.   **How much have you heard about recent reports involving Ukraine, Donald Trump, and Joe Biden?**
Have heard a lot   (-.081)
Have heard a little
Have not heard anything

U2.   **How much have you read or heard about the "rough transcript" issued by the White House of what was said in the call between Donald Trump and Ukrainian President Zelensky?)** (-.035)
I have read the transcript myself
I have not read the transcript myself, but I have read or seen extensive news coverage of what was in it
I have only heard a little about what the transcript actually says
I have not heard anything about the details in the transcript

For the next set of statements, please indicate how much you disagree or agree with each using this scale:

> Very strongly disagree (-4)
> Strongly disagree (-3)
> Moderately disagree (-2)
> Slightly disagree (-1)
> Neither disagree nor agree (0)
> Slightly agree (+1)
> Moderately agree (+2)
> Strongly agree (+3)
> Very strongly agree (+4)

U3. The "rough transcript" of the Trump-Zelensky phone conversation that the White House released shows that the president did NOT specifically ask Zelensky to investigate Joe Biden or his son.(.720)

U4. President Trump stopped the payment of funds for military aid to Ukraine, then called President Zelensky and asked for a favor in order to release those funds. (-.764)

U5. White House officials put the transcript of the Ukraine phone conversation on a top-secret computer to hide it because they were afraid Trump could be damaged politically if it became public. (-.781)

U6. If Barack Obama had made a phone call to the leader of a foreign nation in 2011, suggesting that his likely opponent Mitt Romney should be investigated with the help of the president's personal attorney, Obama should have been impeached and removed from office. (-.628)

For the next set of statements, please indicate how much you <u>disagree</u> or <u>agree</u> with each using this scale:

> Very strongly disagree (-4)
> Strongly disagree (-3)
> Moderately disagree (-2)
> Slightly disagree (-1)
> Neither disagree nor agree (0)
> Slightly agree (+1)
> Moderately agree (+2)
> Strongly agree (+3)
> Very strongly agree (+4)

Censorship Scale

CS1. Should a university professor be allowed to teach an anthropology course in which he argues that men are naturally superior to women, so women should resign themselves to inferior roles in our society?

CS2. Should a book be assigned in a Grade 12 English course that presents homosexual relationships in a positive light?

CS3. Should books be allowed to be sold that attack "being patriotic" and "being religious"?

CS4. Should a racist speaker be allowed to give a public talk preaching his views?

CS5. Should someone be allowed to teach a Grade 10 sex education course who strongly believes that all premarital sex is a sin?

CS6. Should commercials for "telephone sex" be allowed to be shown after 11 PM on television?

CS7. Should a professor who has argued in the past that black people are less intelligent than white people be given a research grant to continue studies of this issue?

CS8. Should a book be allowed to be published that argues the Holocaust never occurred, but was made up by Jews to create sympathy for their cause?

CS9. Should sexually explicit material that describes intercourse through words and medical diagrams be used in sex education classes in Grade 10?

CS10. Should a university professor be allowed to teach a philosophy course in which he tries to convince his students there is no God?

CS11. Should an openly white supremacist movie such as "The Birth of a Nation" (which glorifies the Ku Klux Klan) be shown in a Grade 12 social studies class?

CS12. Should "Pro-Choice" counselors and abortion clinics be allowed to advertise their services in public health clinics if "Pro-Life" counselors can?

For this final set of statements, please indicate how much you <u>disagree</u> or <u>agree</u> with each using this scale:

> Very strongly disagree (-4)
> Strongly disagree (-3)
> Moderately disagree (-2)
> Slightly disagree (-1)
> Neither disagree nor agree (0)
> Slightly agree (+1)
> Moderately agree (+2)
> Strongly agree (+3)
> Very strongly agree (+4)

It is important that you try to answer every question. If you have different reactions to different parts of a statement, select an average response that indicates how you feel on balance.

Religious Fundamentalism scale

RF1. God has given humanity a complete, unfailing guide to happiness and salvation, which must be totally followed.

RF2. No single book of religious teachings contains all the intrinsic, fundamental truths about life.*

RF3. The basic cause of evil in this world is Satan, who is still constantly and ferociously fighting against God.

RF4. It is more important to be a good person than to believe in God and the right religion.*

RF5. There is a particular set of religious teachings in this world that are so true, you can't go any "deeper" because they are the basic, bedrock message that God has given humanity.

RF6. When you get right down to it, there are basically only two kinds of people in the world: the Righteous, who will be rewarded by God, and the rest, who will not.

RF7. Scriptures may contain general truths, but they should NOT be considered completely, literally true from beginning to end.*

RF8. To lead the best, most meaningful life, one must belong to the one, fundamentally true religion.

RF9. "Satan" is just the name people give to their own bad impulses. There really is *no such thing* as a diabolical "Prince of Darkness" who tempts us.*

RF10. Whenever science and sacred scripture conflict, *science* is probably right.*

RF11. The fundamentals of God's religion should never be tampered with, or compromised with others' beliefs.

RF12. *All* of the religions in the world have flaws and wrong teachings. There is *no* perfectly true, right religion.* [End of Religious Fundamentalism Scale]

RFX1. If we have faith in Jesus, accepting him as our personal savior and asking forgiveness of our sins, *we will be saved*, no matter what kind of life we live afterwards. (.322)

Thank you very much for helping with this important research project!

EXPLANATIONS AND DETAILED ANALYSES OF THE AUTUMN 2019 NATIONAL AUTHORITARIANISM POLL UNDERTAKEN BY MONMOUTH UNIVERSITY POLLING INSTITUTE

BOB ALTEMEYER

Table 1 (below) shows how the national sample reacted to all six of our multi-item measures. Personality researchers will know that the most important information lay in the last two columns. The "Average Inter-Item Correlation" tells you how much a person's responses to a test all went together in the same direction, like cars on a one-way street. Low levels of interconnection mean the responses were going in many different directions, like cars in a mall parking lot on Black Friday, and you have a big mess. But the higher the number, the more the cars were lined up heading the same way. Almost all the scales in Monmouth's national survey look like they were fast one-way streets, as these things go. Some were like smooth-flowing superhighways, if not bullet-trains. For example, the 24 diverse prejudice items have 276 intercorrelations. These averaged .519 among our white respondents, which is many times stronger than the bond as appeared in previous studies with similar scales. The wide-ranging sentiments tapped by these statements apparently go together in America now to unprecedented degrees. With relatively minor exceptions, people tend to either reject the whole package, or swallow most of it hook, line and sinker. So, people who complained about "too many people from the wrong sorts of places" were not just backing up the president, they also tended to think blacks are naturally violent and ungrateful for being brought to America, Jews killed Jesus and secretly control the banks, Latinos are lazy, promiscuous, and irresponsible, white people are superior to everyone else, Americans are exceptionally good people, etc. You can find people who are prejudiced against just one group, but they are rare. Where you find one prejudice, you usually find a dozen more tightly connected. It is a wide-ranging disease of the mind.

The last column in Table 1, "Alpha Reliability Coefficient," is determined by the average inter-item correlation and the number of items on the test. It indicates how stable, how trustworthy, the total score on a test is likely to be. A perfect test would have an alpha of 1.00, but nobody has ever gotten there. The best standardized IQ tests have alphas of about .90. Psychologists usually consider .80 "good enough." Nearly all of our tests met that minimum standard, and three of them had simply fantastic, very alpha, alphas. Again, to our knowledge, such numbers have never appeared before, certainly not as broadly, in a study of the general population.

Table 1 Statistical Properties of the Personality Tests Used in the Autumn 2019 National Survey (N=990)

Scale	Number of Items	Possible Range	Actual Range	Average (Mean)	Variance	Average Inter-Item Correlation	Alpha Realiability Coefficient
RWA	20	20-180	20-176	84.0	1577	.516	.955
SDO=DOM	8	8-72	8-71	23.4	136	.396	.840
SDO=ANTI	8	8-72	8-72	29.3	225	.502	.888
Child Rearing	4	0-4	0-4	1.50	1.84	.396	.725
Prejudice*	24	24-216	24-214	92.5	1987	.519	.963
Religious Fundamen.	12	12-108	12-108	50.4	833	.669	.960

*White respondents only (N=810)

(Continuing on with statistical doings) principal axes factor analyses of the instruments used in the survey produced strong evidence of unidimensionality in almost every case. All had one dominant factor in the unrotated solution with subsequent ones so small they were easily dismissed by a Scree test. For example, the first factor extracted from the 24 prejudice items had an eigenvalue of 12.94, while the second amounted to only 1.99. *Most* of the variance in each test, except SDO-Dominance and Child-rearing, was common variance, which is unheard of. It means the factor underlying all the items on the scale was more powerful than the effect of the specific issues raised by the different items plus the error variance. For a psychometrician, that is the thing dreams are made of.

What's an eigenvalue? It's how many eigens you got. Sheesh.

"FIGURE 1" VALUES FOR THE SOCIAL

Dominance Scales

Here are the means for the SDO-Dominance Scale, from the 466 "Strongly Disapprovers" to the 348 "Strongly Approvers:" 16.4, 25.2, 24.6, 27.9, and 31.0). The corresponding values for the "Anti-Equality" SDO scale are 19.3, 30.3, 27.8, 36.1, and 40.4

Correlations Between the Measures

The biggest reason we did the survey was to see what Trump's non-supporters were like, psychologically, compared to those who support him. The statistic that best shows this is called the correlation coefficient. It shows how much two things, like personal prejudice and support for Trump. Go along together in a whole sample. It does not show which causes the other one however (and both could be caused by something else). Correlations vary in strength from 0.00 (no connection whatsoever) to ±1.00 (a perfect connection).

Lots of things in life are correlated. For instance, if you measure the height and weight of all the adult human beings on the planet tomorrow, in your spare time, these two aspects of our physical being will correlate about .50. Generally, tall people tend to weigh more than short people, even though you run into definite exceptions. (I am 5'8" and weigh more than most of the players in the NFL If I were 3" taller, I'd look perfectly round from the front.) Similarly, you may have noticed that bright people do better in school than, uh, unbright people. The correlation between scores on a stellar IQ test and academic success also runs about .50. in studies

Because .50 is halfway between 0.00 and 1.00, you might conclude that height explains about 50 percent of the weight of the population (and potato chips explain the rest). But that would be wrong, it turns out. You *square* a correlation to see how important it is. So, height only explains (.50 x .50 =) .25, or 25 percent of the human tonnage being lugged around the planet. (And the rest is due to potato chips and chocolate.) So, for One Thing to be able to explain *most* of the differences (i.e., the variance) in Another Thing because it goes along with it, the two have to correlate about .71 or higher (because $(.71)^2$ gives you over 50 percent of the explanation). And you know what? A researcher in the social sciences may never discover a relationship that strong in her lifetime. Because nature and nurture affect us in so many different ways, almost nothing interesting about human behavior correlates that much with any one thing. All the big, powerful stuff that does, like who has babies (the females), was noticed a long time ago. There are virtually no simple answers to the remaining Mysteries of Life. Researchers plugging away at their little piece of the Humongous Unknown usually discover small bits of knowledge—which is to be expected because they are trying to find things nobody- but-nobody- has found before. Correlations between .30 and .40 are often considered important finds—even though you're only explaining 10-15 percent of what you're trying to figure out.

If you understand that, then sit down because Table 2 is going to blow your mind to smithereens. (Like Table 1, it still sends chills down my spine the way it did when the numbers first popped up on my monitor.) The table has some big Bad Boy Numbers in it representing some Big Very Bad Connections in America.

Table 2 Correlations Among the Scales, Political Party Preference, and Approval of Trump's Performance [Note: First correlation (xxx/) is for whole sample, N=990; Second correlation (/yyy) is for white respondents only, N=810)]

	RWA Scale	Social Dominance: Orientation	Social Dominance: Anti-Equality	Child-Rearing	Predjudice	Religious Fundamentalism	Political Party Preference [a]	Approve of Trump [b]
RWA Scale	*	.613/ .634	.614/ .643	.645/ .666	.836/ .856	.829/ .841	.748/ .788	.737/ .764
Soc. Dom: Dominance		*	.640/ .642	.439/ .495	.712/ .720	.447/ .483	.568/ .571	.556/ .567
Soc. Dom: Anti-Equal.			*	.389/ .455	.729/ .734	.462/ .515	.627/ .628	.635/ .635
"Child Rearing"				*	.573/ .629	.569/ .593	.489/ .556	.471/ .528
Prejudice					*	.651/ .696	.775/ .787	.812/ .817
Religious Fundamen.						*	.627/ .700	.594/ .654
Party (Dem. Or GOP)							*	.859/ .868

a   Democrats versus Republicans.

b   Figure 1 in Chapter 10 shows that answers to the "Approve of Trump" question were enormously bi-modally distributed, Use of the Pearson product-moment correlation assumes a bi-variate normal distribution. Accordingly, we collapsed the "Approve Trump" data into two categories:, "Disapprove" (by merging "Strongly disapprove" and "Somewhat disapprove,") and "Approve" by following the same tack. Anybody who has ever speed-dated (we hear) knows that "Disapproval" versus "Approval" is at root a "natural," discrete, two-value variable (i.e. you hit or you miss) and therefore can be used to establish point-biserial correlations with continuous variables, which are product-moment values equal in size to Pearsons but which make no assumption, obviously, about normal distributions. The correlations shown in the column headed "Approve of Trump" are point-biserials.

c   There is not much to say about the four-item "Childrearing" Scale discussed in Appendix I.. It had better psychometric properties in this survey than usual (or ever), but it still does not bring anything to the table that is not already there, and it misses a great deal as well. There is a statistical procedure called a multiple regression analysis that's a whiz at showing how important things are by themselves and in combination with other things. If you are trying to predict support for Trump, combining the RWA Scale and the "Four Simple Questions," gets you almost nothing more than what the RWA Scale gives by itself. True, it only takes four items to account by itself for $(.47)^2 = 22$ percent of the variance in people's support Trump and that might impress some. But that is less impressive than it seems. Most (13/20) of the items on the RWA scale accounted for more than that just by themselves as single items. We will accordingly not spend much "ink" on this measure.

Let us start with the final column, which reports correlations that the various measures had with approval of Trump's performance. There are two numbers in each cell, such as .737 and .764. The second numbers (which refers to only the 810-white folk in the sample) can be ignored unless we are discussing white prejudice. As you run your eye down the last column, you see that, most of all, Trump's supporters were Republicans not Democrats. The correlation (found in the bottom cell) was .859. But "Duh." "Duh Squared." Much more to the point (of this book, and other matters), *almost all our scales predicted support of Trump much, much better* than height predicts weight and much, much better than IQ predicts academic success—things we think of in everyday life as important predictors. But they are puny compared to what we've got here. Two of our measures, the degree to which the person is a right-wing authoritarian and the respondent's score on the prejudice items can each explain *most* of the difference we find in voters' reaction to Donald Trump. That is really saying something, given how complicated people's reasons can be for choosing a presidential candidate. But it's a fact, Jack.

You may be wondering how two different tests can each account for more than half of something. Is it like "Reaganomics"? ("Half of the economy is the federal government, and half is the state governments, and half is the private sector.") They cannot, if they are independent of each other. But RWA Scale scores and prejudice are themselves very, very highly correlated (.856 among the white respondents). Which means way more than most (73.3 percent!) of the differences in prejudice among the white respondents in the study can be explained with just the RWA Scale, since .856 x .856 = 73.3 percent. Adding in the additional explanation that the two social dominance scales can contribute raises this to 81.1 percent. After which there's not much left to explain, even though (as we said in Chapter Six), many different kinds of people support Donald Trump. Economic factors for example are often cited. In our poll, as in other surveys, support for Trump had a low correlation with reports of annual family income before taxes (it was .00, DOA.). But a strong correlation (.660 over the whole sample) did appear between supporting the president and feeling that one had benefitted from the recent economic improvement. However, this feeling of moving ahead correlated .554 with prejudice (.539 for whites only). Thus, you could account for lots of the "Benefit-ted's" in Trump's corner with their prejudice scores. But economic improvement added little to our understanding of who supports Trump. A multiple regression analysis found that adding "Benefitted" to Prejudice raised the variance accounted for in Trump support from 65.9 percent to 71.4 percent for the whole sample, and from 66.5 percent to 71.7 percent for white respondents only. The biggest reason by far that people sup-ported Trump was their level of prejudice, but some (not many) relatively unprejudiced subjects approved of him because they thought they were prospering thanks to him.

COMPARISON OF THE SCALE'S PERFORMANCE IN THE MAY AND OCTOBER POLLS.

The alphas for the RWA, Dominance, Anti-Equality, Child-Rearing, Prejudice, and Religious Fundamentalism measures in May were, respectively, .949, .833, .897, .658, .959, and .942. The values for the Autumn sample, as reported in Table 1 above were .955, .840, .888, .725, .963, and .960.

Table 3 gives the comparison of the inter-scale correlations obtained in the May and October polls (May correlation comes first; October correlation comes last)

Table 4. Correlations between the Scales and Trump Approval in May and in October 2019 Polls

	RWA Scale	Social Dominance: Orientation	Social Dominance: Anti-Equality	Child-Rearing	Predjudice	Religious Fundamentalism	Approve of Trump
RWA Scale	*	.630/ .613	.621/ .614	.527/ .645	.816/ .856	.780/ .829	.755/ .737
Soc. Dom: Dominance		*	.644/ .640	.439/ .405	.712/ .720	.490/ .447	.516/ .556
Soc. Dom: Anti-Equal.			*	.389/ .317	.729/ .734	.396/ .462	.659/ .635
"Child Rearing"				*	.516/ .629	.569/ .470	.406/ .471
Prejudice					*	.659/ .696	.812/ .817
Religious Fundamen.						*	.574/ .594

The October Poll Censorship Study

Another search for replication in the Monmouth autumn poll centered on the relationship between RWA and "political correctness." Various conservative politicians in Canada complained at one point about being pressured to be "politically correct," which usually meant not making comments that would offend disadvantaged groups. But conservatives seemed to want to control language and communications just as much, only on different topics. So, a dozen cases were assembled involving the spread of controversial ideas, half of which would anger High RWAs, and half of which would tick off Lows. I thought the two groups would betray equal drives to censor. A large sample of parents of Canadian university students reacted to the twelve cases and their answers stunningly disconfirmed my hypothesis. Disbelieving, I ran the experiment again with a second parent sample and Mother Nature gave the same answer: "You're wrong, Dummy!!"

The "Censorship Scale" was accordingly squeezed onto the end of the Monmouth autumn poll because if any of my past studies would not replicate in the USA, it was probably this one because the previous outcomes seemed so wrong.

The Censorship Test is shown below as it appeared on our survey. Each item was answered on a +4 to -4 basis. The correlation between a desire to censor the material and RWA Scale scores is given in parentheses after each item.

ENDNOTES

INTRODUCTION

1 Michael J. Tansey, "Why 'Crazy Like a Fox' Versus 'Crazy Like a Crazy' Really Matters: Delusional Disorder, Admiration of Brutal Dictators, the Nuclear Codes, and Trump," in Bandy Lee, ed., *The Dangerous Case of Donald Trump* (New York: St. Martin's Press, Updated Edition, 2019), 110.

2 Bandy Lee, ed., *The Dangerous Case of Donald Trump* (New York: St. Martin's Press, 2017).

3 John D. Gartner, "Donald Trump is (A) Bad (B) Mad (C) All of the Above," in Bandy Lee, ed., *The Dangerous Case of Donald Trump* (New York: St. Martin's Press, 2017), 93.

4 On March 19, 2019, George Conway, an accomplished attorney and noted conservative Trump critic since his wife is Trump's 2016 campaign manager and senior White House staff counselor, Kellyanne Conway, posted the medical definitions of both the narcissistic personality disorder and the antisocial personality disorder on his Twitter account. He urged people to consider the possibility that Trump is too mentally ill to continue serving. Some six months later, Conway flushed out his concern in greater detail. See George Conway, "Unfit for Office: Donald Trump's narcissism makes it impossible for him to carry out the duties of the presidency in the way the Constitution requires," *The Atlantic*, October 3, 2019, https://www.theatlantic.com/ideas/archive/2019/10/george-conway-trump-unfit-office/599128/.

5 Bob Woodward, *Fear: Trump in the White House* (New York: Simon & Schuster, 2018).

6 Anonymous, "I Am Part of the Resistance inside the Trump Administration," *New York Times*, September 5, 2018, and Anonymous, *A Warning* (New York: Twelve, 2019).

CHAPTER ONE

1 Stephen Collinson, "Trump Officials Deflect Blame for US Death Toll, Escalate Reopening Push, *CNN*, May 18, 2020, https://www.cnn.com/ 2020/05/18/politics/trump-us-death-toll-blame-reopen/index.html.

2 On May 5, 2020, Dr. Anthony Fauci, the head of the National Institute of Allergy and Infectious Disease and the most famous scientist in America now from his role

on the president's Coronavirus Task Force, said, "If you look at the evolution of the virus in bats and what's out there now, the scientific evidence is very, very strongly leaning toward this could not have been artificially or deliberately manipulated . . . Everything about the stepwise evolution over time strongly indicates that [this virus] evolved in nature and then jumped species." Chris Cillizza, "Anthony Fauci Just Crushed Donald Trump's Theory of the Coronavirus," *CNN*, May 5, 2020, https://www.cnn.com/2020/05/05/politics/fauci-trump-coronavirus-wuhan-lab/index.html.

3   Derrick Bryson Taylor, "How the Coronavirus Pandemic Unfolded: a Timeline," *New York Times*, June 9, 2020, https://www.nytimes.com/article/coronavirus-timeline.html.

4   "Coronavirus: France's First Known Case 'Was in December,'" *BBC*, May 5, 2020, https://www.bbc.com/news/world-europe-52526554.

5   Ashley Collman, "In 2017, Obama Officials Briefed Trump's Team on Dealing with a Pandemic Like the Coronavirus. One Cabinet Member Reportedly Fell Asleep, and Others Didn't Want to Be There," *Business Insider*, March 17, 2020, https://www.businessinsider.com/trump-appointees-trained-pandemic-responsein-2016-2020-3.

6   Eric Lipton et al., "He Could Have Seen What Was Coming: Behind Trump's Failure on the Virus," *New York Times*, April 11, 2020, https://www.nytimes.com/2020/04/11/us/politics/coronavirus-trump-response.html.

7   Our summary of Trump's responses to the coronavirus crisis is based largely on Leonhardt's careful research. David Leonhardt, "A Complete List of Trump's Attempts to Play Down Coronavirus," *New York Times*, March 15, 2020, https://www.nytimes.com/2020/03/15/opinion/trump-coronavirus.html.

8   Caroline Kelly, "The Washington Post: US Intelligence Warned Trump in January and February as He Dismissed Coronavirus Threat," *CNN*, March 21, 2020, https://www.cnn.com/2020/03/20/politics/us-intelligence-reports-   trump-coronavirus/index.html.

9   Marlene Lenthang, "Donald Trump Dismissed Health Secretary Alex Azar's January Warning on Coronavirus as 'Alarmist' and Cut Him Off during a Phone Briefing, Report Says," *Daily Mail*, April 5, 2020, https://www.dailymail.co.uk/news/article-8190167/Donald-Trump-dismissed-Health-Secretary-Alex-Azars-January-coronavirus-warning-alarmist.html.

10 Shane Harris, Greg Miller, John Dawsey, and Ellen Nakashima, "US Intelligence Reports from January and February Warned about a Likely Pandemic," *Washington Post*, March 20, 2020, https://www.washingtonpost.com/national-security/us-intelligence-reports-from-january-and-february-warned-about-a-likely-pandemic/2020/03/20/299d8cda-6ad5–11ea-b5f1-a5a804158597_story.html.

11 David Leonhardt, "A Complete List."

12 Maggie Haberman, "Trade Adviser Warned White House in January of Risks of a Pandemic: A Memo from Peter Navarro Is the Most Direct Warning Known to Have Circulated at a Key Moment among Top Administration Officials," *New York Times*, April 11, 2020, https://www.nytimes.com/2020/04/06/us/politics/navarro-warning-trump-coronavirus.html.

13 Michelle Mark, "Trump learned of a memo in January warning 'half a million American souls' could die of coronavirus, and he was displeased his adviser put it in writing," *Business Insider*, April 11, 2020, https://www.businessinsider.com/trump-peter-navarro-january-memo-coronavirus-deaths-2020-4.

14 David Leonhardt, "A Complete List."

15 Media Matters Staff, "Rush Limbaugh: Coronavirus Is like the Common Cold, and 'All of This Panic Is Just Not Warranted,'" *Media Matters*, March 11, 2020, https://www.mediamatters.org/coronavirus-covid19/rush-limbaugh-coronavirus-common-cold-and-all-panic-just-not-warranted.

16 Bess Levin, "Trump Claims Coronavirus Will 'Miraculously' Go Away by April,"

Vanity Fair, February 11, 2020, https://www.vanityfair.com/news/ 2020/02/donald-trump-coronavirus-warm-weather.

17 Gabriel Sherman, "Inside Donald Trump and Jared Kushner's Two Months of Magical Thinking," *Vanity Fair*, April 28, 2020, https://www.vanityfair.com/news/2020/04/donald-trump-jared-kushners-two-months-of-magical-thinking.

18 "'Maybe I have a natural ability': Trump plays medical expert on coronavirus by second-guessing the professionals," *Washington Post*, March 20, 2020, https://www.washingtonpost.com/politics/maybe-i-have-a-natural-ability-trump-plays-medical-expert-on-coronavirus-by-second-guessing-the-professionals/2020/03/06/3ee0574c-5ffb-11ea-9055-5fa12981bbbf_story.html.

19 The Economist Staff, "Americans Are Not Rallying around Donald Trump during the Pandemic," *The Economist*, April 15, 2020, https://www.economist.com/graphic-detail/2020/04/15/americans-are-not-rallying-around-donald-trump-during-the-pandemic.

20 Bess Levin, "Texas Lt. Governor: Old People Should Volunteer to Die to Save the Economy," *Vanity Fair*, March 24, 2020, https://www.vanityfair.com/news/2020/03/dan-patrick-coronavirus-grandparents.

21 Editorial Staff, "Models Project Sharp Rise in Deaths as States Reopen," *New York Times*, May 5, 2020, https://www.nytimes.com/2020/05/04/us/coronavirus-live-updates.html#link-582f66ac.

22 Jasmine Kim, "Cornoavirus deaths in U.S. projected to surpass 200,000 by October," *CNBC*, June 20, 2020, https://www.cnbc.com/amp/2020/06/17/coronavirus-deaths-in-us-projected-to-surpass-200000-by-october.html.

23 Oliver Laughland, "Donald Trump and the Central Park Five: The racially charged rise of a demagogue," *The Guardian*, February 17, 2016, https://www.theguardian.com/us-news/2016/feb/17/central-park-five-donald-trump-jogger-rape-case-new-york.

24 CNN Staff, "Transcript: President Trump's call with US governors over protests," *CNN News*, June 1, 2020, https://www.cnn.com/2020/06/01/politics/wh-governors-call-protests/index.html.

25 Amanda Macias and Dan Mangan, "Joint Chiefs of Staff Chairman Milley apologizes for appearing with Trump at church photo op," *NBC News*, June 11, 2020, https://www.cnbc.com/2020/06/11/george-floyd-joint-chiefs-chairman-milley-apologizes-for-appearing-with-trump.html.

26 See Quinta Jurecic and Benjamin Wittes, "Yet Another Week of Trump failing to Be an Actual Authoritarian," *The Atlantic*, June 9, 2020, https://www.theatlantic.com/ideas/archive/2020/06/yet-another-week-trump-failing-be-actual-authoritarian/612829/.

27 Trump has been labeled an authoritarian literally thousand upon thousand of times. For example, a Lexis Nexus Boolean search for "Trump w/5 authoritarian" produced 7,182 results going back to only September 30, 2019.

28 See https://richardlangworth.com/worst-form-of-government.

29 Steven Levitsky and Daniel Ziblatt, *How Democracies Die* (New York: Viking Press, 2018).

30 Patrick Healy and Maggie Haberman, "95,000 Words, Many of Them Ominous, From Donald Trump's Tongue," *New York Times*, December 5, 2015, https://www.nytimes.com/2015/12/06/us/politics/95000-words-many-of-them-ominous-from-donald-trumps-tongue.html?searchResultPosition=21.

31 Winston Churchill, "Soapbox Messiahs," Collier's, June 20, 1936, https://www.unz.com/PDF/PERIODICAL/Colliers-1936jun20/11–12/.

32 T. W. Adorno et al., *The Authoritarian Personality* (New York: Harper and Row, 1950). Adorno traveled from Los Angeles to Berkeley occasionally, participated in discussions, and wrote four of the twenty-two chapters in the book (the others authored by

E. Frenkel-Brunswick, D. J. Levinson, and R. N. Sanford). Adorno appears to be the leading investigator of the team because Sanford selflessly gave up first authorship and listed the group alphabetically to end quarrels about who would come after him on the title page. Thus, the book was evermore referenced as "Adorno et al." (So, when someone says "the Berkeley group" was led by Theodore Adorno, you should be careful about believing the rest of what they say.) Ironically, Adorno's original name was Wiesengrund-Adorno, but he shortened it in 1943, moving him from the end of the alphabet to the beginning.

33   If you have heard about research on authoritarianism lately, it may be based on a four-item questionnaire developed by political scientist Stanley Feldman in the early 1990s that asks for your preferences in child-rearing goals (e.g., independence versus respect for elders). Feldman thought people's choices indicated how authoritarian they were, and the four items have been used in many big national surveys over the years. Marc Hetherington and Jonathan Weiler used these findings to argue, in *Authoritarianism & Polarization in American Politics*, (2009) that America was splitting in half because of authoritarianism. Then in 2018 they said in *Prius or Pickup* that Feldman's items did not measure authoritarianism, but instead how "fluid" or "fixed" you are. Also, Matthew MacWilliams, a graduate student working on his dissertation, published an article in *Politico* on January 17, 2016, that said the four items measured authoritarianism and significantly distinguished Trump supporters from nonsupporters. Drawn to the subject, Amanda Taub read up on the political science literature in this area and wrote a piece for Vox a few weeks later titled, "The Rise of American Authoritarianism" (March 1, 2016). If pundits use that label now more often than before, it may be partly because of Taub's essay. We have some significant hesitations about the value of the four-item questionnaire as a measure of authoritarianism, which you can find in Appendix I.

CHAPTER TWO

1   Bob Altemeyer, "The Other 'Authoritarian Personality.'" In Mark Zanna, ed., *Advances in Experimental Social Psychology*, 30 (New York: Academic Press, 1998).

2   Jane Mayer, "Donald Trump's ghostwriter tells all," *New Yorker*, July 25, 2016, https://www.newyorker.com/magazine/2016/07/25/donald-trumps-ghost writer-tells-all. Also, Tony Schwartz, "I Wrote The Art of the Deal with Trump; His Self-Sabotage Is Rooted in His Past." In Bandy Lee, ed., *The Dangerous Case of Donald Trump* (New York: St. Martin's Press, 2017).

3   Jane Mayer, "Donald Trump's ghostwriter tells all," *New Yorker*, July 25, 2016, https://www.newyorker.com/magazine/2016/07/25/donald-trumps-ghost-writer-tells-all.

4   Michael D'Antonio, *The Truth about Trump* (New York: St. Martin's Press, 2016). (Originally published in 2015 as *Never Enough: Donald Trump and the Pursuit of Success*.)

5   Ibid.

6   Michael Kranish and Marc Fisher, eds., *Trump Revealed* (New York: Scribner, 2016.)

7   Ibid.

8   Donald Trump and Tony Schwartz, *Trump: The Art of the Deal* (New York: Random House, 1987), 79-80.

9   David Barstow, Susanne Craig, and Russ Buettner, "Trump engaged in suspect tax schemes as he reaped riches from his father," *New York Times*, October 2, 2018, https://www.nytimes.com/interactive/2018/10/02/   us/politics/donald-trump-tax-schemes-fred-trump.html. See also, Russ Buettner, Susanne Craig and David Barstow, "11

Takeaways From The Times's Investigation Into Trump's Wealth," *New York Times*, October 2, 2018, https://www.nytimes.com/2018/10/02/us/politics/donald-trump-wealth-fred-trump.html.

10   Russ Buettner and Susanne Craig, "Retiring as a Judge, Trump's Sister Ends Court Inquiry Into Her Role in Tax Dodges," *New York Times*, August 10, 2019, https://www.nytimes.com/2019/04/10/us/maryanne-trump-barrymisconduct-inquiry.html.

11   Tony Schwartz, *PBS Frontline* interview, July 12, 2016, https://www.pbs.org/wgbh/frontline/interview/tony-schwartz/.

12   Louise Sunshine, "President Trump," *PBS Frontline*, January 3, 2017, https://www.pbs.org/wgbh/frontline/film/president-trump/.

13   Sandy McIntosh, "President Trump," *PBS Frontline*, January 3, 2017, https://www.pbs.org/wgbh/frontline/film/president-trump/.

14   Donald J. Trump and Charles Leerhsen, *Surviving at the Top*, (New York: Random House, 1990), 63.

15   Donald Trump, *Think Big and Kick Ass in Business and Life*, (New York: HarperCollins, 2007).

16   Michael D'Antonio, 2016, 40.

17   Michael Wolfe, *Fire and Fury: Inside the Trump White House* (New York: Henry Holt and Company, 2018).

18   Michael Kranish and Marc Fisher, 33.

19   "President Trump," *PBS Frontline*, May 8, 2017.

20   Donald Trump and Tony Schwartz, 72.

21   Roy Baumeister, *Evil: Inside Human Violence and Cruelty* (New York: Holt Paperbacks 1999), 149-153. See also, McKayla Arnold, "Five Reasons Teens Become Bullies," https://www.crchealth.com/you-programs-5-resasons-teens-become -bullies/.

22   Paul Schwartzman & Michael Miller, "Confident. incorrigible. bully: Little Donny was a lot like Candidate Trump." *Washington Post*, June 22, 2016, https://www.washingtonpost.com/lifestyle/style/young-donald-trump-military-school/2016/06/22/f0b3b164-317c-11e6-8758-d5.

23   Donald Trump and Tony Schwartz, 71.

24   Philip Rucker and Carol Leonnig, *A Very Stable Genius*, (New York: Penguin Press, 2020) 136.

25   Paul Schwartzman & Michael Miller, 2016.

26   Donald Trump and Tony Schwartz, 72.

27   Schwartzman & Michael Miller, 2016.

28   Michael D'Antonio, 2016, 325.

29   Michael Kranish and Marc Fisher, 35. See also, Paul Schwartzman & Michael Miller, 2016.

30   Sean Illing, "Trump biographer: "He's an actor who's been playing himself for his entire life," *Vox*, January 25, 2017, https://www.vox.com/policy-and-politics/2017/1/25/14357474/donald-trump-2016-election-barack-obamadantonio-mark-media.

31   Krishnadev Calamur, "Nine Notorious Dictators, Nine Shout-Outs From Donald Trump," *The Atlantic*, March 4, 2018, https://www.theatlantic.com/international/archive/2018/03/trump-xi-jinping-dictators/554810/. The desire to appear menacing may have been why Trump improbably hired Tony Schwartz to write what became *The Art of the Deal*. Schwartz had just written a very uncomplimentary article about Trump for *New York Magazine*, with a cover featuring an artist-created picture of an unshav-

en, determined, steely-eyed Trump. Trump loved it, and sent Schwartz a note saying, "Everybody seems to have read it." Schwartz doubted Trump had read it; he just liked the picture. (Schwartz found that Trump reads almost nothing and may not have even read *The Art of the Deal*.)

32 Michael Kruse, "The Mystery of Mary Trump," *Politico*, November 5, 2017, https://www.politico.com/magazine/story/2017/11/03/mary-macleod-trump -donald-trump-mother-biography-momimmigrant-scotland-215779.

33 Michael Kranish and Marc Fisher, 2016, 81. Peale's teachings fit comfortably alongside "prosperity theology"—considered a heresy by some Protestant denominations—which holds that God wants his followers to be wealthy and healthy. They in turn have to show faith, optimism, and make donations to religious causes. So, you can tell who the good people are because they are rich. President Trump likes prosperity theology and has been especially impressed with one of its foremost advocates, televangelist Paula White, since he saw her TV show in 2002. She has frequently had private Bible study sessions with him, and she gave the invocation at his inauguration. Ms. White has had various duties in the administration, and in November 2019, during Trump's impeachment problems, a copy of a book she was writing chock full of praise of him somehow became known to him. She became a special advisor to the Faith and Opportunity Initiative at the Office of Public Liaison. The sometimes-reliable Wikipedia reports that White believes Trump's political opponents operate in sorcery and witchcraft, and Trump may literally believe his charge that the Mueller and impeachment investigations were "witch hunts."

34 Peale, Norman Vincent, *Stay Alive All Your Life* (New York: Simon & Schuster, 1957.)

35 Sandy McIntosh, *PBS Frontline*, September 27, 2016.

36 Ibid.

37 Gwenda Blair, *PBS Newshour*, July 18, 2016.

38 Michael Kranish and Marc Fisher, 42.

39 Ibid., 40-41.

40 Marc Fisher, "'Grab that record:' How Trump's high school transcript was hidden," *Washington Post*, March 5, 2019, https://www.washingtonpost.com /politics/grab-that-record-how-trumps-high-school-transcript-was-hidden/2019/03/05/8815b7b8-3c61-11e9-aaae-69364b2ed137_story.html.

41 Michael D'Antonio, 2016, 43.

42 Ibid., 46.

43 "What Trump interviews with biographer tell us," *BBC News*, October 26, 2016.

44 Donald Trump and Tony Schwartz, 126.

45 Michael E. Miller, "50 years later, disagreements over young Trump's military academy record," *Washington Post*, January 9, 2016, https://www.washingtonpost.com/politics/decades-later-disagreement-over-young-trumps-military-academy-post/2016/01/09/907a67b2-b3e0-11e5-a842-0feb51d1d124_story.html.

46 Ibid.

47 Michael Kranish and Marc Fisher, 44.

48 Ibid., 40.

49 Ibid., 41, and Michael D'Antonio (2016), 45.

50 Sandy McIntosh, *PBS Frontline*, September 27, 2016.

51 Sandy McIntosh, "How young Donald Trump was slapped and punched until he made his bed," *New York Daily News*, August 11, 2017, https://www.nydailynews.com/opin-

ion/donald-trump-fellow-cadet-article-1.3401110.

52   By the time Trump sat down for interviews with Michael D'Antonio in 2014 his baseball accomplishments had grown from hitting a walk-off home run in a non-existent
stadium to his being the greatest player in the state in his youth. "By his own estimate
he was definitely 'the best baseball player in New York,' and he would have turned
pro except that 'there was no real money in it." (Michael D'Antonio (2016), 47. When
asked, his high school baseball coach Major Dobias said a scout for the Philadelphia
Phillies came to watch Trump play, but there is no known evidence anyone ever offered
Trump a contract, or even an invitation to attend a try-out camp. Trump may really
believe he could have been a professional ball player, but he apparently was just the best
player on a high school team that played other small private high schools in the region.

53   Donald Trump and Tony Schwartz, 77.

54   Michael Kranish, "Trump has referred to his Wharton degree as 'super genius stuff.'
An admission officer recalls it differently," *Washington Post*, July 8, 2019, https://www.
washingtonpost.com/politics/trump-who-often-boastsof-his-wharton-degree-says-
he-was-admitted-to-the-hardest-school-to-get-into-the-college-official-who-re-
viewedhis-application-recalls-it-differently/2019/07/08/0a4eb414-977a-11e9-830a-
21b9b36b64ad_story.html.

55   Jonathan Valania, "Fact-Checking All of the Mysteries Surrounding Donald
Trump and Penn," *Phillymag.com*, September 14, 2019, https://www.phillymag.com/
news/2019/09/14/donald-trump-at-wharton-university-ofpennsylvania/.

56   Michael Kranish & Marc Fisher, 49.

57   Raiser Bruner, "Candice Bergen describes her very color-coordinated date with Donald Trump," *Time Newsfeed*, September 14, 2017.

58   Michael Kranish, 2019.

59   *Daily Pennsylvanian*, February 16, 2017. Trump's academic records would probably cast
the gravest doubt on his being a "super-genius," but they are as unavailable as his tax
returns. Michael Cohen testified before the House Oversight Committee on February
27, 2019 that Trump had him threaten the New York Military Academy, Fordham,
and Penn State with lawsuits if they ever revealed his grades. He also promised to
sue the Educational Testing Service if it revealed his SAT scores. On March 6, 2019
the *Washington Post* reported that while Trump was criticizing Barack Obama for not
releasing his grades at Harvard School of Law, insisting that a president owed it to
the country to do so, friends of Trump were trying to get the New York Military
Academy to give them his records so no one could ever see them. https://www.wash-
ingtonpost.com/politics/grab-that-record-how-trumps-high-schooltranscript-was-
hidden/2019/03/05/8815b7b8-3c61-11e9-aaae-69364b2ed137_story.html?utm_ter-
m=.45c5b2db0c7f.

60   Ibid.

CHAPTER THREE

1   Bob Altemeyer, "The Other 'Authoritarian Personality.'" In Mark Zanna, ed., *Advances
in Experimental Social Psychology*, 30 (New York: Academic Press, 1998). This test was
based on the Machiavellianism Scale developed earlier by Richard Christie and Florence
Geis of Columbia University. Dick Christie and M. Brewster Smith were early supporters of my research on authoritarianism and helped get my first book published in 1981.

2   If you think, as we do, that these statements could go on the back of that "Donald Trump Creed" poster you were going to buy in the gift shop at Mount TRUMP in Chapter Two, others agree. Senator Lindsey Graham (R-SC) called Trump dishonest and a "race-baiting, xenophobic, religious bigot," who was totally unfit to be commander-in-chief in December 2015 (https://www.youtube.com/watch?v=2bkDykGhM8c). (Senator Graham became close friends with Trump after Trump was elected.) Retired General Stanley McChrystal told ABC News that Trump was dishonest and immoral. (https://abcnews.go.com/Politics/retired-army-gen-stanleymcchrystal-president-donald-trump/story?id=60065642). Former Republican Presidential candidate Mitt Romney said of Trump before he took office that he lacked honesty and integrity (https://www.washingtonpost.com/opinions/mitt-romney-the-president-shapes-the-public-character-of-the-nation-trumps-character-falls-short/2019/01/01/37a3c8c2-0d1a-11e98938-5898adc28fa2_story.html?utm_term=.0f2bbda9601c). The senior Trump White House official who wrote the anonymous op-ed for the *New York Times* on September 5, 2018 summarized it nicely: "The root of the problem is the president's amorality. Anyone who works with him knows he is not moored to any discernible first principles that guide his decision making." (https://www.nytimes.com/2018/09/05/opinion/trump-white-house-anonymous-resistance.html). A year later "Anonymous" wrote in his/her book, *A Warning*: "In the history of American democracy, we have had undisciplined presidents. We have had incurious presidents. We have had inexperienced presidents. We have had amoral presidents. Rarely if ever before have we had them all at once." *Anonymous, A Warning* (New York: Twelve, 2019) 56-57.

3   Steve Eder, "Did a Queens Podiatrist Help Donald Trump Avoid Vietnam?", *New York Times*, December 26, 2018, https://www.nytimes.com/2018/12/26/us/politics/trump-vietnam-draftexemption.html.

4   Donald Trump and Charles Leerhsen, *Surviving at the Top*, (New York: Random House), 55. Trump probably meant the "Lucky Sons Club." Like many men, he identifies with the sperm that carried DNA from his father to the ovum provided by his mother. But half of a son's DNA comes from his mother. Furthermore, a sperm from (say) a robber-baron industrial magnate could, in the faithful execution of its duty, help produce a male heir who would be born lucky. The sperm however would not be lucky as it has been handed a suicide mission. It would be destroyed the instant it penetrated the ovum's outer coating and released its chromosomes. As we saw in the Introduction regarding the COVID-19 virus, Trump's knowledge of basic biology may be a tad deficient. His strongest defender might be hard pressed to demonstrate that President Trump's knowledge of basic chemistry, physics, geology, astronomy, atmospheric science is better. We acknowledged at the outset that Presidents are not picked by college transcript and GPA. But can a defender name any field of knowledge or artistic attainment in which Donald Trump has shown much knowledge except real estate and borrowing money? It does seem fair to wonder, aloud, "How much "there" is there there, intellectually?"

5   Jeremy Diamond, "Donald Trump Describes Father's 'Small Loan:' $1 million," *CNN*, October 27, 2015, https://www.cnn.com/2015/10/26/politics/donald-trump-small-loantown-hall/index.html.

6   David Barstow, Susanne Craig, and Russ Buettner, "Trump Engaged in Suspect Tax Schemes as He Reaped Riches from His Father," *New York Times*, October 2, 2018.

7   When the *Times* story broke in December 2018, President Trump denied it was true

and expressed outrage that it had been printed. His lawyer said it was "extremely inaccurate." But neither Trump or the lawyer provided any disproof, just denials. See "I started with a million-dollar loan. Taking apart Donald Trump's Taxes," *NPR*, October 25, 2018, https://www.npr.org/2018/10/25/660642593/-i-started-with-a-million-dollar-loan-taking-apart-trumpstaxes.

8   Donald Trump & Tony Schwartz, Trump: *The Art of the Deal*, (New York: Random House: 1987, 94-96).

9   "President Trump," *PBS Frontline*, January 3, 2017.

10   Michael D'Antonio, *The Truth about Trump* (New York: St. Martens Press, 2016, 79-82). (Originally published in 2015 as *Never Enough: Donald Trump and the Pursuit of Success.*).

11   Michael Kranish and Marc Fisher, eds., *Trump Revealed* (New York: Scribner, 2016, 68).

12   Judy Klemesrud, "Donald Trump, Real Estate Promoter, Builds Image As He Buys Buildings," *New York Times*, November 1, 1976.

13   Similarly, Trump acquired great clout by cracking the "Forbes 400" list of wealthiest persons in 1982 by asserting (via "John Barron," an alter-ego he sometimes assumed when telephoning reporters with news of how great Donald Trump was) that his assets totaled twenty times what he actually owned. (Jonathan Greenberg, "Trump lied to me about his wealth to get onto the Forbes 400. Here are the tapes," *Washington Post*, April 20, 2018, https://www.washingtonpost.com/outlook/trump-lied-to-me-about-his-wealth-to-get-onto-the-forbes-400-here-are-the-tapes/2018/04/20/ac762b08-4287-11e8-8569-26fda6b404c7_story.html.

14   Ibid., 73-79, 103-104. 9

15   Michael D'Antonio, 101.

16   Ibid, 109.

17   Trump Tower has 58 floors, with a large atrium on the first floor. But Trump wanted it to (seem to) be the tallest building in the neighborhood. So he jiggled the numbering of the floors and claimed it had 68 floors. It was like getting others to think the girls who visited him at New York Military Academy found him irresistible.

18   Donald Trump and Tony Schwartz, 56.

19   Donald Trump and Charles Leerhsen, *Surviving at the Top* (New York: Random House, 1990, 24).

20   John O'Donnell and James Rutherford, *Trumped! The Inside Story of the Real Donald Trump—His Cunning Rise and Spectacular Fall* (Hertford, N.C., Crossroad Press, 1991, 35).

21   Ibid., 26-27.

22   Ibid., 57.

23   Ibid., 93.

24   David Barstow, Susanne Craig, & Russ Buettner.

25   Steve Reilly, "Hundreds Allege Donald Trump Doesn't Pay His Bills," *USA Today*, April 25, 2018.

26   Tony Schwartz, "I wrote *The Art of the Deal* with Donald Trump. His self-sabotage is rooted in his past," In Bandy Lee, ed., *The Dangerous Case of Donald Trump* (New York: St. Martin's Press, 2019, 71).

27   Tony Schwartz, "I wrote *The Art of the Deal* with Trump. He's Still a Scared Child," *The Guardian*, January 18, 2018, 58. Donald Trump's level of empathy is revealed by a

little-known event concerning his brother Fred's family. By 1993 Fred Sr. was showing signs of dementia and apparently Donald helped him rework his last will and testament. When Fred Sr. died in 1999, Fred Jr.'s family inherited nothing. This was attributed to Donald's influence over his cognitively slipping father. Fred Jr. of course was dead, but his son Fred C. Trump III expected to be a beneficiary in the will, so he sued. Donald responded that his father wanted to disinherit Fred III, in this "Case of the Three Freds," because Fred I did not like Fred II's wife, who was Fred III's mother. This seems strange, because Fred II's wife was never in the will and it seemed unsporting to punish her son because she was out of reach. But Donald Trump was outraged that his nephew had taken the will to court, and to get even (and Donald said this was his motivation) he did something pretty heinous. Fred III had an infant son afflicted with cerebral palsy, and the costly care for the newborn was covered by the Trump Company for the child's lifetime. Donald stopped all payments for the care of the child. He did not care if the baby died. "Why should we give him medical coverage," Donald heartlessly protested publicly to the *New York Daily News*. (Natalie Schreyer, "The Trump Files: When Donald Took Revenge by Cutting Off Health Coverage for a Sick Infant," *Mother Jones*, August 25, 2016, https://www.motherjones.com/politics/2016/08/trump-files-donald-sick-infant-medical-care/. A confidential settlement was reached in 2000, so we do not know how this story ended.

28 Michael Kranish & Marc Fisher, 188-196.

29 Louise Sunshine, "President Trump," *PBS Frontline*, January 3, 2017, https://www.pbs.org/wgbh/frontline/film/the-choice-2016/transcript/.

30 Cal Fussman, "What I've Learned: Donald Trump," *Esquire*, June 16, 2015, https://www.esquire.com/author/5133/cal-fussman/.

31 Michael Kranish & Marc Fisher, 195.

32 Russ Buettner & Charles V. Bagli, "How Donald Trump Bankrupted His Atlantic City Casinos but Still Earned Millions," *New York Times*, August 11, 2016.

33 Drew Harwell, "As its stock collapsed, Trump's firm gave him huge bonuses and paid for his jet," *Washington Post*, June 16, 2016, https://www.washingtonpost.com/business/economy/as-its-stockcollapsed-trumps-firm-gave-him-huge-bonuses-and-paid-for-his-jet/2016/06/12/58458918-2766-11e6b989-4e5479715b54_story.html.

34 Michael Kranish & Marc Fisher, Chapter 10.

35 Ibid., 186.

36 Timothy L. O'Brien, *Trump Nation: The Art of Being The Donald* (New York, Warner Books, 2005).

37 Trump plays a lot of golf, but he is not a good golfer, according to sportswriter Rick Reilly, who has played with him and wrote a book about it (*Commander in Cheat: How Golf Explains Donald Trump*). Trump just cheats a lot. He takes mulligans (second, third, fourth tries) after a bad shot, kicks his ball out of the rough, gives himself putts that he could easily miss, will kick an opponent's ball into a sand trap, and often says it took him fewer shots to finish a shot than it really did. If you played golf at various Trump courses prior to his becoming president, you might have seen a framed photo of him in the lobby that shows him on the cover of Time as "Man of the Year." It was a fake. (David A. Fahrenthold, "A Time Magazine with Trump on the Cover Hangs in His Golf Clubs. It's Fake," *Washington Post*, June 27, 2017.)

38 Paul Schwartzman & Michael E. Miller, "Confident. Incorrigible. Bully: Little Don-

ny was a lot like candidate Donald Trump," *Washington Post*, June 22, 2016.

39   Tony Schwartz, *PBS Frontline*, July 12, 2016, https://www.pbs.org/wgbh/frontline/interview/tony-schwartz/.

40   Russ Buettner & Susanne Craig.

41   John O'Donnell gives an insight into how *The Art of the Deal* rang up big sales and became a publishing sensation as soon as it was released. Trump required each of his casinos to buy 4,000 copies, on a no-return basis, to sell to customers. They did not sell all that well. Eventually O'Donnell gave them away at customer parties and put one in every room in his hotel on New Year's Eve, 1987. (O'Donnell and Rutherford, 24-25.)

42   Donald Trump and Tony Schwartz, 70-71.

43   Tony Schwartz, "I wrote *The Art of the Deal* with Trump. He's Still a Scared Child," *The Guardian*, January 18, 2018, 58.

44   Michael D'Antonio, 212.

45   Patrick Radden Keefe, How Mark Burnett Resurrected Donald Trump as an Icon of American Success: With 'The Apprentice,' the TV producer mythologized Trump – then a floundering D-lister – as the ultimate titan, paving his way to the Presidency," *New Yorker*, January 7, 2019, https://www.newyorker.com/magazine/2019/01/07/how-mark-burnett-resurrected-donald-trump-as-an-icon-of-american-success.

46   John Cassidy, "Trump University: It's Worse Than You Think," *New Yorker*, June 2, 2016, https://www.newyorker.com/news/john-cassidy/trump-university-its-worse-than-you-think/amp.

47   Eliza Relman, "The 25 women who have accused Trump of sexual misconduct," *Business Insider*, May 1, 2020, https://www.businessinsider.com/women-accused-trump-sexual-misconduct-list-2017-12.

48   Bob Woodward, *Fear: Trump in the White House* (New York: Simon & Schuster, 2018), 175.

49   Dan P. McAdams, "A psychologist analyzes Donald Trump," *The Atlantic*, June 2016.

50   Harry Hurt, "Donald Trump Gets Small," *Esquire*, May 1991, https://classic.esquire.com/article/1991/5/1/donald-trump-gets-small.

51   Louis Nelson, "Trump told Howard Stern it's OK to call Ivanka a 'piece of ass,'" *Politico*, October 8, 2016, https://www.politico.com/story/2016/10/trump-ivanka-piece-of-ass-howard-stern-229376, and Nick Ciccone.

52   Stormy Daniels with Kevin Carr O'Leary, *Full Disclosure* (New York: St. Martin's Press, Kindle edition, 2018), Locations 1793-1814.

53   Stuart Greer, "Female engineer behind Trump Tower reveals what it's like working with the President of the United States," *Manchester Evening News*, October 1, 2018, https://www.manchestereveningnews.co.uk/business/business-news/female-engineer-behind-trump-tower15220690

54   Philip Johnson, "Interview with Donald Trump," *New York Magazine*, November 9, 1992.

55   Donald Trump and Kate Bohner, *The Art of the Comeback* (New York: Times Books, 1997).

56   Susan Milligan, "Women Could Cost Trump the Election: The gaping gender gap spells trouble for President Trump, and he's not making progress with women," *U.S. News*, December 17, 2020, https://www.usnews.com/news/elections/articles/2019-12-17/lack-of-support-from-women-could-cost-trump-the-2020-election.

CHAPTER FOUR

1   Erin Schaff, "Full Transcript: Michael Cohen's Opening Statement to Congress," *New York Times*, February 27, 2019, https://www.nytimes.com/2019/02/27/us/politics/cohen-documents-testimony.html

2   Brian Skellenger, "Trump is getting trolled after declaring his presidency 'The Age of Trump,'" August 29, 2019, https://www.comicsands.com/donald-presidency-age-of-trump-2640104500.html.

3   Richard Wolffe, "Trump's spat with the UK reveals the bottomless depths of his insecurity," *The Guardian*, July 9, 2019, https://www.theguardian.com/commentisfree/2019/jul/09/trump-spat-uk-ambassador-darroch.

4   Jim Acosta, *The Enemy of the People* (New York: Harper-Collins, 2019) 205-206.

5   *Politifact*, June 15, 2019, https://www.politifact.com/personalities/barackobama/statements/byruling/false/.

6   Glenn Kessler, Salvador Rizzo, and Meg Kelly, "President Trump made 16,241 false or misleading claims in his first three years, *Washington Post*, January 20, 2020, https://www.washingtonpost.com/politics/2020/01/20/president-trump-made-16241-false-or-misleading-claims-his-first-three-years/

7   Jane Mayer, "Donald Trump's ghostwriter tells all," *The New Yorker*, July 25, 2016, https://www.newyorker.com/magazine/2016/07/25/donald-trumps-ghostwriter-tells-all.

8   Eric Bradner, "Conway: Trump White House offered 'alternative facts' on crowd size," *CNN News*, January 23, 2017, https://www.cnn.com/2017/01/22/politics/kellyanne-conway-alternative-facts/index.html.

9   Caroline Kenny, "Rudy Giuliani says 'truth isn't truth'," *CNN News*, August 19, 2018, https://www.cnn.com/2018/08/19/politics/rudy-giuliani-truth-isnt-truth/index.html

10   Cristian Farias, "No sane lawyer would let Trump sit for an interview with Mueller," *CNBC*, January 9, 2018, https://www.cnbc.com/2018/01/09/no-sane-lawyer-would-let-trump-sit-for-an-interview-with-mueller.html

11   Philip. A Rucker and Carol Leonning, *A Very Stable Genius* (New York: Penguin Publishing Group, 2020), 191-192.

12   Bob Woodward, *Fear: Trump in the White House* (New York: Simon & Schuster, 2018) 320.

13   Anonymous, *A Warning* (New York: Twelve, 2019) 64.

14   The issue on which President Trump has flip-flopped the most originated in a campaign promise to pull out of overseas military commitments. Trump announced in December 2018 that he was going to bring home all American troops in Syria. Two days later, after being publicly chastened by the theater commander, he said the forces would stay. Then in May 2019 he announced he was sending more troops to the Middle East to protect the troops that were already there. Then in October he ordered fifty US troops to withdraw from their positions in Northern Syria, where they had provided a diplomatic shield for their allies the Kurds, whom Turkey had been threatening to attack for months. Trump promised to ruin Turkey's economy with sanctions if it behaved badly toward the Kurds. Of course, the Turks attacked the Kurds almost immediately, forcing them to ally with the Syrian regime that America opposed, and thus with Russia. Trump tweeted that was all right and withdrew all the remaining American soldiers in Northern Syria. As the Kurds were now fighting for their lives

against invading Turkish forces, some of the ISIS prisoners they were holding escaped during a bombing, and Trump suggested the Kurds had let them go deliberately. He blamed "Europe" for not repatriating its citizens who had left to fight for ISIS. Trump explained again the United States had to stop getting involved in "tribal wars" overseas. But the next day he announced he was sending yet more troops to Saudi Arabia to back his ally in its conflict with Iran. Then, in the face of condemnation at home and various military commanders whose honor as comrades-in-arms he had desecrated, he said he would leave some American soldiers in Iraq—to protect oil fields. He said the United States would keep the oil that came out, even though that is against American and International law and considered a war crime. Then he canceled the few sanctions he had imposed on Turkey. In January 2020 he had Iranian general Qasem Soleimani killed in Baghdad and announced he was sending another 3,000 troops to the region to protect Americans from reprisals. The Iraq parliament demanded American troops leave their country, and although the American government had said many times that its forces were in Iraq at Baghdad's request, it replied, in essence, "Go to hell. We're staying." None of this chaotic policy made any sense. Altogether it was a flip-flop-flip-flop-flip-flop-flip with three twists and three somersaults. Degree of difficulty: 3.6 and done blindfolded into a sea of peril. What has Trump's foreign "policy" accomplished in the Middle East? He has betrayed an ally, handed over territory won from ISIS by America and its allies to the Russian-backed dictator of Syria, Bashar al-Assad and the wannabe dictator of Turkey, Recep Tayyip Erdogan, and possibly to a rejuvenated ISIS. He has shown that our word means every bit as much as Trump's junk bonds. He has made the United States look like a plundering colonial power. He has alienated our ally Iraq, increasing its affiliation with Iran. And he has not, by any stretch of the imagination, withdrawn the American troops from the region. He is after the money, not what's right.

15 Guy Snodgrass, "Inside Trump's first Pentagon meeting," *Politico*, October 21, 2019, https://www.politico.com/magazine/story/2019/10/21/inside-trumps-first-pentagon-briefing-229865?utm_source=pocket-newtab.

16 Rucker and Leonning, Chapter Nine, "Shocking the Conscience."

17 Bob Woodward, 271. For another example of Trump's inability to stay focused, see below the excerpt of his news conference of November 7, 2018 which took listeners on a tortuous ride through his mind on a switchback road that went nowhere: Q. "Mr. President, what about healing the divides in this country — addressing those issues, specifically?" THE PRESIDENT: "Well, we want to see — we want to see it healed. And one of the things I think that can help heal is the success of our country. We are really successful now. We've gone up $11.7 trillion in — in worth. If you know, China has come down tremendously. Tremendously. China would have superseded us in two years as an economic power; now, they're not even close. China got rid of their "China '25" because I found it very insulting. I said that to them. I said, "China '25" is very insulting, because "China '25" means, in 2025, they're going to take over, economically, the world. I said, 'That's not happening.' And we've gone way up. They've gone down. And I don't want them to go down. We'll have a good meeting and we're going to see what we can do. But I have to say this: Billions of dollars will soon be pouring into our Treasury from taxes that China is paying for us. And if you speak to Mr. Pillsbury, who probably is the leading authority on China — he was on the other day saying he has never seen anything like it. And you know who else hasn't? China hasn't." See https://

chicago.suntimes.com/politics/transcript-trump-raucous-press-conference-mid-term-election.

18   Eric Lach, "'I didn't need to do this': Donald Trump declares a national emergency," February 15, 2019, https://www.newyorker.com/news/current/i-didnt-need-to-do-this-donald-trump-declares-a-nationalemergency (See "Differential Effects of Intervention Timing on COVID-19 Spread in the United States," https://www.medrxiv.org/content/10.1101/2020.05.15.20103655v1.full.pdf.)

19   Max Read, "5 Theories About Conspiracy Theories," *New York Magazine*, February 6, 2020, https://nymag.com/intelligencer/2020/02/why-do-people-believe -in-conspiracy-theories.html.

20   Robert Mackey, "How Trump pushed Ukraine's president to probe conspiracy theories about Democrats," *The Intercept*, September 28, 2019, https://theintercept.com/2019/09/26/donald-trump-wantsukraines-president-probe-conspiracy-theories-democrats/.

21   Philip Rucker, Josh Dawsey, and Damian Paletta, "Trump slams Fed chair, questions climate change and threatens to cancel Putin meeting in wide-ranging interview with The Post," *The Washington Post*, November 27, 2018, https://www.washingtonpost.com/politics/trump-slams-fed-chair-questions-climate-change-and-threatens-to-cancel-putin-meeting-in-wide-ranging-interview-with-the-post/2018/11/27/4362fae8-f26c-11e8-aeea-b85fd44449f5_story.html.

22   Bob Woodward, 308.

23   Tina Nguyen, "A Brief History Of Trump's Allies Calling Him An Idiot," *New York Magazine*, February 6, 2018, https://www.vanityfair.com/news/2018/02/trump-staffers-who-call-trump-an-idiot.

24   Jim Acosta, *The Enemy of the People*, 7.

25   Bob Woodward, 56.

26   Aaron Blake, "19 things Donald Trump knows better than anyone else, according to Donald Trump," *Washington Post*, October 4, 2016, https://www.washingtonpost.com/news/the-fix/wp/2016/10/04/17-issues-that-donald-trump-knows-better-than-anyone-else-according-to-donald-trump/.

27   John Haltiwanger, "Trump defends abandoning the Kurds by saying they didn't help the US in WWII," *Business Insider*, October 9, 2019, https://www.businessinsider.com/trump-abandoning-kurds-syriadidnt-help-during-wwii-allies-2019-10.

28   Hitler was smarter than his generals when he occupied the Rhineland in 1936. He was not so smart when his intuition told him that Britain would surrender in 1940, or that "racially inferior" Russian soldiers would prove no match for Germans, or when he declared war on the United States on December 11, 1941 because he believed "hybrid America" would play an insignificant role in the war, or that Germany would win at Stalingrad if he went all in, or that the Allies would invade Europe in 1944 at Pas-de-Calais, not Normandy, or that nuclear weapons would not work. The rubble in 1945 that was once Berlin and the burned bodies outside the Chancellery bunker provided conclusive evidence that intuition cannot possibly match knowledge.

29   Teo Armus, "Social distancing a week earlier could have saved 36,000 American lives, study says," *Washington Post*, May 21, 2020, https://www.washingtonpost.com/nation/2020/05/21/columbia-study-coronavirus-deaths/.

30   David Halberstam, *The Best and the Brightest* (New York: Random House, 1972) Chapter 20.

31   Donald Trump & Bill Zanker, *Think BIG and Kick Ass in Business and Life* (New York: Harper Collins, 2007), 160.

32   On January 2, 2019, Trump called an "emergency" Cabinet meeting and invited the press in. The world saw "Trump-pets" on live television. The emergency meeting, which cause everyone to show, turned out to be an hour and 35 minute "mind dump" of whatever was on the President's mind. He was unfocused, rambling, and frequently inaccurate. There was no emergency. The cabinet discussed nothing and most of them never said a word. They were props on his stage, like the (most white) people at his rallies placed behind him to smile, nod, and applaud. So Trump's less than subtle message was, "See all these important and powerful people? I control every one of them." See https://www.nytimes.com/2019/01/02/us/politics/trump-cabinet-meeting-factcheck.html.

33   Bob Woodward, 317.

34   *CBS News*, "Trump asked James Comey to pledge his loyalty to him," May 11, 2017, https://www.cbsnews.com/news/trump-asked-james-comey-to-pledge-his-loyalty-to-him/.

35   Billy House, Evan Sully, & Saleha Mohsin, "GOP members disrupt impeachment hearing with Trump's blessing," *Bloomberg*, October 23, 2019, https://www.bloomberg.com/news/articles/2019-10-23/gop-protest-disrupts-impeachment-hearing-with-trump-sblessing.

36   Domenico Montanaro, "Poll: Americans don't trust what they're hearing from Trump on coronavirus," *NPR*, March 17, 2020, https://www.npr.org/2020/03/17/816680033/poll-americans-dont-trust-what-they-re-hearing-from-trump-on-coronavirus.

37   Nick Gass, "Trump defends loyalty oaths: 'We're having such a great time,'" *Politico*, March 8, 2016.

38   Michael D. Shear & Julie Herschfield Davis, "Shoot migrants' legs, build alligator moat: Behind Trump's ideas for border," *New York Times*, October 1, 2019, https://www.nytimes.com/2019/10/01/us/politics/trump-borderwars.html.

39   Consider the malignant growth of Trump's Enemies List. Whereas earlier his tweets belittled the other Republicans vying for the party's nomination and then Hillary Clinton, and the media, his hit list since being elected has expanded in all directions: President Obama (endlessly), Democratic leaders in Congress (women in particular), insufficiently submissive members of his own cabinet and other appointees, the directors of the FBI and other security agencies, countless journalists who ask him "nasty" questions at news conferences, the few Republican lawmakers who disagreed with him or did not support him (whom Trump called "human scum"), scientists who presented unwelcome facts, sundry judges, Angela Merkel, conservative pundits, Generals, spokespersons for shooting victims, Puerto Rican officials, The National Review, movie stars, the Mayor of London, numerous pro athletes, rape victims, pollsters and fact-checkers including the Fox News Poll, a long list of minorities, the Wall Street Journal, the Federal Reserve, various biographers, Karl Rove, Arnold Schwarzenegger, Meghan McCain, Planned Parenthood, Omarosa Manigault Newman, Megyn Kelly, Colin Powell, Arianna Huffington, Maxine Waters, "Meet the Press," Oprah Winfrey, Harley-Davidson Company, Stephen Colbert, Katie Couric, Joe Scarborough, Mika Brzezinski, John Kasich, Michael Cohen, military widow Myeshia Johnson, Robert Mueller, the four women of color in the House known as "the Squad," Anthony Scaramucci, Meryl Streep, the City of Baltimore, Jewish Americans who support the Democratic Party, the prime minister of Denmark, John Legend and Chrissy Teigen,

Inspector General for Intelligence Michael Atkinson, Jeff Sessions, Rob Rosenstein, Marie Yovanovitch, Greta Thunberg, Nancy Pelosi, The Center for Disease Control, the World Health Organization, Governors Andrew Cuomo, Gretchen Whitmer, Jay Inslee, and one of your authors. (Our apologies to all those whom we left out. There are just so many. See https://www.nytimes.com/interactive/2016/01/28/upshot/donald-trump-twitter-in sults.html for another 500.)

40   Jim Acosta, 235.

41   John Wagner, "Trump lashes out again at whistleblower, questions whether Schiff should be arrested for treason," *Washington Post*, September 30, 2019, https://www.washingtonpost.com/politics/trump-lashes-out-again-atwhistle   blower-questions-whether-schiff-should-be-arrested-for-treason/2019/09/30/932840ba-e370-11e9-a6e88759c5c7f608_story.)

42   The next day Trump attacked Pelosi on Twitter, showing a photo of her standing in the Cabinet Room pointing her finger at him. His caption read, "Nervous Nancy's unhinged meltdown." He had himself been described as "unhinged" and having had a meltdown, and so he probably thought he was turning the tables on Pelosi and his critics. But it fits right in with a Roy Cohn counterattack tactic he used often: "So are you! Only worse!" —a totally unimaginative schoolground retort when you can't think of anything else. Pelosi quickly used the photo as her twitter cover and it went viral. Paul LeBlanc, "Trump tweets a photo attacking Nancy Pelosi. She made it her Twitter cover photo," *CNN*, October 17, 2019, https://www.cnn.com/2019/10/16/politics/nancy-pelosi-trump-twitter-cover-photo/index.html.)

43   Jeremy Stahl, "Trump Just Said His Friends in the Military, Police, and a Biker Group Might Get 'Tough' on Democrats," *Slate*, March 14, 2019, https://slate.com/news-and-politics/2019/03/trump-toughpeople-military-police-bikers.html.

44   See e.g. https://www.telegraph.co.uk/news/2020/05/14/obamagate-donald-trump-calls-barack-obama-testify-officials/.

45   John Wagner, "Trump Says He Has 'Absolute Right' to Pardon Himself of Federal Crimes But Denies Any Wrongdoing," *Washington Post*, June 4, 2018, https://www.washingtonpost.com/politics/trump-says-he-has-absolute-right-to-pardon-himself-of-federal-crimes-but-denies-any-wrongdoing/2018/06/04/3d78348c-67dd-11e8-bea7-c8eb28bc52b1_story.html.

46   Chris Strohm and Shannon Pettypiece, "Trump Says He Can Pardon Himself. Nixon Was Told He Couldn't," *Bloomberg*, June 4, 2018, https://www.bloomberg.com/news/articles/2018-06-04/trump-says-he-can-pardon-himself-nixon-was-told-he-couldn-t.

47   Bobby Allyn, "Trump Still Faces 3 Lawsuits Over His Business Empire," *NPR*, December 12, 2019, https://www.npr.org/2019/12/12/787167408/trump-still-faces-3-lawsuits-over-his-business-empire. (As of this date there were three lawsuits making their way through the federal courts.)

48   Julie Hirschfield Davis, "President Wants to Use Executive Order to End Birthright Citizenship," *New York Times*, October 30, 2018, https://www.nytimes.com/2018/10/30/us/politics/trump-birthrightcitizenship.html.

CHAPTER FIVE

1   Libby Nelson, "Read the full transcript of Obama's fiery anti-Trump speech, 'This is not normal,'" *Vox*, September 7, 2018, https://www.vox.com/policy -and-politics/2018/9/7/17832024/obama-speech-trump-illinois-transcript.

2   Kim Lacapria, "Donald Trump 'Fifth Avenue' comment," *Snopes*, January 24, 2016, https://www.snopes.com/fact-check/donald-trump-fifth-avenue-comment/.

3   Bob Altemeyer, "Donald Trump and Authoritarian Followers," 2016, www.the authoritarians.org.

4   Ibid.

5   Bob Altemeyer, "The Other 'Authoritarian Personality.'" In Mark Zanna, ed., *Advances in Experimental Social Psychology*, Vol. 30 (New York: Academic Press, 1998).

6   Nate Silver, "President Trump's approval rating has been steady. Richard Nixon's once was too," *FiveThirtyEight*, May 8, 2018, https://fivethirtyeight.com/features/president-trumps-approvalrating-has-been-steady-richard-nixons-once-was-too/. On February 4, 2020, the Gallup Poll announced that Trump had hit a 49 percent approval rating in its survey, the highest mark in his presidency. But that was one poll at one time. Others have, on one occasion or another, shown Trump scoring over 50 percent. But over the impeachment period, from December 2019 to February 2020, the highest average approval rating among registered voters across all polls reached 44.9 percent on January 27, as you can see by examining the website above.

7   Official 2016 Presidential General Election Results. General Election Date: 11/08/2016 at https://transition.fec.gov/pubrec/fe2016/2016presgeresults.pdf. White House Press Secretary Sarah Sanders, while chastising reporters on October 29, 2018 for their unfavorable coverage of the president, said Trump "won by an overwhelming majority of 63 million." (https://thehill.com/homenews/administration/413692sanders-says-trump-won-by-overwhelming-majority-of-63-million.) The belief apparently persists among some Administration officials that Trump won the popular vote—which he did not, did not, did not. Clinton got 48.2 percent of the vote, and Trump received 46.1 percent. The fact that Sanders told reporters, of all people, this falsehood while she was bemoaning how dishonest they were appearing to indicate that she thinks it is true. Which makes you wonder just how many people in the White House are living in the "alternate reality."

8   Many states do not collect party preference data when voters register, but for those that do, we can tell that Clinton lost primarily because more Democrats stayed home than Republicans, and independents decided to vote for Trump. The key state of Pennsylvania illustrates this. 49 percent of the registered voters were Democrats, but only 42 percent of the voters were. The Republicans voted in accordance with their numbers: 38 percent of registered, 39 percent of voters. The Democrats—low turnout and all—still might have won, with their 42 percent versus 39 percent of the voters. But Pennsylvania independents turned up big time, being only 13 percent of registered voters, but 20 percent of actual voters, and they broke 48-41 percent for Trump, giving him his narrow triumph. In both Michigan and Wisconsin, other key states that gave Trump his victory in the Electoral College (but which do not identify registered voters by party preference), Independents voted for Trump by sizeable margins (52-36 percent in MI, 50-40 percent in WI) and provided him with his small margins of victory as they did in PA. Most of these margins, we shall see, probably came from independents

who did not think either candidate was qualified to be president but voted Trump. See David Heath & Jennifer Agiesta, "How voters who found both candidates unfit broke," *CNN*, November 11, 2016, https://www.cnn.com/2016/11/11/politics/hillary-clinton-donald-trump-voters-dislike/index.html.] These independents obviously will not all follow Trump to the gates of Hell. Some of them stopped supporting him almost immediately after he took office and sent his approval rating south.

9   John McCain's daughter Meghan told Trump, "No one will ever love you like they loved my father." But you can bet Trump will be revered by multitudes of his supporters for the rest of their lives. As Hitler, Stalin, Chairman Mao, Saddam Hussain, and others were by those who strongly identified with these men's policies. Nothing will ever convince most of Trump's True Believers that he was not as wonderful as he said he was. (And even he did not believe it.)

10   Besides these, a substantial number of people (over 75,000 in Michigan alone) went to the polls but did not cast a vote for president. Trump won Michigan by about 10,000 votes.

11   Other guesstimates can be made. Charles E. Cook (*The Cook Report*, December 14, 2018) prefers just those who tell pollsters they strongly approve of Trump. That amounts to a much smaller base than our figuring because we also include those who say they approve (or somewhat approve but not strongly) of what the president has been doing. If those folks can be shaken loose from their preference by further disturbing acts or revelations, Cook is right, and they are not part of Trump's firm base. We believe however that if these voters still support Trump after the past three years—and they have hardly wavered at all—it is going to take something monumentally disturbing to make them change by November 3, 2020. Not all the 40-45 percent of the registered/likely voters who tell pollsters they approve of Trump will vote. If they all did (and that will be the supreme goal of the Trump campaign), that would amount to 60 to 62 million ballots if the 2020 turnout matches that of 2016. It seems likely however that the turnout will be significantly higher this time.

12   We do not mean that social dominators (and authoritarian followers) are a type of person. They are instead people who score relatively highly in that trait. Typologies usually classify people as one thing OR another, such as introverts or extroverts. That inevitably leaves out lots of people who are neither fish nor fowl. Putting several dichotomies together, the way the Myers-Briggs test does, adds some complexity to the venture, but all of the components suffer from the same "You're either this or that" oversimplification. It is much better to analyze traits on a continuous scale, the way we measure height. "Six foot-ten" tells you a lot more than "tall." When we talk about "high social dominators" and "low authoritarian followers" in this book we are referring to people who score noticeably higher/lower than most in some analysis. But we do not mean to imply there are only a few kinds of people. Approximately 7.7 billion different kinds of people trod the earth right now.

13   F. Pratto, J. Sidanius, L.M. Stallworth, & B.F. Malle, "Social Dominance Orientation: A personality variable predicting social and political attitudes," *Journal of Personality and Social Psychology*, 67 (1994), 741-763.

14   See Chapter 5 of Altemeyer, *The Authoritarians* available at www.theauthoritarians.org.

15   Author Dean reported in *Conservatives Without Conscience* (2006) that authoritarians had grown in the ranks of the Republican conservative movement.

16   Matthew Yglesias, "What really happened in 2016, in 7 charts," *Vox*, September 18,

2017,   https://www.vox.com/policy-and-politics/2017/9/18/16305486/what-real-
ly-happened-in-2016. Mitt Romney also received 62% of the white male vote four
years earlier. You could say from this that Trump did not get a heightened social dominance boost. But Romney was running against a black American. Trump attacked
other minorities as well and was running against a woman which would have helped
him maintain the white male vote at Romney's level.

17   Daniel Cox, Rachel Lienesch, & Robert P. Jones, "Beyond economics: Fears of cultural displacement pushed the white working class to Trump," *PRRI/The Atlantic Report*,
May 9, 2017, https://www.prri.org/research/white-working-class-attitudes-econo-
my-trade-immigration-election-donaldtrump/; and Diana C. Mutz, "Status threat,
not economic hardship, explains the 2016 presidential vote," *Proceedings of the National Academy of Sciences of the United States*, May 8, 2018, https://www.pnas.org/con-
tent/115/19/E4330.

18   Ibid.

19   See,e.g,https://en.wikipedia.org/wiki/Donald_Trump_2000_presidential_campaign.

20   Donald J. Trump, "What I Saw at the Revolution," *New York Times*, February 19,
2000, https://www.nytimes.com/2000/02/19/opinion/what-i-saw-at-the-revolution.
html. (Trump observed of his withdrawal: "I also thought that Americans might be
ready for straight talk and that they would find an unscripted candidate appealing.")

21   "Presidential Campaign Announcement by Donald Trump, *C-SPAN*, June 16, 2015,
https://www.c-span.org/video/?326473-1/donald-trump-presidential-campaign-an-
nouncement&start=657.

22   Interview with Jim Gilmore, *PBS Frontline*, December 20, 2016, https://www.pbs.
org/wgbh/pages/frontline/interactive/trumps-road-whitehouse-frontlineinterviews/
transcript/corey-lewandowski.html.

23   Ibid.

24   Megan Specia, "Donald Trump campaign offered actors $50 to cheer for him," *Hol-
lywood   Reporter*,   https://www.hollywoodreporter.com/news/donald-trump-cam-
paign-offered-actors-803161.

25   "Donald Trump's polling lead means little at this stage, past data shows," *The Guardian*,
December 9, 2015, https://www.theguardian.com/us-news/datablog/2015/dec/09/
donald-trump-polls-pastelections-republican-nomination

26   Jim Acosta, *The Enemy of the People* (New York: Harper Collins, 2019) 264-265.

27   "Donald Trump on protestor: I'd like to punch him in the face,'" *Washington Post*, February 23, 2016, https://www.chicagotribune.com/politics/ct-donald-trump-protester-
punch-face-20160223story.html.

28   Ibid.

29   Melissa Chan, "Trump may pay legal fees of man who sucker-punched protester,"
Time, March 13, 2016, http://time.com/4256809/donald-trump-l/.

30   Julia Manchester & Tatianna Amatruda, "Man reconciles with Trump supporter who
punched him at rally," *CNN*, December 16, 2016, https://www.cnn.com/2016/12/14/
politics/donald-trump-protestersupporter-reconcile/index.html. Even when you have
a signed contract with Donald Trump, it is no guarantee he will feel obliged to honor
his end. Michael Cohen testified to the House Oversight Committee on February 27,
2019 that he often told small business owners that Trump had decided to pay them
only a part, or even none, of what he owed them for work they had done. Their only
recourse was to sue, which many could not afford to do. This "Trump Cheat" goes back

at least to the 1990s, we saw in Chapter Three.

31   Tessa Berenson, "Donald Trump defends torture at Republican debate," *CNN*, March 4, 2016, https://time.com/4247397/donald-trump-waterboarding-torture/.

32   Jim Acosta, 260. The scary thing is that, while we are sure it was not, this could have been sent by aka "John Baron."

CHAPTER SIX

1   Note from Dean: My collaborator developed and refined the RWA Scale, which has long been the gold standard employed by social science in determining authoritarian followers. His modesty precludes me from fully explaining the importance of this scale to this body of science. A full description of the terms in this definition is given in Bob Altemeyer, *Right-Wing Authoritarianism* (Winnipeg: University of Manitoba Press, 1981), 148–155.

2   People who characteristically show lots of rebellion against the established authorities in their lives, "contrarians" sort of like perpetual teenagers only they can be any age, could be considered "left-wing authoritarians" if they were slavishly following some rebel leader. Again, this has nothing to do with any economic or political creed, but whether one is fiercely rebelling against the established authorities. In the 1970s small groups of Maoists appeared on some North American university campuses carrying their little red books of Chairman Mao's sayings. They wanted to overthrow the free-enterprise system and democratic rule. They would be, by the definition above, left-wing authoritarians. The intensely committed followers of Chairman Mao in China would be right-wing authoritarians according to the conceptualization being offered here. Are Antifas left-wing authoritarians by this conceptualization? No, for they do not have an authority (person or ideology) that they submit to. Nor do they insist everyone behave according to conventions endorsed by an authority. They are instead autonomous groups of anarchists and various political left-wingers whose common bond is a militant resistance to white supremacists. Angry and aggressive to be sure. Authoritarian? Not really.

3   Zeesham Aleem, "A new poll shows a startling partisan divide on the dangers of the coronavirus," *Vox*, March 15, 2020, https://www.vox.com/2020/3/ 15/21180506/coronavirus-poll-democrats-republicanstrump.

4   "Trump Drug Hydroxychloroquine Raises Death Risk in Covid Patients, Study Says," *BBC News*, May 22, 2020, https://www.bbc.com/news/world-52779309.

5   If you are interested in how people become low and high RWAs, see chapter 2 of Altemeyer's free online book, *The Authoritarians* at www.theauthoritarians.org. To answer a few FAQs: What is the most powerful factor? Whether a person has had certain experiences in life. Does education affect RWA? Yes, higher education lowers it some. Does your level of RWA change much over adulthood? It can. Becoming a parent seems to make people more authoritarian, for example. Does the level of RWA in a country change over time? Yes, for sure. It was pretty low in the 1970s, then went up noticeably in the 1980s, then slid about halfway back down in the 1990s and 2000s. By the time people enter university, they are "carriers" of their times.

6   See Bob Altemeyer and Bruce E. Hunsberger, *Amazing Apostates: Why Some Turn to Faith, and Others Abandon Religion* (Amherst, NY: Prometheus Press, 1997), 17–20.

You will not be surprised to learn that the religiosity of university students generally reflects how much their parents emphasized the family faith to them as they were growing up. Socialization works. But how does one explain the rare, fascinating cases when students from weak religious backgrounds become very religious, and students from very religious homes become nonbelievers? Research has found that the "Amazing Believers" usually turned to religion because they were facing some crisis in their life, such as overwhelming loneliness, an addiction, or the death of a loved one—and found help in a church group. The "Amazing Apostates," on the other hand, usually gave up their strongly held religion because they could not make themselves continue believing what it taught. It did not make sense given its own contradictions, what they learned from science, their own experiences, and so on. In a way, this resulted ironically from their strong religious socialization. Their families had emphasized that their faith was the true religion, and that nurtured in them a strong valuing for the truth. When their religion then failed the test it had emphasized, they felt they had no choice but to give it up. Usually most reluctantly because it often cost them dearly.

7   Dartunorro Clark, "Report: Trump Told Acting DHS Head He'd Pardon Him If He Were Sent to Jail for Closing the Border, *NBC*, April 12, 2019, https://www.nbcnews.com/politics/white-house/trump-toldacting-dhs-head-he-d-pardon-him-if-n994061.

8   Veronica Stracqualursi, "Trump Told Officials He Would Pardon Them If They Break the Law Building Border Wall," *Washington Post*, August 28, 2019, https://www.cnn.com/2019/08/28/politics/trump-border-wall-election-day/index.html.

9   We do not mean that Trump's approval rating did not change even a scintilla. Even in aggregates, such as Nate Silver's compilation, superficial random fluctuations change the scores a little from day to day. But none of the Trump actions under discussion was followed by a drop of even a minor drop of say 2 percent (e.g., from 43.4 percent approval to 41.4 percent approval), even over two to five days. That just did not happen. In short, his support did not budge.

10 Oliver B. Waxman, "The Poem on the Statue of Liberty Was 'Added Later' but There's More to That Story," *Time*, August 7, 2017, http://time.com/4884799/statue-of-liberty-emma-lazaruspoem/. Stephen Miller reputedly is responsible for Trump's policies on immigration and is known to stiffen the president's resolve when others push back. He may become Trump's go-to guy if Trump decides to dramatically usurp powers not granted the president in the Constitution or American history. As Jim Acosta relates, when Miller appeared on Face the Nation after Trump imposed a travel ban against seven predominantly Muslim countries, he said, ". . . the powers of the president to protect our country are very substantial and will not be questioned." Jim Acosta, *The Enemy of the People* (New York: Harper Collins, 2019), 61.

11 "Scam Exposed: Donations to Clinton Foundation Plummeted after Clinton Lost the Election," *Investor's Business Daily*, November 23, 2018, https://www.investors.com/politics/editorials/clinton-foundation-donations.

12 "Clinton Foundation," Wikipedia, June 15, 2019, https://en.wikipedia.org/wiki/Clinton_Foundation.

13 For example, one of his golf courses has on display an expensive portrait of DJT. Someone paid $60,000 for it at an auction of celebrity portraits. Michael Cohen told the House Oversight Committee that this person had been instructed to bid whatever it cost to make sure Trump's portrait commanded more money than any other. The fake bidder was reimbursed, but not with Donald Trump's money. The $60,000 came

from the Trump Foundation. So Donald got his portrait back and used $60,000 from a "charity" to garner some head-swelling MVP ("Most Valuable Portrait") publicity. Once again, he had "fixed" the system so that he looked far grander than he was—both standard operating procedure for him and a desperate need. (Just to make sure people found out about the MVP, Trump posted a "Gee, guys, guess what just happened!" announcement of his portrait being worth more than anybody else's.) Jack Holmes, "Michael Cohen's Testimony Again Illustrates How Insanely Trump's Charity Operated," *Esquire*, February 27, 2019, https://www.esquire.com/news-politics/a26550118/michaelcohen-testimony-trump-foundation-portrait-60000/.

14 Alan Feuer, "Trump Ordered to Pay $2 Million to Charities for Misuse of Foundation: The President Admitted He Had Used Funds Raised by the Donald J. Trump Foundation to Promote His Campaign and Pay Business Debts," *New York Times*, November 7 and 22, 2019, https://www.nytimes.com/2019/11/07/nyregion/trump-charities-newyork.html.

15 Anthony Zurcher, "Can Hillary Clinton Give a Straight Answer on Emails?," BBC, August 3, 2018, https://www.bbc.com/news/election-us-2016-36960223.

16 Pamela Brown and Kaitlan Collins, "President Pressured Staff to Grant Security Clearance to Ivanka Trump, CNN, April 1, 2019, https://www.cnn.com/2019/03/05/politics/ivanka-trump-securityclearance-pressure/index.html.

17 Trump, of course, loves bombast, and regularly blows things way, way out of proportion. It seems that for him a properly formed sentence must have a subject, a predicate, and an extreme exaggeration. Many people quickly notice this and learn to discount everything he says by something like ten cents to the dollar, a bankruptcy expression with which Trump is very familiar. But his base cheers wildly when his statements misrepresent wildly.

18 Jane C. Timm, "Tracking President Trump's Flip-Flops," *NBC News*, May 12, 2018, https://www.nbcnews.com/storyline/president-trumps-first-100-days/here-are-new-policy-stances-donaldtrump-has-taken-election-n684946.

19 John T. Bennett, "Mueller Report Has Gone from 'Witch Hunt' to 'Gold Standard' at White House," *Roll Call*, March 26, 2019, https://www.rollcall.com/news/at-white-house-mueller-probe-has-gone-fromwitch-hunt-to-gold-standard.

20 John T. Bennett, "Trump Has Been All over the Place on 'Crazy' Mueller Report," *Roll Call*, April 29, 2019, https://www.rollcall.com/news/whitehouse/trump-has-been-all-over-the-place-on-crazy-muellerreport.

21 Philip Bump, "Most Republicans Don't Accept a Basic Mueller Finding: That Russia Tried to Interfere in the 2016 Campaign," *Washington Post*, April 1, 2019, https://www.washingtonpost.com/politics/2019/04/01/most-republicans-dont-accept-basic-mueller-findingthat-russia-tried-interfere-election/?utm_term=.1d59ecc159de. A Monmouth Poll seven weeks later on May 22 found that 56 percent of Republicans by then thought the Russians had tried, but it had almost no effect. https://www.monmouth.edu/pollinginstitute/documents/monmouthpoll_us_052219.pdf/.

22 Stuart Anderson, "Where the Idea for Donald Trump's Wall Came From," *Forbes*, January 4, 2019, https://www.forbes.com/sites/stuartanderson/2019/01/04/where-the-idea-for-donald-trumpswall-came-from /#77923c9c4415. Trump promised to build the wall at the end of his June 16, 2015, candidacy speech: "I will build a great, great wall on our southern border. And I will have Mexico pay for that wall. Mark my

words." On August 31, 2016, in Phoenix he promised that he would begin building the wall "on Day One" of his administration, and again Mexico would pay for 100 percent of it. The promises drew tremendous applause.

23 Bob Altemeyer, "The Other 'Authoritarian Personality,'" in Mark Zanna, ed., *Advances in Experimental Social Psychology 30* (New York: Academic Press, 1998).

24 See, e.g., Rich Barlow, "Racist Americans, Not Trump, Are The Problem. There Might Be A Cure," *Cognoscenti*, November 30, 2018, https://www.wbur.org/cognoscenti/2018/11/30/donaldtrump-racism-supporters-rich-barlow; German Lopez, "The Past Year of Research Has Made It Very Clear: Trump Won because of Racial Resentment," *Vox*, December 15, 2017, https://www.vox.com/identities/2017/12/15/16781222/trump-racism-economic-anxiety-study; and Morgan Gstalter, "Study: Trump Supporters on College Campuses More Likely to Show Prejudice toward International Students," *The Hill*, August 30, 2018, https://thehill.com/blogs/blog-briefingroom/news/404363-study-trump-supporters-on-college-campuses-more-likely-to-show.

25 "First They Came . . ." Wikipedia, https://en.wikipedia.org/wiki/First_they_came_.

26 Bob Altemeyer, "Dogmatic Behavior among Students: Testing a New Measure of Dogmatism," *Journal of Social Psychology*, 142 (2002), 713–721.

27 Karlyn Bowman, "Democrats and Republicans Divide on Climate Change," *Forbes*, April 19, 2019, https://www.forbes.com/sites/bowmanmarsico/2019/04/19/democrats-and-republicans-dividedon-climate-change/#453d42c23198.

28 Dartunorro Clark, "Trump on Measles Vaccination: 'They Have to Get the Shot,'" *NBC News*, April 26, 2019, https://www.nbcnews.com/politics/white-house/trump-measles-vaccination-theyhave-get-shot-n998881.

CHAPTER SEVEN

1 Bob Altemeyer, *Right-Wing Authoritarianism* (Winnipeg, Canada: University of Manitoba Press, 1981), 216, 227–232.

2 Altemeyer, *Right-Wing Authoritarianism*, 224-227.

3 The Leadership Conference on Civil and Human Rights, https://civilrights.org/trump-rollbacks/.

4 This was not an entirely theoretical proposal. There is a bona fide, if extremely small, Communist Party in Canada and a Communist, Joseph Zuken, was elected to public office in Winnipeg (where most of the students lived) from 1941 to 1983. (See https://en.wikipedia.org/wiki/Joseph_Zuken.) To Altemeyer, who arrived in Winnipeg from Nebraska in 1968 and saw an openly socialist party win the provincial election in 1969, it was quite amazing.

5 For example, RWA scale scores of San Francisco State University students correlated highly with support for Posse Homosexuals. A posse after "radicals" similarly captured sizable RWA connections at the Universities of Pittsburgh and Houston. In Omaha, high RWA Creighton University students were significantly less bothered than most by the idea of government persecution of homosexual people, religious cults, and abortionists. These findings led to a series of experiments in Canada to find groups that *low* RWAs would support attacking. Students were first asked about the Ku Klux Klan (which has a toehold in Canada). High RWAs expressed less support

for persecuting the Klan than they did for attacking Communists, homosexuals, cults, and abortionists, but they still proved more willing to do so than lows were. The relationship was weaker—less than half that found in the previous cases—but reliably there. (Note: That is to say, the finding was statistically significant. You may have seen this expression before. It refers to how confident one can be that if the same study was repeated with a different sample drawn from the same population, one would get the same basic result. That does not mean the result is important. When research begins on a topic, you are glad just to find something reliable. But over time the quest should shift to finding the reliable things that are most important, that explain behavior the best. But we seem to get stuck at Phase One. Many statistically significant findings amount to very little. In practical terms they are insignificant, and do not deserve the space on the internet that they get.) Other students were then asked about persecuting various conservative political parties, including the Conservative Party itself, which high RWAs usually support. No matter the victim, authoritarian followers did what you would expect authoritarian followers to do, although again the relationship was muted. Low RWAs' answers in all these studies again were usually −4.

6   Natalie Gallon and Chandler Thornton, "Bodies of Father and Daughter Who Drowned in the Rio Grande Head Home to El Salvador," *CNN*, June 27, 2019, https://www.cnn.com/2019/06/27/americas/drowned-father-daughter-rio -grande-migrants-elsalvador/index.html.

7   John Sides, "The Extraordinary Unpopularity of Trump's Family Separation Policy (in One Graph)," *Washington Post*, June 18, 2018, https://www.washingtonpost.com/news/monkeycage/wp/2018/06/19/the-extraordinary-unpopularity-of-trumps-family-separa-tion-policy-in-onegraph/?utm_term=.dabb0b40e7c9.

8   Dylan Matthews, "Polls: Trump's Family Separation Policy Is Very Unpopular—Except Among Republicans," *Vox*, June 18, 2018, https://www.vox.com/policy-andpol-itics/2018/6/18/17475740/family-separation-poll-polling-border-trump-children-im-migrant-familiesparents.

9   Stanley Milgram, "Behavioral Study of Obedience," *Journal of Abnormal and Social Psychology* (October 1963).

10 Bob Altemeyer, *Right-Wing Authoritarianism*, Winnipeg, University of Manitoba Press, 1981, 233-4.

11 Albert Bandura, *Social Learning Theory* (Englewood Cliffs, NJ: Prentice-Hall, 1977).

12 M. Brewster Smith, "Review of the Authoritarian Personality," *Journal of Abnormal and Social Psychology* (1950): 775–779.

13 If you directly ask high RWAs how moral they think they are compared with other people, most of them will say they are average. But they have been taught a truly righteous person does not vainly declare his righteousness (Luke 18:10-14). If instead you ask them to evaluate someone who happens to have the same beliefs and attitudes as they do, they think that person is wonderful compared to someone who has very different beliefs from their own. Low RWAs make no distinction. See Bob Altemeyer, *Enemies of Freedom* (San Francisco: Jossey-Bass, 1988), 157–161.

14 Theodore M. Newcomb, *The Acquaintance Process* (New York: Holt, Rinehart & Winston, 1961).

15 John Roy, "The Fox News Bubble," *Data for Progress*, March 29, 2019, https://www.dataforprogress.org/blog/2019/3/23/the-fox-news-bubble.

16   Shawn Langolis, "Fans of Rush Limbaugh Top This List of the Most Biased News Consumers," *Marketwatch*, September 27, 2018, https://www.marketwatch.com/story/fans-of-rush-limbaugh-topthis-list-of-the-most-biased-news-consumers-2018-09-27.

17   The results imply that high RWAs might be quite vulnerable to manipulative communicators who tell them what they want to hear, which may trigger a memory because you read it in chapter 3 as an item from the Conman Scale. This result was confirmed in another experiment in which someone running for mayor gave a tough "law and order" speech after learning that 90 percent of the voters favored this approach. High RWAs trusted him, despite the obvious chance he was just saying that to get votes. On the other hand, low RWAs positively distrusted a candidate who gave a "community improvement" speech after learning 90 percent of the voters favored this approach. They would not touch a politician with a ten-foot pole who came out in favor of something everybody was in favor of, even if they agreed with the pitch. Low RWAs are a hard sell. In another experiment subjects were told a traveling evangelist conducted a survey in a city on his route to see what kind of program would get him the most money when he passed the hat. He then put on that kind of show. High RWAs believed the preacher was highly trustworthy. Lows did not, by a long shot.

18   See John W. Dean, *Conservatives Without Conscience* (New York: Viking, 2005).

19   Editor, "Bush Mocks Bush," *BBC News*, March 25, 2001, http://news.bbc.co.uk/2/hi/americas/1241240.stm.

20   Stephen E. Ambrose, *Nixon: Ruin and Recovery 1973–1990* (New York: Simon & Schuster, A Touchstone Book, 1991): 129–130.

21   Bob Altemeyer, *The Authoritarians* (online book available at www.theauthoritarians.org), 100–101.

22   Ian Schwartz, "Trump MAGA Rally Crowd Chants 'Send her back' to Rep. Ilhan Omar," *RealClearPolitics*, July 17, 2019, https://www.realclearpolitics.com/video/2019/07/17/trump_maga_rally_crowd_chants_send_her_back_to_rep_ilhan_omar.html.

23   Bob Altemeyer, "To Thine Own Self Be Untrue: Self-Awareness in Authoritarians," *North American Journal of Psychology* (1999): 157–164.

CHAPTER EIGHT

1   The term *evangelical* is often used differently, so we should explain how we use the term. The original concept obviously involved evangelizing, preaching the Gospels. However, some sources (Wikipedia, for example, on June 15, 2019) say the core of evangelism today is accepting Jesus through grace as your savior who brought you salvation through his death. People who do this are said to be "born again." But not everyone who calls themselves evangelical Christians say they have been born again, and vice versa. So polls, including the exit polls in elections, usually ask voters who say they are Christians, "Are you born again or evangelical?" These are the people whose overwhelming support for Donald Trump we are trying to understand, so when we say "evangelicals," in general, we mean people who would answer the pollster's either/or question with an evangelical answer.

Researchers have tried to pin down evangelicals theologically. The most determined attempt has been made by a hard-working religious pollster named George

Barna. He has developed a nine-item questionnaire, which, if you answer every question affirmatively, makes you an evangelical. For example, "Have you made a personal commitment to Jesus Christ that is still important in your life today?" If you hesitate on one of the items or answer no, you are excused. Barna reports that 8 to 10 percent of his extensive nationwide polls of adult Americans qualify as evangelicals. That is far below the 17–23 percent of evangelicals that other pollsters and demographers estimate live in the United States. So, while Barna's measure gives one an opportunity to study highly evangelical persons, we might miss most of the "religious" Trump supporters we are trying to understand if we used his criterion. We favor the self-report criterion used in most polls. These will be buttressed by scores on the Religious Fundamentalism Scale, which captures fundamentalist beliefs in Christianity and Judaism, Hinduism, and Islam as well. A solid majority of Christian fundamentalists say they are evangelicals or born again. "Survey Explores Who Qualifies as an Evangelical," The Barna Group, January 18, 2007, https://www.barna.com/research/survey-explores-who-qualifies-as-an-evangelical/.

2   Kenneth Phillips, *American Theocracy* (New York: Viking, 2006), xiii, 188.

3   John W. Dean, *Conservatives Without Conscience* (New York: Viking, 2006), xxxiv.

4   Jimmy Carter, *Our Endangered Values: America's Moral Crisis* (New York: Simon and Schuster, 2005), 34.

5   Mark Tran, "Book Reveals White House Contempt for Religious Right," *The Guardian*, October 13, 2006, https://www.theguardian.com/news/blog/2006/oct/13/theartofbein.

6   John W. Dean, *Conservatives Without Conscience*, xxxv.

7   Meredith McGraw, "Inside Donald Trump's Relationship with Rev. Billy Graham: Graham and His Family Have Been Evangelical Defenders of President Trump," *ABC News*, March 2, 2018, https://abcnews.go.com/Politics/inside-donald-trumps-relationship-rev-billy-graham/story?id=53448191.

8   Gideon Resnick, "Donald Trump in 1990: Adultery Is Not a Sin," *Daily Beast*, October 30, 2016, https://www.thedailybeast.com/donald-trump-in-1990-adultery-is-not-a-sin.

9   Philip Bump, "How Fox News Fans Keep Donald Trump Afloat," *Washington Post*, July 12, 2016, https://www.washingtonpost.com/news/the-fix/wp/2016/07/12/how-fox-news-fans-keepdonald-trump-float/?utm_term=.abc8e7961507.

10   Stoyan Zaimov, "Donald Trump: 'Nobody Reads the Bible More than Me. John Kerry Hasn't Read the Bible,'" *The Christian Post*, February 25, 2016, https://www.christianpost.com/news/donald-trump-nobody-reads-bible-more-than-me-john-kerry.html.

11   Tina Nguyen, "Trump Backtracks on Whether He Asks God for Forgiveness," *Vanity Fair*, September 22, 2015, https://www.vanityfair.com/news/2015/09/donald-trump-god-forgiveness.

12   Wikipedia, June 1, 2019, https://en.wikipedia.org/wiki/Nationwide_opinion_polling_for_the_2016_Republican_Party_presidential_p rimaries#Polls_conducted_in_2015.

13   Trump's relationship with Jerry Falwell Jr. had been growing steadily. Falwell invited him to speak at Liberty University, and in his introduction said (honestly, we are not making this up): "Donald Trump lives a life of loving and helping others as Jesus taught in the great commandment." On January 26, 2016, Falwell formally endorsed Trump for president, saying Trump greatly reminded him of his father. This helped Trump garner 21 percent of the evangelical vote in Iowa, while Cruz pulled in 34

percent. If you have read this book this far your Spidey Sense may be tingling now because something else was likely going on behind the scenes here. On May 7, 2019, a story appeared in major news outlets that in 2015 Jerry Falwell Jr. asked Michael Cohen, Trump's "fixer," for help with a personal problem. It seems Falwell and his wife had taken "racy" pictures of themselves, and an extortioner had gotten hold of them. Could Cohen get the photos back? Cohen said he convinced the extortioner to destroy the photos, although he (Cohen) had one on his phone. Later Falwell aides revealed Liberty University had made improper loans to friends of Falwell and although a "nonprofit" the school was actively involved in real estate transactions. "We're not a school, we're a real estate hedge fund," said a senior official at the largest Christian university in the world. Brandon Ambrosino, "'Someone's Gotta Tell the Freaking Truth:' Jerry Falwell's Aides Break Their Silence," *Politico*, September 9, 2019, https://www.politico.com/magazine/story/2019/09/09/jerry-falwell-liberty-university-loans-227914. In short, we do not know the full story of the Falwell Jr. endorsement.

14   Romney speech denouncing Trump, https://en.wikipedia.org/wiki/Mitt_Romney percent27s_2016_anti-trump_speech.

15   Trump has his evangelical leaders in for a meal now and then, where you can be sure they get their picture taken with him. But none of them has any known influence in his government. Everyone in the room knows that they need the president a lot, lot more than he needs them. He's the Pied Piper, and they are the good burghers of Hamelin.

16   "Exit Polls," *CNN*, June 15, 2018, https://www.cnn.com/election/2016/results/exit-polls.

17   Bob Woodward, *Fear: Trump in the White House* (New York, Simon & Schuster, 2018), 33.

18   Steve Mitchell, "Why Evangelicals Support Trump," *Real Clear Politics*, March 6, 2016, https://www.realclearpolitics.com/articles/2016/03/06/why_evangelicals_support_trump_129864.html.

19   As Princeton historian Julian Zelizer has pointed out, Lyndon Johnson foresaw the danger that someone who harnessed white backlash could present to the United States: "I can think of nothing more dangerous, more divisive, or more self-destructive than the effort to prey on what is called 'white backlash . . .'" Johnson prophetically said in 1966. "I think it is dangerous because it threatens to vest power in the hands of second-rate men whose only qualification is their ability to pander to other men's fears. I think it divides this nation at a very critical time—and therefore it weakens us as a united country," *CNN*, June 15, 2019, https://www.cnn.com/2018/11/05/opinions/lyndon-b-johnson-warned-us-about-this-backlash-opinionzelizer/index.html.

20   Tara Isabella Burton, "The Biblical Story the Christian Right Uses to Defend Trump," *Vox*, March 5, 2018, https://www.vox.com/identities/2018/3/5/16796892/trump-cyrus-christian-right-bible-cbnevangelical-propaganda.

21   Tara Isabella Burton, "Trump-Allied Pastor Tells Worshippers 'America Is a Christian Nation,'" *Vox*, June 25, 2018, https://www.vox.com/2018/6/25/17502170/pastor-robert-jeffress-americachristian-nation-trump-dallas-baptist. Jeffress had also said President Obama was paving the way for the Antichrist, Islam promotes pedophilia, Catholicism is a Babylonian mystery religion, and the Church of the Latter Day Saints is a cult. See https://www.nbcnews.com/politics/donald-trump/trump-attackswhistleblower-schiff-tweets-impeachment-would-cause-civil-war-n1060191.

22   Jeremy W. Peters and Elizabeth Dias, "Paula White, Newest White House Aide, Is

a Uniquely Trumpian Pastor," *New York Times*, November 2, 2019, https://www.ny-times.com/2019/11/02/us/politics/paulawhite-trump.html.

23   Ronald J. Sider, *The Scandal of the Evangelical Conscience* (Grand Rapids, MI: Baker Publishing Group, 2005). See also Austin Cline, "Divorce Rates for Atheists Are Among the Lowest in America," *Learn Religions*, August 24, 2018, https://www.learnreligions.com/divorce-rates-for-atheists-248494.

24   "Study of Women Who Have an Abortion and Their Views on Church," Life Way Research, June 15, 2019, https://lifewayresearch.com/wp-content/uploads/2015/11/Care-Net-Final-Presentation-ReportRevised.pdf. The figure in the Life Way Research national poll of 1,038 American women who had an abortion was 21 percent for weekly Christian church attenders, with an additional 5 percent who went to church more often than that. If you think most women who call themselves Christian go to church weekly, then the poll indicates regularly attending women are less likely to have an abortion than other women are. But estimates of how many Christian women attend church at least weekly vary quite a bit. It is probably more than 26 percent, but probably not a whole lot more. And you have to consider the strong possibility that dedicated Christian women who had an abortion would be less likely than most to participate in the study.

25   Dietrich Bonhoeffer, *The Cost of Dictatorship* (New York: SCM Press, 1959).

26   Two groups have particularly noticed the apparent lack of integrity among evangelicals: Teens and young adults are often permanently turned off by what they see in church. Some apologists claim youthful apostates usually come back to the fold with renewed faith. This is disconfirmed by a study of a large sample of Canadian parents who had been given a religious upbringing but who quit their religion and did not raise their children in any faith. When asked why they left their faith, their most common explanation was, "As I grew up, I saw a lot of hypocrisy in the people in my religion." (Bob Altemeyer, 2006, 132). That hypocrisy thus cost the religion at least two generations and appears to be one of the big reasons church attendance is down so dramatically in the United States and the fastest growing religious category is now no religion. Some polls are finding this effect even among fundamentalist faiths that prided themselves on their ability to retain their young people while liberal denominations were losing them hand over fist. Diane Cox and Robert P. Jones, "America's Changing Religious Identity," PRRI, September 6, 2017, https://www.prri.org/research/american-religious-landscape-christian-religiously-unaffiliated/. Again, the big cause is perceived hypocrisy, with the most cited issue being attitudes toward homosexuality.

The second group are evangelical ministers trying to change their religion's course. One of them, Timothy Keller, wrote at the end of 2017, "'Evangelical' used to denote people who claimed the high moral ground; now, in popular usage, the word is nearly synonymous with 'hypocrite.'" "Can Evangelicalism Survive Donald Trump and Roy Moore?" *New Yorker*, December 19, 2017, https://www.newyorker.com/news/news-desk/can-evangelicalism-survive-donald-trump-and-roy-moore.

27   See Chapter 7 in *The Authoritarians*, at www.theauthoritarians.org. ("The Milgram Experiment," starting at page 222.)

CHAPTER NINE

1   See Bob Altemeyer, "The Other 'Authoritarian Personality,'" in Mark Zanna, ed., *Advances in Experimental Social Psychology* 30 (New York: Academic Press, 1998).

2   For example, studies show they almost always support the Conservative Party in Canada. Scoring highly in both traits seems to give them that much more of a reason to prefer the Tories. Similarly, both high SDOs and high RWAs score highly on a Militia Scale developed after the Oklahoma City bombing that measures belief in the conspiracy theory that the country is being taken over by Jews and Communists through the United Nations. But Double Highs score highest of all and agree that armed resistance will probably be needed to fight plots to take away citizens' firearms.

3   A brief but slightly fuller description of the game paraphrased from the game's original website and other sites that seek to explain the game:

    The Global Change Game is a large-scale board game devised in 1991 by a group of students from the University of Manitoba, including the oldest son of Altemeyer. The game has been played throughout the world, largely in secondary schools and occasionally at the college level. It is played on a colorful world map the size of a basketball court. It is a simulation that involves exploring, understanding, and solving some of the global issues of the time. The large map of the world is laid out, and 50 to 70 participants (depending upon the size of the venue) are divided up and randomly assigned by administrators/facilitators to one of the 10 regions of the world: North America, Latin America, Europe, the Commonwealth of Independent States, Africa, India, the Middle East, Southeast Asia, China, and the Pacific Ring. Each region begins the game with realistic assets and real-world problems. For example, North America, Europe, and the Pacific Ring are well-off, but India and Africa are experiencing extreme poverty. Military strengths reflect that of the real-world situation of the region, and Army tokens are given out in relationship to that strength. Food supply, medical facilities and employment opportunity tokens are distributed based on actual figures in reality.

    The game is informed and controlled by administrators/facilitators and played over three hours which represent the passing of thirty to forty years. At the beginning of the game the nuclear powers are asked if they wish to disarm. Players in regions without food, health care, or employment are given black armbands by the facilitators for each of those situations, and when they receive three armbands the facilitator will declare them dead. Regions can also declare refugees, however if no other region offers them asylum, they are perished to the open ocean. When the game is in play the facilitators move around to determine if proposals for dealing with certain problems are feasible and will reward or punish the groups accordingly. For example, the poor management of the environment can result in famine, strife, and pestilence. Facilitators also announce random problems at specified intervals, ranging from ozone depletion to global warming. Leaders are chosen at the beginning of each game for their respective regions. These leaders are given hats to give them the aura of leadership. They control the finances and military strength and are allowed to pocket the wealth of their regions as they deem fit. Leaders can also declare war. Victory is determined by the army tokens. Once victory is achieved the leader's territory and assets belong to the winner. If the Army tokens are equal both sides lose not only the army but their wealth. A victor can control the invaded territory by stationing troops in the conquered land. Nuclear war wipes out the entire Earth's population and ends the game. See, e.g., the Global Change Game at http://ourworld.ca/ow2002/gcgame.html.

4   Bob Altemeyer, *The Authoritarian Specter* (Cambridge, MA: Harvard University Press, 1996), 130–136.

5   Bob Altemeyer, "What Happens When Authoritarians Inherit the Earth? A Simulation," *Analyses of Social Issues and Public Policy* (2003): 161–169.

6   Altemeyer, *The Authoritarians*, www.theauthoritarians.org., 26, 174–176.

7   Altemeyer, *The Authoritarians*, 26.

8   Altemeyer, *The Authoritarians*, 26.

9   Bob Altemeyer, *Enemies of Freedom* (San Francisco: Jossey-Bass, 1988), 253–257.

10   Bob Altemeyer, *The Authoritarian Specter*, (Cambridge, MA, Harvard University Press,1996) chapter 11.

11   Altemeyer, 1996, 260–267.

12   The older and wiser of your authors told the much younger and less perceptive one in 2005 that he thought the Republican Party had been transformed from the conservative party he had joined as a lad into the Authoritarian Party, and it was going to pose a great danger to American democracy. This became the thrust of the bestseller *Conservatives without Conscience*. Altemeyer was informed by the book. Preoccupied by running experiments to test various hypotheses, he had not really noticed how much it was all coming true in the United States. But he said it would take a long time for the threat to materialize, if it ever did. Boy, was he wrong! Boy, are we sorry!

13   McKay Coppins, "How Newt Gingrich Destroyed American politics," *The Atlantic*, October 17, 2018, https://www.theatlantic.com/magazine/archive/2018/11/newt-gingrich-says-youre-welcome/570832/.

14   John W. Dean, *Conservatives without Conscience* (New York: Penguin, 2006), 118–123.

CHAPTER TEN

1   Kevin Coyne, "Monmouth University Pollster Patrick Murray is Making Numbers Meaningful," *New Jersey Monthly*, September 12, 2018, https://njmonthly.com/articles/politics-public-affairs/monmouth-university-pollster-patrick-murray-making-numbers-meaningful/.

2   The Monmouth University Polling Institute has a strong reputation in the polling industry for accuracy and reliability. Nate Silver's "538" website (https://fivethirtyeight.com/) gives it a rating of A+, one of only six polls out of over 400 that get its highest grade. (The others are *ABC/Washington Post*, Marist College, Muhlenberg College, Selzer & Co., and Siena College/*New York Times*. Upshot: https://projects.fivethirtyeight.com/trump-approval-ratings/.) So we were thrilled with Patrick Murray's offer, which came about when author Dean visited Monmouth University for lecture programs and on two occasions was seated at luncheons next to the man who in 2005 created and today serves as the director of the polling institute. Patrick Murray was trained in political science but found his calling in polling. When Dean told Murray of this project, and our interest in testing the major findings on authoritarianism, he offered to conduct a national poll employing Altemeyer's measures, provided he, in turn, would have exclusive control of the data after we crunched it for a book. Murray's interest in the subject is purely intellectual and not social or political. If we had been studying "left-wing authoritarians," he would be just as interested in seeing if a poll could find out things about them. So we became partners in a mission that had one, and only one, goal: To get the most accurate, full-scale measurements possible from a reasonably representative sample of American voters, of various personality traits and political

attitudes believed to be the most significant factors in deciding whether one approves or disapproves of Donald Trump. Believe it or not, nobody had ever done such a study.

We wanted the Monmouth poll to be conducted as late as possible, but we hoped to publish this book well before the 2020 election, so the data collection was undertaken in October and November 2019. By then we had composed the core material in the chapters examining Trump's authoritarian character, and more importantly, the authoritarian nature of his followers and were just sticking fresh examples on the framework every news cycle. To put it as heroically as possible, we bravely predicted the Monmouth poll would find the same sort of things found many times before, albeit to a large extent 60 miles north of the North Dakota border. But the poll might instead reveal the accumulated science on authoritarianism was just a sea of weak overgeneralizations. "Do I really want to know," Altemeyer wondered, "if I'm living in a fool's paradise?" The concerns proved baseless.

3   We know of only one study that collected SDO Scale data from a representative sample of American adults. ("Study 4" in Jake Womick, Tobias Rothmund, Flavio Azevedo, Laura A. King, and John T. Jost, "Group-Based Dominance and Authoritarian Aggression Predict Support for Donald Trump in the 2016 Presidential Election," *Social Psychological and Personality Science* (2018): 1–10. It found correlations in the 30s between SDO scales and preference for Donald Trump during the 2016 campaign. Similarly, only one study has looked at RWA Scale scores in a representative sample of Americans. This poll was conducted by Mick McWilliams and Jeremy Keil for the Libertarian Party in 2005. (See page 14 and page 215 in Altemeyer, *The Authoritarians*.) It too found a modest connection (.34) between RWA scores and being a Republican rather than a Democrat.

4   Thus our poll is not as representative of the electorate as it would be if we had, say, recruited the same percentage of Democrat-voters and Republican-voters who took part in the 2016 election. But we were not trying to predict who would win the next election, but rather trying to understand those who supported Trump today compared to those who opposed him. If you want to know how seriously our sample over-represents Republican voters, the regular national polls taken over the weeks that our survey was "in the field" found more "Disapprovers" (~ 53 percent) than "Approvers" (~ 42 percent) among registered voters. (See https://projects.fivethirtyeight.com/trump-approval-ratings/.) In our study the edge was 52 percent to 48 percent.

5   It is possible that prejudice causes authoritarianism instead, or that both are caused by other, "third" factors. We expect both of these will prove true to some extent, especially the third. But we think we know what causes authoritarianism in a person (see chapter 2 in Altemeyer, *The Authoritarians*), and prejudice is not an important factor. Whereas prejudice is, we think, built to some extent upon an ethnocentric template that many authoritarians first encountered through their parents, who with other authorities in the youth's in-group would have taught stereotypes that put racial and ethnic groups in a bad light.

6   How did this survey achieve such spectacular, unprecedented results? Credit must be given to Monmouth University Polling Institute and its very competent director, Patrick Murray, who developed a smooth, clear, on-line surveying method that obviously minimized measurement error. Also, the length of the survey probably filtered out persons with little concern about politics, leaving the responding to those who have keener, better organized attitudes regarding societal matters. In the same vein, and

likely most important of all, opinions on some of these issues have become polarized in the United States. Extreme points of view tend to be highly organized compared to more la-de-da stances. Extreme viewpoints may be boiling over in your community now, which you might have noticed the last time you got into an argument so heated that you could hardly form sentences.

7   In this and other comparisons using high SDOs, we used the sum of the SDO-Dominance and SDO-Antiequality Scales. If you compute two SDO scores instead, you get the same results, but SDO-Anti-Equality scores usually have stronger relationships than SDO-Dominance ones.

8   We asked our respondents how much they had benefitted economically from Trump's presidency and there was a strong connection between benefit and support for Trump. But not as strong as the connections with authoritarianism and prejudice that we have seen, and when you took those factors into account, economic improvement lost almost all its importance. That is, the authoritarian/prejudiced people who were better off tended to support Trump, but the others who were also better off did not.

9   A prediction for the future. We followed the item about Trump declaring the 2020 election invalid with four other "What if" questions about Trump's possible fate. Should he be investigated for any crimes he may have committed while in office? Should he be put on trial for any such crimes if he is removed from office by the impeachment process? Or if he resigns? Or if he is defeated in November? Trump's *opponents* almost universally said yes, yes, yes, and yes. It's a pretty safe prediction that they would do so if the hypothetical became the actual. But the situation among Trump's base seems less clear because these issues had not been discussed in the media, nor has Trump said anything except the impeachment process was a witch hunt. But even without those influences, 24–29 percent of Trump's supporters in the survey took his side that he should be immune from prosecution. Another 18–19 percent said they had no opinion on the matter, which is not a good sign for support of the rule of law.

10   Sean Collins, "Why These Protests Are Different: There Have Been Uprisings against Police Brutality and Racism before, but This Is the Country at Its Exasperation Point," *Vox*, June 4, 2020, https://www.vox.com/identities/2020/6/4/21276674/protests-george-floyd-arbery-nationwide-trump.

11   See endnote 2.

12   Many readers will recall from their piano lessons, *ffff* comes from musical scoring where *f* stands for *forte*, or *fortissimo*, meaning louder, louder, louder, louder!

13   We put six questions about the Ukraine scandal in the questionnaire. In general (and to Altemeyer's surprise) Trump supporters seemed to be as well informed about the drama as those who disapproved of Trump's performance as president. Which is not to say either side had a good grasp of the matter. Supporters were mistaken about whether Trump had named the Bidens as objects of investigation in his July 25, 2019, telephone conversation with President Zelensky. (He had, but they thought he had not.) Supporters also did not believe the "rough transcript" of that conversation had been put on a very secure computer system because White House aides thought it would damage the president if it became known. (It was.) In turn, Trump opponents were overwhelmingly wrong about whether a quid pro quo of military aid for political investigations was specified by Trump in that conversation. (It may well have been implied, but almost all who disliked Trump thought he had explicitly stated it to Zelensky.)

    Our last Ukraine question gave Trump opponents a second chance to show bias.

We asked everyone if President Obama should have been impeached and removed from office if he had made a phone call to the leader of a foreign nation in 2011 suggesting Mitt Romney should be investigated with the help of Obama's personal attorney. Almost all of those who opposed Trump, who had earlier said Trump should be impeached, said Obama too should have been impeached and removed from office. It appears there is no double standard in those answers. But a quarter of Trump's supporters, who had said Trump should not be impeached, said Obama should have been for doing the same thing, a definite double standard.

CHAPTER ELEVEN

1   Michael Cohen, "Testimony of Michael D. Cohen Committee On Oversight and Reform," *U.S. House Of Representatives*, February 27, 2019, https://www.politico.com/f/?id=00000169-2d31-dc75-affd-bfb99a790001.

2   Corey R. Lewandowski and David N. Bossie, *Let Trump Be Trump: The Inside Story of His Rise to the Presidency* (New York: Center Street, 2017). (At page 43 the authors state: "The boss [Trump] was interviewed about his hiring strategy back in 2014. He surprised the guy interviewing him with his answer, but it wouldn't surprise anyone who has worked for Mr. Trump. When asked what he valued in an employee, Mr. Trump gave the interviewer a one-word answer: loyalty.")

3   Kenneth P. Vogel and Shane Goldmacher, "Trump staffers face threat of blacklist: Some political operatives shy away from the billionaire for fear of being shunned by other Republicans," *Politico*, April 19, 2016, https://www.politico.com/story/2016/04/trump-staffers-face-threat-of-blacklist-222123.

4   Olivia Paschal and Madeleine Carlisle, "A Brief History of Roger Stone: The GOP operative and self-described "dirty trickster," who was convicted today, has been a presence in the president's life for more than 30 years," *The Atlantic*, November 15, 2019, https://www.theatlantic.com/politics/archive/2019/11/roger-stones-long-history-in-trump-world/581293/.

5   Quint Forgey, "Trump promises Stone won't serve prison time: 'He can sleep well at night!'" *Politico*, June 4, 2020, https://www.politico.com/news/2020/06/04/trump-promises-roger-stone-will-serve-no-prison-time-300351.

6   David Bossie later admitted there was such a conspiracy. See, e.g., Daniel Moritz-Rabson, "Former Trump Campaign Manager Admits There Was, In Fact, A 'Vast right-Wing Conspiracy' To Undermine the Clintons," *Newsweek*, November 25, 2018, https://www.newsweek.com/conservatives-engaged-vast-conspiracy-undermine-clintons-1230227.

7   Lewandowski and Bossie, *Let Trump Be Trump*, 24-25.

8   Lewandowski and Bossie, *Let Trump Be Trump*, 37-38.

9   Corey wrote a remarkably laudatory letter to the sentencing judge for Bob Ney possibly because he had been forced to talk to the prosecutors and grand jury to save himself – and anyone who spent as much time with the Congressman as Lewandowski, would likely have some awareness of the conspiracy that started about 2000, since Corey did not leave until February 2001. His letter, in part, read:

I had the privilege of spending 20 hours a day with Bob seven days a week for over three years. In that time, I learned more about life, people, politics, friendships and the importance of family than I ever could have imagined. Bob served as a mentor to me, as a surrogate father, and as a best friend all in one. No one can make excuses for what has occurred, but I know a different Bob than what is portrayed in media accounts.

    Letter of January 1, 2007 from Corey R. Lewandowsky, Former Administrative Assistant, US Congressman Robert W. Ney to the Honorable Ellen Segal Huvelle, U.S. District Court for the District of Columbia, *United States v. Ney*, Criminal Case No. 1:06-cr-00272-ESH.

10   Lewandowski and Bossie, *Let Trump Be Trump*, 47.

11   Ibid., 49.

12   Ibid., 120.

13   Ibid., 146-152.

14   Alexander Burns and Maggie Haberman, "Inside the Failing Mission to Tame Donald Trump's Tongue," *New York Times*, August 13, 2016, https://www.nytimes.com/2016/08/14/us/politics/donald-trump-campaign-gop.html.

15   Gabriel Sherman, "'Crickets. They're Gone': Why the Mercers, Trump's Biggest 2016 Backers, Have Bailed on Him," *Vanity Fair*, June 17, 2019, https://www.vanityfair.com/news/2019/06/why-the-mercers-trumps-biggest-2016-backers-have-bailed-on-him/amp.

16   Jane Mayer, "The Reclusive Hedge-Fund Tycoon Behind the Trump Presidency: How Robert Mercer exploited America's populist insurgency," *New Yorker*, March 17, 2017, https://www.newyorker.com/magazine/2017/03/27/the-reclusive-hedge-fund-tycoon-behind-the-trump-presidency/amp.

17   Lewandowski and Bossie, *Let Trump Be Trump*, 145.

18   Ibid., 140.

19   Jonathan Martin, Jim Rutenberg and Maggie Haberman, "Donald Trump Appoints Media Firebrand to Run Campaign," *New York Times*, August 17, 2016, https://www.nytimes.com/2016/08/18/us/politics/donald-trump-stephen-bannon-paul-manafort.html.

20   Nolan D. McCaskill, Alex Isenstadt and Shane Goldmacher, "Paul Manafort resigns from Trump campaign: The departure of Trump's embattled campaign chairman comes two days after the nominee shook up his leadership team," *Politico*, August 19, 2016, https://www.politico.com/story/2016/08/paul-manafort-resigns-from-trump-campaign-227197.

21   There is no question that Brad Parscale, who designed websites for the Trump Organization, and then joined the Trump campaign to work with data, played a very important role. He and Trump's son-in-law Jared Kushner had set up a data operation for the campaign. As an add-on, for example, he raised $240 million. Parscale was knowledgeable about data, and during a *60 Minutes* interview largely dismissed Cambridge Analytica. He told Lesley Stahl he did not like their methodology but did not deny they were part of the operation. But the Cambridge Analytica guys had the heavy-duty data, and maybe most telling is when Cambridge Analytica closed, they purchased Brad Parscale's interest in his company for $9 million, and he sits on the board of the acquiring company. See, e.g., Ian Schwartz, "Trump Digital Director Brad Parscale Explains Data That Led To Victory on 'Kelly File'," *Real Clear Politics*, November 16, 2016, https://www.realclearpolitics.com/video/2016/11/16/trump_digital_director_brad_parscale_explains_data_that_led_to_victory_on_kelly_file.html. (Transcript of broadcast of *The Kelly File* on the *FOX News Channel*.) And Lesley Stahl, "Facebook 'Embeds,' Russia

and the Trump campaign's secret weapon: Brad Parscale, digital director for Trump's campaign, was a critical factor in the president's election. Now questions surround how he did it," *60 Minutes*, October 8, 2017, https://www.cbsnews.com/news/facebook-embeds-russia-and-the-trump-campaigns-secret-weapon/.

22 Harry Enten, "How Much Did WikiLeaks Hurt Hillary Clinton?" *FiveThirtyEight*, December 23, 2016, https://fivethirtyeight.com/features/wikileaks-hillary-clinton/.

23 See, e.g., Nate Silver, "How Much Did Russian Interference Affect The 2016 Election? It's hard to say," *FiveThirtyEight*, February 16, 2018, https://fivethirtyeight.com/features/how-much-did-russian-interference-affect-the-2016-election/ and Molly McKew, "Did Russia Affect the 2016 Election? It's Now Undeniable: In the wake of the Mueller indictment of a Russian troll farm, any attempt to claim that the 2016 election wasn't affected by Russian meddling is laughable," *Wired*, February 2, 2018, https://www.wired.com/story/did-russia-affect-the-2016-election-its-now-undeniable/.

24 Nate Silver, "The Comey Letter Probably Cost Clinton the Election: So why won't the media admit as much?" *FiveThirtyEight*, May 3, 2017, https://fivethirtyeight.com/features/the-comey-letter-probably-cost-clinton-the-election/.

25 Dareh Gregorian, "'Off the charts:' White House turnover is breaking records," *NBC News*, September 23, 2019, https://www.nbcnews.com/politics/white-house/charts-white-house-turnover-breaking-records-n1056101.

26 Two examples typify the situation and make the point. Trump convinced Rex Tillerson, the CEO and Chairman of ExxonMobil since 2006, to serve as his Secretary of State. Tillerson had no previous experience in the military or government, but he knew the world from decades-long service with a massive company with offices everywhere in the world. His name was suggested to Trump by former Secretary of Defense Robert Gates and former Secretary of State Condoleezza Rice agreed with the recommendation. Tillerson held the State Department post from February 1, 2017 until March 13, 2018, when Trump unceremoniously fired him. Trump did not like Tillerson, because he pushed back on Trump's directives. Tillerson later explained he pushed back because he was not willing to break the law for Trump. Caitlin Oprysko, "'It violates the law:' Tillerson vents about having to repeatedly push back against Trump," *Politico*, December 17, 2018, https://www.politico.com/story/2018/12/07/tillerson-spills-on-trump-1048884. A second example is Gary Cohn, the former president, and CEO, of Goldman Sachs, who took the White House post of director of the National Economic Council, the president's top economic adviser. Donald Trump believes he is an economics genius when, in fact, he could not likely pass an open book exam in Economics 101. Gary Cohn's appointment gave Wall Street and Capitol Hill great comfort that Trump's crazy talk about tariffs during the campaign would not be imposed. Cohn represented traditional GOP economic thinking. He lasted a year. Trump could not argue with someone who actually knew what he was talking about, so he let Cohn go, sparing him one of his ignominious firings. As many thought, and Cohn later publicly worried, with his departure there was no one left to tell Trump no when he pushed one of his half-baked ideas. Abbey Marshall, "Gary Cohn says no one is left in the White House to stand up to Trump," *Politico*, December 2, 2019, https://www.politico.com/news/2019/12/02/gary-cohn-no-one-left-stand-up-to-trump-white-house-074757.

27 Editorial Staff, "Tracking how many key positions Trump has filled so far," *Washington Post* (updated constantly) at https://www.washingtonpost.com/graphics/politics/trump-administration-appointee-tracker/database/. As we write over 150 important

offices throughout government are vacant. Dareh Gregorian, "Help Wanted: Trump administration riddled with vacancies: The president has yet to nominate people for nearly 140 top-level positions, which experts say is hampering his long-term goals," *NBC News*, March 28, 2019, https://www.nbcnews.com/politics/donald-trump/help-wanted-trump-administration-riddled-vacancies-n983036. What Trump has done is allow his cabinet and subcabinet appointees to select people they want in their departments and agencies. Trump's cabinet is the wealthiest in American history. Julianna Goldman, "Donald Trump's Cabinet richest in U.S. history, historians say," *CBS News*, December 20, 2016, https://www.cbsnews.com/news/donald-trump-cabinet-richest-in-us-history-historians-say/. Trump typically selected people to run the organizations who had come from the industries they would be regulating, and they hired lobbyists from the industries to run their departments. All oblivious to the conflicts of interest laws, and all interests but the public interests being represented. Tom Scheck and APM Reports, "Ethics Be Damned: More than half of Trump's 20-person Cabinet has engaged in questionable or unethical conduct," *Marketplace*, February 16, 2018, https://www.marketplace.org/2018/02/16/ethics-be-damned-more-half-trumps-20-person-cabinet-has-engaged-questionable-or/.

28   Governor Mike Pence Twitter account, December 8, 2015, https://twitter.com/GovPenceIN/status/674249808610066433?ref_src=twsrc%5Etfw.

29   Susan B. Glasser, "Mike Pompeo, the Secretary of Trump: How he became a heartland evangelical – and the President's most loyal soldier," *New Yorker*, August 26, 2019, https://www.newyorker.com/magazine/2019/08/26/mike-pompeo-the-secretary-of-trump

30   Heather Digby Parton, "Donald Trump finds an attorney general: But will Bill Barr be his "Roy Cohn"? *Salon*, December 10, 2018, https://www.salon.com/2018/12/10/donald-trump-finds-an-attorney-general-but-will-bill-barr-be-his-roy-cohn/.

31   McKay Coppins, "God's Plan for Mike Pence," *The Atlantic*, January/February 2018, https://www.theatlantic.com/magazine/archive/2018/01/gods-plan-for-mike-pence/546569/.

32   Glasser, "Mike Pompeo, the Secretary of Trump," *New Yorker, supra*.

33   Bill Barr, Memorandum to Deputy Attorney General Rod Rosenstein Assistant Attorney General Steve Engel, "Muller 'Obstruction' Theory,", June 8, 2018, https://int.nyt.com/data/documenthelper/549-june-2018-barr-memo-to-doj-mue/b4c05e39318dd2d136b3/optimized/full.pdf.

34   Marty Lederman, "A First Take on Bill Barr's Memo on Presidential Authority and the Mueller Investigation," *Just Security*, December 20, 2018, https://www.justsecurity.org/61975/legal-arguments-bill-barrs-memo-mueller-investigation/.

35   Paul Waldman, "Pence's unwillingness to be alone with a woman is a symptom of a bigger problem," *Washington Post*, March 30, 2017, https://www.washingtonpost.com/blogs/plum-line/wp/2017/03/30/pences-unwillingness-to-be-alone-with-a-woman-is-a-symptom-of-a-bigger-problem/.

36   Edward Wong, "The Rapture and the Real World: Mike Pompeo Blends Beliefs and Policy," *New York Times*, March 30, 2019, https://www.nytimes.com/2019/03/30/us/politics/pompeo-christian-policy.html.

37   Ibid.

38   Glasser, "Mike Pompeo, the Secretary of Trump," *New Yorker, supra*.

39   Bill Barr graduated from Columbia University in 1971 with a bachelor's degree in

government studies, and a master's degree in 1973 in Chinese studies. He then moved to Washington, DC during the summer of Watergate, to work for the Central Intelligence Agency as an analyst while going to night school at George Washington University Law School, from which he graduated in 1977. (It appears Barr worked at the CIA during George H.W. Bush's tenure as Director.) After law school Barr clerked for a federal judge, then got a job at a top law firm, and a job at the Reagan White House from May 1982 to September 1983 as Deputy Assistant Director for Legal Policy on the domestic policy staff, a position that would have given him a good understanding of the Department of Justice in general, and the Office of Legal Counsel in particular. It was a time of the Iran-Contra scandal, so President George H. W. Bush kept Ronald Reagan's attorney general, Dick Thornburgh, but did add others at the Justice Department, including Bill Barr, who became the assistant attorney general in charge of the Office of Legal Counsel, where he served for sixteen months before becoming the Deputy Attorney General in May 1990. Nineteen months later, when Dick Thornburgh departed, Barr was appointed attorney general, serving until the end of the Bush I administration.

40   Katherine Stewart and Caroline Fredrickson, "Bill Barr Thinks America Is Going to Hell," *New York Times*, December 29, 2019, https://www.nytimes.com/2019/12/29/opinion/william-barr-trump.html.

41   Anne Applebaum, "History Will Judge the Complicit: Why have Republican leaders abandoned their principles in support of an immoral and dangerous president?" *The Atlantic*, July/August 2020, https://www.theatlantic.com/magazine/archive/2020/07/trumps-collaborators/612250/.

42   David Davies, "Journalist Explains Why Republican Leaders Back Trump's 'Proto-Authoritarian Cult'," *NPR's "Fresh Air"*, June 4, 2020, https://www.npr.org/2020/06/04/869722081/journalist-explains-why-republican-leaders-back-trumps-proto-authoritarian-cult.

43   Anne Applebaum, "History Will Judge the Complicit," *supra*.

44   Ibid.

45   Gabby Orr, "Trump looks to reward conservative Catholics for their loyalty: American Catholics supported the Democratic nominee in all but four presidential cycles since 1952. Trump is looking to secure a 2020 repeat of their support for him three years ago, but he could face some roadblocks," *Politico*, January 14, 2020, https://www.politico.com/news/2020/01/14/trump-catholics-reelection-098518; and Lee Fang, "Inside The Influential Evangelical Group Mobilizing To Reelect Trump," *Intercept*, May 23, 2020, https://theintercept.com/2020/05/23/coronavirus-evangelical-megachurch-trump/.

46   Mandy Gillip, "Trump has appointed second-most federal judges through May 1 of a president's fourth year," *Ballotpedia*, May 6, 2020, https://news.ballotpedia.org/2020/05/06/trump-has-appointed-second-most-federal-judges-through-may-1-of-a-presidents-fourth-year/.

47   See, e.g., "Obama tan suit controversy," *Wikipedia* at https://en.wikipedia.org/wiki/Obama_tan_suit_controversy, and "Obama's Tan Suit: The Worst Scandal in Presidential History," *YouTube*, https://www.youtube.com/watch?v=WrTf6CaTTc0.

48   See, e.g., Image at https://www.alamy.com/us-president-barack-obama-tosses-a-football-in-the-oval-office-of-image69015553.html, and *The Astute Blogger*, http://astuteblogger.blogspot.com/2013/09/obama-playing-football-in-oval-office.html.

49   The Editorial Board, "The Republican Guide to Presidential Etiquette," *New York*

Times, January 20, 2018, https://www.nytimes.com/interactive /2018/01/20/opinion/ the-Republicans-Guide-to-Presidential-Etiquette.html. (Here are a few dozen from the hundreds: Imply, without evidence, that a television anchor was involved in a murder; falsely claim the F.B.I.'s reputation is "in tatters—worst in history" and call members of the intelligence community "political hacks;" have your lawyer pay $130,000 in hush money to a porn star with whom you had an affair while your wife was at home caring for your new son; exploit a White House event honoring Native American veterans to mock a senator with a racially charged slur; defend your mental competency by saying that you are "like, really smart" and a "very stable genius;" falsely claim that your predecessor failed to contact the families of fallen soldiers, and then exploit the death of your chief of staff's son to defend yourself; insult people, places and things constantly; absurdly take credit for the fact that no one died on a domestic commercial airliner during your first year in office; praise the delivery to Norway of fighter planes that exist only in a video game; tell more than 2,000 lies in a year, or roughly five a day; watch four to eight hours of cable television a day, mostly the channel that feeds you self-serving propaganda; mock a foreign leader with a demeaning nickname and threaten his country with nuclear annihilation over Twitter; attack a senator battling terminal cancer; spend one of every three days as president visiting at least one of your own properties; deliver a speech to the Boy Scouts of America that includes mockery of a former president and winking references to sexual orgies, and then lie by claiming that the head of that organization called and told you it was the best speech ever delivered in Boy Scout history; force your cabinet members to take turns extolling your virtues in front of television cameras; without consulting anyone at the Pentagon, announce a new policy barring transgender soldiers from serving in the military; pardon a former sheriff who was convicted of criminal contempt of court for refusing to obey the law; continue to leave hundreds of executive branch positions unfilled; profit off the presidency, accepting millions of dollars from foreign government officials, businesses, politicians and other supporters who pay a premium to patronize your properties and get access to you—while also attempting to hide the visitor lists at some of those properties from the public; call the media "the enemy of the American people;" hire relatives for key White House posts and let them meet with foreign officials and engage in business at the same time; and tweet, tweet, tweet, while skipping daily intelligence briefings.

50   Jonathan Martin and Alexander Burns, "Democrats Capture Control of House; G.O.P. Holds Senate," *New York Times*, November 6, 2018, https://www.nytimes. com/2018/11/06/us/politics/midterm-elections-results.html.

51   Speaker Pelosi remembered well the partisan impeachment of President Bill Clinton, which was driven by the endless investigations Republicans mounted against him, until he finally made a fatal mistake and lied under oath about his affair with Monica Lewinsky. The Republican-controlled House voted for articles of impeachment against Clinton on a straight party line and sent them to the Senate, where Clinton was acquitted on a party line vote. It requires only a simple majority of the House members to impeach, but a two-thirds supermajority to convict (and remove a president) in the Senate. The Clinton impeachment and removal undertaking ushered in the era of deep partisan polarization in which we now live. Republican Speaker Newt Gingrich orchestrated the impeachment/removal drive, and its failure forced his resignation. Also, it resulted in the resignation of the Speaker-designate Robert Livingston. At the end of the impeachment proceedings, Bill Clinton's job approval rating reached its high-

est level during his presidency—at 73 percent approval. Frank Newport, "Presidential Job Approval: Bill Clinton's High Ratings in the Midst of Crisis, 1998," *Gallup*, June 4, 1999, https://news.gallup.com/poll/4609/presidential-job-approval-bill-clintons-high-ratings-midst.aspx.

52 Charlie Savage, "Judge Calls Barr's Handling of Mueller Report 'Distorted' and "Misleading,'" *New York Times*, March 5, 2020, https://www.nytimes.com/2020/03/05/us/politics/mueller-report-barr-judge-walton.html.

53 Editorial Staff, "Document: Read the Whistle-Blower Complaint," *New York Times*, September 26, 2019, https://www.nytimes.com/interactive/2019/09/26/us/politics/whistle-blower-complaint.html.

54 See, e.g., Ian Millhiser, "The 4 possible crimes in the Trump-Ukraine whistleblower scandal, explained: Based on what we know so far, Trump and his top aides could be implicated in four different types of federal crimes," *Vox*, September 27, 2019, https://www.vox.com/policy-and-politics/2019/9/27/20885557/criminal-laws-trump-barr-giuliani-ukraine, and Judge Andrew Napolitano, "Trump's call with Ukraine president manifests criminal and impeachable behavior," *Fox News*, October 3, 2020, https://www.foxnews.com/opinion/judge-andrew-napolitano-trump-attacks-presidency.

55 This political and legal check on federal officials arose early in the Constitutional Convention of 1787, and we have a good understanding of it because a leading proponent wrote at some length about it when presenting the Constitution to the people for adoption. Alexander Hamilton addressed it in Federalist Papers No. 65, 66 and 67. His understanding of how the impeachment and removal process would playout was prescient, as this passage from No. 65 reveals:

> The subjects of its jurisdiction are those offenses which proceed from the misconduct of public men, or, in other words, *from the abuse or violation of some public trust.* They are of a nature which may with peculiar propriety be denominated *POLITICAL*, *as they relate chiefly to injuries* done immediately to the society itself. The prosecution of them, for this reason, will seldom fail to agitate the passions of the whole community, and to divide it into parties more or less friendly or inimical to the accused. In many cases it will connect itself with the pre-existing factions, and will enlist all their animosities, partialities, influence, and interest on one side or on the other; and in such cases there will always be the greatest danger that the decision will be regulated more by the comparative strength of parties, than by the real demonstrations of innocence or guilt. (Emphasis added.) Alexander Hamilton, *Federalist Paper No. 65*, https://avalon.law.yale.edu/18th_century/fed65.asp.

56 Remember the "Victory Celebration" in the White House that Trump held the day after he was acquitted by the Senate? (Chapter 4) Trump spouted one half-truth and outright lie after another for over an hour. But everyone clapped, over and over, included Senator Charles Grassley (Iowa), who nodded in agreement when Trump falsely claimed Grassley got James Comey to admit he was leaking, and as far as we know, no one who was there corrected the record on any of the president's factually wrong or false comments. We do not think it was just because they did not want to disagree with a vengeful president whom they had just made more powerful than ever. Instead, videos of the scene reminded us of films of speeches given by many dictators to their compliant officials, from Franco to Kim Jong-un, who are there simply to applaud everything Dear Leader says. That is their job, more than anything else. And it did not happen so much because they were afraid of Trump or because he had outsmarted or corrupted them. Most GOP

leaders lost interest in the truth a long time ago. (Remember again Grassley's "Death Panels.") The Representatives and Senators who led the fight to destroy Congress' constitutional responsibility to check and balance the executive branch have no doubt long wanted to do this for a GOP president.

CHAPTER TWELVE

1　A Republican pollster named David Winston gently pointed this out when the dust had settled after the mid-terms. https://www.rollcall.com/news/opinion/republicans-traded-election-caravans.

2　Gregory A. Smith, "White evangelicals among groups with slipping confidence in Trump's handling of COVID-19," May 14, 2020, https://www.pewresearch.org/fact-tank/2020/05/14/white-evangelicals-among-groups-with-slipping-confidence-in-trumps-handling-of-covid-19/

3　Bob Altemeyer, *Enemies of Freedom* (San Francisco: Jossey-Bass), 289-310.

4　William Cummings, "Americans disapprove of Trump's response to George Floyd death and protests, polls find," *USA Today*, June 4, 2020, https://www.usatoday.com/story/news/politics/2020/06/04/george-floyd-trump-response-disapproved-americans-polls-find/3142639001/.

5　Rosie Perper and Sonam Sheth, "3 self-proclaimed members of the far-right 'boogaloo' movement were arrested on domestic terrorism charges for trying to spark violence during protests," *Business Insider*, June 3, 2020, https://www.businessinsider.com/3-boogaloo-men-terror-charges-george-floyd-protest-riot-conspiracy-2020-6

6　David A. Graham, "The other way the *National Enquirer* helped Trump," *The Atlantic*, December 14, 2018, https://www.theatlantic.com/politics/archive/2018/12/national-inquirer-helped-trump-attacking-clinton/578116/.

7　Sam Levine, "Trump says Republicans would 'never' be elected again if it was easier to vote," *The Guardian*, March 30, 2020, https://www.theguardian.com/us-news/2020/mar/30/trump-republican-partyvoting-reform-coronavirus.

8　Carol Anderson, "The five ways Republicans will crack down on voting rights in 2020," *The Guardian*, November 13, 2019, https://www.theguardian.com/us-news/2019/nov/13/votersuppression-2020-democracy-america.

9　Who votes, who doesn't, and why," *Pew Research Center*, October 18, 2006, https://www.peoplepress.org/2006/10/18/who-votes-who-doesnt-and-why/.

10　Dylan Scott, "Michael Cohen's parting shot: I fear what happens if Trump loses in 2020," *Vox*, February 27, 2019, https://www.vox.com/policy-and-politics/2019/2/27/18243686/michael-cohen-testimony-closing-statement.

11　Anonymous, *A Warning* (New York: Twelve, 2019), 243.

12　Glenn Thrush, "Pelosi Warns Democrats: Stay in the Center or Trump May Contest Election Results," *New York Times*, May 4, 2019, https://www.nytimes.com/2019/05/04/us/politics/nancy-pelosi.html. Daniel Block, "How Trump Could Lose the Election and Remain President: A step-by-step guide to what might happen if he refuses to concede," *Washington Monthly*, April/May/June 2019, https://washingtonmonthly.com/magazine/april-may-june-2019/how-trump-could-lose-the-election-andremain-president/. See also Barbara McQuade, "What Would Happen If Trump Refused to Leave Office? A peaceful transfer of power is necessary for American democracy to survive," *The Atlantic*, February 22, 2020, https://www.theatlantic.com/ideas/archive/2020/02/what-if-he-wont-go/606259/; Aaron Rupar, "The serious but potentially overblown fear that Trump won't leave office, explained: Nancy Pelosi is worried Trump won't leave office if he loses in 2020. She has good reason to be," *Vox*, May 10, 2019, https://www.vox.com/policy-and-politics/2019/5/10/18535212/trump-2020-pelosi-lose-leave-office; and Natasha Bertrand and Darren Samuelsohn, "What if Trump won't accept 2020 defeat? The situations all seem far-fetched, but the president's comments have people chattering in the halls of Congress and throughout the Beltway," *Politico*, June 21, 2019, https://www.politico.com/story/2019/06/21/trumpelection-2020-1374589.

13   See, Jack Maskell and Elizabeth Rybicki, "Counting Electoral Votes: An Overview of Procedures at the Joint Session, Including Objections by Members of Congress," *Congressional Reference Service*, November 15, 2016, https://fas.org/sgp/crs/misc/RL32717.pdf and Thomas H. Neale, "Contingent Election of the President and Vice President by Congress: Perspectives and Contemporary Analysis," *Congressional Reference Service*, November 3, 2016, https://fas.org/sgp/crs/misc/R40504.pdf.

14   Abigail Simon, "President Trump Says He Can Pardon Himself. Most Voters Disagree," *Time*, June 13, 2018, https://time.com/5311182/donald-trump-self-pardon-poll/.

15   Rachel Kleinfeld and David Solimini, "It will take more than an election," *The American Interest*, March 23, 2020, https://www.the-american-interest.com/2020/03/23/it-will-take-more-than-an-election/.

AFTERWORD

1   See "Authoritarianism Among Trump Voters," statement released by Monmouth University Poll on Jan. 19, 2021 at https://www.monmouth.edu/polling-institute/reports/monmouthpoll_authpanel_011921/ (hereafter Monmouth Post-Election 2020 authoritarian survey.)

2   *Ibid.* at p. 2.

3   E.g. Google: "Trump's Big Lie."

4   Jack Holmes, "Sunk Cost King Mike Pence Is Still Pushing the Big Lie After It Nearly Got Him Killed: Sure, the mob was chanting, "Hang Mike Pence." But if you want a future in Republican politics, you've got to push The Lie, and for the former vice president, there's no going back now," *Esquire* (Mar. 3, 2021) at https://www.esquire.com/news-politics/a35711288/mike-pence-big-lie-january-6/

5   David Smith, "'Accomplice' senators who amplified Trump's lies now get a say in his fate: Republicans Josh Hawley, Ted Cruz and others unabashedly endorsed the former president's assault on democracy," *The Guardian* (Feb. 12, 2021) at https://www.theguardian.com/us-news/2021/feb/11/republican-senators-accomplices-trump-impeachment-josh-hawley-ted-cruz.

6   *Ibid.*

7   Jim Rutenberg, Jo Becker, Eric Lipton, Maggie Haberman, Jonathan Martin, Matthew Rosenberg and Michael S. Schmidt, "77 Days: Trump's Campaign to Subvert the Election: Hours after the United States voted, the president declared the election a fraud — a lie that unleashed a movement that would shatter democratic norms and upend the peaceful transfer of power," *NY Times* (Jan. 31, 2021) at https://www.nytimes.

com/2021/01/31/us/trump-election-lie.html.

8   Chris Cillizza, "Three-quarters of Republicans believe a lie about the 2020 election," *CNN Politics* (Feb. 4, 2021) at https://www.cnn.com/2021/02/04/politics/2020-election-donald-trump-voter-fraud/index.html.

9   Monmouth Post-Election 2020 authoritarian survey, summary table "Authoritarian and Non-Authoritarian Trump Voters – Key Differences.

10   See, e.g., Staff, "Counting Electoral Votes: An Overview of Procedures at the Joint Session, Including Objections by Members of Congress," *Congressional Reference Service* (updated Nov. 15, 2016) at https://crsreports.congress.gov/product/pdf/RL/RL32717/12.

11   There is no more reliable a collection of the relevant information relating to Trump's pre- and post-election behavior than the Trial Brief prepared by the House Managers for the Impeachment Trial of Donald J. Trump. See https://judiciary.house.gov/uploadedfiles/house_trial_brief_final.pdf?utm_campaign=5706-519. [Cited hereafter as House Impeachment Brief."]

12   Within days of the announcement of Trump's losses in key states, his campaign's legal team began filing lawsuits in state and federal courts, one after another, contesting the results in Arizona, Georgia, Michigan, Nevada, Pennsylvania, and Wisconsin. Save for one action in Pennsylvania which had no impact on his loss there, all sixty-one of these lawsuits were dismissed. As one federal judge, who had been appointed to the bench by Trump, wrote when dismissing the action, ". . . calling an election unfair does not make it so. Charges require specific allegation and then proof. We have neither here." (Jeremy Roebuck, "'Voters, not lawyers, choose the president': Federal appeals court rejects Trump's last significant challenge to Pa. election": "'Calling an election unfair does not make it so. Charges require specific allegations and then proof. We have neither here,' the court wrote." *Philadelphia Inquirer* (Nov. 27, 2020) at https://www.inquirer.com/politics/election/pennsylvania-lawsuit-trump-election-third-circuit-appeal-supereme-court-20201127.html.) Nor did Trump have evidence anywhere that there had been election irregularities, fraud, or that anything had been stolen from him, anywhere. To the contrary, Christopher Krebs, the Department of Homeland Security director appointed by Trump to spearhead false rumors about voter fraud, announced by mid-November that the 2020 election was "the most secure in American history." Krebs added: "There is no evidence that any voting system deleted or lost votes, changed votes, or was in any way compromised." Promptly, Trump fired Krebs. (David E. Sanger, Matt Stevens and Nicole Perlroth, "Election Officials Directly Contradict Trump on Voting System Fraud: A group of federal, state and local officials working with a Department of Homeland Security agency declared flatly that the election was the most secure in the nation's history," *New York Times* (Nov. 12, 2020) at https://www.nytimes.com/2020/11/12/us/politics/election-officials-contradict-trump.html.) By December 1, 2020, Attorney General William Barr, who had been Trump's chief apologist and fixer, and who had, contrary to Department of Justice policy, sent United States attorneys looking for election irregularities, declared: "To date, we have not seen fraud on a scale that could have effected a different outcome in the election." (Ryan Lucas, "Barr: DOJ Has No Evidence Of Fraud Affecting 2020 Election Outcome," *NPR.com* (Dec. 1, 2020) at https://www.npr.org/sections/biden-transition-updates/2020/12/01/940786321/barr-doj-has-no-evidence-of-fraud-affecting-2020-election-outcome.) When later pressed about Trump's claims

of massive voting fraud and misconduct, Barr accurately described the president's contentions as "Bullshit." (Jesse Byrnes, "Barr told Trump that theories about stolen election were 'bulls---': report," *The Hill* (Jan. 18, 2021) at https://thehill.com/home-news/administration/534672-barr-told-trump-that-theories-about-stolen-election-were-bulls-report.)

13   Notwithstanding the fact that Biden defeated Trump by more than 7 million popular votes, Trump was only 38 electoral votes short of the 270 needed for a majority in the Electoral College. Trump's lawsuits focusing on just seven states reveal some strategic thinking about where he and his attorneys believed they might miraculously reverse the results. With the exception of Nevada with its 6 electoral votes, Trump was focusing on states he had won in 2016 and had only lost by a relatively small margin in 2020: Arizona with 11 electoral votes he had been lost by 10,457 popular votes; Georgia with 16 electoral votes he lost by 11,779 popular votes; Michigan with 16 electoral votes he lost by 154,188 popular votes; Pennsylvania with 20 electoral votes he lost by 80,555 popular votes; and Wisconsin with 10 electoral votes he lost by 20,682.

14   See, e.g., "Federal Prosecution of Election Offenses," Seventh Edition May 2007 (Revised August 2007) Written by: Craig C. Donsanto, Director Election Crimes Branch Public Integrity Section and Nancy L. Simmons, Senior Counsel for Policy Public Integrity Section at https://www.justice.gov/sites/default/files/criminal/legacy/2013/09/30/electbook-rvs0807.pdf. (There may be a later edition of this outline of applicable federal laws.)

15   House Impeachment Brief at 8.

16   Christa Case Bryant, "Trump wants states to overturn results. Michigan was the first test," *The Christian Science Monitor* (Nov. 23, 2020) at https://www.csmonitor.com/USA/Politics/2020/1123/Trump-wants-states-to-overturn-results.-Michigan-was-the-first-test.

17   Jeremy Roebuck and Jonathan Lai, "Trump and his allies tried to overturn Pennsylvania's election results for two months. Here are the highlights: There was a lot of noise in the time between Biden winning the 2020 election in Pennsylvania and the final certification of that victory in Congress," *The Philadelphia Inquirer* (Jan. 7, 2021) at https://www.inquirer.com/politics/election/pennsylvania-2020-election-lawsuits-timeline-20210107.html. See also William Bender and Angela Couloumbis, "President Trump invited Pa. lawmakers to the White House. Then everyone went silent. President Donald Trump summoned state lawmakers to the White House to talk about the election, but those who went weren't talking about it late." *The Philadelphia Inquirer* (Nov. 26, 2020) at https://www.inquirer.com/news/president-trump-invited-pa-lawmakers-white-house-then-everyone-went-silent-20201126.html.

18   Amy Gardner, "Trump pressured a Georgia elections investigator in a separate call legal experts say could amount to obstruction," *The Washington Post* (Mar. 11, 2021) at https://www.washingtonpost.com/politics/trump-call-georgia-investigator/2021/01/09/7a55c7fa-51cf-11eb-83e3-322644d82356_story.html.

19   House Impeachment Brief at 9.

20   Examples of Trump's reference to Fulton Country during his January 20, 2021 call to Georgia Secretary of State Brad Raffensperger are striking. If this is not an effort to interfere with an election, I am not sure what would qualify. If Trump is not prosecut-

ed, it will be surprising. This is not a president, it is a mob boss:

Trump: . . . We have . . . anywhere from 250 to 300,000 ballots were dropped mysteriously into the rolls. Much of that had to do with Fulton County, which hasn't been checked. We think that if you check the signatures — a real check of the signatures going back in Fulton County — you'll find at least a couple of hundred thousand of forged signatures of people who have been forged. And we are quite sure that's going to happen.

Trump: . . . Then the other thing they said is in Fulton County and other areas. And this may or may not be true . . . this just came up this morning, that they are burning their ballots, that they are shredding, shredding ballots and removing equipment. They're changing the equipment on the Dominion machines and, you know, that's not legal.

Trump: . . . Do you think it's possible that they shredded ballots in Fulton County? Because that's what the rumor is. And also that Dominion took out machines. That Dominion is really moving fast to get rid of their, uh, machinery.

Trump: So why did you do Cobb County? We didn't even request — we requested Fulton County, not Cobb County. Go ahead, please. Go ahead.

Germany: We chose Cobb County because that was the only county where there's been any evidence submitted that the signature verification was not properly done.

Trump: No, but I told you. We're not, we're not saying that.

Mitchell: We did say that.

Trump: Fulton County. Look. Stacey, in my opinion, Stacey is as dishonest as they come. She has outplayed you . . . at everything. She got you to sign a totally unconstitutional agreement, which is a disastrous agreement. You can't check signatures. I can't imagine you're allowed to do harvesting, I guess, in that agreement. That agreement is a disaster for this country. But she got you somehow to sign that thing, and she has outsmarted you at every step.

Trump: . . . But in Fulton, where they dumped ballots, you will find that you have many that aren't even signed, and you have many that are forgeries. Okay, you know that. You know that. You have no doubt about that. And you will find you will be at 11,779 within minutes because Fulton County is totally corrupt, and so is she totally corrupt. And they're going around playing you and laughing at you behind your back, Brad, whether you know it or not, they're laughing at you.

Trump: . . . But you have to go back to check from past years with respect to signatures. And if you check with Fulton County, you'll have hundreds of thousands because they dumped ballots into Fulton County and the other county next to it. So what are we going to do here, folks? I only need 11,000 votes. Fellas, I need 11,000 votes. Give me a break. You know, we have that in spades already.

Amy Gardner and Paulina Firozi, "Here's the full transcript and audio of the call between Trump and Raffensperger," *Washington Post* (Jan. 5, 2021) at https://www.washingtonpost.com/politics/trump-raffensperger-call-transcript-georgia-vote/2021/01/03/2768e0cc-4ddd-11eb-83e3-322644d82356_story.html.

21   House Impeachment Brief at 20.

22   House Impeachment Brief at 20.

23   One of the exceptions to the hush over social science's discussion of Trump's authoritarianism I was delighted to discover is John R. Hibbing's *The Securitarian Personality:*

What Really Motivates Trump's Base and Why It Matters for the Post-Trump Era (Oxford University Press, 2020). John Hibbing is a widely respected political scientist, and I am familiar with some of his work. To study those most attracted to Donald Trump, John attended Trump rallies, and talked with these people. Next he got the most ardent Trump enthusiasts to participate in focus groups and then he polled them to further examine their thinking. Here is a thumbnail of his findings from his publisher:

Drawing from participant observation, focus groups, and especially an original, nationwide survey of the American public that included over 1,000 ardent Trump supporters, Hibbing demonstrates that what Trump's base really craves is actually a specific form of security. Trump supporters do not strive for security in the face of all threats, such as climate change, Covid-19, and economic inequality, but rather only from those threats they perceive to be emanating from human outsiders, defined broadly to include welfare cheats, unpatriotic athletes, norm violators, non-English speakers, religious and racial minorities, and certainly people from other countries. The central objective of these "securitarians" is to strive for protection for themselves, their families, and their dominant cultural group from these embodied outsider threats.

John Hibbing does not think Trump's core followers are authoritarians. Those he dealt with did not strike him as inclined to submit to anyone. I called John (via Zoom) to discuss his findings. And after re-reading his work and talking with him I concluded his findings are not uniquely different from ours; rather, the differences are definitional and focus. I suspect he is correct that many of Trump's most ardent followers do not fit Bob Altemeyer definition of Right-Wing Authoritarian followers, but I know from our national survey many Trump followers do fit. In short, I found Hibbing's work adds context to our findings. His "securitarians" – the ardent Trumpists who sought security from threatening "others" (e.g. people of color) – appear to me those we write about in Chapter 9 and describe as "double highs." Suffice it to say, hopefully my collaborator will address Hibbing's work on his webpage as he continues to share his science. I believe the more social scientists looking at Trump and his base the better. Of course contemporary authoritarians are unlike to learn anything about themselves from social science because they are now anti-science. They are currently refusing the COVID-19 vaccine, which hopefully is simply thinning the herd of fools. Meanwhile the rest of us never every social scientist concerned about democracy to do what Bob Altemeyer and John Hibbing and a few others are doing, and that is probe and explain these people so we can deal with the threat they pose. The authoritarian nightmare is far from over, and these authoritarian personalities, with the threat they pose our democracy at our collective peril, cannot be ignored. May this book provoke many more addressing these anti-democratic Americans.

APPENDIX IV

1   These 990 were all the respondents who reached the Demographic questions toward the end of the questionnaire. Whereas sometimes researchers drop participants from a study because they skipped a lot of questions or are judged to have given random or nonsensical answers, no one who got to the Demographics was excluded so that we might "take" as complete a picture of the sample involved as possible.

2   Our survey was conducted in late 2019 before the first Democratic caucus in Iowa

and we listed the top five candidates in this question. Michael Bloomberg had not announced his candidacy yet. Persons who said they were Republicans were excluded from this analysis. The results have very little meaning because of sample limitations. Only persons who had voted in previous elections were likely to be contacted, so many Sanders supporters had no chance of being polled. Recall also that the sample was biased toward older white men. Also, the small differences and small sample sizes mean few of the differences below are statistically significant. So why did we include this breakdown? We thought people would ask for it if we did not.

Candidate	Number of Supporters	% Females	Mean AGE	Mean Pref-24	Mean RWA	Mean SDO-DOM	Mean SDO-Anti
Biden	129	48%	63.0	63.8	64.2	18.3	23.9
Buttigieg	106	49%	57.7	57.2	52.3	16.6	19.7
Sanders	54	41%	48.8	64.7	54.7	19.6	21.8
Warren	89	60%	55.3	51.9	49.4	16.4	16.9

INDEX

abortion, 130–31, 174, 177, 182–83, 187, 208, 362n24

Abramoff, Jack, 234

Abrams, Stacey, 292, 377–78n20

Access Hollywood tape, 183

Acosta, Jim, 79, 121, 355n10

Adelson, Sherman, 142–44, 217

Adorno, Theodor W., 28, 337–38n32

Affordable Care Act. *See* Obamacare (Affordable Care Act)

African Americans: Black Evangelicals, 172; housing discrimination, 55–56, 68; vote suppression, 267–69, 271, 295. *See also* Black Lives Matter protests

Ailes, Roger, 239–40

alt right, 119, 121

Altemeyer, Bob, xii, xiii, 29, 103, 191, 357n4, 364–65n2, 364n12

American National Election Surveys (ANESs), 298–99

American University (Washington, DC), 234

Americans for Prosperity, 234–35

Anderson, Christopher, 276

"Anonymous" (administration official and op-ed author), xviii, 84, 247, 275, 342n2

antifa, 89, 264, 354n2

antisocial personality disorder, 335n4

Apostles' Creed, 218

Applebaum, Anne, 246–48, 249

The Apprentice (television series), 72–73, 74, 115–16, 117–18, 229, 233

Aristotle International, 310

al-Assad, Bashar, 346–47n14

Associated Press, 305

Atkinson, Michael, 276, 349–50n39

Atlantic City casinos, 60–67, 96

attachment theory, 33

authoritarian followers. *See* right-wing authoritarians (RWAs) (authoritarian followers)

The Authoritarian Personality (Adorno et al.), 28, 337–38n32

The Authoritarian Specter (Altemeyer), 126

authoritarianism, defining, 25–27

authoritarianism, social science research on, xiii–xiv, xx, 27–29, 107–11, 142–44, 338n33, 378–79n23; Con Man Scale, 51–52, 109, 115,